T0140202

IFIP Advances in Information and Communication Technology

601

Editor-in-Chief

Kai Rannenberg, Goethe University Frankfurt, Germany

Editorial Board Members

TC 1 – Foundations of Computer Science
  Luís Soares Barbosa, *University of Minho, Braga, Portugal*

TC 2 – Software: Theory and Practice
  Michael Goedicke, University of Duisburg-Essen, Germany

TC 3 – Education
  Arthur Tatnall, Victoria University, Melbourne, Australia

TC 5 – Information Technology Applications
  Erich J. Neuhold, University of Vienna, Austria

TC 6 – Communication Systems
  Burkhard Stiller, University of Zurich, Zürich, Switzerland

TC 7 – System Modeling and Optimization
  Fredi Tröltzsch, TU Berlin, Germany

TC 8 – Information Systems
  Jan Pries-Heje, Roskilde University, Denmark

TC 9 – ICT and Society
  David Kreps, University of Salford, Greater Manchester, UK

TC 10 – Computer Systems Technology
  Ricardo Reis, Federal University of Rio Grande do Sul, Porto Alegre, Brazil

TC 11 – Security and Privacy Protection in Information Processing Systems
  Steven Furnell, Plymouth University, UK

TC 12 – Artificial Intelligence
  Eunika Mercier-Laurent, University of Reims Champagne-Ardenne, Reims, France

TC 13 – Human-Computer Interaction
  Marco Winckler, University of Nice Sophia Antipolis, France

TC 14 – Entertainment Computing
  Rainer Malaka, University of Bremen, Germany

IFIP – The International Federation for Information Processing

IFIP was founded in 1960 under the auspices of UNESCO, following the first World Computer Congress held in Paris the previous year. A federation for societies working in information processing, IFIP's aim is two-fold: to support information processing in the countries of its members and to encourage technology transfer to developing nations. As its mission statement clearly states:

IFIP is the global non-profit federation of societies of ICT professionals that aims at achieving a worldwide professional and socially responsible development and application of information and communication technologies.

IFIP is a non-profit-making organization, run almost solely by 2500 volunteers. It operates through a number of technical committees and working groups, which organize events and publications. IFIP's events range from large international open conferences to working conferences and local seminars.

The flagship event is the IFIP World Computer Congress, at which both invited and contributed papers are presented. Contributed papers are rigorously refereed and the rejection rate is high.

As with the Congress, participation in the open conferences is open to all and papers may be invited or submitted. Again, submitted papers are stringently refereed.

The working conferences are structured differently. They are usually run by a working group and attendance is generally smaller and occasionally by invitation only. Their purpose is to create an atmosphere conducive to innovation and development. Refereeing is also rigorous and papers are subjected to extensive group discussion.

Publications arising from IFIP events vary. The papers presented at the IFIP World Computer Congress and at open conferences are published as conference proceedings, while the results of the working conferences are often published as collections of selected and edited papers.

IFIP distinguishes three types of institutional membership: Country Representative Members, Members at Large, and Associate Members. The type of organization that can apply for membership is a wide variety and includes national or international societies of individual computer scientists/ICT professionals, associations or federations of such societies, government institutions/government related organizations, national or international research institutes or consortia, universities, academies of sciences, companies, national or international associations or federations of companies.

More information about this series at http://www.springer.com/series/6102

Rajendra K. Bandi · Ranjini C. R. ·
Stefan Klein · Shirin Madon ·
Eric Monteiro (Eds.)

The Future of Digital Work: The Challenge of Inequality

IFIP WG 8.2, 9.1, 9.4 Joint Working Conference, IFIPJWC 2020
Hyderabad, India, December 10–11, 2020
Proceedings

 Springer

Editors
Rajendra K. Bandi
Indian Institute of Management Bangalore
Bangalore, India

Stefan Klein
University of Münster
Münster, Germany

Eric Monteiro
Norwegian University of Science
and Technology
Trondheim, Norway

Ranjini C. R.
Ramalingaswami Centre on Equity
and Social Determinants of Health
Bangalore, India

Shirin Madon
London School of Economics
and Political Science
London, UK

ISSN 1868-4238   ISSN 1868-422X   (electronic)
IFIP Advances in Information and Communication Technology
ISBN 978-3-030-64699-8   ISBN 978-3-030-64697-4   (eBook)
https://doi.org/10.1007/978-3-030-64697-4

Preface

The papers in this volume constitute the proceedings of a joint working conference organized by the IFIP Working Groups 8.2, 9.1, and 9.4. The conference, entitled "The future of digital work: the challenge of inequality," was planned to take place during December 9–10, 2020, in Hyderabad, India. Due to the COVID-19 pandemic the conference was held virtually.

The call for papers resulted in a total of 29 submissions. Of these, 22 full papers were finally selected for presentation at the working conference. The submissions were selected through a blind-review process involving two reviewers and the editors. Authors of submissions that were selected for the next round were requested to revise their contributions in accordance with the reviewers' and the editors' recommendations. The revised submissions were then reviewed for publication in this volume. An introductory paper by the editors provides a thematic overview of these papers.

The papers published in this volume are complemented by contributions from the two keynote speakers at the conference: Renana Jhabvala and Michael Barrett.

Renana Jhabvala, Chairperson SEWA Bharat and Grih Rin Ltd, is an Indian social worker, who has been active for decades in organizing women in the informal economy into trade unions, co-operatives, and financial institutions in India, and has been extensively involved in policy issues relating to poor women and the informal economy.

Michael Barrett, Professor of Information Systems and Innovation Studies at the Cambridge Judge Business School, UK, has a long track record of engaging with social aspects of digital technologies, also with a view to the global south.

The editors would like to take this opportunity to thank all the contributors to this volume. We are very grateful to all the members of the Program Committee who participated in the review process. We give special thanks to Arunima S. Mukherjee and Divya Sharma for all their hard work on the conference organization. We would also like to recognize Eija Karsten, who has initiated the joint conference, working closely with the conference chairs Rajesh Chandwani, Shirin Madon, and Jungwoo Lee, who also took responsibility for the RIP stream, and Miriam Costales and her colleagues at Springer, who helped in producing these proceedings.

The local host organizations are the Indian Institute of Management, Ahmedabad, India, and Society for Health Information Systems Program – HISP India, New Delhi, India.

October 2020

Rajendra K. Bandi
Ranjini C. R.
Stefan Klein
Shirin Madon
Eric Monteiro

Organization

Program Chairs

Rajendra K. Bandi	Indian Institute of Management Bangalore, India
Ranjini C. R.	Ramalingaswami Centre on Equity and Social Determinants of Health, India
Stefan Klein	University of Münster, Germany
Shirin Madon	London School of Economics and Political Science, UK
Eric Monteiro	Norwegian University of Science and Technology, Norway

Organizing Chairs

Arunima S. Mukherjee	University of Oslo, Norway

Program Committee

Steve Sawyer	Syracuse University, USA
Brian Nicholson	The University of Manchester, UK
Silvia Masiero	Loughborough University, UK
Neil Pollock	The University of Edinburgh, UK
Sundeep Sahay	University of Oslo, Norway
Carla Bonina	Surrey Business School, UK
Suzana Brown	SUNY Korea, South Korea
Richard Heeks	The University of Manchester, UK
Fareesa Malik	NUST Business School, Pakistan
Nathalie Mitev	Paris Dauphine University, France
Abayomi Baiyere	Copenhagen Business School, Denmark
Matti Rossi	Aalto University, Finland
Séamas Kelly	University College Dublin, Ireland
Ella Hafermalz	Vrije Universiteit Amsterdam, The Netherlands
Anastasia Sergeeva	Vrije Universiteit Amsterdam, The Netherlands
Panos Constantinides	Alliance Manchester Business School, UK
Chrisanthi Avgerou	London School of Economics, UK
Jan Ljungberg	Gothenburg University, Sweden
Eivor Oborn-Barrett	University of Warwick, UK
Yingqin Zheng	Royal Holloway, University of London, UK
Daniel Fuerstenau	Freie Universität Berlin, Germany
Jonny Holmstrom	Umeå University, Sweden

Matthew Jones	University of Cambridge, UK
Ineke Buskens	Research For the Future CC, Macau
M. Lynne Markus	Bentley University, USA
Petter Nielsen	University of Oslo, Norway

Contents

Transforming Healthcare

The Dark Side of Digitalisation

Introduction

The Future of Digital Work: The Challenge of Inequality

Rajendra K. Bandi[1], Stefan Klein[2], Shirin Madon[5], Eric Monteiro[3]([✉]), and C. R. Ranjini[4]

[1] Indian Institute of Management Bangalore, Bangalore, India
[2] University of Muenster, Muenster, Germany
[3] Norwegian University of Science and Technology, Trondheim, Norway
Eric.monterio@ntnu.no
[4] Public Health Foundation of India, Bangalore, India
[5] London School of Economics and Political Science, London, UK

1 Introduction

The worlds of work and organisation are increasingly being pervaded by digital technologies which provide opportunities to generate new sectors and work tasks, increase productivity and deliver effective public services but create many challenges for society. The COVID-19 crisis has caused the largest global digitalization experiment, forcing almost everyone to work, study or learn from home. On the optimistic side, the development of automation enabled by technologies including robotics and artificial intelligence brings the promise of higher productivity and economic growth. This is assumed to enable firms to scale up or down quickly thereby challenging traditional production patterns based on ownership of resources and blurring the boundaries between firms [8]. Digital platform firms adopt new business models that differ from traditional production processes based on input, process and output generating value instead by creating a network effect connecting customers, producers and providers while facilitating interactions in a multi-sided model. In order to trade goods and services on an online platform, individuals and firms need only a broadband connection, which offers economic opportunities also for small traders in developing countries. In terms of sectoral changes, digital technologies have shifted employment in different ways. In advanced economies, the past few decades have seen a decline in industrial employment and a shift from manufacturing to services. The trend in low-and-middle income countries has been different as the share of industrial employment primarily in manufacturing has remained stable and in some East Asian countries has risen. The World Bank [19] explains this trend as resulting from the falling cost of connectivity enabling emerging economies to produce more capital-intensive exports as well as due to increasing patterns of consumption of products and demand for new products as a result of rising incomes. In terms of skills, while the demand for less advanced skills that can be replaced by technology is declining, the demand for advanced cognitive skills, socio-behavioural aptitude needed to participate in global teams, and the ability to employ agile methods to maintain flexibility and adaptability to fast-changing demand is rising. While this trend has been evident for

© IFIP International Federation for Information Processing 2020
Published by Springer Nature Switzerland AG 2020
R. K. Bandi et al. (Eds.): IFIPJWC 2020, IFIP AICT 601, pp. 3–10, 2020.
https://doi.org/10.1007/978-3-030-64697-4_1

some time in developed countries, the same pattern is emerging in developing countries as the share of employment in high-skill occupations is rising [15].

In contrast, there are critical voices that express concerns about the future of digital work for business organisations, consumers, workers and individuals. Platformization has in many cases de facto led to monopolization, in line with a winner-takes-it all logic of network effects. Many SMEs are forced to trade on platforms in order to not lose out, yet they have become easy prey to the monopolistic platform providers. For consumers we observe two effects: on the one side they benefit from allocation efficiencies (for instance, transparency, low transaction costs) the platforms provide, yet on the other side they are subjected to value extraction [4] as their digital traces are collected, analysed and monetized by the platform, who claim ownership of their customers' data [21]. For workers, this raises challenging issues of division of labour between the human and the machine - the algorithm. While automation and replacement of human labour is happening in some areas, the majority of cases, however, point towards various forms of transformation of work and symbiotic agency [7]. Lessons learnt from the productivity paradox or the digital divide decades ago revealed how it is the interwoven character of labour, technology and work processes that leads to productivity gains. However, new institutional responses such as globally-distributed teams which have emerged bring uncertainties as a result of geographical and temporal distance as a result of how dispersed teams are configured and the diversity of workers [6]. From the perspective of workers, two-thirds of people living in advanced economies are anxious about the sweeping impact of technology on employment [5]. A main cause for anxiety is identified to be related to rising inequality compounded by the advent of the gig economy in which organisations contract with independent workers for short-term work that encourages a race to the bottom in working conditions. There has been a rapid increase in the number of companies with zero employees where individuals provide services through some form of independent contractual relationship with firms. This type of work which responds to the increasing call for a range of on-demand services like food delivery and transportation could account for millions of workers within a few years. While bringing flexibility, this perceived advantage is indeed a double-edge sword. Despite offering workers diverse income sources and ability to control work schedules, gig economy platforms have been criticised for being unpredictable and associated with poor wages and work conditions, particularly in the context of developing countries where informality characterises a large set of economic activities [18]. Large corporations such as RyanAir have adopted a similar approach by designing freelance contracts for pilots. Google, Facebook and Twitter have created (at least) two tier employment models, with loads for perks at the high end and dismal working conditions for individuals employed by outsourcing operators, portrayed in the documentary The Cleaners[1]. Those workers and their dismal working conditions are hidden by non-disclosure agreements, they become invisible and are seen and treated as non-persons [13].

Of essence with these critiques is the fundamental argument about how digital technologies are diminishing the value of labour in society. Digital technologies have enabled the rise of tech titans, which do not hesitate to use their monopoly power to further their

---

[1] https://www.theverge.com/2018/1/21/16916380/sundance-2018-the-cleaners-movie-review-facebook-google-twitter.

businesses[2], they also make it their business to undermine antitrust regulation, privacy protection and social/welfare protection under the umbrella of digital disruption [10]. As several scholars have argued, transaction platforms established to mediate work such as Uber, Upwork and Deliveroo treat labour as a commodity that can be bought rather than human capital that is socially-embedded within networks of inter-personal trust and safeguarded by state policies and legal frameworks [2, 20]. Uber has worked relentlessly to defend their claim that their drivers are not their employees, who would be eligible for protection guaranteed by labour laws, but merely as "consumers" of "algorithmic technology" [11]. A claim, which has been refuted by the European Court of Justice[3] and lately in California[4].

As digital technologies become ever-more pervasive in organisational life and work, they are serving to reconfigure the relationship between time, space and place. There is growing realisation of a reconfiguring of time and space as the separation of work-life and home life is becoming indistinct. Information systems enable work to occur anywhere and anytime. This reconfiguration of space and time is frequently seen as a source of freedom, entrepreneurial opportunity and escape from organisational controls and structures. However, discussions about the interpenetration of professional activities and duties into the private sphere have so far been lacking [1]. [9] have collected cases of algorithmically supported work which show a profound loss in work life quality. Moreover, one person's freedom from time or space constraints by enabling work to be done anywhere and anytime may become another person's constraint as home life is invaded with work considerations. Digital technologies also reconfigure the relationship between space and place in the workplace environment. IT-enabled globalization has resulted in a transfer of knowledge about operations from the place of work into the space of managers who take decisions about how best to organise production work based on global standards [12]. At the same time, work-related changes brought about by digital technologies in peripheral locations can only take hold if they mesh with the practices, tactics, local contextual factors and human motivation that occur within local workplace situations. Herein lies the crucial insight that despite the proclaimed, potential benefits of digitalization, the realization of these possibilities comes only with considerable attention to local situations, resources and circumstances. Hence, a constant process of reformation takes place at local level as social actors validate new work spaces introduced as a result of technology deployment in sectors as disparate as banking, public service delivery and healthcare. As digital technologies enable labour to become increasingly commodified and traded across the world, this reconfiguration of work and organisations tends to be biased against place, labour and tradition. Technology hubs and online work centres tend to be located in urban centres encouraging investment by policy makers in infrastructure such as roads and transport while neglecting to support more traditional sectors such as agriculture, artisanal industry and primary healthcare.

---

[2] https://www.theverge.com/2020/7/29/21335706/antitrust-hearing-highlights-facebook-google-amazon-apple-congress-testimony.

[3] https://www.nytimes.com/2017/12/20/business/uber-europe-ecj.html.

[4] https://thehill.com/policy/transportation/512137-california-ruling-against-uber-lyft-threatens-to-upend-gig-economy.

Eventually, the future of digital work and the challenge of inequality that emerges hold important implications for public policy. New digital forms of industrial organization raise critical issues in the areas of privacy, competition and taxation as the virtual nature of productive assets prevents the ability of governments to raise revenues. The contemporary phenomenon of smart cities across the world raises important issues about privacy as digital infrastructure is used to monitor and steer aspects such as tracking movements of residents and visitors, energy usage, and estimating neighborhood sentiment. [17] studies Rotterdam's smart city initiative raising issues of who has legitimate access to data, which data should be in the public domain and what are appropriate privacy frameworks to put in place to support the changing nature of city governance. The importance of policies to regulate competition and taxation surfaces as another public policy concern. The case of Uber, as revealed in a study by [14], demonstrates how government policy in Germany and Sweden supported the operating of Uber so long as it respected national laws on licensing and taxation. With the gig economy occupying ever-greater presence, the payroll-based insurance model is increasingly challenged by working arrangements outside standard employment contracts calling for new ways of protecting people's jobs. In recent years, the ILO [3] has been conducting surveys of crowd-workers to gauge their overall levels of vulnerability and make recommendations for introducing international public policy measures to improve their income security. In the context of low-and-middle income countries, the lack of quality private sector jobs leaves talented young individuals with few pathways to wage employment [16]. This requires the creation by the government of formal jobs to seize the benefits of technological change and better learning opportunities to enable those who have left school to reskill according to changing labour market demands. In many developing countries, however, despite open trade and improvements in the business regulatory environment most workers remain in low-productivity employment often in the informal sector with little access to technology. Government investment in hard and soft infrastructure is also needed to ensure that the 'value' generated from digital technologies in the workplace is equitably distributed. Most obvious is investment in affordable access to the internet for those who remain unconnected. Equally important is government investment in roads, transport and the built environment which supports organisations to exploit new technologies. Finally, addressing the challenge of inequality requires huge investment to improve human capital outcomes of basic schooling and primary healthcare which are currently sub-optimal. In sum, public policy needs to be geared towards broad, infrastructural capacity boosting, not different from other investments in public good.

The IFIP Working Groups 8.2, 9.1 and 9.4 have a long history of supplementing the dominant technology-push accounts of digitalization with socially informed ones. This joint conference brings together these three groups for the much-needed analysis of the social pre-conditions, engagement and consequences of digitalization visibility. They have a tradition to highlight that the negative consequences of technology are not inevitable (deterministic) but typically the result of human intent and design. A critical assessment of the price societies are paying for the dark side of digitalization is called for as much as a reconsideration of societal values that are worthwhile to protect. This implies to ask what type of world we, people all over the world including future generations, would like to live in. With increasingly vocal proclamations of the consequences of digitalisation, there is a need for socially informed analysis of the uptake of digitalisation for work and everyday life in the manner traditionally promoted by all three of the IFIP working groups. The conference seeks to stimulate and encourage critical discussion of potential shifts in the changing world of work, organisations and its implications in the developing world. This conference seeks to open a space for the exploration of the ethics and politics of information systems in contemporary work and organisation and stimulate critical discussion about their implications for individuals, organisations and society at large. As a joint conference that combines three different working groups together, our overall goal has been developmental and inclusive in order to enable the nurturing of ideas, critical engagement with issues and eventual discussion of emerging topics that intersect the interests of the three working groups. The theme of the conference is particularly appropriate within the current extraordinary context of COVID-19 in which organisations around the world are having to adapt to new ways of working in order to continue functioning through the use of digital artefacts. The organisation of this IFIP Joint Working Conference has, in turn, also had to adapt to preparing for and running the conference in an online mode. Over the course of the past few months, the pandemic has resulted in disruptions to many academics as a result of health concerns, difficulties in travelling, adhering to quarantine procedures and the stress of uncertainties in terms of planning for the future affecting the submission of articles.

The proceedings in this volume include 22 full research papers. For the purpose of overview, the papers may be seen to fall into the following broad set of themes (although, of course, more often than not really cutting across several themes):

Innovation and Entrepreneurship: Influenced by a Schumpeterian approach to innovation, this set of papers forefront the generative potential of digital technologies to offer new services but also ways of organizing their offerings. New opportunities for entrepreneurial activities and actors emerge but these should not obscure the role that humans play as intermediaries in promoting trust in business activities.

The Social Significance of Digital Platforms: Digital platforms and their associated ecosystem is a novel organisational phenomenon that reshapes the nature of service work and, not the least, the relationships between implicated actors in the ecosystem. Of paramount importance is the need to capture the attitudes and experiences of digital workers in order to improve understanding of how digital platforms impact lives, communities and society.

Transforming Healthcare: With healthcare, especially in resource-scarce regions and countries of the world, constituting an essential service aspiring to reach all corners of society, the scope - potentially - for digital technologies to enhance quality, efficiency and coverage is significant. At the same time, limitations of technology deployment need to be addressed related to the wider contextual realities and structural impediments that shape health outcome.

The Dark Side of Digitalisation: A characteristic aspect of all contributions to all three of our IFIP working groups is their critical perspective. However, we have here collected together papers which make the critical agenda more explicit.

In addition to the full research papers, the conference has two panels.

Panel on AI in Healthcare: Once thought as a futuristic threat to humankind, Artificial intelligence (AI) is now part of everyday life. AI applications are nearly in all spheres of human activity from the banal to the fantastic, from mundane smartphone apps to controversial autonomous weapons, from playing chess to sports reporting, on the road as self-driving cars or in the ICU assisting in surgeries. AI is projected to have an unprecedented impact on the future of work, governance, warfare, education, medicine, and overall, the way we live.

The COVID-19 pandemic has highlighted the importance of the inter-connections of health systems and technological innovation. AI's most powerful use is to enhance human capabilities and not replace them. Three main areas in which AI is expected to contribute in healthcare are AI-powered predictive care, networked and connected care and in improving patient and provider experiences. This panel will focus on the application of AI-based interventions in healthcare, both in the public and private sector. The aim is to understand how AI is being used in healthcare, how could it be used in the near future and what are the ethical, social, policy and implementation challenges that these current and prospective uses present for work. The panelists will be drawn from a wide range of expertise including clinical, technical, private sector, public sector, non-government and academia who will describe the unique opportunities and challenges for AI and digital health in India. Apart from analysing the current trends, they will share their particular experiences and describe their success stories. For example, one of the panelists will describe the 'people first, technology last' inclusive approach that they adopted to reverse the paradigm and convince policymakers while implementing a malnutrition programme in childcare centres.

Panel on Delivery of Digital Services to the Citizens: Delivery of digital services has never been more important than during the current COVID-19 pandemic times, with two phrases 'social distancing' and 'contactless delivery' dominating the public discourse.

Governments world-wide have made significant investments in the past couple of decades, in taking the government services to the citizens doorstep using digital technologies. These efforts have met with varying success based on a number of factors such as the e-governance readiness, extent of citizen's participation, prevailing digital divide, process reengineering of service delivery processes, and the appropriate mindset required for digital transformation. The challenges in this have been studied and documented by researchers.

COVID-19, and lockdowns around the world, has pushed governments to turn to digital technologies to ensure business continuity and offer newer services, in differing ways and with varying success. Countries that had developed sound, dependable e-governance infrastructure, capabilities and policies are finding it easier to provide contactless digital services for citizens and businesses. On the other hand, countries that have a gap in their policies and IT capabilities are struggling to respond to the pandemic-imposed challenge.

Governments have been deploying a variety of technologies such as the development of contact tracing apps, usage of drones and robots, tele-medicine, making digital payments, use of AI and data analytics to analyse and to predict spread of COVID-19 etc.

However, some of these initiatives have come under intense scrutiny for a wide variety of problems. Some of the issues raised include, widening the digital divide, violation of privacy of the citizens and ignoring the basic principles of privacy by design, creation of a surveillance state and having a blind faith in the technologies.

This panel will focus on the challenges and opportunities in designing and delivering digital services in general with particular emphasis on unexpected emergencies like the current Pandemic. The panellists will be a mix of senior government officers involved in e-governance initiatives and researchers who have been studying these developments.

Key Notes: Finally, our conference has two prominent keynote speakers. The abstracts of their talks are provided in this proceedings. Renana Jhabvala, Chairperson SEWA Bharat and Grih Rin Ltd, is an Indian social worker, who has been active for decades in organising women in the informal economy into trade unions, co-operatives and financial institutions in India, and has been extensively involved in policy issues relating to poor women and the informal economy.

Michael Barrett, Professor of Information Systems & Innovation Studies at the Judge Business School at University of Cambridge, has a long track record of engaging with social aspects of digital technologies, also with a view to the global South.

References

1. Ciolfi, L., Lockley, E.: From work to life and back again: examining the digitally-mediated work/life practices of a group of knowledge workers. Comput. Support. Coop. Work **27**, 803–839 (2018). https://doi.org/10.1007/s10606-018-9315-3
2. Graham, M., Anwar, A.: The global gig economy: towards a planetary labour market? First Monday **24**, 4 (2019)
3. ILO. Income Security in the On-Demand Economy: Findings and policy lessons from a survey of crowdworkers, Working Paper, Conditions of Work and Employment Series No. 74, May 2016, International Labour Organisation, Geneva (2016)
4. Mazzucato, M.: The value of everything: Making and taking in the global economy. Penguin; Public Affairs, New York (2018)
5. McKinsey.: Technology, Jobs, and the Future of Work, Briefing Note. McKinsey Global Institute (2017)
6. Morrison-Smith, S., Ruiz, J.: Challenges and barriers in virtual teams: a literature review. SN Appl. Sci. **2**(6), 1–33 (2020). https://doi.org/10.1007/s42452-020-2801-5
7. Neff, G., Nagy, P.: Agency in the digital age: using symbiotic agency to explain human-technology interaction. In: Papacharissi, Z. (ed.) A Networked Self and Human Augmentics, Artificial Intelligence, Sentience, pp. 97–107. Routledge, New York (2018)
8. Research and Markets. Digital Transformation of the Future of Work. Report (2019)
9. Riemer, K., Peters, S.: The robo-apocalypse plays out in the quality, not the quantity of work. J. Inf. Technol. (2020). https://doi.org/10.1177/0268396220923677
10. Rogers, B.: The social costs of uber. Univ. Chicago Law Rev. Online **82**(1) (2015). https://doi.org/10.1787/9789264065307-en
11. Rosenblat, A.: Uberland: How Algorithms are Rewriting the Rules of Work. University of California Press, Oakland (2019)
12. Schultze, U., Boland Jr., R.J.: Knowledge management technology and the reproduction of knowledge work practices. J. Strateg. Inf. Syst. **9**(2–3), 193–212 (2000)

13. Star, S.L., Strauss, A.: Layers of silence, arenas of voice: the ecology of visible and invisible work. Comput. Support. Coop. Work (CSCW) **8**(1–2), 9–30 (1999). https://doi.org/10.1023/A:1008651105359
14. Thelen, K.: Regulating Uber: the politics of the platform economy in Europe and the United States. Perspect. Politics **16**(4), 938–953 (2018)
15. UNCTAD. Digital Economy Report 2019 Value creation and capture: Implications for developing countries, United Nations Conference on Trade and Development (2019)
16. UNDESA. World Youth Report: Youth and the 2030 Agenda for Sustainable Development, New York (2018)
17. Van Zoonen, L.: Privacy concerns in smart cities. Gov. Inf. Q. **33**(3), 472–480 (2016)
18. Vasilescu, M.D., Serban, A.C., Dimian, G.C., Aceleanu, M.I., Picatoste, X.: Digital divide, skills and perceptions on digitalisation in the European Union—towards a smart labour market. PLoS ONE **15**(4), e0232032 (2020)
19. World Bank. The changing nature of work, Wordl development report (2019)
20. Wood, A.J., Graham, M., Lehdonvirta, V., Hjorth, I.: Networked but Commodified: the (dis)embeddedness of digital labour in the gig economy. Sociology **53**(5), 931–950 (2019)
21. Zuboff, S.: The Age of Surveillance Capitalism: The Fight for a Human Future at the New Frontier of Power. Public Affairs, New York (2019)

Keynotes

Overcoming Gender Inequality in the Digital World

Renana Jhabvala[✉]

SEWA Bharat, New Delhi, India
renanajhabvala@gmail.com

I thank the International Federation for Information Processing (IFIP) for inviting me to this conference and would like to commend it for taking up the difficult task of addressing issues of digital inequality. There are many forms of digital inequality, which I am sure the conference will address. However, in this talk I would like to focus on a particular form, that is gender inequality in the digital world.

I come from SEWA, Self Employed Women's Association, which started as a trade union in India working with women in the informal sector and has developed into a family of organisations which include all kinds of social enterprises and direct capacity building reaching out to SEWA's 1.7 million members for a variety of functions, from fighting for rights, especially economic rights, to delivering services such as micro-finance, health care, child care and helping women to form social enterprises to access the markets. The women who are members of SEWA include rural women such as small farmers, agriculture workers livestock producers and urban workers such as domestic workers, street vendors and of course many more trades. These women constitute over 90% of the female workforce in India. And SEWA is confined not only to India but has also founded international networks and federations such as HomeNet, the international network of homebased workers, StreetNet, the network of street vendors and the International Domestic Workers Federation.

These are the women I am going to be talking about today. They are the women at the base of the economic pyramid and so already face social as well as economic inequality, which are now compounded by digital inequality. Digital inequality is both a consequence of the socio-economic inequality, as well as a cause to deepen these other inequalities.

In order to tackle digital inequality, it is really important that we understand the degree of inequality, and are able to measure it. There are many different estimates of gender digital inequality and it becomes quite difficult to actually put all these figures together to come to one conclusion. For example the Kantor IMRB study [2] says that only 30% of women use internet services and 38% use mobile phones as opposed to 71% of men, whereas the GSMA study [4] says only 16% of women were using internet services. The Pew centre tells us that 34% of men and 15% of women have smartphones [5], whereas the IAMAI (internet and mobile association of India) tells us that double the number of men use the internet as compared to women [2]. There are many more studies which I will not quote here. But looking at the welter of statistics we have, it is obvious that we need reliable figures on the degree of inequality.

© IFIP International Federation for Information Processing 2020
Published by Springer Nature Switzerland AG 2020
R. K. Bandi et al. (Eds.): IFIPJWC 2020, IFIP AICT 601, pp. 13–16, 2020.
https://doi.org/10.1007/978-3-030-64697-4_2

Regardless of the exact numbers, it is obvious that there is a high level of difference between men and women on the use of the most common digital assets such as mobile phones, smartphones and all means of accessing the internet. There is no existing data, but observation shows that these differences are even higher among the families who are at the base of the economic pyramid.

The reasons for these differences are well known and mirror the socio-economic inequality that exists in the world in general and in India in particular. Women have lower levels of education, and especially among older women, a higher level of illiteracy; patriarchal mind-sets which do not allow women freedom to explore the outside world; product contents on digital devices which are more male oriented; a fear of online harassment; lack of digital literacy; a reluctance to spend family funds on women– when there is a smartphone in the house, it is usually the men who use it.

Although the digital gap affects both the social and economic aspects of a woman's life, here I would like to focus more on women's economic status, as women are particularly disadvantaged economically. According to the National Sample Survey (NSS), the female labour force participation rate is only 27%, and women earn, on the average, about 50% of a man's earnings [3]. If women are to reduce this gap, they need access to digital assets. Digital Assets can be defined as- a) digital infrastructure, tools, hardware or devices, for example, mobile phones, personal computers, digital kiosks etc., that enable access to digital technology, as well as b) digital platforms, processes or entities, for example, e-marketplace, mobile banking, information channels, digital documents, that help access opportunities of gainful employment and entrepreneurship. In other words, digital assets are both tools and processes that facilitate access to information, resources, opportunities for employment, and better income.

Digital assets do not, however, exist on their own, they need to be embedded into the larger system. An important part of our economy, indeed of our daily life, is the financial sector, and women need to be part of it, as in today's world, money is the oil which keeps life running. Worldwide there is inequality in financial inclusion although financial inclusion has been a priority in India, and the Government made a big effort to open bank accounts for all. However, with the widespread use of debit and credit cards, and the introduction of fintech, financial inclusion has acquired a digital aspects which excludes most women. Our experience has shown that with some digital literacy women can overcome these barriers and begin to use digital tools with ease. SEWA has trained digital sakhis who work mainly in rural areas and train women (and also men when they request it), in how to use ATM machines, how to access their bank accounts through Bhim and other applications and how to apps like Paytm for all kinds of payments. These digital sakhis are not only highly regarded in their villages, but they themselves perform many digital services for the villagers, thereby earning a living.

Many of the digital sakhis in different states in India have attached themselves to banks as business correspondents and are able to provide important banking services. During the COVID-19 crisis and lockdown for example, most people were unable to access banks due to lack of transport, and it was these women who reached families with their pensions, with cash relief from the Government and helped them access their savings.

Over 65% of India's population still lives in villages, and a large proportion of them is dependent on agriculture. In fact, about 75% of rural working women are engaged in agriculture [1]. There is a feminization of agriculture as men move to more lucrative employment, or migrate to urban areas, women have been taking care of the farms and the livestock. Digitization has played an important part in imparting information and in marketing of crops, vegetables and milk, and the digital gender gap means that these women farmers tend to get left behind with lower productivity and lower prices for their produce. Our interventions in these areas have shown that agriculture can be made more productive. Firstly, we have collaborated with meteorological department to bring women weather updates on their mobile phones, which enables them to decide when to plant, when to give water, when to harvest etc. Second we have linked them with available apps and websites which give the prices on that day in the local mandis. This has made a big difference as mostly women farmers tend to sell their produce to local traders, and by knowing the price at the mandi they can obtain a fair price. Thirdly, we have an IVR system whereby they receive messages and small talks from experts about existing agricultural practices in their area, which can increase their yield.

In both urban and rural areas, many women are self employed micro entrepreneurs, and often the whole family is involved in the enterprise. They need to reach the market to sell their products. Marketing is getting increasingly digitised too, many of us order our food, clothes and other items from marketing platforms such as Amazon, Big Bazaar, Swiggy and many many more. These too, are causing increasing gaps, as the goods which are supplied on these platforms tend to be from bigger enterprises which are controlled by men. Women's enterprises tend to be small, often micro, and they are unable to access these platforms. However many women microentrpreneurs have found a way around this by using free apps such as Whatsapp and Facebook and have created local marketing channels through which they have been able to service their customers. Some platforms have been able to reach out to women who provide services, for example Urban Clap has on-boarded beauticians who will offer personalised services in people's houses. Other services include child care, domestic work and old age care.

India is a young country, with about one-third of its population being below the age of 24 years. Girls education has grown by leaps and bounds, primary education is near universal, and although girls lag behind boys in middle, secondary and college education, this too has grown tremendously for girls in the last two decades. These girls are better prepared to access the internet than their previous generation. However, for young girls there is an additional barrier. Their families are over protective, and do not want to allow them access to the internet or to smartphones. We have found that young girls often have to depend on their brothers even to get important information like their own exam results.

When young educated girls are able to overcome the barrier of family they use it to enhance both their knowledge and their opportunities. For example, some girls earn extra money by doing tuitions, having learnt on how to teach others through Youtube videos; others take designs off the internet to stitch clothes for themselves and others; still others use Youtube to learn to dance or sing or cook. Some young girls have learnt Kobo, a data collection digital tool and collect data for research agencies; others help their families and

Riskscapes and the Scaling of Digital Innovation: Trajectory Dynamics of Mobile Payments in Times of Crisis

Michael Barrett[✉]

Cambridge Judge Business School, University of Cambridge, Cambridge CB2 1AG, UK
m.barrett@jbs.cam.ac.uk

Keywords: Digital innovation · Trajectory · Dynamics · Scaling · Riskscapes · Climate change · Mobile payments · Crisis

Over the last decade, a wave of crises – financial crisis, climate change, and COVID-19 pandemic, antiracism movement - have amplified and made visible the challenges of inequality in our society and global economy. In the West, the scale of covid-19 pandemic has made visible the inequality in access to healthcare by ethnic minorities. For example, black Americans are 3.5 times more likely to develop COVID-19 and to have a poor outcome from the infection while Latino Americans are almost twofold higher in that probability. In a developing countries context, the development and scaling of mobile payments have been deployed to address challenges of financial exclusion [9] to reduce inequalities associated with accessing financial markets. However, the trajectory of mobile payments as it scales across different geographical places is not uniform in addressing inequality of financial exclusion. Mobile technology are also being used to enable carbon payments to farmer networks in developing countries who are participating in reforestation programmes to help address the riskscape associated with the crisis of climate change. We propose that the conceptual merging of riskscapes and scaling are useful in conducting practice-based studies which seek to contribute to our understanding of the challenges of inequality in contemporary contexts.

In this talk, I will explore the challenges (and opportunities) of using mobile payments to promote financial and social inclusion, as well as in supporting climate action in crises of sustainability. The role of mobile payments as a digital innovation in promoting economic and social development has garnered considerable attention [2] over the last decade. Studies have examined the quality of healthcare [4], access to financial services [3, 7, 11] amongst many other areas of deployment. A central focus of the digital innovation literature has been on the characteristic nature of convergence (across digital platforms) and generativity (associated with reprogrammability) in enabling different forms of innovation across time and in different contexts. Studies have noted the potential of user innovation and new capabilities being incorporated after initial design [12, 13] in scaling the digital innovation [5]. At the same time, other studies [10] have recognized that there may be significant challenges in the scaling of digital innovation in addressing financial exclusion across different contexts.

© IFIP International Federation for Information Processing 2020
Published by Springer Nature Switzerland AG 2020
R. K. Bandi et al. (Eds.): IFIPJWC 2020, IFIP AICT 601, pp. 17–20, 2020.
https://doi.org/10.1007/978-3-030-64697-4_3

In examining the empirical phenomenon of scaling the deployment of mobile payments for financial inclusion we draw on the concept of trajectory dynamics [9] to theorize the ways in which the innovation trajectory intermingles with and is transformed by interactions with local trajectories in a specific place. We discuss how this concept can be used to explore the challenges in scaling mobile payments across similar yet distinct developing country contexts. In so doing, we build on the insight that phenomena are shaped by different trajectories that influence outcomes (Timmermans 1998), and suggest that place(s) has an important influence on the innovation trajectory [9]. Such trajectory dynamics emerge in and over time and place.

We discuss the wider implications of our findings for developing practice-based studies that explore the scaling of digital phenomena. Specifically, we suggest that the sociomaterial enactment of contemporary digital phenomena must account for the multiple, situated places where work is now being performed through emerging technologies, for example, the provision of correspondent banking services in remote locations [6]. With respect to mobile payments, [9] adopts a sociomaterial practice perspective to understand how a digital innovation (mobile money) was transformed in multiple and unexpected ways as it moved from a specific locale of development (in the UK) to distant places of implementation and use (different countries in sub-Saharan Africa) where it interacted with multiple different local conditions and practices. This enactment over time and in multiple places reconfigured both the specific digital innovation as well as the conditions of possibility for financial inclusion. The study highlights that while digital innovations are transferable across contexts, it is the active engagement of the innovation with local conditions that matter for the specific accomplishments that are enacted in practice. These insights underscore the criticality of asking where, when, and how specific digital innovations are developed, implemented and engaged with on the ground.

We discuss the different enactments of scale of mobile money in Kenya and Tanzania which yielded different trajectory dynamics in these developing country contexts despite the similarities of geography (neighbouring countries in sub-Saharan Africa), and which were expected to yield a similar scaling dynamic [10]. Furthermore, we reflect on and discuss the scaling of digital innovations in addressing different riskscapes [1]. For example, in addition to addressing financial exclusion, mobile payments can enable social inclusion such as access to clean energy through business models that combine mobile loans and payments (e.g. M-Kopa). Furthermore, mobile money can help address climate change through the provision of carbon payments at scale across different places over time.

In addition to scaling, we suggest that practice-based studies should better account for riskscapes which focus on the consequentiality of risk to account for crisis in contemporary society. Risk is more than just a concept which helps to rationalize future gains and losses, but also a concept which performatively shapes practice and space. While phenomena such as climate change may well be global in extent, their impacts are spatially differentiated. Riskscapes include a scalar dimension of risk. More specifically, riskscapes recognize the mutually constitutive relations between risk and space and can be understood as socially produced 'temporalspatial' phenomena. They are temporalspatial phenomena, because they combine the material and practice components of risk and relate them to space. They link the material dimension of physical threats, the discursive dimension of how people perceive and communicate risks, and the dimension of agency, i.e. how people are dealing with risk. We suggest that riskscapes, like the nexuses of practice, are open and fluid, multiple and subjective. And they overlap, leading to the emergence of new com-binations and dynamics of risk. Practice based studies which examine riskscapes should therefore account for connections between risk, meaning, practice, time and space [8].

We propose that the conceptual merging of riskscapes and scale allows us to appreciate the consequentiality of risk in practice-based studies through its focus on the scalar negotiations of risk [1]. Empirically, we draw on ongoing research which examines how mobile money may provide carbon payments to scale farmer networks. These farmers in developing countries are participating in climate action efforts globally through the development of reforestation networks. In so doing they are participating together with large corporations in the West to help address climate change as a quintessential crisis of our times. The case study examines how farmer networks through their reforestation projects are providing carbon offsets for organizations in the West who are aiming to achieve carbon neutrality.

In these carbon sequestration projects, mobile money is an important mechanism by which farmers can receive carbon payments for trees planted. Moreover, our study shows how mobile payments are also integral to the organizing of farmer network meetings, and are a critical enabler to scaling sustainable growth across farmer networks over time. While the use of mobile payments is important for facilitating the disbursement of financial resources to farmers in a timely manner it is not necessarily sufficient for responsible scaling. There are challenges and risks to scaling the reforestation program responsibly. For example, as a bottom up partnership guided by the local subsistence farmers, there is a need to assure a commitment to core values by keeping the farmers vision and needs central while reinforcing local leadership. Our ongoing study is also exploring the risks and challenges of ensuring timely payments which depend on effective quantification strategies and capabilities on the ground while depending on the volatile and unpredictability of carbon markets which are at an early stage of development.

In addition to these conceptual developments on riskscapes and scaling, we reflect on the practical challenges of conducting practice-based studies to examine the scaling of digital innovations. Specifically, we discuss the challenges of conducting practice-based studies to examine the rapid scaling of the digital innovation deployed in different places and over time, and in times of crisis characterized by evolving riskscapes.

References

1. Aalders, J.T.: The scale of risk: conceptualising and analysing the politics of sacrifice scales in the case of informal settlements at urban rivers in Nairobi. Erdkunde **72**(2), 91–102 (2018)
2. Aker, J.C., Mbiti, I.M.: Mobile phones and economic development in Africa. J. Econ. Perspect. **24**(3), 207–232 (2010)
3. Duncombe, R., Boateng, R.: Mobile phones and financial services in developing countries: a review of concepts, methods, issues, evidence and research directions. Third World Q. **30**(7), 1237–1258 (2009)

4. Hoffman, J.A., et al.: Mobile direct observation treatment for tuberculosis patients: A technical feasibility pilot using mobile phones in Nairobi, Kenya. Amer. J. Prevent. Med. **39**(1), 78–80 (2010)

5. Huang, J., Henfridsson, O., Liu, M., Newell, S.: Growing on steroids: rapidly scaling the user base of digital ventures through digital innovation. Manage. Inf. Syst. Q. **41**(1), 301–314 (2017)

6. Leonardi, P.M., Bailey, D.E., Diniz, E.H., Sholler, D., Nardi, B.: Multiplex appropriation in complex systems implementation: the case of Brazil's correspondent banking system. Manage. Inf. Syst. Q. **40**(2), 461–473 (2016)

7. Mas, I., Morawczynski, O.: Designing mobile money services lessons from M-PESA. Innovations: Tech., Governance, Globalization **4**(2), 77–91 (2009)

8. Mueller-Mahn, D., Everts, J., Stephan, C.: Riskscapes revisited-exploring the relationship between risk, space and practice. Erdkunde **72**(3), 197–214 (2018)

9. Oborn, E., Barrett, M., Orlikowski, W., Kim, A.: Trajectory dynamics in innovation: developing and transforming a mobile money service across time and place. Organ. Sci. **30**(5), 1097–1123 (2019)

10. Orlikowski, W., Barrett, M.: Digital innovation in emerging markets: a case study of mobile money. MIT Center Inf. Syst. Res. Brief. **14**(6) (2014)

11. Shamim, F.: The ICT environment, financial sector and economic growth: a cross-country analysis. J. Econom. Stud. **34**(4), 352–370 (2007)

12. Von Hippel, E.: The Sources of Innovation. Oxford University Press, Oxford (1988)

13. Yoo, Y., Boland, R.J., Lyytinen, K., Majchrzak, A.: Organizing for innovation in the digitized world. Organ. Sci. **23**(5), 1398–1408 (2012)

Innovation and Entrepreneurship

Review of the Nexus Between Trust and Respect in Entrepreneurs' Information-Seeking Behaviour

Thao Orrensalo[✉] and Shahrokh Nikou

Faculty of Social Science, Business and Economics, Åbo Akademi University, Turku, Finland
{thao.orrensalo,shahrokh.nikou}@abo.fi

Abstract. In an information-based society, having accurate and timely information can influence the success of entrepreneurs in their business. Often, due to limitations in their resources and capabilities, entrepreneurs rely on their social capital to satisfy their information need. Moreover, trust and respect are two fundamental factors that not only influence the information seeking behaviour (ISB) but also the inter-actions within the social capital of an entrepreneur. However, despite the significance and relevance of these concepts, there is a lack of systematic reviews regarding the nexus between trust and respect in entrepreneurs' ISB. Consequently, this study aimed to conduct a literature review on the ISB of entrepreneurs with an emphasis on the roles trust and respect play in their decision-making when viewed through the lens of social capital theory (SCT). The review findings indicated that both trust and respect influence entrepreneurs' ISB, especially in their decision-making in selecting their information sources. Entrepreneurs select in-formation sources that they trust, respect and feel respected by in return. The influence of trust and respect in entrepreneurial information source selection is also related to the seeker's perception of the social cost/risk. Lastly, the review findings showed that when viewed through the lens of SCT, respect plays a key role in forming and nurturing trust within relationships. Based on the review findings, we also point out the gaps in the current entrepreneurship literature and suggest a number of themes for future research.

Keywords: Entrepreneurs · Entrepreneurship · Trust · Respect · Social capital theory · Information seeking behaviour

1 Introduction

Entrepreneurship is widely recognised as one of the primary drivers of industrial dynamism, economic and social sustainability, and growth [1]. A vast majority of prior studies in entrepreneurship research have shown great interest in identifying the factors and conditions that influence the success or failure of a business. Information has been identified as one of the critical factors among those [e.g. 46]. The acquisition and effective use of information positively influence business strategies, operations and

R. K. Bandi et al. (Eds.): IFIPJWC 2020, IFIP AICT 601, pp. 23–37, 2020.
https://doi.org/10.1007/978-3-030-64697-4_4

performance evaluation [67–69]. Information can be generated internally and externally. Internal information includes the knowledge and information accumulated within an enterprise, such as the incorporation of financial, technical and managerial data. External information is information obtained from outside sources, such as information about the market price, product quality requirements, existing and potential customers, sources of finance, and innovations. Both internal and external information are essential for businesses to survive and develop [2, 67–69]. Friedman [3] highlighted the role of information in enabling entrepreneurs to make rational decisions, while Popovič et al. [4] elaborated on its importance in managerial decisions and organisational improvements. Entrepreneurs need information to help them overcome pressure, adapt to market changes and to develop their enterprises in the business world [5]. According to Mueller [6], entrepreneurs' information-seeking behaviour [hereinafter referred to as ISB] and the process they follow for gathering information have a significant impact on the outcomes of their decision-making and ultimately on their business success. However, despite the importance of ISB in the entrepreneurship context, the current literature lacks sufficient contributions on this particular phenomenon.

Often, due to the shortage of information infrastructure and resources, entrepreneurs tend to rely on their networks to access and obtain information. Their networks are based on personal relations, trust and reciprocity. Trust is a crucial factor in entrepreneurial activities, such as in promoting the company, transferring information, enhancing customer relationships, reducing transaction costs and especially for nurturing entrepreneurial networks to acquire resources, opportunities and cooperation. Moreover, the literature on information behaviour acknowledges the significance of trust in knowledge and information sharing among entrepreneurs [7]. According to Hislop [8], the lack of trust results in human withdrawal from the information-sharing process. Connaway [9] furhter conceded the importance of trust in human information-seeking and using-information behaviours [9]. In entrepreneurship study, although trust has been discussed, to the best of our knowledge, the effect of trust and the conditions under which trust works have not been sufficiently explored, especially from an entrepreneurs' information practices standpoint [e.g. 15, 71].

Furthermore, regarding the establishment of trust in interpersonal networks, many researchers have mentioned the role of respect in the trust-building process [10]. In spite of differences in values, trust and respect always act jointly in interpersonal relationships, as a person can only trust someone who he/she respects. Regarding entrepreneurship, Kuratko [11] emphasised that trust and respect are both crucial for entrepreneurs to achieve and maintain success for their enterprises and their personal careers. In some cultures, such as the Chinese and Japanese cultures, the showing of respect is critical to creating a good impression, and results in developing trust within a business relationship [12, 13]. In those cultures, respect is strongly correlated with trust and has been argued that it brings clear benefits to entrepreneurs [13]. This concept has been discussed in various academic disciplines, e.g. social and organisational psychology, leadership, nursing, ethics and education. Yet, it has not been sufficiently addressed in the entrepreneurship research.

Considering the literature gap, this paper presents results from an extensive re-view of the relevant literature, with a specific focus on the significance and relevance of trust and respect in entrepreneurs' information-seeking behaviours. While, performing the literature search, social capital theory (hereafter referred to as SCT) [14] was used as a theoretical lens to investigate the nexus between trust and respect in entrepreneurs' ISB. This theory emphasises how the quality of social resources available within an individual's social network affects his/her success and achievements. Moreover, it has been argued in SCT that an individual's social capital facilitates the individual's behaviour, such as the exchange of information, sharing of capital and reduction of risk [46]. Through their social capital, an entrepreneur can obtain business contacts and advisors that are essential for them performing entrepreneurial activities [46]. Prior studies have acknowledged the merit of other theoretical frame-works, such as resource-based view (RBV) theory [47], in entrepreneurship research. However, as social capital entails interpersonal relationships and the resources embedded in such relationships, we made an explicit choice to use SCT in this paper. Social capital theory allows conceptualising trust and respect and helps to understand how these work and affect entrepreneurs' ISB. SCT provides an understanding of the structural and relational dimensions of information-seeking behaviour [14]. Moreover, this theory helps to study the effect of social structures on information access and its flow. By determining the relationship between information seekers and information sources, in addition to the social position of the information source, the theory provides a framework for monitoring the information behaviours, i.e. information-source preferences.

The main objectives of this study are twofold: (i) to perform an extensive review of the literature to understand the significance and relevance of trust and respect in entrepreneurs' ISB through the lens of SCT, and (ii) to provide the literature review results regarding entrepreneurs' ISB and to suggest themes for future research in this line of research. Based on the above discussions, the following research questions were formulated:

- What is the current state-of-the-art research regarding the role of trust and respect in entrepreneurs' ISB?
- What are the roles of trust and respect and how do they influence entrepreneurs' ISB when viewed through the lens of SCT?

We expect the results of this review paper to contribute to the field of knowledge of information-behaviour studies and entrepreneurship research. In particular, this research, by devoting its focus to an emerging and yet growing stream of research, aimed to provide new insights on the role of trust in the success of entrepreneurs while tackling how respect strengthens it. These two concepts have been studied individually in some depth, but have not been studied together within entrepreneurship studies or in information-behaviour studies.

In the following, we provide an overview of the core concepts, including trust, respect, social capital theory and information-seeking behaviours. Then we present a discussion on the role of trust and respect in entrepreneurs' ISB and their interplay when viewed through the lens of SCT. Finally, we provide some conclusions to re-mark on the important findings from our research and, based on those, we recommend some themes for future research agenda.

2 Definitions of the Concepts

2.1 Trust

Trust has been conceptualised and defined through multiple dimensions in different scientific domains. Prominently, the definitions of trust still maintain its effectiveness and relevance in the current research [15]. Of the many views on trust, for example, psychologists perceive trust as an individual trait or as a psychological state where a person accept uncertainties [16]. From a sociological perspective, trust is a form of social cohesion for the nature of interpersonal relationships [17]. For social psychologists, trust is a psychological condition whereby a person is willing to be vulnerable because he/she has a positive expectation of another's motives and/or conduct [18]. Moreover, economists see trust through a rationale in which a person evaluates the possibility of an event based on its alignment with agency theory [19]. In this review paper, we use Sabel's definition of trust. According to Sabel [20], trust refers to the faith and high hope one holds in others that they will not exploit any adverse selection, moral hazard or any other vulnerability. In other words, each member of a trustful relationship sacrifices his/her short-run benefit and self-interest for joint goals or longer-term objectives. Trust is often analysed through three main disciplines: cognitive, emotional and intentional behaviour [21, 22]. The cognitive aspect indicates a belief or an expression of it that the trustor holds towards a trustee, while the emotional aspect relates to the feeling of security, both physically and psychologically. Finally, the intentional behaviour aspect reflects the trustor's reliance on the trustee's words and actions. This reliance is determined by the level of trust among the parties.

In business relationships, trust reflects a strong belief and expectation in only positive outcomes [15]. In business activities, the trustor is reliant on the trustee's words to fulfil his/her obligation in a business exchange [23]. Additionally, trust also acts as a governance factor for a business owner to overcome uncertainty or to reduce the potential risks existing in a commercial transaction [24]. In a trustful relationship, business owners and entrepreneurs expect their partners to act based on their interest too, or at least to consider those interests. Although, they might be uncertain about how satisfied they will be with the end-results, they still need to have confidence that they will not be disappointed. Those expectations are based on the attributions that the trustor places on the trustee with regard to their trustworthiness [25]. Trustworthiness is defined as the attributes that the trustor uses in the evaluation process to decide if someone is trustworthy or not. The level of trustworthiness is shown through three characteristics: benevolence, competence and integrity.

Benevolence refers to the extent to which a trustee is believed that he/she is determined (willingly) to do good for the trustor. Competence considers one's ability to serve the trustor's interests. Integrity refers to temporal continuity, in which one's readiness and capacity to serve another's interests do not change or stop over time or require supervision. In other words, a person is trustworthy when he/she shows consistency (integrity) in proving his/her willingness (benevolence) and ability (competence) to fulfil the trustor's interests ethically [26]. The trustworthiness of a business partner is shown through his/her personal characteristics, past behaviour and emotions, such as demonstrated honesty, loyalty, sympathy and empathy [27]. It can also be derived from the referral from a community or organisation, i.e. ethnic groups, professions, networks, firms, associations or whole industries in the form of recommendations [20], reputation and image [28]. Particularly in the business world, trust is also gained from the security of political, legal or economic frameworks, as well as the norms, values and codes of conduct inherent within society [15]. Often, entrepreneurs recognise trust through a personal evaluation of the losses and gains in a relationship (calculative trust) [19] or the social interaction (relational trust) [29].

2.2 Respect

Respect can be shown in various forms, including from expressing an attitude, a feeling, to following a norm, a duty, an entitlement, a recognition and a principle [30]. In this paper, respect refers to a relationship in which a subject (respecter) properly responds to the object (respectee) [31]. Respect is often considered object generated rather than wholly subject generated, as the act of respect is owed to, called for, deserved, elicited or claimed by the object [30]. This way of viewing respect allows distinguishing it from other feelings, such as fear, sadness or excitement, as they originate wholly from the subject. This can be explained by 'a deontic experience' [32], which makes respect a must-manner in many situations [33]. Respect is not simply a fundamental moral emotion, but also an effective response to the other as a rational agent. Respect also regards behavioural components. Through appropriate behaviours, the respecter shows his/her conduct, thoughts and feelings towards others or things. Appropriate behaviours include engaging and restricting the response in certain ways, which considers it being suitable, exemplary or indebted to a particular object. The performance of respect can vary from supporting, complimenting, obeying, not violating or interfering, and caring [30]. For further clarification, Darwall [34] introduced two kinds of respect: (i) recognition respect and (ii) appraisal respect. The former respect is the intention to evaluate and give due consideration regarding an object, and thus to adjust one's personal behaviours accordingly. The object of recognition respect is often related to laws, dangerous issues, other's feelings, social institutions or persons in diverse contexts; whereas, the latter respect refers to a positive attitude towards a person because of his/her personal characteristics or achievements.

For entrepreneurs, respect often appears in the list of useful advice that emphasises the importance of entrepreneurs to show and earn respect. However, this concept has been given less attention in academic studies. Researchers, in general, have underestimated this domain when addressing the factors that influence entrepreneurial success or failure. The current literature mostly discusses the role of respect in cross-cultural business [12–36]. To illustrate; for example, Jeanne and Tyree [36] view respect as a key to successfully forming business relationships in Middle Eastern and South Asian cultures. Specifically, managers from these cultures favour doing business with those who respect their values. Respect, thus, supports the flow of relation-ships and interpersonal interactions. This view has been further elaborated by other researchers [12, 13] through studies in different Asian cultures, such as Japanese and Chinese. However, it should be noted that, respect is one of the most basic human manners and is the basis for every sustainable relationship, not just in business activities. As such, entrepreneurs need to show respect to their business partners to increase their chance of success in negotiation, transaction, sustaining their business relationships or expansion of their network. Furthermore, respect is frequently mentioned in leadership and organisational studies. According to those studies, respect positively influences the effectiveness of teamwork, organisational communication and job satisfaction. Hess [37] further added that entrepreneurs as leaders need to show respect to their followers to motivate their contribution and commitment to the enterprise.

2.3 Information-Seeking Behaviour

In the contemporary and information-based society of today, people seek and make use of information in various formats on a daily basis. Research on information-seeking behaviour (ISB) shows how people search, locate and use information to afford their desired information need or to fill a gap in their knowledge. This includes how people make choices regarding where and how to find information, as well as the way they reflect or act based on the information they obtain [38]. Information-seeking behaviour research allows exploring a set of actions, emotions and attitudes that a person goes through in order to obtain the needed information [39]. According to Wilson [40], ISB refers to human behaviour in relation to the sources and channels of information, including both active and passive information seeking and information use. In other words, it encompasses ISB through interpersonal communication as well as in the passive reception of information; for example, from reading a newspaper, watching TV or surfing the Internet without any intention to acquire specific information. Case [39] argued that ISB covers the entirety of both intention-al/unintentional information, as well as purposeful non-search-related behaviour, such as avoiding information.

All businesses need timely, accurate and relevant information for their various business activities. The information needs of entrepreneurs vary over time, according to the stage of the entrepreneurial lifecycle. For instance, the needs of enterprises prior to start-up, or during the start-up phase, will differ from those that are in the growth and expansion phase or for businesses that are in danger of imminent collapse. All these business situations differ in their need for information and in the urgency of that need. Entrepreneur's need for information and their information landscape are thus always emerging and changing. Thus, the need for information makes entrepreneurs seek information in a professional way and on a daily basis. That is why an understanding of entrepreneurs' information-seeking behaviour is essential in relation to understanding the nexus between trust and respect in entrepreneurship. By studying ISB, we can learn how entrepreneurs conceptualise their information needs, the process of selecting the information sources, and their preferences towards the omni-channel of information retrieval. The results of this ISB study can serve as a framework for designing and developing information packages, as well as information services that can directly contribute to entrepreneurial success.

3 The Role of Trust and Respect in Entrepreneurs' Information-Seeking Behaviour

Entrepreneurs rely on their networks when seeking information and affirm social relationships as their preferred sources for business information [41]. As such, it can be assumed that trust forms the foundation of social relationships, and binds people to benevolent and reciprocal interactions. These interactions in social relationships lead to the success of the relational exchange of information. Moreover, the nature of the entrepreneurial environment is often unstable, hazardous and lacks the resources for making only rational choices. Thus, entrepreneurs sometimes need to rely on trust to create a sense of safety for their decisions and actions [15]. In their ISB, entrepreneurs intentionally consider the strength of their social relationships (i.e. trust) when choosing their information sources, and the selected ones are those that they trust.

Furthermore, digitalisation has shifted the nature of ISB and has reduced the barriers of time and space. Information can be broadcast, at least partially, so it can be easily monitored and accessed through multiple sources and channels. In the digital world, trust is an essential determinant for many aspects of enterprises, especially small and medium-sized enterprises (SMEs), including their information processes and communication technology (ICT) adoption [42]. Some researchers have also highlighted the role of trust in adopting e-government and e-entrepreneurship [43, 44]. According to the authors, one of the reasons for some entrepreneurs' refusal to make use of the Internet is due to their lack of trust in the security and reliability of systems and legal frameworks. Trust is often discussed through three modes: institution-based, characteristic-based and process-based trust. The characteristic-based dimension refers to managerial competence and the organisational support of information technology. Meanwhile, institution-based trust refers to individual perceptions of the institutional environment, including the structures, regulations and legislation that make an environment feel safe and trustworthy. Finally, process-based trust concerns the accumulation of trust over time. Trust also connects with the perceived risk in influencing a user's decision to adopt ICT. In other words, users might refuse to adopt ICT if they have unpleasant feelings about it, such as uncertainty, anxiety, conflict, psychological discomfort and/or cognitive dissonance [45].

Regarding respect and its importance, one can argue that respect and showing respect are vital in all business behaviours, as respect forms the basis of all relationships in entrepreneurial activities. The act of respect concerns supporting professional development, showing appreciation, collaboration and caring for others. Respect involves emotional support, appraisal and affirmation, and it strengthens social ties and ensures the information flow [48]. Respect increases the feeling of belonging; thus, a lack of respect would lead to a person's isolation and withdrawal from social interaction. Consequently, in the business environment, the lack of respect would hinder people from sharing their information and knowledge. The showing of respect is not only essential in face-to-face settings, but also in online environments. In the digital information realm, respect also refers to personal data privacy and its governance [49]. Moreover, the role of respect in entrepreneurs' ISB is displayed through its correlation with trust. Respect is a premise of trust. When individuals feel respected, their brains will instantly generate an increased level of the neurotransmitters serotonin and oxytocin, which are associated with a sense of pleasure, trust and belonging [50]. Additionally, Ross and Parks [51] pointed out that the showing of respect results in the evolvement of true caring/cared for social relationships, which further enhances trust between the parties. Additionally, respect is a core determinant of a safety culture [52]. This type of culture refers to an environment with high levels of mutual trust, collaboration and personal and institutional accountability.

4 The Nexus Between Trust, Respect and Information-Seeking Behaviour Through Social Capital Theory

Social capital theory (SCT) is expressly rooted in the notion of trusts, norms and in-formal networks, in which it recognises social ties as valuable resources and powerful means for economic advancement [53]. According to the SCT, social resources are available in personal networks. They can be either in a tangible form, i.e. financial capital, public spaces, private property, or in an intangible form, i.e. social status, human and cultural capital, collaboration, information, reputation, credibility, access to networks, and social and environmental responsibility. The theory suggests that people must form and invest in building strong social ties in their networks and inter-personal relationships in order to obtain social resources, thus receiving rewards like collaboration or economic and social benefits. Social ties are valuable and powerful means of achieving economic enhancement [54] and refer to the interpersonal bonds, which are essential for sharing information, knowledge, emotions and experiences. Social ties can be shown as weak or strong ties [55, 70]. On the one hand, strong ties refer to the close social relationships that one has with others, such as family, friends or colleagues. Members in strong social ties tend to communicate more often and share a great deal of trust in the relationship. Weak ties, on the other hand, are social contacts with whom an individual tends to have a looser connection, such as acquaintances or a stranger with a common background. This looseness may be due to the short duration of the relationship, infrequent interaction or a personal feeling of a lack of closeness [55]. Johnson [14] pointed out that social relationships provide an individual with a better possibility to attain relevant and valuable information to meet their needs.

Trust is a critical driving force in SCT as behaviours within social networks will be more efficient when the trust is high [54, 56]. Trust is the premise for social capital, as it helps forming relationships, societies, partnerships and mutual commitment, all characterising the social capital. Trust reflects the bonds (strong ties) within a social relationship [15]. The degree of trust determines the level of interpersonal interaction within the social network. With trust present, people are more confident in predicting and expecting others' actions, and thus they are more open to act in the relationship. For entrepreneurs, trust, as a relational form of social capital, is imperative to overcome risky business behaviours [57, 58]. The process of entrepreneurship frequently relies on unfamiliar and dysfunctional socio-economic ties [57]. Trust, in this case, transforms complicated and structured transactional relations into fluid and informal relationships. Especially in ISB, entrepreneurs often seek information from those they hold strong social ties with or in other words, with people whom they have established trust and respect. Therefore, they habitually develop and rely on their informal networks, and these are trusted sources of business information, advice and learning [41]. The role of trust in encouraging and facilitating the flow of business information has been widely recognised in previous studies [e.g. 14, 59, 60]. People are more willing to give and receive information when trust exists. In entrepreneurial activities, trust is an instrument that supports the feeling of safety (social cos/risk) while reducing the feeling of uncertainty in certain business circumstances, i.e. the absence of a contract, an incomplete contract or the lack of a guarantee [61, 74].

In terms of the role of respect in entrepreneurs' ISB and especially when viewed through the lens of SCT, it can be argued that respect develops and maintains the social capital of an entrepreneur by helping them form and sustain trust within their social relationships. It also creates good harmony between information seekers and information providers during the information-exchange process [48, 52]. In addition, respect also encompasses the social cost and risk entrepreneurs face when seeking information. The social cost/risk is an individual natural avoidance of embarrassment, the loss of face or the revelation of incompetence, while thriving to achieve social benefits [72, 73]. Respect is a fundamental social manner that entrepreneurs need to feel when approaching and selecting an information source [62]. Silver [63] also revealed that people refuse to ask for information when they sense neglection, or in other words, disrespect. Furthermore, showing respect can significantly influence the enrichment of the entrepreneurial network and its expansion. It contributes to developing and maintaining the social capital of an entrepreneur, which in return grants her/him a greater and better choice of information sources. A respectful manner creates a positive impression of the entrepreneur, which can help her/him also approach new relationships from different social and professional backgrounds through referrals [64]. A large network is useful for entrepreneurs to access wider in-formation through a variety of sources, thus opening the door for greater business opportunities [65].

Moreover, to assess the nexus between trust and respect through the lens of SCT, one must understand that respect and trust positively and jointly influence entrepreneurs' ISB, especially regarding their preference for the information sources. According to social capital theory and in the context of entrepreneurship, respect forms and enhances trust within social relationships, while trust enables the flow of information. Together, they reduce the social cost/risk that occurs during the information-acquisition and information-sharing processes. The information seekers choose a certain information source because they believe that the source has the information they need. Additionally, they have confidence in their ability to understand and accurately interpret the information. More importantly, the information seekers trust that the information providers are willing to give entire and honest information to the seekers without inappropriate judgment or behaviours. As such, from the information providers' perspective, information seekers are more open to those with whom they feel comfortable. In other words, information providers are more confident to place their trust in those who show appreciation and respect to them.

5 Conclusion

This paper provides an overview of the literature highlighting the importance of trust and respect in entrepreneurs' information-seeking behaviours. We affirm the vital role of information for entrepreneurs throughout all stages of their careers, from their entrepreneurial intentions to their entrepreneurial growth and expansion. The nexus between trust and respect and their impact in entrepreneurial success have been seldom discussed in the entrepreneurship research, thus giving rise to its relevance to be pursued in academic research [2, 3]. Consequently, through an extensive review of the literature, we found that both trust and respect play crucial roles in the formation of entrepreneurs' information-seeking behaviour. When viewed through the lens of social capital theory, the review findings indicated that an understanding of entrepreneurs' information-seeking behaviours could contribute to the implementation of a supportive information environment for entrepreneurship. The current literature, however, underestimates the significance of ISB in entrepreneurial success and, more importantly, ignores the nexus between trust and respect in various entrepreneurial activities. This paper thus raises the awareness of academia in this research domain.

This review paper contributes to the literature by showing how trust and respect influence entrepreneurs' ISB, especially their preference for information sources; thus calling for further research and inviting researchers to conduct more research on this topic. The literature review results show that trust and respect are critical factors for entrepreneurs to build and advance various social relationships. These relationships can then be considered as social capital for entrepreneurs and as sources for their information needs [53]. Trust encourages entrepreneurs to overcome their uncertainty and their shortage of resources for making rational choices; whereas, respect is a basic social manner that makes social interactions (i.e. information exchange) fluid. This review paper further demonstrated that trust and respect not only influence entrepreneurs' information-seeking behaviours in the traditional business context, but also in the high-tech environment of digital information, digital devices and digital platforms [43–47]. Especially in the modern era when information is abundant due to the advancement of the Internet and ICT, entrepreneurs could easily enter the era of "fake news", making them sceptical with all the information that comes to them [66]. Trust then becomes an important determinant in nurturing and facilitating the level of participation and an ethical sharing behaviour for information through online communities. Information seekers are more confident in their information evaluation when they have trust in the information providers.

Furthermore, this review paper demonstrated the importance of social capital theory in entrepreneurial activities, particularly from the ISB perspectives. Within the SCT framework, trust is found to have both relevance and the importance in strengthening social relationships. When viewed through the lens of SCT, we found that both trust and respect affect the entrepreneurial sources selections as well as the perception of the social cost/risk. Our literature review findings showed that trust acts as an entrepreneurial shield to protect entrepreneurs from the negative consequences of their social interactions. In addition, we found that respect reduces the sense of the social cost/risk by generating a comfortable and supportive environment for entrepreneurs. Trust and respect further help entrepreneurs to select the rightful information sources for achieving a better quantity and quality. Therefore, we assume that maintaining trust at any cost will naturally bring benefits to firms and their operations. In an entrepreneurship context, most activities are reciprocating, and trust is accumulated through time and experience. Therefore, it is essential for entrepreneurs to act as trustworthy regardless of their role – either as information seekers or as in-formation providers. Inappropriate behaviours or attitudes can cause the entrepreneurs unfavourable consequences, like a loss of trust or respect. Therefore, it is useful for them to pay attention to their behaviour both online and offline to protect and develop their personal and organisational images.

Lastly, the review results showed that there is scarce research in both the entrepreneurship and information-seeking behaviour literature focusing predominantly on the nexus between trust and respect. While explaining its concept, we disclosed that respect is an instrument that nurtures trust within relationship formation and in fostering the extension of social capital for entrepreneurs. On a more practical level, the literature review results implicated that both information seekers and information providers need to pay attention and to perform respectfully throughout their entrepreneurial communications and interactions. Respect is an essential social skill for entrepreneurs to obtain information and to expand their information network. Whereas for information providers, e.g. governments or entrepreneurial organisations, respect is necessary to attract, facilitate and maintain the use of their services. In the digital world, the showing of respect not only covers interpersonal interactions but also concerns maintaining user privacy, data security and the honesty of the information, thus making users feel comfortable and safe while sharing or asking for in-formation on the Internet. This review of the literature also has some practical implications. For example, the findings suggest that information providers need to spend time and effort in relationship building with their users at the very beginning of the initial stage. However, we found that there is a gap in the extant literature; thus, suggesting a number of avenues for future research.

6 Future Research Agenda

This research thoroughly reviewed the prior studies that had investigated the role of trust and respect in entrepreneurs' information-seeking behaviours. However, it seems that the research regarding this topic is fragmented when considering the field of entrepreneurship. Additionally, most of the literature only pays attention to the benefits of trust in relation to social networks, rather than investigating it from an entrepreneurial activities perspective, such as regarding information-seeking behaviours and information-source preferences. Our review findings also revealed that information-seeking behaviour is a sub-concern rather than the main focus of the entrepreneurship literature. This gap in the literature suggests that scholars should develop and pursue this topic empirically. We suggest that researchers interested in this topic should take the initiative in their future research to examine how trust influences the information-seeking behaviours of entrepreneurs, such as their preferences towards the information sources, their ignorance, and their intention to use digital tools to search for information on the Internet.

Furthermore, entrepreneurs' roles in their social networks and their information-seeking behaviours can be interchangeable. They can act as a trustee, a respectee and as an information source. Therefore, we suggest further studies should concentrate on how entrepreneurs build and maintain their trustworthiness and respect in terms of their interpersonal and virtual relationships through social media. In the modern era of an abundance of information and where the spread of fake news in digital networks and over the Internet can lead to an absence of trust, trustworthiness has become a critical issue for enterprises, thus, raising the question of how to trigger the recovery of trust. Moreover, we suggest future research could investigate how to create and maintain a respectful/safe environment for sharing and exchanging in-formation online. This could be examined through a study that focuses on the roles that governmental agencies, service providers and digital platform administrators play.

We also recommend that future studies should investigate the downside of trust in information-seeking behaviours [15, 35, 74, 75]. For instance, looking into issues such as overtrust, mistrust and distrust problems, and examining the possible consequences of these on a business, and alternative solutions for how to avoid these issues. In such a research endeavour, we suggest that researchers pay attention to what could potentially happen to entrepreneurs' ISB when they overtrust, mistrust or distrust their information sources. Moreover, despite the fact that digital information sources are becoming increasingly popular for entrepreneurs and entrepreneurial activities, trust is an essential factor in the adoption or resistance of such sources. Therefore, researchers would benefit from exploring how trust influences entrepreneurial intentions and the usage behaviour of digital information sources. Future research should continue to develop the theoretical framework to study the role of trust in ICT adoption in relation to entrepreneurs' ISB. Additionally, it is essential to draw investigations on what affects trust in entrepreneurs' ISB, i.e. culture, personal traits, risk perception and the role of security, privacy.

Furthermore, the entrepreneurship literature seems to neglect the proper study of respect. The role of respect in the entrepreneurship context is only recognised in cross-culture studies for entrepreneurship and organisational performance. However, it is rarely mentioned in the information-seeking behaviour literature what role respect plays in the decision of an entrepreneur in selecting information sources. Our literature review results indicated that the discussion regarding respect is quite narrow and insufficient. Scholars often consider it as fundamental for building trust but fail to monitor its independent effects on relationship formation. The absence of respect in entrepreneurship research and information-behaviour study hereby opens a broad scope of subjects for future research. For instance, future research could investigate the role that respect plays in building social capital in different contexts (nations, regions, industry, tradition/online environment). Finally, we call for future research on the positive and negative sides of respect in terms of entrepreneurship through both quantitative and qualitative approaches.

References

1. Audretsch, D.B., Cunningham, J.A., Kuratko, D.F., Lehmann, E.E., Menter, M.: Entrepreneurial ecosystems: economic, technological, and societal impacts. J. Technol. Transf. **44**(2), 313–325 (2018). https://doi.org/10.1007/s10961-018-9690-4
2. Nikou, S., Brännback, Malin E., Orrensalo, T.P., Widén, G.: Social media and entrepreneurship: exploring the role of digital source selection and information literacy. In: Schjoedt, L., Brännback, Malin E., Carsrud, Alan L. (eds.) Understanding Social Media and Entrepreneurship. EDE, pp. 29–46. Springer, Cham (2020). https://doi.org/10.1007/978-3-030-43453-3_3
3. Friedman, M.: Essays in Positive Economics. University of Chicago Press, London (1953)
4. Popovič, A., Hackney, R., Tassabehji, R., Castelli, M.: The impact of big data analytics on firms' high value business performance. Inf. Syst. Front. **20**(2), 209–222 (2016). https://doi.org/10.1007/s10796-016-9720-4
5. Heilbrunn, S., Kushnirovich, N.: The impact of policy on immigrant entrepreneurship and businesses practice in Israel. Int. J. Public Sect. Manage. **21**(7), 693–703 (2008)
6. Mueler. D.: Information, mobility and profit. Kyklos **29**(3), 419–447 (1976)
7. Chow, W.S., Chan, L.S.: Social network, social trust and shared goals in organizational knowledge sharing. Inf. Manage. **45**(7), 458–465 (2008)

8. Hislop, D.: Knowledge Management in Organizations: A Critical Introduction, 3rd edn. Oxford University Press, Oxford (2013)
9. Connaway, L.S.: The Library in the Life of the User: Engaging with People Where They Live and Learn. In: OCLC Research, Ohio, USA (2015)
10. Hakanen, M., Soudunsaari, A.: Building trust in high-performing teams. Technol. Innov. Manage. Rev. **2**, 6 (2012)
11. Kuratko, D.F.: Entrepreneurship: Theory, Process, and Practice, 8th edn. Southwestern Cengage Learning, Mason (2009)
12. Grzegorczyk, M.: The role of culture-moderated social capital in technology transfer – insights from Asia and America. Technol. Forecast. Soc. Chang. **143**, 132–141 (2019)
13. Khan, Y.: Tips on Doing Business in Japan. Global Bus. Lang. **2**(16), 187–196 (2010)
14. Johnson, C.A.: Nan Lin's theory of social capital. In: Fisher, K.E., Erdelez, S., McKenie, L.E.F. (eds.), Theories of Information Behaviour, pp. 323–327. Information Today Inc., Melford (2006)
15. Welter, F.: All you need is trust? A critical review of the trust and entrepreneurship literature. Int. Small Bus. J. **30**(3), 193–212 (2012)
16. Luhmann, N.: Trust and Power. Wiley, New York (1979)
17. Granovetter, M.: Economic action and social structure: the problem of embeddedness. Am. J. Sociol. **91**, 481–510 (1985)
18. Das, T.K., Teng, B.S.: Between trust and control: developing confidence in partner cooperation in alliances. Acad. Manage. J. **23**(3), 491–512 (1998)
19. Williamson, O.E.: Calculativeness, trust, and economic organization. J. Law Econ. **34**, 453–502 (1993)
20. Sabel, C.F.: Studied trust: building new forms of co-operation in a volatile economy. Hum. Relat. **46**(9), 1133–1170 (1993)
21. Goel, S.A., Karri, R.: Entrepreneurs, effectual logic, and over-trust. Entrepreneurship Theory Pract. **30**(4), 477–493 (2006)
22. Johnson, D.S., Grayson, K.: Cognitive and affective trust in service relationships. J. Bus. Res. **58**(4), 500–507 (2005)
23. Alfred, S., Wen, X.: The importance of trust in the development of entrepreneurship. Int. J. Advancements Res. Technol. **2**(12), 230–244 (2013)
24. Mickiewicz, T., Rebmann, A.: Entrepreneurship as trust. Found. Trends Entrepreneurship **6**(3), 244–309 (2020)
25. Pirson, M.A., Malhotra, D.: Foundations of organizational trust: what matters to different stakeholders? Organ. Sci. **22**(4), 1087–1104 (2011)
26. McKnight, D.H., Cummings, L.L., Chervany, N.L.: Initial trust formation in new organizational relationships. Acad. Manage. Rev. **23**(3), 473–490 (1998)
27. Nooteboom, B.: Trust: forms, foundations, functions, failures, and figures. Edward Elgar, Cheltenham, UK (2002)
28. Inka, H., Orrensalo, T.: Brand Image as a facilitator of relationship initiation: case studies from business practice. In: Koporcic, N., Ivanova-Gongne, M., Nyström, A.-G., Törnroos, J.-Å. (eds.) Developing Insights on Branding in the B2B Context: Case Studies from Business Practice, pp. 97–112. Emerald Publishing Limited, Bingley (2018)
29. Bromiley, P., Harris, J.: Trust, transaction cost economics, and mechanisms. In: Bachmann, R., Zaheer, A. (eds.) Handbook of Trust Research, 124-143. Edward Elgar Publishing, Northampton (2006)
30. Dillion, R.S.: Respect for persons, identity, and information technology. Ethics Inf. Technol. **12**(1), 17–28 (2010)
31. Banks, S., Gallagher, A.: Ethics in Professional Life: Virtues for Health and Social Care. Palgrave MacMillan, New York (2009)

32. Birch, T.H.: Moral consider ability and universal consideration. Environ. Ethics **15**(4), 313–332 (1993)
33. Rawls, J.: In: Herman, B. (ed.) Lectures on the History of Moral Philosophy. Harvard University Press, Cambridge, Mass (2000)
34. Darwall, S.: Two Kinds of Respect. Ethics, 88: 36–49. Reprinted. In: Dillon, R.S. (ed.) Dignity, Character, and Self-Respect. Routledge, New York (1977)
35. Huvila, I.: Distrust, mistrust, untrust and information practices. Information research, 22(1) (2017)
36. Jeanne, B., Tyree, M.: Research: how to build trust with business partners from other cultures. Harvard Bus. Rev (2020). https://hbr.org/2020/01/research-how-to-build-trust-with-business-partners-from-other-cultures
37. Hess, E.: Growing an Entrepreneurial Business: Concepts & Cases. Stanford University Press, Stanford (2011)
38. Choo, W.C.: The Knowing Organization: How Organizations Use Information to Construct Meaning, Create Knowledge, and Make Decisions. Oxford University Press (2005)
39. Case, O.D.: Looking For Information: A Survey of Research on Information Seeking, Needs and Behaviour, 3rd edn. Emerald, UK (2012)
40. Wilson, T.D.: Human information behaviour. Inf. Sci. Spec. Iss. Inf. Sci. Res. **2**(2), 49–55 (2000)
41. Fielden, S.L., Hunt, C.: Online coaching: an alternative source of social support for female entrepreneurs during venture creation. Int. Small Bus. J. **29**(4), 345–359 (2011)
42. OECD: ICT, E-Business and Small and Medium Enterprises, OECD Digital Economy Papers, No. 86. OECD Publishing, Paris (2004)
43. Al Khattab, A., Al-Shalabi, H., Al-Rawad, M., Al-Khattab, K. Hamad, F.: The effect of trust and risk perception on citizen's intention to adopt and use e-government services in Jordan. J. Serv. Sci. Manage. **8**(03), 279–290 (2015)
44. Bennani, A., Oumlil, R.: Acceptance of e-entrepreneurship by future entrepreneurs in developing countries: case of Morocco. J. Entrepreneurship Res. Pract. 2–10 (2014). https://doi.org/10.5171/2014.700742
45. Featherman, M.S., Pavlou, P.A.: Predicting e-services adoption: a perceived risk facets perspective. Int. J. Hum Comput Stud. **59**(4), 451–474 (2003)
46. Kungwansupaphan, C., Leihaothabam, J.K.S.: Capital factors and rural women entrepreneurship development: a perspective of Manipur state, India. Gender Manage. **31**(3), 207–221 (2016)
47. Burt, R.S.: Structural Holes: The Social Structure of Competition. Harvard University Press, Cambridge (1992)
48. Mineo, D.L.: The importance of trust in leadership. Res. Manage. Rev. **20**(1), 1–6 (2014)
49. Rantanen, Minna M., Koskinen, J.: Respecting the individuals of data economy ecosystems. In: Cacace, M., Halonen, R., Li, H., Orrensalo, T.P., Li, C., Widén, G., Suomi, R. (eds.) WIS 2020. CCIS, vol. 1270, pp. 185–196. Springer, Cham (2020). https://doi.org/10.1007/978-3-030-57847-3_13
50. Meshanko, P.: The respect effect: leveraging emotions, culture, and neuroscience to build a better business. Dog Ear Publishing, Indianapolis (2012)
51. Ross, D.G., Parks, M.: Mutual respect in an ethic of care: a collaborative essay on power, trust, and stereotyping. Teach. Ethics **18**(1), 1–15 (2018)
52. Lucian, L., Miles, S., Jules, D., Robert, M., Edgman-Levitan, S., Meyer, G., Healy, G.: Perspective: a culture of respect, part 2: creating a culture of respect. Acad. Med. J. Assoc. Am. Med. Coll. **87**(7), 853–858 (2012)
53. Bhandari, H., Yasunobu, K.: What is social capital? A comprehensive review of the concept. Asian J. Soc. Sci. **37**(3), 480–510 (2009)

54. Luoma-aho, V.: Social capital theory. In: Carroll, C. (ed.) The SAGE Encyclopaedia of Corporate Reputation, pp. 760–762. SAGE Publications Inc., Thousand Oaks (2016)

55. Granovetter, M.: The strength of weak ties: a network theory revisited. Sociol. Theory **1**, 201–233 (1983)

56. Putman, R.D.: Bowling Alone: The Collapse and Revival of American Community. Simon & Schuster, New York (2000)

57. Shi, H., Shepherd, D., Schmidts, T.: Social capital in entrepreneurial family businesses: the role of trust. Int. J. Entrepreneurial Behav. Res. **21**(6), 814–841 (2015)

58. Manolova, T.S., Gyoshev, B.S., Manev, I.M.: The role of interpersonal trust for entrepreneurial exchange in a transition economy. Int. J. Emerg. Markets **2**(2), 107–122 (2007)

59. Zolin, R., Kuckertz, A., Kautonen, T.: Human resource flexibility and strong ties in entrepreneurial teams. J. Bus. Res. **64**(10), 1097–1103 (2011)

60. Welter, F., Smallbone, D.: Institutional perspectives on entrepreneurial behaviour in challenging environments. J. Small Bus. Manage. **49**(1), 107–125 (2011)

61. Smith, D.A., Lohrke, F.T.: Entrepreneurial network development: trusting in the process. J. Bus. Res. **6**(4), 315–322 (2008)

62. Borgatti, S.P., Cross, R.: A relational view of information seeking and learning in social networks. Manag. Knowl. Organ. Creating, Retain. Transferring Knowl. **49**(4), 432–445 (2003)

63. Silver, M.P.: Patient perspectives on online health information and communication with doctors: a qualitative study of patients 50 years old and over. J. Med. Internet Res. **17**(1), 19 (2015)

64. Fisher, K.E., Durrance, J.C., Hinton, M.B.: Information grounds and the use of need-based services by immigrants in Queen. NY: a context-based, outcome evaluation approach. J. Am. Soc. Inf. Sci. Technol. **55**(8), 754–766 (2004)

65. Su, Y., Zahra, S., Li, R., Fan, D.: Trust, poverty, and subjective wellbeing among Chinese entrepreneurs. Entrepreneurship Reg. Dev. **32**(1–2), 221–245 (2020)

66. Albright, J.: Welcome to the era of fake news. Media Commun. **5**(2), 87–89 (2017)

67. Simon, C.: Corporate information transparency: the synthesis of internal and external information streams. J. Manage. Dev. **25**(10), 1029–1031 (2006)

68. Cooper, A.C., Folta, T.B., Woo, C.: Entrepreneurial information search. J. Bus. Ventur. **10**(2), 107–120 (1995)

69. Anand, V., Manz, C.C., Glick, W.H.: An organizational memory approach to information management. Acad. Manage. Rev. **23**(4), 796–809 (1998)

70. Ren, S., Shu, R., Bao, Y., Chen, X.: Linking network ties to entrepreneurial opportunity discovery and exploitation: the role of affective and cognitive trust. Int. Entrepreneurship Manage. J. **12**(2), 465–485 (2014). https://doi.org/10.1007/s11365-014-0350-3

71. Welter, F., Smallbone, D.: Exploring the role of trust in entrepreneurial activity. Entrepreneurship Theory Pract. **30**(4), 465–475 (2006)

72. Kauer, S.D., Mangan, C., Sanci, L.: Do online mental health services improve help-seeking for young people? A systematic review. J. Med. Internet Res. **16**(3), 66 (2014)

73. Morrison, W.E., Vancouver, B.J.: Within-person analysis of information seeking: the effects of perceived costs and benefits. J. Manage. **26**(1), 119–137 (2000)

74. Kwon, I., Sohn, K.: Trust or distrust: entrepreneurs vs. self-employed. Small Bus. Econ., 1–18 (2019). https://doi.org/10.1007/s11187-019-00278-y

75. Jukka, M., Blomqvist, K., Li, P.P., Gan, C.: Trust-distrust balance: trust ambivalence in Sino-Western B2B relationships. Cross Cult. Strateg. Manage. **24**(3), 482–507 (2017)

Entrepreneurs and ICT Technology in the Dzaleka Refugee Camp

Suzana Brown[1](✉) and Patience Desire[2]

[1] SUNY Korea, Incheon, Korea
suzana.brown@sunykorea.ac.kr
[2] SNHU, Dzaleka, Malawi

Abstract. This paper aims to investigate whether ICT technologies can have an enabling impact by creating opportunities for self-reliance and self-employment for refugees while they rebuild their lives. In the process, we explore the challenges refugee entrepreneurs in Dzaleka refugee camp in Malawi face. Drawing on 25 structured interviews with successful refugee entrepreneurs, the findings suggest that refugee entrepreneurs frequently use digital tools. However, digital literacy is the main obstacle towards accomplishing the full potential of ICT tools and achieving the full benefits of this technology. With one exception, data collection using ICT tools regarding current customers is not common. Given the chance, almost all respondents are eager to obtain customer feedback so they can improve customer satisfaction. Among 25 entrepreneurs 7 are female and among them one with a non-traditional female business.

Keywords: Refugee entrepreneurship · Self-reliance · ICT

1 Introduction

With a growing global refugee crisis, the total population of forcibly displaced people has risen to a record high of 70.8 million people as of 2019 [1]. Despite popular fearmongering and presentations in the media, the burden of refugees, 84% of them, has fallen on developing countries [2]. Uganda alone currently hosts almost 1.4 million refugees and asylum seekers [3]. Similarly, to the south, the UNHCR found Malawi has taken on over 37,000 refugees as of March 2018 [4], many fleeing from the Democratic Republic of the Congo, and the number in Malawi has grown. Malawi's largest refugee camp, Dzaleka, alone hosts more than that even a year later, as this paper will discuss later.

Impoverished developing countries, like Malawi with an annual GDP per capita of nearly $1,300 [5], can face difficulties with supporting refugee and asylum seeker populations, and the refugees and asylum seekers can face quite a bit of difficulty themselves. Refugees often face structural difficulties with entering their host country's labor market, often legal in nature. Having left their homes fleeing war, natural disasters, or prosecution, these refugees are forced to start from scratch, frequently lacking in money or possessions. These problems can both make it difficult for their host countries to take

R. K. Bandi et al. (Eds.): IFIPJWC 2020, IFIP AICT 601, pp. 38–49, 2020.
https://doi.org/10.1007/978-3-030-64697-4_5

care of them and make life difficult for them. To escape these problems, self-reliance and financial security provide them with the tools to succeed. The New York Declaration for Refugees and Migrants of the UN issued in September 2016 emphasizes the importance of this self-reliance [6].

However, the barriers which self-reliance is meant to overcome are also barriers to self-reliance, leaving few options for refugees. One such option is entrepreneurship. This entrepreneurship helps the refugees who engage in it escape the unemployment that faces these populations thanks to institutional difficulties mentioned above. It also provides them with autonomy they would not otherwise have, even among those who can find jobs. Finally, they provide benefits to their host countries by promoting social cohesion and changing the perception of refugees among host populations. As a result, this approach has been a growing tool for international organizations and focus of study for researchers [7].

Refugee entrepreneurs can benefit from the use of ICT technology in many ways, including facilitating their business. As such, it's important to examine the benefits and difficulties around the use of ICT technology among refugees to help policymakers better understand how to handle the problems, and potential solutions, they face in caring for a refugee population.

1.1 Literature Review

There is existing research, both on refugee entrepreneurship and on the use of ICT technology among refugees. It is important to put our research into the context of this existing research.

To begin with, existing research has demonstrated the benefits of refugee populations to host countries [8, 9]. In addition, while research isn't comprehensive on refugee entrepreneurship, the Organisation for Economic Cooperation and Development (OECD) estimated in 2010 that refugee entrepreneurship is higher than normal [10]. A 2011 study of the Kakuma refugee camp in Kenya finds that informal business activity, including entrepreneurship and employment of other refugees, emerged despite difficulties [11]. A 2014 study found that Ugandan refugee entrepreneurs contribute to local economies, both through paying local taxes and rent to local property owners [12]. Finally, a 2017 study in Zambia found that refugee entrepreneurs also contributed jobs to the local economy [13]. Other studies have examined the pressures faced by entrepreneurs in a refugee camp and the ability to begin their entrepreneurial activity [14, 15]. In all these ways, the existing literature demonstrates the willingness and ability of refugees to engage in entrepreneurship and a slew of benefits from refugee entrepreneurship.

Existing studies examine the use of ICT technology in aiding marginalized populations like refugees [16, 17], but this research has been unfortunately limited in scope to developed countries where a minority of refugees reside [18].

Some studies have examined refugees' innovative approaches to entrepreneurship. A study titled "Refugee Entrepreneurship a Case-based Topography" examined 17 case studies of refugee entrepreneurs [19]. Another study examined the use of technology in refugee entrepreneurship based on interviews with refugee entrepreneurs in Berlin [20]. This spurred on panel discussions on the topic at ICIS 2016 and ECIS, two of the largest information Systems Conferences, which explored themes of refugee ability to enter labor markets, their access to information, and opportunities they had for entrepreneurship [20]. These explorations have only begun to scratch the surface of the topic, but already show the benefits of ICT technology to refugee entrepreneurship.

This existing research has established the benefits of refugees to host countries, the ability, difficulties, and benefits of refugee entrepreneurship, and the use of technology by refugee entrepreneurs. Many have focused on developed nations with a minority of refugees. Others have broken ground on research allowing for more in-depth studies in the future.

In addition, there is no consensus on the benefit of entrepreneurship for development. The school that questions benefits of it is discussing the dark side of social entrepreneurship [21], considering terrorists as entrepreneurs [22], and indicating environmental dimension as being negatively affected by entrepreneurship [23]. The most relevant to the present case is the issue of legal identity as an obstacle, and similar to other instances where host country forbids refugee labor [24], inducing refugees to use inventive strategies.

However, the dark side of social entrepreneurship is not in itself a reason to reject more positive uses of entrepreneurship. Positive results of entrepreneurs do not rely upon entrepreneurship being always good. Furthermore, the legal difficulties present a problem to refugee entrepreneurship, but it is a problem overcome with legal fixes to the situation instead of an abandonment of refugee entrepreneurs. Refugee self-reliance would benefit from getting legal access to work and operating a business.

This study seeks to add to existing literature by exploring themes developed before in more depth. It also seeks to add more examinations of developing countries to the analysis. To this end, it will seek to answer: How have the circumstances in the Dzaleka refugee camp in Malawi and the of ICT technology has impacted entrepreneurship? To this end, it will examine a series of interviews with refugee entrepreneurs. In addition, it will show the impacts of refugee entrepreneurship on self-reliance and recovery from crisis.

1.2 Theory

The theoretical basis for the current paper is in the same lines as Tonelli et al. [25] who analyze entrepreneurship by exploring the implications of the theoretical-methodological assumptions of the Actor-Network Theory (ANT). This theory unlike other theoretical perspectives for entrepreneurship, considers all entities as hybrids, diverging from the asymmetric way of accessing reality, recognizing that both, subjective and objective, aspects contribute to the success or failure of entrepreneurial initiatives. Actor-network theory (ANT) holds that social forces do not exist in themselves, and therefore cannot be used to explain social phenomena. Instead, strictly empirical analysis should be undertaken to "describe" rather than "explain" social activity. ANT represents a single circulating entity, instead of the idea dualized between two notions, micro versus macro; individual versus structure, or even subjective versus objective [26]. In addition, the actors are configured according to their position. The perception of its existence only occurs through the connection with other human and non-human elements that make up the network [27].

Furthermore, following the classification from Marti and Mair [28] about brining change to poor via entrepreneurship outside traditional boundaries, which indicates that actors, often powerless and under-resourced, sometimes leverage the following approaches: (1) engage in experimental projects; (2) probe for weaknesses and exploiting small advantages; (3) work – often behind the scenes.

Therefore, this study considers entrepreneurs in the Dzaleka refugee camp, participants in this case study, as actors who along with the other technological and non-human entities form a network in an attempt to exploit small advantages and work behind the scenes to improve their unfavorable position and become more self-sufficient.

2   Background, Methodology, and Data Collection

2.1   Culture and Location Background

Dzaleka camp is located 45 km outside of the capital of Malawi, Lilongwe (see Fig. 1). The camp is small, congested and surrounded by local villages, with no adequate access to agricultural land (see Fig. 2). Refugees in the camp are from Ethiopia, Somalia, Rwanda, Burundi, and Congo. This has resulted in a multicultural community as refugees brought with them their own local cultural practices. In addition, this means that French, English, Kinyarwanda, Kirundi, and Kiswahili are all spoken in the camp, among other languages. These were the languages our interviews were conducted in. Kiswahili is the most popular language in the camp and is the language most business is conducted in. This multiculturalism has produced a diverse landscape of refugees and allowed for many to leverage their unique skills.

Fig. 1. Location of Dzaleka

The UNHCR, the World Food Program (WFP), Churches Action for Relief and Development (CARD), Welt Hunger Hilfe (WHH), World Food Program (WFP), Jesuit Refugee Services (JRS), Plan International Malawi jointly coordinate activities within the camp. A 2019 report from WHH put the population of the camp at 45,095, far outstripping the refugee population in Malawi even the year before.

Fig. 2. Dwellings in the camp

The Malawi government has made it illegal for refugees to get jobs or conduct businesses outside of the camp. However, Malawi does not restrict conducting business in the camps themselves. These legal barriers have created illegal business activity by the refugees outside of the camp and opportunities within the camp for refugees.

2.2   Network Access

It is important for ICT use to consider access to communications networks. There are two cellular internet providers available in Dzaleka, TNM, and Airtel. They bundle voice and internet separately and options are often unaffordable for residents of the camp. Even cheap internet plans carry a large cost. The cheapest is the equivalent cost of two months' rations of maize from the UNHCR. Significantly cheaper plans exist, but they are cheaper because they only allow the use of the internet-based messaging app WhatsApp. However, similar to other locations, internet speeds are less than advertised when residents actually use them. There is not any Wi-Fi in the camp, further restricting the access of residents to the internet.

Digital literacy is low, but a few organizations help build it. The Jesuit Refugee Service provides classes on computer use. AppFactory helps to teach app development. However, these are not yet comprehensive, and neither provide refugees with Wi-Fi.

2.3   Interview Methodology

Interviews were conducted by a student researcher who is also a refugee in the camp and has resided there since January 2015. The interviews began on October 5th, 2019. They were semi-structured in-depth face to face interviews. Interviews were conducted in the native language of the interviewee with a native speaker as a translator. The interviews lasted between 45 min and an hour each and the interviewees were asked to elaborate on some questions.

The interviews were conducted to determine the effect, positive or not, of ICT technology on self-reliance. To this end, the subjects were asked about the general state of entrepreneurship in the camps and the possibility of expansion outside of the camp and integration in the broader society of the host country. The subjects were also asked about the biggest hurdles in their business. Foremost, they were asked about their use of technology, both regarding how they used ICT technology for their business and if they used digital tools for data collection about their customers. Their answers form the basis of the discussion in the next section. Interviews were analyzed for the response patterns by finding common answers for the above questions.

3   Discussion of Interview Data

The refugee camp is estimated to have between 40 and 50 entrepreneurs. The attempt was made to interview all of them but eventually succeeded to talk only to 25 of them, about half. The interview subjects owned a variety of businesses. Some were in the hospitality industry, owning restaurants, bars, or gambling establishments. Others were in retail, owning clothing or produce stores (see Fig. 3). Some were in the service industry, owning barbershops, or providing educational services. Indeed, there was a broad variety in their entrepreneurial activity among the subjects.

Fig. 3. Corner store

A majority of the entrepreneurs had been entrepreneurs prior to entering the refugee camp. Usually they were engaged in a business before they became refugees. One of them described how he had a restaurant in his home country before coming to the refugee camp. He said:

> "It is not the first business, but I was also having the same business in my mother country which is the Democratic Republic of Congo. I was also having a well-known restaurant in Kinshasa which was not in a refugee camp."

Some had businesses at other refugee camps as well. One entrepreneur said:

"This is not the first business I was having a bar in Rukore Refugee Camp which was located in Tanzania."

Having previous experience allowed them to carry over skills and expertise they already had. Their prior experience and carrying over of skills doubtless contributed to the observed diversity of their entrepreneurial activity. However, some who had businesses at home did not have a business in the same industry as before. Most viewed their entrepreneurship as a path to economic security.

In addition, many entrepreneurs talked about their use of ICT. For example, one participant said:

"I normally use my phone to communicate with my customers and even publish some of my services online to attract many new customers. I use mostly WhatsApp and Facebook since they are the only apps with less data consumption compared to other apps."

In addition, some entrepreneurs built their business around ICT and education. One had a business helping refugees with computers, while the other had an education business. Both participants used a wide variety of applications:

"Mostly, I use the android studio for android development, Eclipse, Netbeans, Notepad++ and Microsoft office package."

"I use some applications in communication such as WhatsApp and Slack. I use also Chrome in order to search for some books online."

The major complaints are cost and security. One participant summarizes it:

"I only have two difficulties. The internet bundle is expensive and it is very slow that is why many people are not using many applications. The second problem is security. Some of the refugees can be tracked easily by using technology."

3.1 Gender Data

Of the 25 interview subjects, 7 of them (28%) were women, proportionally much less than the female population in Dzaleka as a whole (46%). With nearly half of women in the general population but a much smaller proportion among entrepreneurs, this shows a lot of difficulties women face in becoming entrepreneurs. Among the women entrepreneurs, 6 out of 7 owned businesses related to food and clothes. Retail is the most common business sector for women ownership [29, 30]. The one remaining business was interesting because it was in welding. The owner, Anna, was interviewed in depth.

Describing how she got into welding, Anna said:

"I was trained by an organization called 'There is Hope' and applied what I have learned. Also, I wanted to support my family and my children because I am a widow."

Describing the challenges, she faced, Anna talked about having a lack of confidence, initially, and the conflicts it had with raising her children as a single mother. Male domination in business also posed a challenge and made it more difficult to raise capital as a woman. Finally, she described men expecting sexual favors from her in exchange for their support of her. When asked about how she stays motivated, she said:

> *"I know what I want, and the social norms and other discouragement are nothing to my business. I am supposed to prove people wrong by showing the result of what I am doing. The profit and the evolution of my business are the things that help me to stay motivated in my business."*

3.2 The Internet and WhatsApp

Almost all the subjects used the internet to conduct their business. WhatsApp was the most popular app for this. WhatsApp was preferred for its security since many of the businesses were not sanctioned by the government and because of phone plans which give WhatsApp use for free. It was both used to communicate with customers and to advertise their business (see Fig. 4).

Fig. 4. WhatsApp adds

They varied considerably if they collected data on their customers, what data they collected, and how they collected it. Some recorded names, addresses, and purchases and others did not. Most businesses wanted to know how their customers thought their services could be improved, and how satisfied their customers were with their business. Some were also interested in demographic information about their customers' information include purchasing power and personal preferences in products and services. Most statements are along these lines:

"I want to know what they think about the services that I offer to them. I would then work on their thoughts to improve my business."

Some of the participants used digital tools for this, but not all. Sophisticated use of digital tools for data collection was extremely uncommon among the participants. One of the exceptions to this was an entrepreneur who worked on ICT technology education. His students developed apps for collecting customer data benefiting him and other entrepreneurs willing to use digital tools for this purpose.

The biggest difficulty to use ICT technology was a lack of digital literacy. Most subjects who had not used sophisticated tools for information gathering cited a lack of skills and expertise as their main reason. Many thought they were making full use of their smartphones but were only using part of their functionalities. As one participant stated it candidly:

"The difficulty that I have is that most of my customers do not know anything about technology. They have smartphones but they are using them for playing music and calling because they do not have knowledge about them."

3.3 Broader Integration

While their business activity was restricted to inside the camp, some reported getting customers from outside of their camp. An entrepreneur who runs a liquor business talked about how he knew he would be successful even outside of the refugee camp because people came into the camp to buy his liquor.

Most were interested in expanding their business outside of Dzaleka and confident they could. A barber talked about his plans of opening a salon in Mzuzu, Malawi's third largest city. Speaking of the viability of this, he said:

"I believe that my skill and experience would be what brings people to my saloon and once I open this salon elsewhere apart from the refugee camp people would still come."

A food and drink shop owner said:

"I want to build my business in various districts here in Malawi once I get the capital I would be able to expand my business to its maximum potential."

Others were not so confident. One participant said:

"chapatti is a staple food for most refugees, therefore, they are prone to buying it. This is a different case with Malawians since their staple food is nsima hence they don't find chapatti as interesting in the same way that refugees do."

However, those lacking in confidence were less numerous and even they wanted to expand out of the camp.

Many would benefit from more access to ICT in expanding their business activity outside of the camp. One participant talked about what he would need to expand out of the refugee camp:

"I have to open a website that will help me to sell my products online."

In addition, some would benefit from increased access to ICT and the electricity in order to expand their business outside of the refugee camp. One computer repairman claimed:

"Electricity would help me to expand my business because its availability would enable me to always send music and songs which would increase my profitability."

4   Conclusion and Future Research

While many entrepreneurs were able to improve their situations, they faced important institutional barriers such as legal barriers that are preventing them from using their entrepreneurship to participate in broader society. A lack of digital literacy precluded many from taking full advantage of ICT technology which would benefit their business. Fitting with the assumptions of ANT, we find all three approaches discussed above among the entrepreneurs examined. We found experimentation, such as a female offering welding services; exploiting weaknesses in the system, such as lack of food variety in the camp; working behind the scenes, such as taking advantage of WhatsApp to get around the illegality of their business.

This reinforces the existing literature's understanding of the difficulties of becoming an entrepreneur as a refugee and the accompanying benefits of it. It further shows that, while existing literature demonstrates benefits to the use of ICT technology, many, especially in developing nations, can experience institutional difficulties accessing that technology, such as a lack of knowledge about how to use them. Further research would benefit from examining how we can increase digital literacy in those extreme settings. In addition, an examination of e-commerce by refugee entrepreneurs would be able to show any further effects of substantial use of ICT technology.

Finally, this demonstrates that policymakers would do well to enhance ICT technology in refugee camps. Programs to increase digital literacy would create multiple benefits for refugee populations. A reduction of legal barriers would be a tremendous help too. The participants have shown a desire to expand their businesses outside of the camps as well as the desire to integrate into the broader society. Doing so would help increase civic participation by refugees and benefit both, host countries and the refugees themselves.

References

1. United Nations: Figures at a Glance. UNHCR. https://www.unhcr.org/en-us/figures-at-a-glance.html. Accessed 23 Apr 2020
2. Resettlement is a critical lifeline for refugees and needs strengthening - UNHCR Philippines: UNHCR. https://www.unhcr.org/ph/16162-unhcr-resettlement-is-critical-lifeline-for-refugees-and-needs-strengthening.html. Accessed 23 Apr 2020
3. 1.4 million refugees set to need urgent resettlement in 2020: UNHCRIUN News: United Nations. https://news.un.org/en/story/2019/07/1041632. Accessed 23 Apr 2020
4. UNHCR data on Malawi. https://www.unhcr.org/malawi.html. Accessed 05 Aug 2020

5. IMF Report for Selected Countries and Subjects. https://www.imf.org/external/pubs/ft/weo/2019/02/weodata/weorept.aspx?sy=2020&ey=2020&scsm=1&ssd=1&sort=country&ds=.&br=1&pr1.x=82&pr1.y=12&c=676&s=PPPPC&grp=0&a=. Accessed 05 Aug 2020
6. United Nations: New York Declaration for Refugees and Migrants. UNHCR. https://www.unhcr.org/new-york-declaration-for-refugees-and-migrants.html. Accessed 23 Apr 2020
7. Wauters, B., Lambrecht, J.: Refugee entrepreneurship in Belgium: Potential and practice. Int. Entrepreneurship Manage. J. 2(4), 509–525 (2006)
8. Maxmen, A.: Migrants and refugees are good for economies. Nature News, 20 June 2018. https://www.nature.com/articles/d41586-018-05507-0. Accessed 23 Apr 2020
9. Jacobsen, K.: Can refugees benefit the state? Refugee resources and African state building. J. Mod. Afr. Stud. 40(4), 577–596 (2002)
10. Entrepreneurship and Employment Creation of Immigrants: OECD. https://www.oecd.org/migration/entrepreneurshipandemploymentcreationofimmigrants.htm. Accessed 23 Apr 2020
11. Oka, R.: Unlikely cities in the desert: the informal economy as causal agent for permanent 'urban' sustainability in Kakuma Refugee Camp, Kenya. In: Urban Anthropology and Studies of Cultural Systems and World Economic Development, vol. 40, no. 3/4, pp. 223–262. JSTOR (2011). www.jstor.org/stable/23339794. Accessed 23 Apr 2020
12. Hakiza, R.: Entrepreneurship and innovation by refugees in Uganda. In: Forced Migration Review Supplement-Innovation and refugees (2014)
13. Nyamazana, M., Koyi, G., Funjika, P., Chibwili, E.: Zambia refugees economies: Livelihoods and challenges. UNHCR, Geneva (2017)
14. Heilbrunn, S.: Against all odds: refugees bricoleuring in the void. Int. J. Entrepreneurial Behav. Res. 25(5), 1045–1064 (2019)
15. Alexandre, L., Salloum, C., Alalam, A.: An investigation of migrant entrepreneurs: the case of Syrian refugees in Lebanon. Int. J. Entrepreneurial Behav. Res. 25(5), 1147–1164 (2019)
16. Qureshi, S.: Are we making a better world with information and communication technology for development (ICT4D) research? Findings from the field and theory building. Inf. Technol. Develop. 21(4), 511–522 (2015)
17. Qureshi, S.: Improving outcomes from information and communication technology for development (ICT4D) studies. Inf. Technol. Develop. 23(4), 645–647 (2017)
18. De Vreede, G.J., Mgaya, R.J., Qureshi, S.: Field experiences with collaboration technology: a comparative study in Tanzania and South Africa. Inf. Technol. Develop. 10(3), 201–219 (2003)
19. Freiling, J., Harima, A., Heilbrunn: Refugee entrepreneurship a case-based topography. In: Refugee Entrepreneurship, pp. 255–277 (2019)
20. Abujarour, S., et al.: ICT-enabled refugee integration: a research agenda. Commun. Assoc. Inf. Syst. 44, 874–891 (2019)
21. Williams, D.A., Kadamawe, A.K.: The dark side of social entrepreneurship. Int. J. Entrepreneurship 16, 63 (2012)
22. Abdukadirov, S.: Terrorism: the dark side of social entrepreneurship. Stud. Conflict Terrorism 33(7), 603–617 (2010)
23. Dhahri, S., Omri, A.: Entrepreneurship contribution to the three pillars of sustainable development: what does the evidence really say? World Devel. 106, 64–77 (2018)
24. Marti, I., Mair, J.: Bringing change into the lives of the poor: entrepreneurship outside traditional boundaries. In: Institutional work: Actors and Agency in Institutional Studies of Organizations, pp. 92–119 (2009)
25. Latour, B.: On actor-network theory: a few clarifications. Soziale Welt 47, 369–381 (1996)
26. Geels, F.W.: Technological Transitions and System Innovations: A Co-Evolutionary and Socio-Technical Analysis. Edward Elgar Publishing (2005)

27. Tonelli, D.F., de Brito, M.J., Zambalde, A.L.: Entrepreneurship from the actor-network theory perspective: exploring alternatives beyond the subjectivism and objectivism/Empreendedorismo na otica da teoria ator-rede: explorando alternativa as perspectivas subjetivista e objetivista. Cadernos EBAPE. BR **9**(S1), 586–604 (2011)
28. Brees, I.: Refugee business: strategies of work on the Thai-Burma border. J. Refugee Stud. **21**(3), 380–397 (2008)
29. Rhodes, C.: Business statistics. Briefing paper, p. 6152 (2015). https://www.limeconsultancy.net/wp-content/uploads/2015/02/sn06152-1.pdf
30. Davis, P.S., Babakus, E., Englis, P.D., Pett, T.: The influence of CEO gender on market orientation and performance in service small and medium-sized service businesses. J. Small Bus. Manage. **48**(4), 475–496 (2010)

Perceptions of Rwanda's Research Environment in the Context of Digitalization: Reflections on Deficit Discourses

Pamela Abbott[(✉)] [iD] and Andrew Cox [iD]

University of Sheffield, Sheffield S1 4DP, UK
{p.y.abbott,a.m.cox}@sheffield.ac.uk

Abstract. Digitalization of research processes, like those related to open science, for example, has had mixed outcomes for the visibility of African scholarship. One reason for this may be that ICT-based interventions aimed at improving African research systems presume a country deficit model, that is, a view that Africa's research environment is inherently under-resourced, and failing. Our study set out to explore, through a collaborative rich picture exercise, how research practices are viewed in Rwanda in the light of digitalization by a mixed group of global North and South information specialists. Through an in-depth qualitative inductive analysis of the participants' accounts, we uncovered not only a dominant discourse of "deficit", but also an underlying but hidden counter-narrative of resistance to this. We extrapolate how this view could be seen as having the potential for more optimistic outcomes in promoting a more inclusive African research paradigm. We then suggest a research agenda to explore the potential for the digitalization of research processes to provide a means of enabling a dialogue between Western and indigenous forms of knowledge.

Keywords: African research systems · Digitalization · Deficit discourses

1 Introduction

There is a persistent discourse around African research that labels it as sub-standard (Arowosegbe 2016). Within this discourse, African scholars are often considered invisible through not participating in global research networks (ibid.). An oft-quoted statistic is that authors from sub-Saharan Africa produce less than 1% of the world's research outputs (e.g. Fonn et al. 2018). Research about Africa that does become known is often co-authored by scholars from the global North, with the role of the African researcher being relegated to data collection or other secondary tasks (Tijssen 2007). This has led to critiques of global North researchers in collaborative research projects based in Africa as being 'extractive' and exploitative (Bai 2018).

The digitalization and globalization of research and scholarship has had mixed outcomes for the visibility of African scholarship. For example, open access/open science programs have been initiated to make African scholarship more visible (McKay 2011),

© IFIP International Federation for Information Processing 2020
Published by Springer Nature Switzerland AG 2020
R. K. Bandi et al. (Eds.): IFIPJWC 2020, IFIP AICT 601, pp. 50–64, 2020.
https://doi.org/10.1007/978-3-030-64697-4_6

but their success is dubious, since openness may expose African scholarship to further exploitation and/or inequalities that mirror or amplify existing digital divides (Schöpfel and Herb 2018). Projects such as Research4Life, funded by international aid agencies, have been set up to enable African scholars access at no, or lower costs, to up-to-date research from the global North. These may, however, be seen as creating a 'market' for global North scholarship and playing into the already North-dominated scholarly publishing system, creating a new form of dependency in a digital economy of knowledge production and dissemination (Chan 2018). Other foreign-aid funded projects aimed at digitally 'strengthening' Africa's research infrastructures (e.g. the EU-sponsored Africa-Connect initiative[1] or Canada's IDRC ICT4D program[2]) and research systems (e.g. SIDA in Rwanda[3]) seem to make only short-term impacts on what appears to be an intransigent problem (Malapela 2017).

It seems that many of these interventionist programs are based on a country deficit model, i.e. a view that Africa's research systems are inherently under-resourced, and failing (Gwynn 2019). Yet this discourse seems to echo the view of development as modernization (Escobar 2012), assuming that there is a common path of development for all countries and ignoring more positive alternatives that would reflect the local needs and strengths of the country. Our study set out to explore how people in one such country saw the status of research there and whether alternative models could be uncovered.

The paper reports on our own attempts in the Information School, University of Sheffield, UK, to start a research collaboration with Rwandan higher learning institution (HLI) librarians and a pan-African information specialist training organization supporting capacity-building efforts in a range of African countries, including Rwanda. Led by our own ethos to engage in participatory and inclusive research, we employed a group discussion method using rich pictures (Checkland and Scholes 1990) to help frame participants' understandings of the research situation in Rwanda. We found that even though the findings revealed underlying patterns of subordination of African research and persistence of the perception of 'failure' as described above, there was an alternative thread that gave a voice to a counter-discourse that is often absent in these debates. What is promising about this counter-narrative is its linkages with other alternative literatures that offer a more optimistic view of research and scholarship in African contexts, some of which also enroll digital technologies in complementary ways (e.g. Piron et al. 2016).

The aim of the paper is to explore discourses around Rwanda's research environment in the context of ongoing digitalization of research processes through the vehicle of an incipient North-South research collaboration. The following research question is thus raised: *What practical issues/challenges can be found in participants' accounts of doing research in Rwanda?*

The following section reviews the literature that presents African research and scholarship as a discourse of deficiency. We then present the methodology of our research

---

[1] This initiative provides ongoing support for research and education networking in sub-Saharan Africa (see: https://www.africaconnect.eu/Pages/Home.aspx).

[2] The IDRC's ICT4D programme initiated a series of infrastructure connectivity programmes aimed at improving access to digital services in several African regions (Elder et al., 2013).

[3] The Swedish government sponsored programmes to strengthen the main research institution in Rwanda (University of Rwanda) including emphasising the role of ICTs (Tvedten et al. 2017).

study followed by in-depth accounts of the findings. We discuss those findings in the light of the dominant 'deficit' discourse while also presenting the counter-discourse for comparison, after which we offer a medium for pursuing a research agenda on this topic. We conclude on this point while also acknowledging the limitations of the study.

2 Literature Review

We take a broad interpretation of the term 'digitalization' in this paper to refer to the processes by which social norms and structures are increasingly influenced by the use of digital technologies (Brennen and Kreiss 2016). In the practices of academic research and scholarship, digitalization can manifest itself as the application of digital technologies and processes to any aspect of these practices, e.g., publication of research outputs, or the underlying bases that enable them, e.g. research infrastructures. One good example of the potential transformative effect of digitalization on research processes is the development of open science, a movement towards more collaborative engagement in knowledge creation and dissemination, underpinned to a great extent by digital technologies (Fecher and Friesike 2014). It has sometimes been positioned as a beneficial development for African scholarship by elevating its status (Raju et al. 2015).

Literature on the paucity or presumptive 'failure' of research from sub-Saharan Africa, though, tends to present it from a "country deficit" perspective. This places center-stage a web of in-country issues that are assumed to create research environments that are inimical to the smooth functioning of the research process (Ngongalah et al. 2018). This perspective emphasizes what the country lacks and how it can "catch up" to more developed country research contexts, which we refer to as a 'deficit' discourse in this paper, where deficit denotes lack or failure in comparison to the contexts of those generating the discourse (Aikman et al. 2016). It does so, however, without necessarily positioning these issues within broader systems of imbalance such as the inequalities created by the international scholarly communication system (Chan 2018). Rather, it focuses on the way that a weaker in-country environment for research makes it more difficult to perform research on par with external scholars. In development contexts such discourses can be enduring and help to reproduce the very conditions which they describe, through so-called discursive practices, sustained by regimes of knowledge and power (Escobar 2012). Below we highlight how these discourses present countries' research environments as a problem to be 'fixed'. Research environments (also referred to as systems) encompass the institutions, infrastructures, processes and other contextual factors that provide support for in-country knowledge creation and dissemination (GDN 2017).

2.1 The Country Deficit Perspective Explained

The country deficit perspective portrays the State's commitment and investment in research in Africa as weak. According to (Fonn et al. 2018), investment in education including Higher Education was a priority immediately after independence; however, since the 1980s, African governments reduced spending on higher education and research, in favor of primary and secondary education. This trend was reinforced by economic policies imposed via the IMF and World Bank. More recently, the World Bank has recognized the need to create local knowledge economies in Africa (Fonn et al. 2018; Collins and Rhoads 2010), thus resulting in a slight increase in the subcontinent's contribution to research output (Fonn et al. 2018). In comparison to more advanced economies, however, the level of government investment in research remains low, below 0.5% of GDP (Beaudry et al. 2018). Where research policies exist, they tend to mimic those of the global North, ignoring local conditions (Boshoff 2009). This may be influenced by the fact that North-South interventionist programs meant to improve research systems in the global South tend to employ models of performing research from the global North (e.g. UNESCO 2009). Universities seem unable to prioritize research, following instead a strategy of massification, which is evidenced by increased growth in student numbers, with accompanying pressures on academic workloads (Beaudry et al. 2018).

This extensive focus on teaching precludes much inspiration for research as a career (Ngongalah et al. 2018). The country deficit perspective also highlights lack of funding, of equipment and of support and mentoring as key barriers for young scholars (Beaudry et al. 2018). Teaching in research methods is deemed to be lacking (Ngongalah et al. 2018) and a lack of influence of research on policy further reduces the motivation to undertake research. These societies are also portrayed as lacking free self-expression, which could be interpreted as a precondition for scholarly debate. The low rewards for research and lack of a research environment are implicated in the "brain drain", with many talented individuals being drawn to migrate (Ondari-Okemwa 2007). The number of scholars moving away from Africa could have been as much as 30% in the 1980s and 90s (Beaudry et al. 2018).

Another important issue in the country deficit model is basic infrastructure. There are fundamental problems in terms of reliable electricity supply, computer ownership, internet access and bandwidth (e.g. Malapela 2017). Even within universities, which are relatively well resourced, facilities are not comparable to those in the Global North. In addition to the international digital divides, there are significant differences in access to resources and skills between institutions, between subject areas of study and geographically within countries (Gwynn 2019). Women are under-represented in scholarly output (Gwynn 2019). While considerable investment is being made in internet infrastructure and digital skills (Nwagwu 2013), African infrastructure consistently lags behind that taken for granted in the Global North.

From the perspective of access to scholarly content, low investment in research as a whole is reflected in a failure to license access to relevant literature. Digitalization does not necessarily provide a solution either, e.g., with open access, scholars often lack the bandwidth or digital and information literacy skills to access content. A country deficit view also prevails regarding the provision of digital infrastructure for open access repositories, which are deemed weakly developed in Africa due to lack of funding, awareness and support from senior management and poor technical infrastructure (Dlamini and Snyman 2017). African institutions have also struggled to fund and retain the expertise to run open access systems effectively (e.g. Christian 2008). These problems are not unique to Africa, but they are often portrayed as barriers causing Africa to lag significantly behind the global North. The consensus is that, fundamentally, the relatively weak research environment in Africa makes it hard for scholars there to benefit from digitalization efforts in the research process.

In the same vein, scholarly publishing within Africa itself is also seen to be weak due to lack of sustainable business models or funding. African authors are reluctant to publish in local journals because the journals lack prestige; indeed African institutions tend to require publication in "international journals" with impact factors. Local publications are effectively invisible since they are not effectively indexed within the scholarly communication systems (Chan 2018). Language is also particularly a barrier for scholars from Sub-Saharan Africa; there are many local languages, but few are used for research publication (Ondari-Okemwa 2007). In the realm of the sharing of research data, Bezuidenhout et al. (2017) identify a large number of barriers in low-resourced research environments. The whole infrastructure for data sharing is seen to be disadvantageous, however, researchers may also not profit from sharing their data for fear of being scooped. Some deficit issues raised are the cost of hardware and software, slow internet speeds and lack of technical support.

2.2 Global South Research Systems

The country deficit perspective is also apparent in the growing literature on the assessment of research environments in countries of the global South. Such literature seems to be predicated on the need to replicate similar systems evidencing the link between science and policy as exists in the global North (GDN 2017). A perceived wide and growing research capacity deficit between so-called 'developed' and 'developing' countries is prompting efforts to establish underlying causes (Mouton and Waast 2009; GDN 2017). A number of tools, techniques and frameworks have been devised to undertake these assessments, but they tend to be based on conceptualizations of research systems as they may work in advanced economies (GDN 2017; Gaillard 2010; UNESCO 2009). There is a recognition that such models may not be entirely congruent with the research environments in low-resource contexts: "...developed research systems – such as those that exist in advanced countries – broadly present different issues from developing ones, especially when it comes to the question of change… The main difference between developed and developing research systems is that, with the former, all or most constitutive elements of a highly productive, international grade research environment are active and effective, while with the latter, some elements are more active and others are either inchoate or non-existent" (Idrissa 2016, p. 3).

These incongruences result in an inability to collect enough reliable data on indicators thought relevant to measuring the performance of the research environment (Gaillard 2010; Mouton and Waast 2009), thus leading to efforts to capture other forms of data that are more processual and qualitative (Gaillard 2010). There is also a question as to whether a 'system' is the best way to describe what is actually occurring in research environments in lower-resourced contexts: "It is even debatable whether one can talk of a science 'system' in many of these countries, as they do not exhibit typical systemic characteristics… Rather, the image of an 'assemblage' of fragile, somewhat disconnected and constantly under-resourced institutions is perhaps a more apt metaphor to describe the science arrangements in some of these countries, particularly in many countries of sub-Saharan Africa" (Mouton and Waast 2009, p. 167).

Although these assessments attempt to capture a view of the social and political contexts in which these research systems operate, their tendency to try to find one-size-fits-all indicators and to compare across countries means that only a superficial analysis can be made. Additionally, such comparative models undoubtedly reinforce the rhetoric of deficiency and dysfunction at play in 'developing country' research environments and the message that they need 'rescuing' or 'fixing'. In turn, this discourse then also falls into the realm of "development as modernization" and encourages a culture of dependency, especially on foreign knowledge regimes (Andrews and Okpanachi 2012). ICT4D literature has already critiqued modernization views of technology-based innovation in the global South and promoted the importance of embeddedness in the local context for a more meaningful engagement with local actors (Avgerou 2010). We take a similar view with regard to the development of research systems in Africa, especially in the light of digitalization, which has often been shown to amplify divides and inequalities, rather than ameliorate them (Toyama 2011). We also align with the spirit of counter-narratives to development as modernization, which take a more context-sensitive approach to improving life conditions in low-resourced settings (Escobar 2012).

3   Methodology

Qualitative data for this paper were collected as part of a project to initiate engagement with the higher learning institution (HLI) librarian community in Rwanda. We (2 University of Sheffield, Information School researchers) contacted 4 librarians from 3 HLIs in Rwanda: University of Rwanda (2 participants), University of Lay Adventists of Kigali (1 participant) and Ruhengeri Institute of Higher Education (1 participant). All were directors of their respective libraries. Prior to travelling to Sheffield, we co-developed a questionnaire which they used to conduct informal enquiries in their institutions. These enquires, together with their own experience as service providers, gave the librarians a broad understanding of their research environment. Our participants also included a representative of Information Training and Outreach Centre for Africa (ITOCA), an NGO targeting capacity-building in information skills for a range of library and information specialists across Africa. ITOCA's knowledge of regional contextual issues around research practice would also inform the data collection. Three of the four invited librarians, the ITOCA representative and the two Information School researchers participated in the weeklong workshop.

We conducted daily group interviews involving the participants. Altogether, we collected around 12 h of recorded material over the weeklong period supplemented by 6 "rich pictures", 10 flipcharts representing discussions and 30 A4 pages of notes. The focus of this paper is on the rich picture collaborative group exercise (similar to Walker et al. 2014) which took place on Day 2 of the weeklong engagement workshop. For this exercise, all participants were asked to prepare a 'picture' of the challenges/issues of doing research in Rwanda. Each participant then presented their rich picture for the benefit of the group and then led a discussion about it. Each presentation and discussion session was recorded and documented, while the flipcharts representing the rich pictures were collected, stored and scanned for later reference. For analysis purposes, each rich picture, its discussion notes and recording were treated as a separate case. Separate in-depth inductive analyses of the cases were done to draw out themes across all of the cases and relate them back to the research question. Table 1 presents the data that were analyzed for each case.

Table 1. Rich picture data collected.

ID	Title of rich picture	Participant [CODE]
RP1	Challenge: availability of content	Rwandan librarian 1 [RL1]
RP2	Challenges: lack of motivation fees & money to be used in research activities	Rwandan librarian 2 [RL2]
RP3	Researchers' skills development	Rwandan librarian 3 [RL3]
RP4	Publishing in low-resource environment	ITOCA representative [IR]
RP5	Global south collaborations	Information school researcher 1 [ISR1]
RP6	Research across two continents	Information School Researcher 2 [ISR2]

Reflecting on our method after the workshop, we began to ask whether framing the rich picture exercise around "issues and challenges" might itself have been influenced by the country deficit discourse. We sought for ways to reassess this as a starting point. We were inspired as a result, to consider how far within the participants' accounts there was evidence for an alternative counter-narrative framing of research practice.

4 Results: Key Points from the Rich Picture Cases

Synopsis of RP1. The main topic of this rich picture was about the (lack of) availability of, and access to, relevant content in many aspects of the Rwandan research environment. The issue was presented from the viewpoint of a Rwandan HLI librarian and their perceptions of the challenges to a Rwandan researcher working in this environment. Presented in a very factual/literal manner, some key issues raised were:

- High costs of subscription to international content;
- Lack of access to locally produced Rwandan content;
- Comparably greater proportional availability of international to local content;
- Low incidence of Rwandan researchers publishing in open access repositories;
- Poor maintenance of these open publishing infrastructures in Rwandan HLIs.

Related to the issue of relevant content was that of impediments to implementing local Rwandan research outcomes due mainly to language barriers. The research outputs are generally produced in English, while policymakers may not be literate enough in that language to be able to convert these findings into implementable outcomes. This leads to what the RL1 referred to as an "information divide", where the results of locally-produced research are rendered inaccessible to the potential beneficiaries.

"...when it comes to the population, they are out of what's going [on], they don't have anything of what's going on, so it's like..., it seems that the project talks about them and is intended to solve their problem even, but at the end of the day... they are also absent as audience" [RL1]

Synopsis of RP2. The main topic of this rich picture was about the financial constraints facing the Rwandan researcher when conducting research locally. The issue was presented from the viewpoint of a Rwandan researcher undertaking field or laboratory-based research. In a very pragmatic way, RL2 proposed "fees" as a key issue to enable (motivate) a local researcher to conduct research and publish the results. The various types of "fees" were broken down into components roughly matching various stages of the research process. The overall implication was that without the availability of "fees" at these various stages, no research was possible.

The discussion revealed that financial constraints both at the level of the HLI (insufficient budgets to fund research) and at the individual level (low salaries) contributed to the need for research funding to subsidize researchers' incomes and those of the many people dependent on the ancillary jobs at each stage of the research process. As RL2 put it, it is a matter of supporting livelihoods:

"Every researcher needs money for a better life... better life means everyone needs money, money from funders so when you get money, you do everything but when you are hungry you can stay at home [laughing in background] for better life" [RL2]

Without these incentives, researchers are likely to seek top-ups to their income by taking on consultancies or extra teaching at other institutions. When funded, they also need to be mindful of financially supporting the "pecking order" of research assistants as mentioned above.

Synopsis of RP3. RP3 was mainly about the lack of a reading and writing culture to support researchers in building up their skills in order to publish their research. This was presented from the perspective of a Rwandan HLI librarian's view of a Rwandan researcher. Like RL1, the key points were presented in a factual/literal manner underpinned by a sort of logical portrayal of the successful pathway to this end: resources/content → search skills → reading → writing → publishing.

RL3 noted 2 key barriers to achieving the above goals: institutional weakness in supporting training and availability and access to content; and the traditional oral society, which RL3 believes is hampering the development of a reading culture:

"So the oral tradition, I think, is another burden on the academician. To spend time reading, reading is time-consuming and sometimes for some literature, it requires concentration. So, there are many things which cause ... in their home, in their houses, there is no other room because there are many people there, you can't read" [RL3]

Rwandan culture and the oral tradition continued to be a major thread of the discussion on this rich picture topic, with other key points being made such as: the large extended families in which researchers are embedded and to which they must contribute financially; the coded messages used to transmit knowledge from generation to generation in traditional Rwandan oral culture; the crowded family homes in which there is no room for reading quietly; and the ineffectiveness of the library as an institution, e.g., in:

> *"When it comes to libraries like the national library, you realize that they exist by name [in name only] but [are] not working properly. Public libraries, also, they have created recently, again are not working properly. So materials on Rwanda, they are there but not well organized." [RL1 in RP3 discussion]*

Synopsis of RP4. This rich picture was presented from a dual point of view, first, from the perspective of the researcher from a low-resourced setting, such as Rwanda, and second, from the perspective of the NGO that is implementing the research project in that low-resourced setting. This rich picture was presented in the form of a force-field analysis with incentives to do research (publish) on one side of the flipchart and barriers against it on the other side. In general, the forces constraining the 'publish' goal were stacked up against the incentive forces and the situation was presented as a challenging "terrain" for a "survival"-oriented type of researcher who has learnt to negotiate this challenging environment.

From the NGO's perspective, the main challenge was to provide a bridging role between the local research environment and the external funding agencies. In this regard, IR raised the issue of the powerlessness of local actors to advance their own research agendas:

> *"External funders drive the research agenda. So the research agenda is not yours. You are going to write that agenda according to what the [external] researcher is willing to fund, so you tell them what they want to hear and therefore then you will be accepted and you are likely to get some funding. So it's not to address the local challenges as such. It's to address what the funder wants to hear" [IR]*

Synopsis of RP5. RP5 was about building global North-South collaborations and was presented from the point of view of a global North researcher. The rich picture was organized in the form of a mind map with the key phrase "Global South Collaborations" in the center and other concepts linked to it around the flipchart. It thus gave the impression of presenting a complex, holistic picture of the situation of doing research in the Rwandan context.

In the presentation and discussion of this rich picture, there were many points critiquing the above, especially, the motivations for ODA (development-focused) funding by the UK government and the pressures to do more and more (potentially extractive) research in the global South:

> *"The other thing that they are pushing now in GCRF [Global Challenges Research Fund] is they want to spend the money in even lower resource countries. This is a good thing for Rwanda, really, but again that is pushing you as a researcher now to go into countries which are so very different in their contexts from where you come from, that it's going to be so hard for you to understand what the problems and the issues are there. And they don't give you time to understand this." [ISR1]*

Synopsis of RP6. The last rich picture analyzed was that of the differences between the research contexts of the global North (UK) and the global South (Rwanda). The perspective here was also that of a global North researcher and presented a dichotomous view of the two research contexts, attempting to depict:

- Cultural issues (language and contexts) – e.g. plurilingualism vs. monolingualism, diversity vs. homogeneity
- Organizational decision-making – hierarchical vs. flat
- Level of economic development – low-tech, agriculture-based vs. highly-industrialized, information-rich
- Environmental sustainability – high level, low level
- Connectivity – low-level vs. high-level of technology infrastructure

A key point raised in this rich picture concerned the overwhelming power wielded by the resource-rich global North, with its historically dominant position based on an imperialist past, which still exerts neo-colonial influences in the global South. A key enforcer of this power differential in the research context is the imperative to write and publish in English, which, as noted by previous rich pictures, is a key weakness in Rwandan cultural traditions. This position is expressed candidly in the following:

> "I think you're being sucked into a system; you are at the margin of a system that we are at the center of. We've got the privilege of writing in our own language. I'm the editor of a journal. I can get my things published relatively easily, but we're thinking of the people on the other side. They can't even write in their own language. There's something very wrong about that. And it's also creating this uniform worldwide culture." [ISR2]

5   Discussion

5.1   Rich Picture Discussions as Deficit Discourses

All six rich picture accounts collected in the workshop, in their own way, shared an explicit deficit view of Rwanda; they all made assumptions that a global North model of research was appropriate to Rwanda and that by this standard their system had failed. Reflecting on our own research practice, we realized, however, that we (a) influenced the co-development of the informal questionnaire by assuming challenges *would* be found and (b) influenced the topics of the rich picture discussions by explicitly asking for their perceptions of these challenges, i.e., *seeded* the challenge idea. Thus, it is hardly surprising that various 'deficit' viewpoints surfaced as described below.

Knowledge and Content Deficit: RL1 bemoaned the failure of the library infrastructure to provide scholars access to the content they needed. There were not enough funds to buy content. Local publishing was weak. The open access infrastructure was poor. For this participant, the basic knowledge infrastructure that academic librarians are tasked with creating barely existed.

Financial Deficit: RL2 perceived Rwanda's deficit in research in terms of poverty; the accumulating costs of research make it impossible for most scholars to afford to do it. This participant's vision of Rwanda is simply as a poor country.

Skills Deficit: RL3 mourned Rwandan scholars' lack of skills in finding content, in reading, in writing in English and in getting published. Fundamentally there was no reading and writing culture because the society's norms were still rooted in orality. His picture of Rwandan researchers was a view of them lacking in skills.

Research Infrastructure Deficit: Bringing these points together into an overview, IR articulated a dilemma of researchers being trapped between the standards of global North scholarship (to gain funding and to publish for tenure) and the range of deficits in the research infrastructure which effectively prevented them succeeding: teaching load, lack of local funding, competition for international funding and misdirected funder research priorities. The whole research infrastructure is condemned as in deficit.

Sustainability Deficit: While ISR1 and ISR2 focused more on the context for international collaboration, both also expressed a sense of deficit. ISR1's account focused on creating a house of collaboration, but revealed a lack of confidence in the UK infrastructure to truly support equal and ethical international research partnerships.

Power Deficit: ISR2's account expressed a sense of a huge gap of understanding between contexts overlaid by a historical and continuing power differential. Rwanda suffers from a power deficit. The deep roots of the deficit in Rwandan research are revealed.

Participants in the workshop had thus effectively reproduced the dominant country deficit discourse as discussed in the literature review, shaped in part by how we had framed the grounds of debate. The *Financial Deficit, Sustainability Deficit* and *Power Deficit* views aligned to the first point of the country deficit model as summarized in the literature review, namely, that concerning inadequate investment in higher education and subsequent dependency on foreign aid (Collins and Rhoads 2010). The *Knowledge and Content Deficit* and *Skills Deficit* views aligned with the second point concerning lack of institutional and suprainstitutional support (Ngongalah et al. 2018). Finally, the *Research Infrastructure Deficit* views aligned to the third point concerning inadequate support for research infrastructures (Gwynn 2019).

5.2 Alternatives to the Deficit Discourse

Having recognized during the analysis process that we had ourselves set up the discussion premised on deficit, it seemed appropriate to actively search analytically for counternarratives. We argue that in the participants' statements and the discussion around the points within the group we can glimpse the outline of a form of resistance to a neocolonial model of research.

Thus, RL2's account hinted at the figure of the potential researcher simply refusing to do research when it did not provide them with a living for a "good life". It appeared that the needs of the extended family that depended on the researcher were valued more than a research career. Thus, fundamental household structures are pictured as preventing the penetration of global North values around research. Although presented as a deficit, it also points to the basis for a refusal to participate in neo-colonial globalization.

Similarly, while RL3 damned the lack of a reading and writing culture, what was simultaneously revealed was the survival of indigenous oral culture. At the most fundamental level the extended household seemed to prevent the creation of quiet spaces for private reading. The "barriers" of language begin also to seem like a form of protection.

Scholars struggled to express themselves for publication in English, seemingly translating their thoughts to English from French, after first having had to translate them from their indigenous tongue, Kinyarwanda, to French. Presented as a barrier to the writing of English these layers could also be read as the insulation of indigenous ways of knowing behind a barrier of language. IR, for example, talked eloquently about how his earliest memories, related to values and morals, are strongly associated with his first language.

During the discussion of RL1's rich picture, it also emerged that because research results are published in English, a language 90% of Rwandans do not read, communities are increasingly reluctant to participate in new research. They are tired of researchers helicoptering in to collect data but never returning to share the results and benefits of their research. This resonated with IR's point that external funders failed to base their funding on in-country need. We can hear echoes here of Tuhiwahi Smith's (2012: 1) shocking statement that research is a dirty word for indigenous people, "inextricably linked to European colonialism and imperialism". Thus, resistance to doing research for the global North publishing behemoth spreads beyond scholars to the subjects of research too.

ISR2's account for all its sense of dualism at least made clear the gap of context and daily life between the contexts as a potential for rich alternative voices. While this casts doubt on international collaboration as a vehicle for research, it also acknowledges profound ignorance of "the other" and articulates a desire to hear different ways of thinking surviving at the global "periphery". While ISR1 felt skepticism about the infrastructure to support true participatory research with Rwanda, she did have a clear vision of what this would look like, if only by virtue of the difficulties of creating it.

Thus, our analysis uncovers elements of resistance to the global North model of research as defined by successfully publishing in an "international" English language journal. While we do not directly see anything of the indigenous knowledge infrastructure or what indigenous research might look like, we do see how shallowly the neocolonial model has penetrated.

Thus, there are hints of resistance to the influences of globalization buried within our data. We would argue that a continuing subjection of endogenous knowledge is apparent in the explicit references to a deficit discourse (Nyamnjoh 2012). Nyamnjoh has traced the deprecation of African knowledge within Africa itself to the violence of colonialization, and argued that it is a form of epistemicide. Endogenous ways of knowing were seen under colonial rule as other, inferior and primitive and reflecting the continuing power of neo-colonialism, African education retains "epistemological xenophilia and knowledge dependency" Nyamnjoh (2012: 143) suggests. African institutions continue to place their scholars in a publish or perish dilemma, where they conduct research at great disadvantage compared to those in the global North. Scholars try to make sense of local problems through the global North's knowledge system, rather than develop their own theory (Andrews and Okpanachi 2012). Much of our data reflects the continuing power of these assumptions, cf. Escobar's (2012) discursive practices.

In this context, evidence of resistance can be seen as a positive starting point for research infrastructures which are a hybrid of African epistemologies and global North science. For example, research subject resistance to extractive research is a positive driver to reconsider the best ways of doing research and publishing the results appropriate to the local context. Revaluing oral ways of knowing would empower local researchers and create potential for new knowledge alliances with scientists working in modes usual in the global North (e.g., Puri 2007). Such optimism has resonances in some work around open science. Mboa Nkoudou (2016) and Piron et al. (2016) see positive prospects in a version of open science for Africa, though one understood in rather different ways from how the term is used in the global North, which has tended to reinforce the hegemony of the existing scholarly publishing system (Okune et al. 2016). In this manifestation, open science would give more emphasis to publishing in local languages and emphasizing public involvement in science. In a similar vein, OCSDNet (2017) propose a manifesto for an inclusive and sustainable form of open science where African ways of knowing gain recognition.

6 Conclusion and Study Implications

The paper explores how "development as modernization" assumptions can take root in thinking about African research, in the form of the country deficit perspective. We find this discourse prevalent in both literature about African research and research evaluation. We also find it deeply embedded in attitudes in the field. Both participants and the researchers themselves began the current study by taking a deficit model for granted. Nevertheless, applying a reflexive turn, we argue that the data generated in our discussions does contain evidence for a counter-narrative which hints at points of resistance to adopting models of research built purely from those of the global North. It points to the potential existence of a resource in orality and indigenous ways of knowing insulated from globalization and neo-colonialism. Regarding theory, this study demonstrates the need to challenge pervasive deficit models in relation to research in the global South and to search for counter narratives that unlock positive opportunities for hybrid approaches sensitive to local contexts, and which can harness digital technologies. In so doing, we may avoid the pitfalls of digitalization being responsible for amplifying 'deficit' discursive practices. Regarding practical implications, a potential follow-own to this work could be bringing together stakeholders both local to, and external from, the research contexts who embody different epistemological positions and engaging them in a rich dialogue to better inform policy that is sensitive to local needs.

References

Aikman, S., et al.: Challenging deficit discourses in international education and development. Compare J. Comp. Int. Educ. **46**(2), 314–334 (2016)

Andrews, N., Okpanachi, E.: Trends of epistemic oppression and academic dependency in Africa's development: the need for a new intellectual path. J. Pan Afr. Stud. **5**(8), 85–104 (2012)

Arowosegbe, J.O.: African scholars, African studies and knowledge production on Africa. Africa **86**(2), 324–338 (2016)

Avgerou, C.: Discourses on ICT and development. Inf. Technol. Int. Dev. **6**(3), 1–18 (2010)

Bai, Y.: Has the Global South become a playground for Western scholars in information and communication technologies for development? evidence from a three-journal analysis. Scientometrics **116**(3), 2139–2153 (2018)

Beaudry, C., Mouton, J., Prozesky, H.: The Next Generation of Scientists in Africa. African Minds, Cape Town (2018)

Bezuidenhout, L.M., Leonelli, S., Kelly, A.H., Rappert, B.: Beyond the digital divide: towards a situated approach to open data. Sci. Public Policy **44**(4), 464–475 (2017)

Boshoff, N.: Neo-colonialism and research collaboration in Central Africa. Scientometrics **81**(2), 413–434 (2009)

Brennen, J.S., Kreiss, D.: Digitalization. In: The International Encyclopedia of Communication Theory and Philosophy, pp. 1–11. American Cancer Society (2016)

Chan, L.: Asymmetry and inequality as a challenge for open access – an interview with Leslie Chan. Litwin Books (2018). https://tspace.library.utoronto.ca/handle/1807/87296

Checkland, P., Scholes, J.: Soft Systems Methodology in Action. Wiley, Hoboken (1990)

Christian, G.E.: Issues and challenges to the development of open access institutional repositories in academic and research institutions in Nigeria (2008). https://idl-bnc-idrc.dspacedirect.org/handle/10625/36986

Collins, C.S., Rhoads, R.A.: The world bank, support for universities, and asymmetrical power relations in international development. High. Educ. **59**(2), 181–205 (2010)

Dlamini, N.N., Snyman, M.: Institutional repositories in Africa: obstacles and challenges. Libr. Rev. **66**(6–7), 535–548 (2017)

Elder, L., Emdon, H., Fuchs, R., Petrazzini, B. (eds.): Connecting ICTs to Development: The IDRC Experience. Anthem Press, London (2013)

Escobar, A.: Encountering Development: The Making and Unmaking of the Third World. Princeton University Press, Princeton (2012)

Fecher, B., Friesike, S.: Open science: one term, five schools of thought. In: Bartling, S., Friesike, S. (eds.) Opening Science, pp. 17–47. Springer, Cham (2014). https://doi.org/10.1007/978-3-319-00026-8_2

Fonn, S., et al.: Repositioning Africa in global knowledge production. Lancet **392**(10153), 1163–1166 (2018)

Gaillard, J.: Measuring research and development in developing countries: main characteristics and implications for the Frascati manual. Sci. Technol. Soc. **15**, 77–111 (2010)

GDN: Doing Research Assessments: Understanding Research Systems in Developing Countries. Global Development Network (2017). http://www.gdn.int/sites/default/files/GDN%20-%20Theoretical%20Framework.pdf

Gwynn, S. (2019). Access to research in the Global South. INASP. https://www.inasp.info/publications/access-research-global-south-reviewing-evidence

Idrissa, R.: Wanting Knowledge: Social Science Research and the Demand Factor in a Low-Income Country – The Case of Niger. Global Development Network (2016). http://www.gdn.int/sites/default/files/GDN_-_Working_Paper-90-Niger_-_final_ba1.pdf

Malapela, T.: Access to scholarly research information in Sub-Saharan Africa: a review. Libri **67**(1), 1–13 (2017)

McKay, M.: Improving access to scholarly research in Africa: open access initiatives. Ser. J. Ser. Commun. **24**(3), 251–254 (2011)

Mouton, J., Waast, R.: Comparative study on national research systems: findings and lessons. In: Meek, V.L., Teichler, U., Kearney, M.L. (eds.) Higher Education, Research and Innovation: Changing Dynamics: Report on the UNESCO Forum on Higher Education, Research and Knowledge 2001–2009, pp. 147–169 (2009)

Mboa Nkoudou, T.H.: Les injustices cognitives en Afrique subsaharienne: réflexions sur les causes et les moyens de lutte (2016). https://corpus.ulaval.ca/jspui/bitstream/20.500.11794/14541/1/Chapitre%202.pdf

Ngongalah, L., Niba, R.N., Wepngong, E.N., Musisi, J.M.: Research challenges in Africa – an exploratory study on the experiences and opinions of African researchers. BioRxiv, 446328 (2018)

Nwagwu, W.E.: Open access initiatives in africa - structure, incentives and disincentives. J. Acad. Librarianship **39**(1), 3–10 (2013)

Nyamnjoh, F.B.: 'Potted plants in greenhouses': a critical reflection on the resilience of colonial education in Africa. J. Asian Afr. Stud. **47**(2), 129–154 (2012)

OCSDNet: Open Science Manifesto. OCSDNET (2017). https://ocsdnet.org/manifesto/open-science-manifesto/

Okune, A., Hillyer, B., Albornoz, D., Sambuli, N., Chan, L.: Tackling Inequities in Global Scientific Power Structures (2016). https://tspace.library.utoronto.ca/handle/1807/71107

Ondari-Okemwa, E.: Scholarly publishing in sub-Saharan Africa in the twenty-first century: challenges and opportunities. First Monday **12**(10) (2007). https://journals.uic.edu/ojs/index.php/fm/article/view/1966

Piron, F., Dibounje Madiba, M.S., Regulus, S.: Justice cognitive libre accès et savoirs locaux. [Cognitive justice, free access and local knowledge]. Science and Commonwealth Editions (2016). https://zenodo.org/record/205145/files/Justice-cognitive-libre-accès-et-savoirs-locaux-15 décembre 2016.pdf?

Puri, S.K.: Integrating scientific with indigenous knowledge: constructing knowledge alliances for land management in India. MIS Q. **31**(2), 355–379 (2007)

Raju, R., Adam, A., Powell, C.: Promoting open scholarship in Africa: benefits and best library practices. Libr. Trends **64**(1), 136–160 (2015)

Schöpfel, J., Herb, U.: Open Divide: Critical Studies on Open Access. Library Juice Press, Sacramento (2018)

Smith, L.T.: Decolonizing Methodologies: Research and Indigenous Peoples. Zed Books, London (2012)

Tijssen, R.J.W.: Africa's contribution to the worldwide research literature: new analytical perspectives, trends, and performance indicators. Scientometrics **71**(2), 303–327 (2007)

Toyama, K.: Technology as amplifier in international development. In: Proceedings of the 2011 IConference on - IConference 2011, pp. 75–82 (2011)

Tvedten, I., Byabagambi, A., Lindström, J., Tedre, M.: Evaluation of the SIDA supported research capacity and higher education development programme in Rwanda, 2013–2017 (SIDA Decentralised Evaluation 2018:3). SIDA (2017)

UNESCO. Mapping research systems in developing countries Essential Bibliography: S&T in African countries (2009). https://unesdoc.unesco.org/ark:/48223/pf0000183365

Walker, D., Steinfort, P., Maqsood, T.: Stakeholder voices through rich pictures. Int. J. Manag. Proj. Bus. **7**(3), 342–361 (2014)

The Social Significance of Digital Platforms

Surviving the Gig Economy in the Global South: How Cape Town Domestic Workers Cope

Boitumelo Lesala Khethisa[✉], Pitso Tsibolane[✉], and Jean-Paul Van Belle[✉]

Centre for Information Technology and National Development in Africa,
University of Cape Town, Cape Town, South Africa
lslboi001@myuct.ac.za,
{pitso.tsibolane,jean-paul.vanbelle}@uct.ac.za

Abstract. The gig economy continues to disrupt different traditional markets such as transport, accommodation, and domestic work in the global South. The gig economy offers flexibility, autonomy and higher earning potential for gig workers. However, it is not without its challenges such as precarious working arrangements, occupational hazards and employment uncertainty. This study explores key survival strategies employed by domestic workers offering their services through one of South Africa's prominent gig platforms that specializes in domestic work. The study used semi-structured interviews with questions based on an adapted conceptual framework based on Folkman's cognitive theory of stress and coping. Three main categories of challenges face domestic workers in the gig economy: application induced technology challenges such as platform usability; occupation-specific challenges such as exposure to dangerous and unhealthy environments; and gig work induced service perceptions such as unrealistic expectations. These challenges result in negative consequences such as personal trauma, exhaustion and financial loss. Workers report feeling exploited and unsure about their relationship with the platform. The workers adopt various problem-focused, emotion-focused, support-seeking, and meaning-making survival strategies that include avoiding bookings by previously problematic customers, negotiating alternative terms with customers outside of the app, enduring traumatic experiences and complying with unreasonable demands. Platforms should consider financial and relationship transparency in their relationship with gig workers as well as affording gig workers more choice and flexibility regarding client bookings.

Keywords: Gig economy · Gig worker challenges · Domestic workers · Coping mechanisms · Survival strategies · South African labour

1 Introduction

Digital platforms mediate between service providers and consumers on an on-demand basis; a trend that continues to date and is sometimes referred to as uberization [1]. Examples of such platforms range from global giants such as Airbnb and Uber, from which the term uberization is derived; to local South African platforms such as Freelance

© IFIP International Federation for Information Processing 2020
Published by Springer Nature Switzerland AG 2020
R. K. Bandi et al. (Eds.): IFIPJWC 2020, IFIP AICT 601, pp. 67–85, 2020.
https://doi.org/10.1007/978-3-030-64697-4_7

Cape Town or M4Jam. Collectively, these platforms and their eco-systems are referred to as the gig economy [2].

Globally, there are over 67 million domestic workers [3] of which at least 1 million are based in South Africa [4]. With such as sizeable population and as is the case with other traditional service sectors such as transport and accommodation; domestic work has also attracted a number of digital platforms that are on a quest to revolutionize it for the better [3]. Though the exact wording differs per platform, most claim to offer affordable domestic services for households and flexible well compensated economic opportunities for domestic workers [5]. Based on the fact that one of the gig work platforms in South Africa already boasts of over 7 million cleaning hours and has over 11000 signed up domestic workers [6], it can be concluded that a considerable number of South African consumers and domestic workers are convinced by the benefits. However, the sector is also known for substandard employment conditions, limited employment benefits and low occupational prestige [7]. Considered as the last bastion of colonialism, perceptions about domestic worker exploitation are rife in South Africa – one of the most unequal countries on the planet [8]. This research serves to give voice to the workers in light of their continued marginalization and exploitative work arrangements.

The objective of this study was to gather information on challenges modern day Cape Town domestic workers that use gig platforms to secure jobs face, and their coping strategies and processes. To achieve this objective, two main questions were posed: What challenges do Cape Town domestic workers that utilize gig platforms encounter? How do they cope with the challenges they face?

Following the literature review, a discussion of the theoretical framework and an explanation of the research methodology, the paper presents an in depth set of findings focussing on occupational challenges, coping strategies, outcomes and platform recommendations. The paper ends with recommendations for future research.

2   Literature Review

This section puts the study into perspective by explaining core concepts underlying this study and providing historical and theoretical contexts under which the study occurred.

2.1   Gig Economy

The term gig economy is often used interchangeably with other terms like sharing-economy, crowd-work, on-demand economy, freelance economy, and platform economy [9]. This research adopts Donovan et al. [2]'s definition of the gig economy as a collection of internet accessible markets that match service providers to service consumers on a gig or job basis. Services offered on such platforms can range from highly specialized services such as software development to services that do not require specialization such as house cleaning and transportation services. In their view, gig economy platforms have three distinctive characteristics: they keep a proportion of job-earnings; they control the brand and thus regulate who operates on their platform and they control relationships between service providers and service consumers.

Based on data collected from seven African countries, Rwanda, Tanzania, Kenya, Mozambique, Ghana, Nigeria and South Africa, estimated that only 2% of the population in these countries has earned money from gig platforms [10]. Although one study estimated there were roughly 7000 domestic workers registered on gig platforms in South Africa [11], the CEO of a domestic cleaning gig platform disclosed that there were over 11000 domestic workers registered on the company's platform alone [6].

The emergence of gig economy has disrupted a number of traditional sectors and in the process created income opportunities for multitudes of people across the globe, albeit it too has challenges [12, 13]. Although gig economy has a lot of positives such as job creation and scheduling flexibility, the working conditions fall short of International Labor Organization (ILO) Decent Work Standards [14]. Bajwa et al. [15] categorize gig economy challenges into three groups:

- **Platform challenges,** which arise due to design, functional and business model flaws of gig platforms. These include functionalities that are not inherently bad such as rating systems employed by most gig platforms to establish trust between service consumers and providers but can inadvertently subject gig workers to prejudice, customer-bias and stress [16]. Other common challenges in this category are information asymmetry; and no-control over the rates platforms charge [15].
- **Precarity challenges,** which arise due to the short-termism and contingent nature of gig work. These include lack of employment benefits often associated with traditional jobs; deprivation of ability to engage in collective bargaining [5]; limited career growth opportunities [17]; low wages; limited legal protection [18]; anxiety and depression arising from precarious nature of gig work [17].
- **Occupational challenges,** which are associated with the kind of work they are performing. These include the danger of entering unfamiliar houses for domestic workers; musculoskeletal injuries for gig workers that perform repetitive tasks such as typing; and increased likelihood of car accidents for ride-sharing applications' drivers [15, 19].

The Fairwork Foundation uses five global core principles for fair work in the platform economy (fair pay, fair conditions, fair contracts, fair management and fair representation) to measure how fair platforms are [20]. In its second year of South African ratings, the foundation scored three local platforms 8 out of a possible score of 10 (SweepSouth, NoSweat, GetTOD), which was significantly better than well-known gig platforms such as Uber, Uber Eats and Bolt who scored 4 out of 10, 3 out of 10 and 1 out of 10 respectively [20].

2.2 Domestic Workers

Convention No. 189 of the ILO [21] defines domestic work as work that is performed in or for a single household or multiple households, and a domestic worker as any individual that is engaged in domestic work within an employment relationship. Examples of domestic work provided by the convention are tasks such as house cleaning, preparing meals, doing laundry, taking care of children, elderly and sick members of a family, gardening, guarding the house, driving for the family, and taking care of household pets.

However, this study focused exclusively on domestic workers that specialize in house cleaning.

The sector is well-established and substantial in size. According to a report by Overseas Development Institute (ODI), there were around 67 million domestic workers globally in 2016 of which 80% were women and 17% were migrants. In that year, domestic work contributed 7.5% of global women's wage employment [3]. According to ILO [22], of the 5.2 million domestic workers in Africa, 1.1 million were in South Africa. This statistic has since dropped to approximately 995 000 according to Statistics South Africa [4].

The post-apartheid governments sought to redress domestic workers' historically dismal working conditions by stipulating regulated working hours, contracts, minimum wages, and unemployment benefits [7]. However, the sector remains characterized by low wages, few employment benefits and low occupational prestige. In addition, racial distribution of domestic workers remains highly uneven in South Africa: 91% are classified as Black Africans and the remaining 9% as Coloured [22].

2.3   Domestic Work and the Gig Economy

There are numerous gig platforms that specialize in domestic work in operation across the globe and in the global South. Examples include MyDidi in India; UberCare and Find-A-Babysitter in Australia. Until recently, South Africa had two specialist domestic worker gig platforms; SweepSouth and Domestly (as this manuscript was being prepared, news broke that Domestly is closing operations). The consumer's motivations for using domestic work gig platforms include:

- **Perceived convenience:** given that traditional ways of sourcing domestic workers often involve relying on referrals or engaging placement agencies [23].
- **Better service quality:** platforms take quality measures including domestic work knowledge examinations, requiring prior paid domestic work experience, and in some cases providing training to service providers [3].
- **Reliability:** a major attraction since platforms can send alternative workers if pre-arranged workers are unable to fulfill the task [3].
- **Non-committal relationship:** the relationship with on-demand workers is less personal than the traditional employer-employee relationship and does not require the employer to get involved in the worker's affairs [23].

Benefits for workers include:

- **Flexibility:** Domestic workers in the gig economy have the liberty to choose when and for how long they want to work [24]. In addition, a two-way rating system allows for domestic workers to choose who they want to work for [6].
- **Higher earning potential:** In South Africa, the National Minimum Wage Act [25], stipulates that domestic workers are legally entitled to a minimum hourly rate of R15, Dreyer et al. [23] established that domestic workers in the South African gig economy receive an hourly rate of between R25 and R30.

In addition to challenges that are common across all gig platforms the following challenges are more amplified on domestic work gig platforms:

- **Biases** effected by platforms' recruitment strategies and rating systems. One-sided, customer-only rating systems used by most platforms can encourage discrimination and even violent treatment of domestic workers who can endure mistreatment in exchange for high ratings [26]. However, some platforms are tackling this rating system bias by introducing two-sided rating systems whereby domestic workers can rate their customers.
- **Exclusion due to digital divide:** women without smartphone are denied access to platforms [27].
- **High operational costs for domestic workers:** platform-based domestics use a significant portion of their earnings to cover operational costs such transport and mobile data costs [3]. The cost of transport is particularly high in South Africa due to apartheid legacy which has left poorer communities, where most domestic workers are based, living considerably long distances from affluent suburbs where consumers are saturated [23].
- **Travelling difficulties:** Unlike in traditional settings where domestics work at a few regular locations, gig economy domestic workers are more likely to find themselves having to find new locations in quick succession [23].

3   Theoretical Framework

Occupational stress is an old phenomenon that precedes the emergence of the gig economy, and as a result a number of theoretical frameworks and models that differ in popularity and statistical support have been developed to study it [28]. This study was informed by Folkman's Cognitive Theory of Stress and Coping [29]. The employed constructs and rationale are provided in Table 1, while the schematic presentation is shown in Fig. 1. The theory views coping as "a phenomenon that involves both cognitive and behavioral responses that individuals use in an attempt to manage internal and/or external stressors perceived to exceed their personal resources" [30]. In this study, the workers

Table 1. Conceptual framework constructs and their relevance to the study.

Constructs	Description
Influencing factors	These are factors such as fear and loss that trigger stress in an environment: they are influenced by personal (e.g. demographics) and environmental circumstances
Coping	Coping refers to cognitive and behavioral efforts taken to combat or tolerate situations and events one appraises as stressful. Problem focused coping strategies are concerned with the alteration and management of the problem that is causing distress whereas Emotion-focused coping strategies employed by individuals to manage their emotional state and distress
Outcome	The results of the strategy that has been employed

response to occupation-induced stress (their coping) is theorized as both a cognitive and behavioral reaction to the precariousness of gig platform labour. The theory provides a solid framework that facilitates a critical and systematic elaboration of the influencing factors, the coping strategies (survival approaches) as well as the outcomes of the survival strategies.

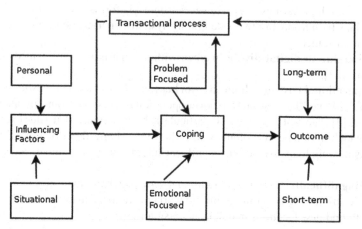

Fig. 1. Conceptual framework developed from Folkman's cognitive theory of stress [29].

4 Research Methodology

This research viewed its subject matter, occupational stress, as a social phenomenon whose perceptions differ from one individual to the next; are highly influenced by personal and situational factors; and cannot be studied without incorporating the worldview of research subjects. This research was therefore interpretivist and followed a qualitative approach as it sought to gain deeper understanding of challenges individual gig economy domestic workers face and how they cope with them by focusing on the underlying reasons expressed by participants, thoughts, experiences and opinions. We applied semi-structured interviews whose questions were based on the conceptual framework explained above; the research protocol is available on simple request. However, the chronological order of the questions differed per interview. All interviews were conducted face to face in locations most convenient for interviewees.

The respondents *(N = 15)* all worked in Cape Town (South Africa) as domestic workers through "Platform1" (not the real name of the platform for purposes of anonymization). Platform1 is accessible through web and mobile applications to connect households and offices with vetted cleaning professionals referred to as GigCleaners (also not the real designation, for anonymity).

A typical gig economy domestic worker in South Africa is a black female that comprehends written English (since the platforms are available in English only), owns a smartphone and is capable of using third-party applications such as Whatsapp [3].

In developing countries, the rising middle class is the main consumer of on-demand domestic work.

Because Platform1 does not publicize their contact details, snowball sampling was used by booking a few domestic workers on the platform, then asking to refer acquaintances that also used the platform. The initial interviewees were purposively selected (sufficiently knowledgeable and experienced gig worker) from different regions of Cape Town metropolitan area to encourage diversity; each participant was asked to refer two acquaintances at most; and the referral chain was stopped at the third level. Each interview was voice recorded, translated and transcribed; coded and analyzed using NVivo Software following a thematic analysis technique as defined by Braun and Clarke [31]. The analytical was repeated until data saturation was reached [32]. Ethical clearance was secured from the University's Ethics in Research Committee (EiRC); consent was explained and obtained prior to every interview. Names have been changed to ensure anonymity. Table 2 below shows the interviewee overview.

Table 2. Overview of interviewees

Pseudonym	Age	Origin	Dependents	Education attained	Additional income source
Abby	30	RSA	3	Incomplete tertiary	Social grants
Lizzy	34	ZIM	2	Currently doing degree	Spouse
Caroline	25	ZIM	1	< Grade 12	None
Julie	37	ZIM	2	Post-School Diploma	None
Ayanda	33	RSA	3	< Grade 12	Social grants
Shelly	35	ZIM	2	< Grade 12	None
Nicky	30	RSA	3	< Grade 12	Spouse
Puly	30	RSA	3	< Grade 12	Social grants
Thato	31	RSA	3	Post-School Diploma	Social grants
Asanda	54	RSA	2	Post-School Diploma	None
Mercy	27	ZIM	0	Post-School Diploma	None
Monica	39	RSA	3	< Grade 12	Social grants
Mosa	43	RSA	1	Grade 12	None
Sam	32	RSA	1	Grade 12	Social grants
Cammy	30	ZIM	2	O-Level	Spouse

Origin: RSA = South Africa, Zim = Zimbwabwe

5   Findings, Analysis and Discussion

5.1   Demographics

Data was collected from 15 female GigCleaners based in different areas of Cape Town. Only one identified as Coloured, the rest identified as Black Africans. This is in line with findings by the ILO's [22] findings that 91% of South African domestic workers are Black Africans and the other 9% Coloureds. Only two participants were born in Cape Town; majority were either domestic migrants from the Eastern Cape or Zimbabwean immigrants. The youngest participant was 25 years old while the oldest was 54 years old: majority were in their thirties. Two participants were widowed, five married and the rest were single. Only one participant did not have any dependents, and most had three dependents. Their education levels ranged from incomplete secondary education to one currently doing her first year of a bachelor's degree. In addition to earnings from domestic work, most South African participants also relied on social grants to make ends meet. Except for the married ones, domestic work was the sole income source for Zimbabwean participants' households. Participants' experience using the platform ranged from 3 years to a few weeks at the time of interviewing.

5.2 Situational Factors - Benefits

There are four main themes of perceived benefits:

Flexibility and Autonomy. Most participants perceived using the platforms gives them a high degree of flexibility and autonomy. They appreciate that they are able to take time off as required; decide their availability to accept bookings; work in their preferred locations; and to a certain extent can decline unfavorable bookings. Two participants in particular emphasize this in their responses:

> ... I need more time to study, you see now when I do these jobs I finish half day then I come home I do my studies. So it's not like all about their money it was just for their flexibility..[Julie]

> ...I can tell them how many hours I want to work and when I want to work. Because if you do not want to go to work tomorrow, you can just go on your App say day off; [...] You just manage your own things, you are not forced to work...[Lizzy]

Income Opportunity. With a third of potential employees currently unemployed in South Africa [4], participants were generally appreciative that the platforms has granted them an opportunity to earn some income. As Caroline put it, "... I can say it's good for us, we can get some jobs because to stay at home you know it's not nice so you can get jobs there and you can work nicely...".

Convenience. Some participants prior to joining Platform1 used to convene at popular informal labor hotspots to seek jobs on a daily basis: an exercise that was costly and had slim chances of securing jobs on any day. Thato highlighted this in her response:

> ...because where I was before, going by the road and asks jobs, sometimes I get sometimes I'm not, I am staying too far I have to travel, I don't have money to go home. It's very better because I receive a job while I am staying at home, I don't need to go out if I don't get a job I am at home I didn't spend anything...[Thato]

Exposure to Different World Views. Opportunity to go into different households with diverse backgrounds, and different income levels and lifestyles was also perceived beneficial by some participants. They regarded it as an opportunity to get a glimpse into lifestyles of individuals they would not normally interact with and as an opportunity to learn to operate different household appliances. As Shelly puts it, "…I just like to see what the different things are in people's lives, that learning new things every day, like using the machine…"

All the above benefits with the exception of exposure to different world views are in line with findings of previous studies as discussed in the literature review section of this report. Appraising an opportunity to get a glimpse into different households' lifestyles as a benefit might be unique to South Africa as it is likely influenced by persisting apartheid era city structures which to date still enforce segregation along economic class lines.

5.3 Situational Factors - Challenges

Challenges encountered by participants can be classified into three main themes, challenges related to nature of the gig economy; occupational challenges, and occupational challenges exacerbated by nature of the gig economy (Fig. 2).

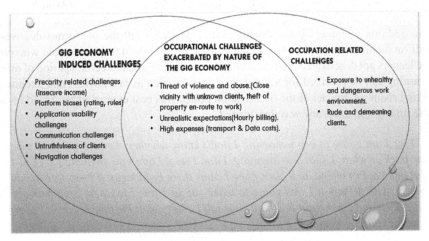

Fig. 2. Challenges encountered by GigCleaners.

Gig Economy Induced Challenges. This theme encompasses challenges that are induced by the business and operational model of gig platforms, here Platform1.

Navigation Challenges. The most appraised group of challenges under gig economy induced challenges was navigation related challenges. The fact that most participants were migrants in Cape Town compounded by not being tech savvy enough to use navigation applications such as Google Maps effectively, resulted in participants often getting lost on their way to bookings.

... getting lost because every time you are going to a new place and I am not a Capetonian, I really don't know some places and I am finding it difficult to use google because they only send you the address and you have to use google maps so oh it's very difficult, you get lost like yesterday I got lost and I have to walk you know? [Cammy]

Other common reasons behind participants having troubles navigating to bookings included clients not updating their physical addresses on their profiles, and clients not providing correct physical addresses.

Platform Biases. In line with De Stefano [16]'s findings, many participants perceived the rating system was unfair and biased in favor of clients. Participants perceived some clients used the rating system to punish them for not complying with clients' taxing demands. One participant suggested the platform could require clients to justify low ratings.

...on the rating like if the client rate you 4 stars then your reliability score goes down on the 4, it must always be 5 who's perfect? No one is perfect. Sometimes you can clean the house then the client you just clean for 5 h then if you not done you just tell the client no I'm not done within that 5 h then you just leave. The client will rate you 3 or 4, they don't ask the client why did you rate this... [Ayanda]

In addition to rating systems many participants also felt the platform rules were unfair on them. One rule that was mentioned the most is the deactivation rule whereby GigCleaners got deactivated after receiving three warning within a certain period of time. A warning can be received for a number of reasons such as late arrivals and declining booking requests. Impact of the deactivation policy was best expressed by Asanda who at the time of the interview was deactivated

...Like I am going to beg tomorrow, I don't know whether they are going to take me back or what. I didn't do anything, I don't steal I don't do anything [...] I just got late I didn't offend, and after when I came there Boitumelo! If I was late to you maybe with 30 min if I was going to leave you at 1 pm, I leave at 2 pm between 13:30 pm and 2 pm, yes I finish all your job I don't count the time because I knew I am at fault... [Asanda]

Application Usability Challenges. Many participants also expressed frustrations with the usability of the application. The application often froze, preventing participants to complete administrative tasks such as confirming arrival at a booking.

...Two or three times it happens, I'm there at the clients house the App is not working is saying Error, and now I can't say arrived because the client don't know I'm there. I can't access to get the contact of the client, so I can call the client I can't do anything. Then I have to call the office, I'm at the client's house, now they say give me booking ID, I can't access my App.[Julie]

Communication Challenges. Another challenge that was appraised by many participants and was an enabler of other challenges, is the communication challenge. This challenge was multi-faceted: it included clients and Platform1 not responding to Gig-Cleaners on time and booking cancelations not being communicated to GigCleaners on time, resulting in financial losses.

> *...On my way to Sea Point I received a message that the booking has been cancelled then I had to call the lady have you cancelled the booking? No, I am waiting for you, I went there when I reached her place I started calling her, No I have cancelled it... I didn't have money R50 was all that I had that day then I had to walk from Sea Point to Cape Town again. [Cammy]*

Precarity Related Challenges. As highlighted in the literature review, precarity is one of the leading challenges of the gig economy. Expectedly, many participants experienced it. One participant, Ayanda narrated how, at one point, she went for two weeks without receiving a single booking. This was compounded by inconsistency of rates. Participants complained that their rates fluctuated:

> *...Because it's not like a fixed I'm supposed to earn like R26/hour they will tell you it's not gonna be R26 some will get to R25 some will get to R24, even that one who have reached 400 h some is 33 some is 32 some is R30. So, you never work like knowing how much you are gonna earn its just working, you don't budget with that money...[Mercy]*

It is worth mentioning that Platform1 platform has recurring bookings functionality and all GigCleaners that had recurring bookings did not appraise precarity as a challenge.

Untruthfulness of Clients. Some participants complained that other clients deliberately lied by understating the number of bedrooms and bathrooms when booking to get lower quotes. Nicky emphasized this in her response, "... some do lie customers do lie then they maybe say they have 2 bathrooms, 2 bedrooms but when you come to their house then it's like a mansion". Closely related to understating the size of their houses was the issue of clients with pets overlooking that a GigCleaner had declared on her profile that she did not work around dogs or cats and booking her anyway.

Occupation Related Challenges. Domestic work in developing countries is often associated with substandard working conditions and low occupational prestige. This is especially true for South Africa due to Apartheid legacy. Unfortunately, this study has revealed that some of these historic challenges and perceptions about domestic work still persist. This theme covers such challenges.

Exposure to Dangerous and Unhealthy Environments. Some participants narrated how some clients exposed them to environments that were potentially detrimental to their health and well-being. These included clients expecting them to clean with no proper protective gear; being expected to use step ladders to clean windows against Platform1's policy; at times being expected to get rid of used sanitary towels and to clean off blood stains. This was particularly emotive for Mercy as she recalled one such experience:

... There was like blood all over the bathroom the mirrors, the walls I said what's going on? In the dinning there was like cigarettes and the house everywhere there are spoons under the bed and everything was like a mess. I ask him, how are you expect me to touch the blood? It's not even healthy I don't know where this blood is coming from.[Mercy]

The only silver lining is that very few participants appraised this challenge.

Rude and Demeaning Clients. A number of participants narrated how demeaning and rude some clients were. One participant, Mosa, has had a horrible experience of being referred to as a "kaffir", a derogatory term that is illegal in South Africa as per the Promotion of Equality and Prevention of Unfair Discrimination (Act No.4 of 2000). Other examples of rude and demeaning behaviors GigCleaners endured were: being given rotten and stale food under the pretext that they are being helped; being continuously monitored while working; being asked to leave their hand bags with lunch boxes in toilets or outside the house; and being offered tea in disposable cups. As it can be inferred from Sam's response, "... you see? I must put my bag in the toilet. They treat us like we are not human beings. The human beings to them is the dogs and the cats..."; this is emotionally taxing for GigCleaners. This inhuman treatment towards domestic workers is unfortunately deep rooted in South African history [33].

Occupation Related Challenges Exacerbated by the Nature of Gig Economy.

This theme covers well known challenges that are inherent to domestic work in South Africa and, based on the participants' responses, are worsened by nature of the gig economy.

High Expenses. Apartheid era city structures saw residential areas of Blacks and Coloureds being on the outer edges of cities, meaning long commute distances to get to workplaces. The resultant city structures unfortunately remain largely unchanged to date. Many participants appraised high operating costs as a major drawback of using the platform: "sometimes they force you to take the booking like 3 h booking it's R80 something and you must travel with R46, how much are you gonna be left with? You gonna be left with R43" [Ayanda]. In addition to high transport costs, using the platform required them to always have access to the internet to complete administrative tasks such as accepting bookings and navigating to unfamiliar areas: "... every 2 days I must buy data for R17 it's about 120 data so after 2 days its finish, it's a weekly data but after 2 days its finish..." [Sam]. It is worth mentioning that Platform1 has attempted to reduce the impact of this challenge by introducing a zero-rated application that should in principle reduce the burden of data costs. However, not all participants were aware of the presence of such an alternative application.

Threat of Violence and Exposure to Abuse. Most participants were of the opinion that using the platform increased their vulnerability to being victims of crimes such violence, abuse and theft. 7am bookings meant GigCleaners had to leave their homes very early; this was especially threatening in Winter due to delayed sunrise. Having to use their mobile phones to navigate to bookings also made them easy targets to thieves. Threat of violence is unfortunately not restricted to when GigCleaners are en-route to bookings;

GigCleaners are not any safer in the homes of clients where some have experienced unwelcomed sexual advances.

> ... *He asked me do you drink? I told him no, I don't drink at all, then he said to me no! no! just only for today you can drink wine, so I told him no! I don't touch any wine. Then I said okay because I was like to be honest I was desperate to earn that money for that day, I just told him that okay if you say so its fine, just one glass of wine cause I didn't want to like let's say maybe that client will say this GigCleaner of yours did like this so I don't want her I am chasing her back and the office won't understand that because they were not there at the time that happens. I would sit down and take the glass and then the client would go further and say you are looking so beautiful...[Abby]*

This challenge is exacerbated by information asymmetry created by the platform operation model. Although information asymmetry is not unique to Platform1 [15], its potential consequences are particularly chilling for GigCleaners given that the prevalence of gender based violence in South Africa is so high.

Unrealistic Expectations. As stated in the literature review, historically, domestic workers have been subjected to unrealistic expectations such as being expected to work long hours a day [33]. Most participants narrated how some clients required them to complete a lot of work within humanly impossible timeframes. This behavior seemed to be largely influenced by the hourly billing model of the platform which drove clients to attempt to get as much value as possible out of their bookings. The frustration unrealistic expectations cause to GigCleaners is best encapsulated in Lizzy's response:

> *...some other clients, they just rude, they are just rude. Maybe I come to your house with big houses, I am not a machine, you understand? I am not a machine. So, you can't expect me to do everything in maybe 8 h that you booked me: I will only do what I can. [Lizzy]*

5.4 Coping

An overview of main coping mechanisms applied by participants for appraised challenges is provided in Table 3. Problem focused theme encompasses strategies that attempt to either alter or prevent a challenge from recurring, while emotion focused theme covers those that do not necessarily act on the challenge but rather manage emotions associated with the challenge.

While there were many problem-focused coping alternatives, the most employed coping mechanism was endurance. In addition, in most cases problem focused strategies did not yield positive results as discussed in the outcomes' section.

Table 3. Overview of coping strategies and challenges.

Coping strategy	Strategy description	Challenges applied on	Examples of application
Problem-focused coping strategies			
Avoidance	Avoiding encountering the challenge once previously encountered or known of	Platform biases (bad ratings by clients); High Expenses (low margin jobs); Threat of violence and abuse	Abby: "...No! even if I am desperate for money I will never [....] I told the office that I don't want to go to that client anymore..."
Negotiation	Having discussions with clients to come up with workable schedules	Unrealistic expectations	Julie: "... So we agreed she won't complain [...] I was doing something else"
Deviating behavior	Making private arrangements with clients through the platform and ignoring platform's rules and regulations to make situations better	Precarity related challenges; navigation challenges (contacting clients against the rules); Unrealistic rules (using step ladders)	Sam: "...Yah that one is my private. I take from Platform1."
Peer assistance	Requesting assistance or financial help from other GigCleaners and acquaintances	Navigation challenges; Application usability challenges	Thato: "...we have a group of WhatsApp so that we can chat, now I am struggling guys I am here then I can't find this place... "
Reporting	Informing platform administrators	Communication challenges; Rude and demeaning clients; Application usability challenges	Mosa: "...So I tell the company yoh that client was very rude they call me a "kaffir" so the Platform1 was very-very sad..."
Improvising	Utilizing ad hoc methods to solve or better challenges	Exposure to dangerous and unhealthy conditions; High expenses; Threat of violence and abuse	Julie: "...I just took a plastic bag and wear it so I could start to pick the blood pads..."
Persisting	Keep trying	Application usability; Navigation challenges	Asanda: "...I walked by foot 3 h you cannot believe and I am still going to work, I followed the directions. I went, I went, I went...I got to the place"

(continued)

Table 3. (*continued*)

Coping strategy	Strategy description	Challenges applied on	Examples of application
Abandoning bookings	Giving up bookings while en-route or already at clients' places	Navigation challenges; communication challenges; threat of violence and abuse	*Abby: "...I just told him you know what, I didn't come here to do what now you require me to do, let me just go home, and then he said to me no its fine let me just sign in that you did work for the 3 h and then you can go home. And then I left, I go home..."*
Emotion-focused coping strategy			
Endurance	Ignoring the challenge and continuing with whatever one was doing or had to do	Exposure to dangerous and unhealthy conditions; Platform biases; Threat of violence and abuse; Unrealistic expectations; Untruthfulness of clients	*Asanda, "...you come early, and the client will tell you I said 8'oclock you are here at 07:30am, you will stand outside..."*
Submission	Yielding to clients and platform's requirements	Platform biases; Rude and demeaning clients; Unrealistic expectations	*Thato: "...I am scrubbing what you want me to scrub although I see it's unnecessary, it's fine I'm just do it..."*
Fake smiling	Smiling while hurt to please clients	Rude and demeaning clients; Unrealistic expectations	*Sam: "... when they say I must do this and this to keep my rating and I'm always put a smile on my face for my ratings, even if you don't want to smile you must smile."*

5.5   Outcome

Outcomes of participants' coping mechanism can be grouped into five main groups:

No Change. This group encompasses situations where the undesirable situation continued unabated despite active attempts to better the conditions by GigCleaners. Based on participants responses, this is the most likely outcome of any coping mechanism. It is concerning that even reporting challenges to the platform administrators did not result in positive outcomes for participants in most cases. Abby also raised this in her response, *"... But my question is, I told them about the client but on my app I will see them sending that clients booking I will just ask haibo! why these people, they keep sending me this client booking cause I told them that I don't want this client."*

Financial Loss. This group covers outcomes where participants lost partial or full earnings. It was the second most common outcome. Coping mechanisms that resulted in loss of income included abandoning jobs; declining bookings; and taking out loans from peers. Enduring also resulted in financial loss especially when used to cope with unrealistic expectations as implied by Sam, *"...Yah if she complains I must do for free cause I don't have a choice."*

Better Conditions. This covers situations whereby coping mechanisms resulted in better conditions. Although better conditions is undoubtedly the ultimate aim for attempting any problem focused coping strategy, only negotiation yielded this outcome. Julie's response best shows this: *"... So we agreed she won't complain if there is nothing done, she must just understand I was doing something else. And yes, she does understand, but that was a very big challenge to make her understand..."*

Trauma. *"...I am telling you I was, I couldn't even eat when I got home, it was very bad and until now I can still feel it. The bathroom was something else and there were no gloves to use, nothing..."*, this was Julie narrating the trauma she experienced after one of her bookings. Mercy also had similar experiences after being exposed to an unhealthy environment. Though only two participants experienced such trauma, their narrations were quite emotive. The platform should consider either setting guidelines on minimal protective equipment clients should have before making bookings or consider supplying GigCleaners with protective equipment itself.

Exhaustion. Like trauma, this outcome was appraised by few participants. It was triggered by walking long distances to bookings and working extended hours without breaks. Participants walked long distances to either cut costs or because they did not know convenient public transport route to take.

5.6   Platform Recommendations

Most participants expressed a wish to have more control on what bookings to accept. They were not particularly eager to accept 3 h bookings which they deem to be non-profitable. Was it not because of possible repercussions, they would never accept such bookings. Some would prefer picking which bookings to take instead of the platform auto-assigning them.

Most participants did not fully comprehend their relationships with the platform. Although the platform explicitly stated in its published terms and conditions that it did not have an employment relationship with its workers, most participants were under the impression that there was an employer-employee relationship between them and the platform. Some participants narrated how the platform had on past occasions arranged taxi rides for them to ensure they get to bookings on time. The platform should communicate more with the workers to clarify the nature and status of their relationship.

Despite most participants acknowledging that the platform ensured they earn more than the stipulated legal minimum wage per hour, there was an overwhelming believe amongst participants that the platform kept more than its fair share of booking fees. This dissatisfaction was best expressed by Monica when she said, "… they are making lots of money but they give us very little …."

6 Conclusion

This study's primary objective was to gather information on challenges that the modern-day Cape Town domestic workers who use gig platforms to secure jobs face, and their coping strategies and processes. This study posed two questions which it deemed were important to answer in order to achieve its objective.

Firstly, what challenges do Cape Town domestic workers that utilize gig platforms encounter? Domestic workers experience three types of challenges, namely; gig economy induced challenges, occupational challenges, and occupational challenges exacerbated by the gig economy nature. Gig economy-induced challenges are those introduced by the business and operational models of gig platforms such as navigation and communication challenges, application usability, precarity and untruthfulness of clients. Occupational challenges are those that are specific to domestic work regardless of it occurring in the gig economy context or in a traditional domestic work context: examples are exposure to dangerous and unhealthy environments, and rude and demeaning clients. Occupational challenges exacerbated by the gig economy are high expenses, threat of abuse and violence, and unrealistic expectations by domestic work service consumers.

Secondly, how do they cope with challenges they face? Domestic workers in the gig economy employ a wide range of mechanisms to cope with challenges they face. The main emotion focused strategies which they employ are endurance, submission and fake smiling. The main problem focused coping strategies employed by domestic workers are avoidance, negotiation, deviating behavior, peer assistance, reporting, improvisation, persistence, and abandoning bookings.

Ensuring workers comprehend their relationship with the platform, the pricing model of the platform and the value the platform adds, and adding more flexibility for workers to reject unprofitable or disliked jobs would go a long way in clearing the believe that the platform somewhat exploits them and increase their job satisfaction. This research contributes to the overarching discussion relating to the gig economy by providing insights into challenges global South domestic workers working in the sector face and how they deal with them. In addition, this paper serves as input for gig platform owners, developers and policy makers globally on how to potentially institute occupation-specific protections for gig workers.

The main limitation of this research is the focus on one platform (although this is currently the only major domestic platform in existence in South Africa) and one region (Cape Town). Future research can be longitudinal – investigating the evolution of the identified issues over time; widen the sampling to other regions or platform types; or contrast the views of the workers with those of the consumers and platform managers.

References

1. Van Doorn, N.: Platform labor: on the gendered and racialized exploitation of low-income service work in the 'on-demand' economy. Inf. Commun. Soc. **20**(6), 898–914 (2017)
2. Donovan, S.A., Bradley, D.H., Shimabukuru, J.O.: What Does the Gig Economy Mean for Workers? CRS Report R44365, 2 May 2016
3. Hunt, A., Machingura, F.: A good gig? The rise of on-demand domestic work. Overseas Development Institute, London (2016)
4. Statistics South Africa: Quarterly Labour Force Survey Quarter 2: 2019, Statistics South Africa, Pretoria (2019)
5. Dokko, J., Mumford, M., Schanzenbach, D.W.: Workers and the online gig economy. The Hamilton Project, pp. 1–8 (2015)
6. Pandor, D.A.: Interview, Rand Merchant Bank Solutionist Thinking. [Interview], 1 April 2019
7. Burger, R., Von Fintel, M., Van der Watt, C.: Household social mobility for paid domestic workers and other low-skilled women employed in South Africa. Feminist Economics **24**(3), 29–55 (2018)
8. Fish, J.N.: Engendering democracy: domestic labour and coalition-building in South Africa. J. South. Afr. Stud. **32**(1), 107–127 (2006)
9. de Reuver, M., Sørensen, C., Basole, R.: The digital platform: a research agenda. J. Inf. Technol. **33**(2), 124–135 (2018)
10. Mothobi, M., Schoentgen, A., Gillwald, A.: What is the state of microwork in Africa? A view from seven countries. Research ICT Africa, Cape Town (2017)
11. Bamu, P.: A pluralistic approach to organizing migrant domestic workers: the case of the Zimbabwe-South Africa global care chain. Int. J. Comp. Labour Law Ind. Relat. **34**(3), 313–344 (2018)
12. Healy, J., Nicholson, D., Pekarek, A.: Should we take the gig economy seriously? Labour Ind. J. Soc. Econ. **27**(3), 232–248 (2017)
13. Sutherland, W., Jarrahi, M.H.: The sharing economy and digital platforms: a review and research agenda. Int. J. Inf. Manage. **43**, 328–341 (2018)
14. Macaulay, T.: Could a working conditions rating system protect gig economy workers?, 9 April 2019. https://www.techworld.com/tech-innovation/new-rating-system-for-digital-platforms-aims-protect-gig-workers-3694758/
15. Bajwa, U., Knorr, L., Ruggiero, E.D., Gastaldo, D., Zendel, A.: Towards an understanding of workers' experiences in the global gig economy. University of Toronto, Toronto (2018)
16. De Stefano, V.: The rise of the just-in-time workforce: on-demand work, crowdwork, and labor protection in the gig-economy. Comp. Lab. L. Pol'y J. **37**, 471 (2015)
17. Ashford, S.J., Caza, B.B., Reid, E.M.: From surviving to thriving in the gig economy: a research agenda for individuals in the new world of work. Res. Organ. Behav. **38**, 23–41 (2018)

18. Howard, J.: Nonstandard work arrangements and worker health and safety. Am. J. Ind. Med. **60**, 1–10 (2017)
19. Mpofu, T., Tsibolane, P., van Belle, J.P.: Risks and risk-mitigation strategies of gig economy workers in the global south: the case of ride-hailing in Cape Town. In: 2020 IFIP WG 9.4 European Conference on the Social Implications of Computers in Developing Countries Proceedings, Salford, UK (2020)
20. Fairwork Foundation, Second round of Fairwork's yearly platform ratings in South Africa launched! (2020). https://fair.work/second-round-of-fairworks-yearly-platform-rat ings-in-south-africa-launched/
21. International Labour Office: Convention No. 189 Decent work for domestic workers. International Labour Office, Geneva (2011)
22. International Labour Office: Domestic workers across the world: Global and regional statistics and the extent of legal protection. ILO, Geneva (2013)
23. Dreyer, B., Lüdeke-Freund, F., Hamann, R., Faccer, K.: Upsides and downsides of the sharing economy: collaborative consumption business models' stakeholder value impacts and their relationship to context. Technol. Forecast. Soc. Chang. **125**, 87–104 (2017)
24. Todolí-Signes, A.: The 'gig economy': employee, self-employed or the need for a special employment regulation. Eur. Rev. Labour Res. **23**(2), 193–205 (2017)
25. Government of the Republic of South Africa: Act No.9 National Minimum Wage Act, Government of the Republic of South Africa, Cape Town (2018)
26. Moore, P.: The threat of physical and psychosocial violence and harassment in digitalized work. International Labour Organisation, Geneva (2018)
27. Florito, J., Aneja, U., de Sanfeliu, M.B.: Gender economic equity and the future of work: a future of work that works for women. CIPPEC, Buenos Aires (2018)
28. Sohail, M., Rehman, C.A.: Stress and health at the workplace-a review of the literature. J. Bus. Stud. Q. **6**(3), 94–121 (2015)
29. Folkman, S.: Personal control and stress and coping processes: a theoretical analysis. J. Pers. Soc. Psychol. **46**(4), 839–852 (1984)
30. Echemendia, R.J., Webbe, F.M., Merritt, V.C., González, G.: Assessment in sports: psychological and neuropsychological approaches. In: Handbook of Psychological Assessment, pp. 275–304. Academic Press (2019)
31. Saunders, M., Lewis, P., Thornhill, A.: Research Methods for Business Students, pp. 122–161. Pearson Education Limited, Harlow (2016)
32. Braun, V., Clarke, V.: Successful Qualitative Research: A Practical Guide for Beginners. Sage, Thousand Oaks (2013)
33. Ginsburg, R.: Come in the dark: domestic workers and their rooms in apartheid-era Johannesburg, South Africa. Perspect. Vernac. Archit. **8**, 83–100 (2000)

Social Enablers and Constraints Related to the Publication and Use of Open Government Data in a Developing Country

Hubeidatu Nuhu[1]($\boxtimes$), Jean-Paul Van Belle[1], and Marita Turpin[2]

[1] University of Cape Town, Cape Town, South Africa
NHXHUB001@myuct.ac.za, jean-paul.vanbelle@uct.ac.za
[2] Department of Informatics, University of Pretoria, Pretoria, South Africa
marita.turpin@up.ac.za

Abstract. The promise of Open Government Data (OGD) rests on the publication, availability, use and reuse of government data. This research focused on how social factors such as data ownership, network creation and power enabled or constrained the publication and use of OGD in Ghana, a developing country in West Africa. Ghana's government data was expected to be both legally and technically open. However, socially constructed behavioral patterns and practices such as power, data ownership and network creation played critical roles in influencing the institutionalization of OGD in Ghana. An interpretive descriptive case study analysis helps understand how social processes influenced the institutionalization of OGD publication and use in Ghana. Giddens' Structuration Theory was used as the main theoretical lens in this study because of its ability to investigate the dynamic interplay between social agency and social structures. Findings from the study indicated that power within Ghana's OGD ecosystem is associated with legitimatized practices and behaviors such as data ownership, culture and networks.

Keywords: Open Government Data (OGD) · Open data · Structuration Theory (ST) · Power · Data ownership · Network creation · Ghana

1 Introduction

The process of adoption and advancement of e-government led to the birthing of the Open Government Data (OGD) movement that has been embraced by both developed and developing countries [1]. OGD is government or public data that is available, usable, reusable and accessible at the least cost possible; such data should be both technically (in machine-readable formats) and legally available [2]. The concept and practice of OGD were introduced as a means of avoiding secrecy in government by making government data technically and legally available to citizens [3].

OGD can be regarded as "machine-readable data which is discoverable, available, and downloadable through dedicated internet portals without cost to potential data users"

R. K. Bandi et al. (Eds.): IFIPJWC 2020, IFIP AICT 601, pp. 86–101, 2020.
https://doi.org/10.1007/978-3-030-64697-4_8

[4]. The OGD ecosystem's main stakeholders are Data Publishers (DP) and Data Users (DU), who have differing roles and views of data [5]. These stakeholders are required to collaborate despite their differences in roles and views of OGD to enable effective implementation [6]. The expected outcome of implementing OGD is to create and generate public value [7]. Governments who want to formally engage in the OGD movement, join by signing as partners of the Open Government Partnership Initiative (OGPI) and by completing biennial Action Plans.

Ghana joined the OGPI in 2011 and has developed and completed multiple Action Plans since 2011, however the publication and use of OGD remained limited. This has been attributed to inadequate intermediaries (or Data Users) and challenges of data quality [8]. Data quality is concerned with validity, confidentiality, privacy concerns, liability, completeness, metadata, technical and semantic interoperability [9]. Data quality in developing economies is a challenge [10] that influences both the publication and use of government data.

Although OGD research has received a lot of attention in Information Systems (IS) research [1, 2], there is still a paucity of contextualized research on how socially constructed behavioral patterns and practices influence the institutionalization of OGD publication and use in sub-Saharan Africa. Such factors have been recognized as important determinants of the successful institutionalization of IS [11]. While data ownership is regarded as important in IS research [12], this is lacking in OGD research.

While the factors that influenced OGD in Ghana may have included data quality, there existed underlying socially created and recreated patterns and practices that were influencing the publication and use of OGD and its institutionalization. For this reason, a case study was performed that drew on theories such as Giddens' structuration theory in order to meet this study's research objective, namely *to understand how social processes have influenced the institutionalization of OGD publication and use in Ghana.*

The paper is structured as follows. First, key concepts are introduced and the case setting explained. Subsequently, the research method and theoretical underpinnings are provided. This is followed by an analysis and discussion of the findings. Finally, the conclusion of the study reflects on the findings and provides recommendations and suggestions for future research.

2   Background: Key Concepts

Open Government Data (OGD) is linked to open data as well as open government. An amalgamation of these two terms gives rise to the concept of OGD [13]. Open data refers to the free, unrestricted access, use and reuse of data [14] while the open government is an initiative by governments to make their data available on data web portals to promote transparency, accountability and to increase collaboration with stakeholders [15]. However, OGD should not only be associated with the availability of data on government web portals but also with the provision of data that has reusable capabilities [16].

Actors in the OGD ecosystem include public administrators, bloggers, NGOs, academic researchers, data journalists, international organizations, donors and beneficiaries [5]. Actors in this study are individuals who fit into the description of Data Publishers and

Data Users. The OGD ecosystem actors' understanding of OGD is shaped by contextual factors such as interest and power [5].

Institutionalization refers to the process of routinizing cultural practices, rules and norms [17]. Institutionalization attempts to explain how institutional rules, cultural practices and norms become accepted or rejected in a social system or structure [18]. Institutionalizing OGD practices and policies in public institutions has become a challenge due to the inability of government to merge openness into known rules, norms and cultural practices [19].

The significance of understanding the role of *power in IS* cannot be underestimated. Power is often used by actors (Data Publishers, Users and Public Sector Intuitions) as a way of influencing each other [20]. The process of information dissemination and control among actors in organizations unearths issues of how power is distributed within the organization [21]; how actors acquire this power determines how they disperse it. The innovation and routinization of IS by actors in an organization, unravels different notions of power; hence the need to combine different theories for suitable interpretation and conceptualization [20].

Ownership has been difficult to define due to its complexity [22]. Understanding the concept of ownership is regarded to be as important as the acquisition of technical skills, education, finance and infrastructure in the era of openness [23]. An organization's perception of data ownership influences critical decision-making such as IS outsourcing, centralization or decentralization [22].

Networks are created through the social interaction between actors in an organization as well as between organizations [24]. Actors play different roles and occupy different authoritative positions in the networks [24]. Such roles and positions create an atmosphere of perceived trust between members of the network. Networks vary in size and are dependent on the actors in the social connection and their interaction. Organizational success is dependent on social networks [25]. In the context of knowledge management, networks are created to transfer tacit knowledge and develop new knowledge, which organizations depend on for future endeavors and transfer of skills [26]. In the knowledge network, organizations support a repository of both explicit and tacit knowledge which is distributed among actors [27]. Research in OGD has thus far paid limited attention to network aspects. This study considers the role of network creation in the successful use of OGD by Data Users. Networks can enable Data Users access to funding support, international exposure, determine data quality and access to data.

The primary *theoretical lens* used in this study to highlight the social processes influencing the institutionalization of OGD is Structuration Theory (ST) [28]. The relevance of ST to the study lies in its ability to surface underlying social factors that influence people's behavior and practices over time [29]. Castells' [30] and Honoré's [31] theoretical explanations to power in networks and data ownership were used to provide additional theoretical explanations to the empirical findings. The combination of theories is recognized as an acceptable practice in IS research [32].

3   Case Study Context

Ghana is a country in West Africa with an estimated population of 28 million people. The country is associated with democracy since 1992. Ghana has an elected president, a parliament, an independent judiciary, electoral commission and different public sector institutions. The public sector institutions are in charge of implementing government initiatives and fostering the relationship between government and citizens.

Ghana became a signatory to the 'Open Government Partnership Initiative' (OGPI) in September 2011. This was a way of strengthening prevailing open government frameworks incorporated in the practice of democracy [33]. The OGPI seeks to attain these goals through government commitments. The completion of the first Action Plan set the motion for the development and implementation of subsequent Action Plans. Lessons learnt, gaps identified, and fissures recognized from the previous Action Plans informed the activities of subsequent ones. Recent developments of the OGD initiative in Ghana can be traced to several activities such as workshops that focused on creating data awareness and increase in stakeholder engagement with data. The workshops also aimed at training participants on how to use available government data to create mobile and web applications through hackathons and advocacy activities. For example, a hackathon challenge was held in April 2019, this led to creating a "waste to gold" platform with an aim of tackling waste management in Ghana [34]. The workshops also discussed how to promote collaboration between different institutions, identification of data needs, promoting data use and improving data quality [35].

The Ghana OGD ecosystem has two government approved publishers. The two publishers are the Ghana Statistical Service (GSS) and the National Information Technology Agency (NITA). The **Ghana Statistical Service (GSS)** is regarded as the 'Government Statistician'. After Ghana's signatory to the OGPI, the responsibility of GSS has extended beyond just a collection and disseminating of statistical data. GSS is mandated to ensure that government data is open, accessible and in user-friendly formats. GSS is now also charged with the responsibility of developing, collecting, disseminating and reporting government data and further assessing it based on the indicators of the Sustainable Development Goals (SDGs). The **National Information Technology Agency (NITA)** was established in 2008 under the Ministry of Communication. The agency was mandated to act as a backbone for e-government in Ghana and the implementation of government ICT policies. After Ghana became a signatory to the OGPI, the responsibilities of NITA were extended to include developing the open data web portal in 2011. NITA was expected to coordinate and publish data from the various government institutions (Ministries Departments and Agencies). This was required to remove data redundancy and create a unified platform that makes government data available and accessible and at the least cost possible.

DUs (intermediaries) include Non-Governmental Organizations (NGOs), data enthusiasts, data analysts and data journalists, who create mobile-based technology solutions and educate citizens with the help of data. Their demand for and use of government data is critical because they can create and trigger major impacts. Some key NGO's are Mobile Web Ghana, Esoko, Famerline, as well as data enthusiasts, data scientists and data journalists. These NGOs have been actively involved and collaborated with government and international organizations due to the OGD movement. For example, Mobile Web Ghana has been actively involved with organizing the Ghana Open Data portal upload challenge and hackathon in 2019 and mapping for the Open Cities Accra Project [34]. The Open Cities Accra Project uses OpenStreetMap, field data collection and remote mapping to make flood-prone areas in Accra more resilient to flooding. Mobile Web Ghana has been involved in a workshop on domestic violence, child labor and Data Management and Publication Training for Government Agencies and Ministries. Likewise, Esoko partnered with government to collect and publish data on about 10,000 farmers in 10 districts. This data was linked with a social interventionist program called Livelihood Empowerment Against Poverty (LEAP) [36].

4 Research Methodology

The research strategy for this study entailed a single descriptive case study [37], namely the case of OGD in Ghana. The study was executed in an interpretive fashion.

Data were initially collected from the two main OGD publishers in Ghana and several OGD users (academia, data journalists, profit and non-profit Non-Governmental Organizations; citizens; international researchers and observer groups and organizations; technology enthusiast). The initial data sample was changed due to emerging themes, for instance, the researcher added other government institutions who were not regarded as OGD publishers. The sample population of OGD users were mostly based in the Greater Accra, Ashanti and Central regions. These three regions are urban cities and well populated. The Greater Accra region, for instance, is the capital city and also the seat of government, the region houses all the government institutions.

Semi-structured interviews were conducted with the assistance of an interview guide. Table 1 provides a summary of the interview participants and data sources.

Giddens' structuration theory was used as the main theoretical underpinning for this study. However, during the analysis of the empirical findings additional explanations were required. The findings indicated that data ownership, power and network creation were socially constructed and thus had been created and recreated over time. Data ownership, power and network creation were already existing structures that kept routinized activities the same, which is line with the Giddens' structuration theory [28]. However, Ghana's signatory to the OGD movement triggered changes which were not in-tune with these routinized existing structures. Thus, these existing structures instead of aiding the OGD movement rather led to the un-institutionalization of OGD. This affected both the publication and use of OGD in Ghana. Thus, in the discussion of the findings, the study blended structuration theory [28] with Castells' categorization of networks [30] and Honoré's categorization of data ownership [31].

Giddens' structuration theory is concerned with the reciprocity between human agency and social structure [28]. Structuration theory highlights the duality of interaction between social practices and human actors. The interaction between human actors and social behavioral patterns are produced and reproduced over time [29]. Social structure, in terms of rules and resources, can either facilitate or constrain social activity [29]. There is, therefore, a recursive relationship between structure and actions [28]. Structuration theory is used by researchers to understand social occurrences and the reproduction of behavior and practices across space and time [29]. The repetitive nature of these behavior and practices overtime become institutionalized as part of the social system. Structuration theory can be summarized by the dimensions of the duality of structure namely structures of signification, domination and legitimation, linking respectively to

Table 1. Data sampling

Category	OGD stakeholders	# Interviewees	Source of data
Data Publishers (DP)	Data Publisher 1	8	Group interviews, observation, website, documents
	Data Publisher 2	2	Group interviews, observation, website, documents
Public Sector Representatives (PS)	Public Sector 1	1	Individual interviews
	Public Sector 2	1	
	Public Sector 3	1	
Data Users (DU)	Data User 1	2	Group interviews, websites and participant observation
	Data User 2	2	
	Data User 3	2	Group interviews, websites and observation
	Data User 4	2	
	Data User 5	3	
	Data User 6	3	
	Data User 7	3	
	Data User 8	3	Group interviews, observation, website, documents

interactions of communication, power and sanction [28]. Table 2 lists the theoretical constructs of structuration theory that are applied in this study.

Castells [30] categorizes four types of networks namely:

1. "Networking Power: the power of the actors and organizations included in the networks that constitute the core of the global network society over human collectives and individual who are not included in these global networks.
2. Network Power: the power resulting from the standards required to coordinate social interaction in the networks. The exercise of power is dependent on rules of inclusion and not by network exclusion.
3. Networked Power: the power of social actors over other social actors in the network. The forms and process of networked power are specific to each network.
4. Network Making Power: the power to program-specific networks according to the interest and values of the programmers, and the power to switch different networks following the strategic alliance between dominant actors of various networks".

These types of power in networks exist in social systems where actors perceive they have power over other actors due to the personalization of the control of data. However,

Table 2. Concepts of structuration theory applied in this study

Construct	Propositions	Particularization
Agency	Also referred to as human, social actors, individuals or people. Giddens' assumed and recognized the knowledgeability of actors within the social system. Agency also determines acceptable and unacceptable behavior within a structure plus its accompanying rewards or sanction. Actions are replicated recursively	The ecosystem has multiple actors with different roles and varying meanings attached to OGD activities [5]
Structure	The structure consists of rules and resources. The existence of structures is dependent on the intertwined relationship between structures and agency. Structures enable the *recursive* production and reproduction of social systems [28]	Different rules and resources are used by actors with the aim of either publishing or using OGD. There national, international and organizational rules that have been produced and reproduced over time
Domination	The *structure of domination* is evident in every *social system* and noticed via the unevenness of allocative and *authoritative resources* [28]	Social actors (DUs, PSs, DPs) perceived data as a resource which needed to be controlled. Observations during the group interviews showed the existence of actors' ability to control others based on positions of authority and symbolic capital
Communication	Individuals within a structure communicate based on commonly acceptable schemes. Individuals are conscious schemes as they part of the structure of signification (rules based on which meanings are produced)	Actors created networks purposely to get access to government data, exposure, funding and determine the quality of datasets
Legitimation	Norms are part of the legitimation structure which allows sanctions to be evolved if not adhered to. Actors within the social system are aware of such norms as well as the sanctions	Organizational actors were aware of the norms that guide data publication and use as well as the sanctions. But suctions in this context was symbolic

the type of network is determined and defined by the particular network actors are involved in within the social system.

Honoré's [31] categorization of ownership includes: "The right to use whatever is owned; the right to control the use of whatever is owned; and the right to remain in control of what is owned, without interference from others". Honoré's [31] grouping identifies ownership from the perspective of property that requires identification and personalization by individuals. Honoré's work is relevant to this study, since it was found that actors' perception of data led to individual personalization of data which constrained data sharing and publication.

5 Findings

5.1 Thematic Analysis

A thematic analysis was performed [38]. "Thematic analysis is a method for identifying, analyzing, and reporting patterns (themes) within data" [38] p. 79. The thematic analysis in a study already starts when transcribing the data and ends with the completion of the study. Table 3 lists the themes and how often they were referenced.

Table 3. Coding references for themes generation

Themes & Number of coding referencing			
Node	# of references	Node	# of references
Actors	150	**Network creation/Data sharing culture**	98
Experiences, history	90	National	55
Roles	89	Organizational	90
Views	50	Trust as a challenge	98
Control\Power	120	Unintegrated and semi-integrated systems	68
Social construction	98	Unreactive nature of data sharing	98
Individual control	77	Publication of data by DPs	80
Institutional control	100	Submission of data by PSs	50
Organizational Control	97	**Resources DPS, PSS**	100
Resources, time and money	100	Data as a resource	117
Right to control use	110	Human skills and knowledge needed	98
Data ownership	200	Laws	50
Citizens data	70	Technological resources	100
Government data	200	Resources DUs	120
Organizational data	100	Human skills and experiences	150
Right to control the use	110	Technological	99
Right to control use	100	**USE**	70
		Publication	80

94 H. Nuhu et al.

Data Ownership. Ghana's signatory to the OGPI has unearthed some contextual issues which were related to who owns the data. DPs and PSs were conscious of the concerns surrounding data ownership. The issue was frequently mentioned in interviews. Data owners were contextually defined to be the actual government institutions in charge of collecting, processing and storing citizen's data. PSs perceived that institutional resources were used to accumulate and store citizen's data. This gave institutions a sense of ownership over data. Also, the existence of unintegrated and manual processes in the public sector was explained as a contributing factor. Both DUs and DPs explained the importance of giving recognition to the sources of data during use and publication. To DUs this acts as a form of protection. OGD publishers and users identified public institutions and online portals as critical primary sources of data.

The contextual explanation of ownership resulted in complexity with the inception of the OGD movement. OGD required signatory governments to develop a web portal aimed at publishing government data. However, critical attention has not given to data ownership. Consequently, there was empirical evidence of various arguments about who owned data within the OGD ecosystem. These arguments on data ownership were unearthed due to the inadequate nature of the published data. While some of the interview respondents believed that government data belonged to "government" others believed it belonged to the citizens. However, in a report on the impact and status of Open Data in Africa, the authors explained that "data belonged to the citizens" [39]. While some interview participants explained that data on the government-mandated web portal was regarded as government data, others asserted that, though the data was available on government web portals, the data is about the people, hence it belongs to them. As emphasized by some of the interview respondents:

"The misconception is, who does the data belong to? This is a critical discussion that we need to have but has not been seen as important. It is like it is difficult for the very people whose data has been accumulated to get access to it" (DU10; also representing the views of DU1, DU5, DU7, DU20).

DUs recognized the value of understanding data ownership within the local OGD ecosystem. Data was understood as a powerful tool of which the owners or publishers should be recognized. Understanding data ownership enabled DUs to disassociate themselves from issues that arose after publishing stories. Identifying and recognizing data owners was essential as it provides a type of credibility in situations where sensitive stories had to be told. Recognizing data owners within the OGD ecosystem by DUs enabled them to identify which DPs' data to use. The interview participants explained that data was obtained and accessed from different sources. These sources ranged from national to international websites. While some of the DUs had a pre-determined mindset on their sources of data, others could be categorized as "freelancers" who used government data from any source; to such DU the most important aspect is the availability of the data. An interview participant stated the following:

"I sometimes get it from data.gov.gh, which is down at this moment. In the last two years, if I need government data, that is where I got to first. I also check the website of DP1 and the websites of other government institutions. I check there to see if I can find the data I want." (DU9).

Actors' perception of Data Ownership led to data control. Controlling data led to institutional personalization of data and the desire to control the data both within and outside the institutional boundaries. Institutional personalization followed from the use of resources such as organizational time, money and skills used in collecting, process and storing data; there was a desire to exert some kind of influence. In addition, the subtle autonomy and integrated system led to the development of the concept of institutional personalization. Some of the participants elucidated that time and money invested in data gathering, processing, storage and disseminating data influenced the attitudes towards control. Institutional personalization of data also resulted in an attempt to control data use by potential and actual users. Some OGD publishers explained that it was essential to control data both within the institution and outside the institutions for ethical reasons including data ownership. Institutional personalization of government data further resulted in the desire to continuously monitor or control data use. It influenced both OGD publication and use.

"If I give you my data, I have the right to know what you are going to use it for and be acknowledged. I need to feel it is still mine. But the moment I give it out I lose that feeling [...]." (PS1, also supported by PS3).

Network Creation. Networks were intentionally and unintentionally created by Data Users. Networks were social connections created between DUs, international donor organizations, national technology enthusiasts as well as government institutions. These networks were created for different purposes. The purposes included financial and technical resources as well as data access. These networks provided a type of social connectedness, which were established as a means to express domination with regards to access to data (that should otherwise be open) and as a source of competitive advantage. Competitive advantage existed among DUs within the OGD ecosystem. This social connectedness was established either based on friendship, social engineering or professional standards. Creating social connections within the OGD ecosystem was deemed as a requirement because it provided the DU both social and technological exposure. Most of the DUs used available data either to tell stories or create technological mobile applications that were intended to trigger social conversation and create an impact. However, most of the DUs were in existence before the introduction of the OGD movement in Ghana. The OGD movement and created networks led to an increase in the incorporation of government data into their routinized activities and structures.

"We are supported by different organizations, it is needed for exposure. When you go to our website you will see them [...] they are mostly international. You must be connected since your connections give you an advantage over other organizations in this thing that we are doing. Knowing the right people in this space is necessary, not just nationally but outside Ghana" (DU 18, also supported by DU 20).

Created networks were used as a means of interaction between data publishers and users. This interaction was required to either enable quick access to data or provide additional understanding of the available data. The networks created by DUs were: 1) National Networks, this was sub-categorized into network created between DUs, PSs and DPs and Networks created among DUs; 2) International Networks.

Power in Networks. The networks created by DUs transcended beyond the local environment to include international networks or connections. The networks, both local and international, were established to ensure that government data was technologically and legally opened and to reuse data to create value for citizens. Reasons for creating international networks also included funding and exposure. These networks led to the creation and creation of power-related structures that were founded on access and use of government data plus other resources. The type of power emanated from the ability of the DU to control or influence the activities of DP and government at large. The power within the networks was used to trigger responses from both local and international OGD communities. The changes and responses that have occurred within the OGD ecosystem would not have been possible without the actions of the socially created power in networks. For example, by using and analyzing different government data from parliament, Odekro (a Ghanaian civic organization promoting government transparency) was able to establish trends that critiqued parliament attendance by parliamentarians from 2013 to 2016. The report also exposed the performance of parliamentarians, this was debated as a key determinate of elections. The report of Odekro was one example of power within networks that critiqued government representatives and made citizens aware through the use of government data.

"[…] providing citizens, communities, media and civil society with the necessary data with which to hold parliament and MPs accountable […]. This report was critical because the lack of quorum brings to a halt government business and may delay or even rush the consideration or passage of crucial bills[…]" [40].

6   Application of Theory to Findings

In this section, the theories introduced in Sect. 4 are applied deductively to the empirical findings.

Agency and Structure. The OGD ecosystem consists of multiple actors with multiple roles and responsibilities who engage in social practices through social interactions. The interactions within social practices are shaped by commonly understood interpretive schemes, sanctions and communication [29]. The actors could be broadly categorized into Data Publishers, Public Sector Institutions and Data Users. OGD actors also include public administrators, bloggers, NGOs, academic researchers, data journalists and their beneficiaries [5]. Within each of these broad categories existed social actors with varying roles and responsibilities [29]. These actors existed and interacted in various ways within the OGD ecosystem. Such interactions lead to the creation and re-creation of both meaning and untended effects of Data Ownership, Power and Network Creation. The interaction between actors was shaped by rules and resources [28]. For example, actors' perceptions of data ownership can be derived from the identification of data as a resource which is guided by different socially constructed legitimation criteria in a network. Data Users interact in a given network to determine data quality before use via a set of acceptable rules and available resources.

Structures of Signification. Actors within the OGD ecosystems have produced and reproduced subjective meanings associated with Data Ownership, Power and Network Creation over time. For example, Public Sector Institutions have both organizational and individually personalized and subjective view of organizational data which resulted in the desire to control it. Such created meanings influenced the actors' interaction within the social structure or OGD ecosystem and thereby continuously affecting the lack of institutionalization of OGD publication and use in Ghana. Interaction between actors in a social system has a recursive effect on how social systems are shaped over time [28]. While DPs and Public Sectors recognized their respective institutions as owners of data, Data Users also recognized government and citizens as owners of data. The concept of data ownership is linked with the perceptions and behavioral patterns of actors inside rather than outside organizations [41].

The perception of Data Ownership has contributed to the un-institutionalization of OGD publication in Ghana. This can be attributed to fear of losing control and relevance as 'Data Owners'. Using ST to understand the concept of ownership reveals the difference between equity and dialectic control existing between actors in a network as well as the influence of power in such institution [42]. From the perspective of ST social behaviors were to result in sanctions; but the inadequate publication of OGD in Ghana by DUs and PSs which can be linked with specific social behaviors was yet to attract such sanctions.

By blending Giddens' ST with Honoré's [31] work, data ownership can be further explained. From the findings, DPs and PSs expressed their right over data in their possession due to the resources used in the accumulation of data. It was assumed that data belonged to such institutions which gave them institutional and individual right of the data. This influenced data control, use and quest to continuously remain in control of data in their possession. Honoré [31] explained that the perception of ownership gives actors three rights: usage rights, controlling usage rights and continuously remaining in control. From the findings, actors held the perception that data belonged to their respective organizations; in some cases individuals in authority, thus they had the right to use, control and continuously be in control of data use. Consequently, such actors reserved the right to determine when data can be released.

Structures of Legitimation and Domination. The creation of networks by DUs became a type of legitimation criterion for data access, determination of data quality, funding and international exposure. Although network creation became a norm among DUs, there were no clear sanctions attached. ST explains the link between norms and the structure of legitimation plus its attributed sanctions [29]. Organizational actors' perspectives on data ownership and networks created two forms of power: collective and individual power. Collective power extended beyond the quest to control data; it also included access and use of organizational resources needed in the process of accumulating and storing data from a collective standpoint. Data or information distribution often brings out issues of control and power [20]. Organizational actors used their institutionalized power to affirm their positions and control over data, this led to the creation of bureaucratic data request structures that were legitimized overtime. Domination was exercised on external actors who needed data for social intervention programs or publication.

Findings from this study explained that actors had different perceptions of power, relating to actors' affiliate organizations, roles and historical factors surrounding data ownership. Knowledge about the existing complexities with the theme of data ownership needs contextual explanations in this era of openness due to large amounts of data being produced and the multiple sources of data [23].

Data ownership and network creation revealed the concept of power, and its implications were expressed by the actors involved. Actors perceived data as an authoritative resource, this led to the creation of bureaucratic structures to control its accumulation, publication and use. Giddens explains power as a social construction, expressed via the use of resources [28]. The creation of networks showed the existence of power relations between OGD actors and international donor partners. Actors, through network creation, exercised power based on the number of international partners they had, funding and ability to access data.

Power in created networks can be explained from the perspective of Castells [30]. Networks were not formed in a vacuum, as such there existed evidence of power within these created networks. Although Castells categorized the power in networks into four types, the findings from this study supported three: 1) From the findings, it was evident that DUs created and valued networks created on the global level. It was perceived as a form of international exposure and power, the number of such networks created including the type of international organization meant was used as a form of power over DUs. Castells categorized this type of network power as 'Networking Power'. 2) DUs also considered their ability to have access data which was not published through social interaction as an exercise of power. To Castells, such power was 'Network Power'. 3) DUs, DPs and PSs exercised the third categorization of Castells' grouping. To Castells 'Networked Power' exists when actors perceive to have power over other actors within a social system which is defined by a particular network.

7 Conclusion

This research set out to understand and explain the factors influencing OGD publication and use in Ghana. Despite Ghana's signatory to the OGPI in 2011, OGD publication and use is yet to be institutionalized by DPs, PSs and DUs. An interpretive case study was performed, drawing from document analysis and stakeholder interviews.

The research demonstrated the need for both OGD practitioners and researchers to have adequate knowledge of the contextual backgrounds and ecosystems of countries prior, and during the implementation of OGD. An understanding of the different contextual backgrounds revealed different behavioral patterns and practices that were created and recreated by actors within the various structures. Although these behavioral patterns and practices have existed for many years, the possibility of transitioning must be considered as important.

The empirical findings revealed that Data Ownership, Network Creation and Power were socially created and re-created over time by DPs, PSs and DUs. These social patterns and practices existed prior to the implementation of OGD and were recognized as critical factors that influenced the institutionalization of OGD publication and use in Ghana. Actors within the OGD ecosystem had personalized the interpretation and meanings associated with Data Ownership. Ownership of data was seen in three ways by actors: government, organizational and citizen's ownership. The perception of Data Ownership led actors to view data as an organizational and individual property whose access and use needed to be controlled continuously by the 'owners'. The issues surrounding Data Ownership were attributed to the inadequate transitioning from manual, un- or semi-integrated systems to fully automated systems.

The implication of Data Ownership on OGD publication led to the creation and recreation of networks by DUs. These networks were used by DUs as a means to obtain data that should have been published as per the OGD signatory. The Networks had both national and international partners; national DUs relied on social connections to enable them to have access to data and determine data quality. International networks were used as a form of exposure and to secure funding. Within these networks existed a socially constructed perception and mutually communicated understanding of power relations that influenced OGD acquisition and use. Castell's explanation of Power in Networks provides an understanding of this part of the findings: 1) DUs created international networks (partners) for exposure and a way of expressing power over other DUs. Such networks were displayed on websites as a sign of prestige: this is referred to as 'Networking Power'. 2) Some DUs, thanks to their networks, had access to data that others did not possess; such data was used to trigger national debates and changes: 'Networked power'. 3) DUs also created networks that gave them the power to partner with government and organizes training workshops for civil right advocacy groups. Such networks were based on interactions and principles of social inclusion.

In summary, this study uncovered that social patterns and practices around Data Ownership, Network Creation and Power have a major influence on the institutionalization of OGD. This study, therefore, recommends the inclusion of change management principles that take explicit cognizance of these practices to achieve OGD implementation (publication and use) in developing countries due to the disruptive nature of the phenomenon. Future research can focus on the application of change management principles in OGD implementation and quantitative analysis of these themes. Future research could also focus on reasons behind the use of symbolic sanctions.

References

1. Jetzek, T., Avital, M., Bjorn-Andersen, N.: Data-driven innovation through open government data. J. Theor. Appl. Electron. Commer. Res. **9**, 100–120 (2014)
2. Saxena, S.: Summarizing the decadal literature in open government data (OGD) research: a systematic review. Foresight (2018)
3. Srimuang, C., Cooharojananone, N., Tanlamai, U., Chandrachai, A.: Open government data assessment model: an indicator development in Thailand. In: 2017 19th International Conference on Advanced Communication Technology (ICACT), pp. 341–347. IEEE (2017)

4. Dawes, S.S., Vidiasova, L., Parkhimovich, O.: Planning and designing open government data programs: an ecosystem approach. Gov. Inf. Q. **33**, 15–27 (2016)
5. Gonzalez-Zapata, F., Heeks, R.: The multiple meanings of open government data: understanding different stakeholders and their perspectives. Gov. Inf. Q. **32**, 441–452 (2015)
6. Mungai, P., Van Belle, J.-P.: Understanding the Kenya open data initiative trajectory from an actor-network perspective, pp. 1–7 (2018)
7. Saxena, S., Muhammad, I.: Barriers to use open government data in private sector and NGOs in Pakistan. Information Discovery and Delivery (2018)
8. World Bank Group: World Bank Support for Open Data (2017)
9. Dawes, S.S., Helbig, N.C.: The Value and Limits of Government Information Resources for Policy Informatics. Routledge, Abingdon (2015)
10. Verhulst, S.G., Andrew, Y.: Open Data in Developing Economies: Toward Building an Evidence Base on What Works and How. African Minds (2017)
11. Bernardi, R.: Health information systems and accountability in Kenya: a structuration theory perspective. J. Assoc. Inf. Syst. **18**, 931–957 (2018)
12. Khan, Z., Pervez, Z., Ghafoor, A.: Towards cloud based smart cities data security and privacy management. In: 2014 IEEE/ACM 7th International Conference on Utility and Cloud Computing, pp. 806–811. IEEE (2014)
13. Sáez Martín, A., Rosario, A.H.D., Pérez, M.D.C.C.: An international analysis of the quality of open government data portals. Soc. Sci. Comput. Rev. **34**, 298–311 (2016)
14. Zuiderwijk, A., Janssen, M.: Open data policies, their implementation and impact: a framework for comparison. Gov. Inf. Q. **31**, 17–29 (2014)
15. Bates, J.: The strategic importance of information policy for the contemporary neoliberal state: the case of Open Government Data in the United Kingdom. Gov. Inf. Q. **31**, 388–395 (2014)
16. Robinson, D.G., Yu, H., Zeller, W., Felten, E.: Government data and the invisible hand. Yale J. Law Technol. **11**, 160–175 (2009)
17. Mekonnen, S.M., Wubishet, Z.S.: An institutional perspective to understand FOSS adoption in public sectors: case studies in Ethiopia and India. Am. J. Inf. Syst. **4**, 32–44 (2016)
18. Avgerou, C.: IT and organizational change: an institutionalist perspective. Inf. Technol. People **13**, 234–262 (2000)
19. Mungai, P.W.: Causal mechanisms and institutionalisation of open government data in Kenya. Electron. J. Inf. Syst. Dev. Ctries. **84**, 1–13 (2018)
20. Silva, L.: Epistemological and theoretical challenges for studying power and politics in information systems. Inf. Syst. J. **17**, 165–183 (2007)
21. Bariff, M.L., Galbraith, J.R.: Intraorganizational power considerations for designing information systems. Acc. Organ. Soc. **3**, 15–27 (1978)
22. Van Alstyne, M., Brynjolfsson, E., Madnick, S.: Why not one big database? Database **15**, 267–284 (1995)
23. de Beer, J.: Ownership of Open Data: Governance Options for Agriculture and Nutrition, 13 pages (2017)
24. Tsai, W., Ghoshal, S.: Social capital and value creation: the role of intrafirm networks. Acad. Manag. J. **41**, 464–476 (1998)
25. Jenssen, J.I., Koenig, H.F.: The effect of social networks on resource access and business start-ups. Eur. Plan. Stud. **10**, 1039–1046 (2002)
26. Bergman, J., Jantunen, A., Saksa, J.M.: Managing knowledge creation and sharing – scenarios and dynamic capabilities in inter-industrial knowledge networks. J. Knowl. Manag. **8**, 63–76 (2004)
27. Miller, K.D., Waller, H.G.: Scenarios, real options and integrated risk management. Long Range Plan. **36**, 93–107 (2003)

28. Giddens, A.: The Constitution of Society. University of California Press, Los Angeles (1984)
29. Jones, M.R., Karsten, H.: Giddens's structuration theory and information systems research. MIS Q. **32**, 127–157 (2008)
30. Castells, M.: A network theory of power. Int. J. Commun. **5**, 773–787 (2011)
31. Honoré, A.M.: Ownership. In: Oxford Essays in Jurisprudence, p. 107 (1961)
32. Gregor, S.: The nature of theory in information systems. MIS Q. **30**, 611–642 (2006)
33. Secretariate, P.S.R.: The Open Government Partnership Initiative, National Action Plan for Ghana (2016)
34. Sabblah, E.: Data Upload Challenge and Hackathon (2019)
35. BusinessGhana: Workshop on Open Data and Development Opens (2018)
36. Fuger, S.: Tales from the Field: Data Collection for LEAP (Livelihood Empowerment Against Poverty) (2018)
37. Baxter, P., Jack, S.: Qualitative case study methodology: study design and implementation for novice researchers. Qual. Rep. **13**, 544–559 (2008)
38. Braun, V., Clarke, V.: Using thematic analysis in psychology. Qual. Res. Psychol. **3**, 77–101 (2006)
39. Van Belle, J.-P.: Africa Data Revolution Report 2018: Status and Emerging Impact of Open Data in Africa (2018)
40. Odekro: Absenteeism rates in Ghana's Sixth Parliament of the Fourth Republic Introduction 97 (2016)
41. Hart, D.: Ownership as an Issue in Data and Information Sharing: a philosophically based review. Australas. J. Inf. Syst. **10**, 23–29 (2002)
42. Coad, A.F., Glyptis, L.G.: Structuration: a position-practice perspective and an illustrative study. Crit. Perspect. Account. **25**, 142–161 (2014)

Attitudes Toward and Experiences of Digital Labour in South Africa

Cuthbert Chidoori[✉] and Jean-Paul Van Belle

CITANDA, University of Cape Town, Rondebosch, Cape Town, South Africa
chdcut001@myuct.ac.za, Jean-Paul.VanBelle@uct.ac.za

Abstract. Digital labour is viewed as having the capacity to drive the technological and economic development by addressing critical issues that often encountered in African countries like South Africa, such as high unemployment, low local wages, lack of local demand and others. As such, it is seen as a crucial steppingstone towards (South) Africa's move towards the Fourth Industrial Revolution (4IR). However, digital labour could also bring significant drawbacks such as exploitation of workers, unguaranteed or no remuneration. This research investigates the attitudes toward digital labour, intention to participate in digital labour; initial experiences from participating in digital labour and continued participation in digital labour practices. We propose, validate and empirically test a new integrative model, and supplement our model with qualitative findings. Digital workers' attitudes and experiences toward digital labour did, unsurprisingly, correlate significantly with the intention and participation of people in digital labour with key aspects of digital labour pertaining to the Global South being identified. Most individuals responded positively toward their experience with digital labour, particularly based on the compensation that they expected or experienced for their digital work.

Keywords: Digital labour · Digital work · Fourth Industrial Revolution · 4IR · Attitudes · Digital platforms · Gig economy · Crowdsourcing · Microwork

1 Introduction

Digital work is described as the creation of new products and services through the use of the human mind, speech and various forms of digital media [1]. Often, digital labour (or gig economy) can include various forms of paid and unpaid digital work forms [1, 2]. [2] distinguished between two types of gig economy work, namely digital gig economy, where the work is primarily digital and the on-demand gig economy, where the work is manual even though the it is partly supported on a digital platform (e.g. AirBnb, Uber). This research was focused particularly on digital gig economy platforms.

Major barriers that often inhibit economic and technological developments in African developing countries include a lack of development of telecommunications infrastructure [3], a lack of appropriate ICT investment policies, insufficient development of skilled

© IFIP International Federation for Information Processing 2020
Published by Springer Nature Switzerland AG 2020
R. K. Bandi et al. (Eds.): IFIPJWC 2020, IFIP AICT 601, pp. 102–116, 2020.
https://doi.org/10.1007/978-3-030-64697-4_9

labour, and limits to foreign-trade imports [4]. Digital labour activities such as crowd-sourcing tend to be beneficial for addressing challenges in African countries by harnessing the skills of multiple workers on online platforms, enhancing operational efficiency in organisations and providing more employment opportunities through crowdsourcing initiatives such as microwork [5].

However, there are also significant drawbacks experienced by people participating in digital work which include exclusion based on traits such as race, religion, successful digital workers exploiting other workers, business knowledge restrictions and others [1, 6].

The main purpose of this research on digital labour is about investigating the attitudes and experiences of people who get paid for their digital work (digital labourers), concerning digital labour with a particular focus on the practice of crowdsourcing, particularly in South Africa. According to [7] although studies that examine digital labour in the Global South are present, the actual and continued practice of digital labour is still a growing area in the Global South and is still in need of further investigation. Therefore, this research investigates the attitudes toward digital labour, intention to participate; initial experiences from participating and continued participation in digital labour practices to contribute to the body of growing research. We propose, validate and empirically test a new integrative model and supplement our model validation with qualitative findings on the barriers experienced by digital labourers in South Africa.

This paper first sketches the background of digital labour in Africa, including its perceived benefits and issues. Then follows the research methodology which also introduces the theoretical model, which was adopted for the research and, based on the model, the detailed research questions. This is followed first by the quantitative analysis section which seeks to validate the model, then by a qualitative analysis section which adds further detail and insight to the analysis. The analysis is then discussed in more detail. The conclusion highlights recommendations and limitations of the research.

2 Background

Often in African countries there is a significant lack of technology infrastructure that is required for economic and ICT development. As an example, often low-end feature phones are used by a lot of people in poor communities in countries like South Africa, where in most cases, people cannot afford to purchase ICT infrastructures and smartphones [3]. However, [8] noted that countries like South Africa have more advanced ICT and mobile infrastructure than other developing countries. According to [9], in South Africa, 64.7% households nationally had at least a single person with access to the internet in various places or outlets such as home, work, internet cafes or study place.

In many developing countries, though, there is a lack of appropriate policies which are critical for enhancing ICT adoption, innovation, education, research and development [10]. According to [11], developing countries seek for foreign investments regarding uptake of technology, but often lack necessary components in their policies such as contractual agreements, foreign alliances, in order to effectively collaborate with other foreign entities. [12] further mention that because of the segregation of education system in South Africa, which led to many people being deprived of learning subjects, such as Mathematics and English, numerous South Africans become less aware of the implication of policies that exist concerning technology usage.

Another challenge in African countries is that basic ICT skills are often unequally spread among different population groups in developing countries, particularly in South Africa [13]. [14] highlighted that in certain African countries, students, including adults tend to struggle with basic language literacy skills due to lack of successful language teaching approaches which leads to missed employment opportunities.

2.1 Digital Labour Initiatives

The implementation of digital labour initiatives is crucial for addressing the major circumstances in countries like South Africa such as unemployment, poverty and others. Some of the digital labour initiatives that are practised include crowdsourcing and microwork [6].

Crowdsourcing, for instance, is known to be the digital labour activity where numerous people can reach out to each other through a network on an ICT platform in order to share and exchange ideas and resources flexibly [5, 6]. The idea of sharing and collaborating crowdsourcing information has been witnessed on global digital platforms such as Facebook, LinkedIn, YouTube, Wikipedia and Upwork which all rely on the contribution of various content by clients around the world, even from developing countries [15]. Regarding microwork, also regarded as crowdsourcing initiative, it is described as an activity used in organisations for breaking down a complex task of a certain size into smaller micro-tasks which could also be performed by people who do not have advanced mobile infrastructures. Microwork can be beneficial even for people who do not possess smartphones or personal computers [5]. Commonly used microwork platforms used by internet users include South African digital platforms such as Mintor, Hooros, Crew Pencil and several others [16].

Crowdsourcing initiatives can present notable benefits such as knowledge sharing, increased networking and communication amongst business colleagues, new job opportunities, enhanced consumer interaction and several others [5, 6]. While there are key benefits in crowdsourcing, there are also significant drawbacks experienced by digital workers, such as low renumeration for online labour provided, exploitation of online labour, lack of formal agreement for ensuring workers' rights [1].

2.2 Digital Labour Issues

Putting into practice digital labour activities could still give rise to significant challenges for digital workers in South Africa. One significant problem is that people using digital and social media platforms can be excluded from certain labour markets due to race, gender or economic status and thus be economically excluded from certain digital platforms [1].

Another notable challenge with digital labour is that successful, highly-skilled digital workers could employ and aggregate and exploit other less experienced or skilled digital workers to undertake digital work that may be burdensome and low-paying, in a process called re-intermediation [1, 17]. However [6] also described the idea of disin-termediation, where workers could gain the opportunity through the internet to directly interact with their clients without requiring a mediating agent [1, 18].

Moreover, digital workers in companies may be barred from accessing knowledge about business processes and thus deprived of the opportunity to enhance their skills and gain knowledge especially if they have a low skill set and also may feel less secure in their jobs [2]. Also, on digital platforms, workers tend to lack the ability to govern and communicate with each other and therefore are unable to unite, form unions and harness bargaining power in order to obtain fair work conditions [19]. [20] highlighted that, as employers tend to favour higher-skilled workers and divert resources and opportunities away from lower-skilled workers to higher-skilled workers, low-skilled workers would have their wages reduced and lose their bargaining power.

3 Research Methodology

The theoretical model used for conducting this research was constructed using concepts mainly from the various sources of literature used for this article and from a popular theory known as Self-Determination Theory (SDT). SDT was used for describing the attitudes and expectations in the Fig. 1 model. SDT examines the extent to which one becomes self-motivated without any external influence [21]. SDT describes the different kinds of motivations, from the extrinsic motivations which are affected by external rewards or punishments to intrinsic motivation where an individual becomes self-determined to undertake a behaviour without requiring external agent [22]. The greater in-depth analysis on the types of motivations that encourage participation in digital labour particularly relating to individuals' attitudes and expectations was the major justification for the use of SDT in the Fig. 1 model. Other Fig. 1 constructs, namely intention to participate, initial participation and continued participation were used as adaptations of Technology Acceptance Model (TAM) and Theory of Reasoned Action (TRA) concepts, to pertain more to adopting a technology practice(s) than to the use of a particular technology [21, 22].

For the theoretical model, the macro construct was used to describe the issues that would affect digital labour practices regionally or even countrywide such as policy and education [13]. For the micro construct, the aspects that could digital labour specific to individuals such digital literacy. The barriers construct consisted of aspects that would occur when there is a full participation in digital labour participation such as lack of digital skill, as shown in the Fig. 1 model [1, 2].

The main constructs in Fig. 1 which were investigated in the research were namely the barriers, initial expectations, the experiential expectations, intention to participate in digital labour, initial participation and the continued participation in digital labour.

The research questions were concerned with how the attitudes and experiences of individuals around digital labour along with the intention to participate, would shape their actual participation and their continued participation.

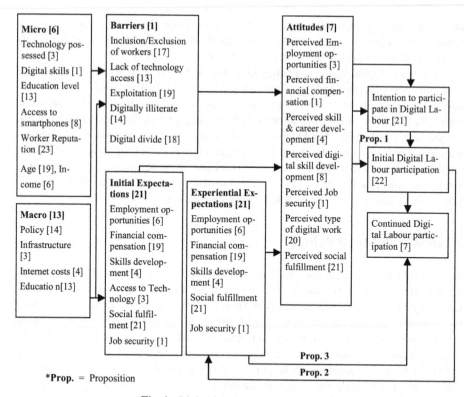

Fig. 1. Digital labour theoretical model

1. What is the relationship between digital labour attitudes with people's initial participation or experience of digital labour?
2. How do some aspects of digital labour affect people's experience of digital labour?
3. What is the relationship between people's initial participation in, or past experience with digital labour with the continuation of their digital labour practices?

The propositions that were investigated in the quantitative data analysis were based on the main constructs for the research model and were used to address the main research questions. The propositions are stated as follows.

- Proposition 1: Attitudes of digital workers and the intention to participate in digital labour both have a positive relationship with their initial participation in digital labour.
- Proposition 2: Initial Participation in Digital Labour has a positive relationship with the experiential expectations around digital labour.
- Proposition 3: Experiential expectations of digital workers concerning digital labour has a positive relationship with the Continued Participation in Digital Labour.

The empirical data to test the model was obtained by means of a survey involving a sample consisting of 70 South Africans who possess basic ICT skills such as blogging, web browsing. The individuals participating in the survey sample were undertaking digital work on platforms relating to crowdsourcing such as htxt, entrepreneurmag, LinkedIn and Upwork, and being paid at any amount for doing digital work. Incentives, such as Electronic Funds Transfer (EFT) payments, offer and mobile airtime were used to encourage participation in the research survey from as many respondents as possible.

The questionnaire used for the research survey had both Likert and open-ended questions and was administered after pilot-testing. The questionnaire for the research was generated and distributed to respondents in the survey sample using an online web survey tool called Qualtrics and the respondents would fill in the questionnaire online. The questionnaire contained questions that were guided by the theories described in the Fig. 1 model. The questionnaire was anonymous and therefore did not collect sensitive personal information from the respondents. Ethics clearance was obtained from the University's Ethics Department. The research data was gathered from the questionnaire responses and analysed using a mixed methods approach involving various quantitative and qualitative techniques. The quantitative analysis was used in order to examine and validate theories described in the Fig. 1 model. The qualitative analysis techniques were used to gain deeper insights about the experience of digital workers that might reinforce or contradict the significant quantitative analysis results, and possibly discover new insights for the proposed model (Fig. 1).

4 Quantitative Data Analysis

The data used for the quantitative analysis was quantified from the responses given by all the survey respondents to the Likert-scale questionnaire questions, which were asked based on the Fig. 1 constructs. The Fig. 1 constructs investigated included expectations, barriers, attitudes intention to participate, the initial participation and continued participation in digital labour. The quantitative analysis methods were conducted using TIBCO Statistica and Microsoft (MS) Office Excel 2010.

The final sample size, after removal of incomplete responses, consisted of 70 respondents. Forty-six of them had crowdsourcing experience whereas 24 of them did not. Most respondents were under the age of 45 years. There were 39 females and 30 males with one respondent refusing to disclose their gender. Concerning education, most of the respondents had tertiary education as their highest education level, with 41 respondents having a bachelor's degree. The quantitative analysis methods and tests conducted are described in the sections that follow.

4.1 Reliability Analysis

The Cronbach Alpha method was used to test how well the variables representing the survey questions fit together in each of the main digital labour model constructs in Fig. 1. The variables were derived from multiple Likert-scale questions and the constructs of initial (0.79) and experiential expectations (0.82), and attitudes (0.84) all held up well apart from barriers with a relatively low 0.60, reflecting some diversity in the barriers. However, each of the constructs had sub-constructs and we wanted to keep the detail of these sub-constructs to enable more fine-grained analysis and, hopefully, policy recommendations. Thus, exploratory factor analysis was done on each of our major model 'grouping' constructs to identify and/or validate our sub-constructs.

4.2 Using Factor Analysis to Refine the Variables in the Initial Model

The factor analysis method was performed to test if valid factors could be formed from the large number of questions that were asked for the main constructs (and whether they corresponded to the initial model). The Factor Analysis was performed separately for each of the main constructs. Therefore, four sets of factor analysis results for the main constructs barriers, initial expectations, experiential expectations and attitudes where produced as a result.

For each of the factor analyses tables, the final sub-constructs that emerged are shown below, along with a short description of our 'final' model sub-constructs.

4.3 Regression Analysis Results

Regression analysis was conducted to determine the nature of the relationship between the Fig. 1 model constructs relevant to each research question. The variables analysed were the sub-constructs from Fig. 1 and Table 1 which were relevant for the research questions. In order to ensure that multicollinearity was not an issue, the backward step-wise regression was performed for each of the following regression models to ensure that only independent variables that were not heavily correlated with each other would remain in the regression models.

Table 1. Final model constructs.

	Initial expectations factors
ExpctSocialMedia	The perceived expectation of being able to use social media for sharing ideas and promoting innovation would consequently affect the perceived expectation of benefitting from knowledge creation and sharing amongst communities on digital labour platforms
ExpctSocial-Belonging	The perceived expectation of obtaining a social belonging on digital labour platforms
ExpctLivingWage	The perceived expectation of being able to earn a living on digital labour platforms
ExpctSecurity	The expectation that there would be security and privacy of personal information when participating in digital labour platforms
	Experiential expectations factors
ExpctLiving-Wage	The experiential expectation of continuing to earn a living wage for performing digital work in the future
ExpctSocial-Belonging	The expectation of continuing to find or experience a social belonging on digital labour platforms

(continued)

Table 1. (*continued*)

	Experiential expectations factors
ExpctSecurity	Continued expectation of experiencing security and privacy of personal information on digital labour platforms
ExpctRealWorld-Impact	The experiential expectation of digital work causing a real-world impact in communities
ExpctInternet-Access	The experiential expectation that there would be sufficient internet access available
	Barriers factors
BarCitizenship	The barrier of citizenship or nationality on being able to participate in online employment opportunities
BarInternetCost	The barrier of the cost of internet access due to government policy and its effect on internet access across South Africa
BarDigitalSkills	Digital skills determining the amount of payment and benefit that is received for participating in digital labour
	Attitudes factors
AttCompetence	Digital work activities are considered suitable for an individual's competence and professional skills, and gaining pleasure from performing digital work
AttInfoSecurity	Not being too worried overall about personal information security would affect the attitude of lacking any overall worries about online fraud
AttTechnologyUse	Attitude towards owning and using more technologies in digital work activities, significantly explains factor 3
AttCommunication	Prepared to considerably change the ways of communicating to participate in digital labour
AttCrowdwork-JobSecurity	Prepared to pursue long-term crowdsourcing jobs would influence the attitude of obtaining opportunities to build career and skills through digital labour participation
AttWork-Location	Prepared to perform digital work from any location

Regarding the first proposition, backward stepwise regression was performed for "InitialParticipation", the attitudes variables and "ParticipationIntention" (Table 2).

The p-value signified that the regression model was very significant and that the claim by the second proposition holds. From the beta values, "ParticipationIntention" had a very strong relationship with the "InitialParticipation" whereas "AttCommunication" had a significant, but weak relationship with "InitialParticipation". The R^2 value signified that the "ParticipationIntention" variable and the "AttCommunication" variable explained a large portion of the variation in the "InitialParticipation" variable.

Pertaining to the second proposition, the expectations and the initial participation in digital labour were investigated using backward stepwise regression (Table 3).

Table 2. Regression model for initial participation, participation intention and attitudes.

Regression summary for dependent variable: InitialParticipation
$R = .843$ $R^2 = .711$ Adjusted $R^2 = .702$ $F(2,67) = 82.46$ $p < .00$ Std. Error of estimate: .487

N = 70	b*	Std. Err. (b*)	b	Std. Err. (b)	t(67)	p-value
Intercept			0.29	0.31	0.95	0.35
ParticipationIntention	0.81	0.07	0.79	0.06	12.37	0.00
AttCommunication	0.16	0.07	0.14	0.06	2.44	0.02

Table 3. Regression model for expectations.

Regression summary for dependent variable: ExpectationsAvg (Prop3)
$R = 0.626$ $R^2 = 0.392$ Adj $R^2 = 0.379$ $F(1,44) = 28.4$ $p < 0.000$ Std. Error of est: 0.504

N = 46	b*	Std. Err. (b*)	b	Std. Err. (b)	t(44)	p-value
Intercept			2.26	0.32	7.11	0.000000
InitialParticipation	0.63	0.12	0.42	0.079	5.33	0.000003

Concerning the regression model, the p-value indicated that the regression model was very significant and justified the claim made by the third proposition. From the beta value, "InitialParticipation" had a notably strong relationship with "Expectations". The R^2 value indicated that "InitialParticipation" explained a notable, moderate amount of the variation in the "Expectations".

With regards to the third proposition, the continued participation in digital labour, the experiential digital labour expectations and the initial participation in digital labour were examined using the backward stepwise regression (Table 4).

Table 4. Regression model for continued participation

Regression summary for dependent variable: ContinuedParticipation
$R = 0.81$ $R^2 = 0.65$ Adjusted $R^2 = 0.64$ $F(2,43) = 40.74$ $p < .00000$ Std. Error of estimate: 0.59

N = 46	b*	Std. Err. (b*)	b	Std. Err. (b)	t(43)	p-value
Intercept			0.49	0.40	1.22	0.23
ExpctLivingWage	0.29	0.10	0.28	0.10	2.77	0.0082
InitialParticipation	0.63	0.10	0.65	0.11	6.12	0.0000

The regression model in Table 4 was significant from the p-value which also justified the statement by the fourth proposition. From the beta values, the "InitialParticipation" variable had a strong relationship with the "ContinuedParticipation" variable whereas

"ExpctLivingWage" had a modest relationship with the "ContinuedParticipation" variable. From the R^2 value, the "InitialParticipation" variable and the "ExpctLivingWage" explained a large amount of the variation in "ContinuedParticipation".

5 Qualitative Data Analysis

The survey questionnaire also contained some open-ended questions where respondents could share their views mainly around particular digital labour experiences. The responses from 20 different respondents were analysed. The qualitative analysis was necessary for addressing the main research questions, especially the second question and further exploring theories tested in the quantitative analysis.

For the qualitative analysis, thematic analysis was used to analyse the responses shared by the respondents in the survey questions. Key digital labour themes which related to digital labour experiences were identified from the respondents' views. The digital labour themes were analysed along with key corresponding statements, thoughts, sentiments and emotive words from respondents. The thematic analysis was conducted using the tools, namely, Microsoft Office Excel and NVIVO Software. The themes and the corresponding responses are described and analysed below.

5.1 Fair Compensation

Regarding compensation for digital work, many respondents mentioned that compensation was the primary incentive for digital labour participation. A significant number of respondents felt that the monetary reward received for producing online work was very little. As an example, Respondent 16, "I am a writer we are often underpaid and overworked". Similarly, Respondent 9 also expressed, "Globally, sites like UpWork exploits freelancers". The respondents' reactions would agree with the literature which emphasizes that workers could get hired very cheaply by employers and earn low compensation depending on the labour market they are in, and competition with other workers for opportunities [1].

Conversely, some respondents expressed that they could obtain opportunities for higher wages, as in the case of Respondent 5 when they mentioned the following point, "great earning potential for writers... This is why I contribute to Wikipedia...other info. portals". The respondents' positive views would coincide notably with the literature which points out that workers tend to have to compete for opportunities with other workers and could obtain higher or lower wages based certain skills being demanded [18].

5.2 Digital Skill

For the digital skill of respondents, a significant number of respondents viewed digital platforms as an opportunity to showcase, utilise and develop their skills for interesting online jobs. Certain respondents also mentioned that they can obtain access to certain opportunities through their skills on digital platforms such as the Southern African Freelancers' Association and Fiverr as well as collaborate with other online professionals with similar skillsets from other countries such as the United States (US). As an example, Respondent 3 stated, "Exposure and promotion of skills…easy access to potential work". Respondent 11 suggested "Digital work is an excellent way for creative people to use their skills while making money; interesting, fulfilling work".

However, some respondents in their views mentioned that people could have their skills exploited without being offered fair payment for performing digital labour, which illustrated the concept of exploitation of workers due to their skill level in the literature [1, 19]. Respondent 17 says "Spec work would be design/creative work briefed openly on the internet and the only the winning work is paid for…. This is exploitation of creative workers".

5.3 Internet Cost and Access

Concerning internet access and cost, most respondents had some access to the internet, and many had smartphones, Wireless and Fibre Internet Connections. As an example, Respondent 15 explained "Cape Town has fast fibre internet available almost anywhere, outside of Cape Town is more affordable, but quality internet connection is not as available". South Africa, according to literature has among the most advanced ICT and network infrastructure in the African continent, even with internet costs problems and infrastructure in many African countries as also expressed by the survey respondents [8].

Most respondents however found internet access very expensive. Respondent 4: "Internet is very expensive in South Africa compared to other 3rd world countries.", "I mean you can get 20meg line in Bali for half the price". Respondent 18 stated the "It is holding back the ability to interact with crowdsourcing platforms from disadvantaged segments of South African society". Respondents' views agreed with the literature which emphasizes how poorer communities in South Africa struggle to afford high-quality internet access [3].

5.4 Networking

Many of the respondents felt that they should connect with clients even abroad. They felt that they could obtain opportunities for interesting digital work, of social fulfilment and higher ("fairer") compensation. Respondent 5: "great earning potential for writers, can secure international clients who can pay in foreign currency", and "working online was quite lonely I felt isolated from the world."

A few respondents however expressed frustration over their interactions with clients. Respondent 20 expressed his frustration, "there is no human contact, the client simply does not see you as a person, just a faceless workhorse… Clients always look for a bargain". The result resembles the idea literature that expresses that digital workers could be exploited by having their work to clients by platform providers while workers are deprived of fair compensation and client interaction [24].

5.5 Work Opportunities

Most respondents felt that work opportunities were readily available, more so on global platforms than local digital platforms. Respondent 14: "I'd rather freelance overseas than work locally". Some respondents found global opportunities to be more rewarding concerning compensation earned in stronger currencies (compensation theme). The positive views related to the literature which expressed that initiatives such as crowdsourcing could present various new job opportunities [8].

However, some respondents had less desirable experiences. Respondent 9 mentioned that "global crowdsourcing sites are extremely competitive and usually the 'cheapest' rates get the jobs. Global - not a good experience. Local - good experience". Respondent 5 suggested that global sites tend to exploit digital workers' labour and underpay workers whereas with certain local sites like NoSweat tend to reward workers more fairly. This view resonates with the literature finding workers on global platforms get lower payments from clients or are underbid by workers charging lower rates for similar services [1].

6   Discussion and Interpretation

The purpose of the quantitative and the qualitative analysis was to use data gathered to investigate the significance and effect of the relationships between the main model constructs (Fig. 1) in digital labour. The data analysis, particularly with the qualitative analysis, was also aimed at further exploring certain aspects of digital labour experiences in order to discover other relevant theories which could either reinforce the hypothesized relationships in the model, contradict or add to them. The refined research model produced after combining the qualitative and quantitative analysis findings is summarized in Fig. 2.

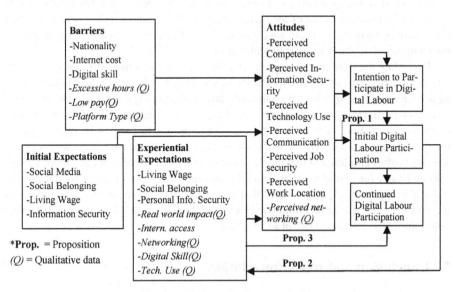

Fig. 2. Refined digital labour model

Considering the first research question, the attitude concerning communication, along with the intention to participate (Table 3) had a notably very strong relationship with the actual participation in digital labour. This agreed partially with the qualitative results, as some respondents mentioned that networking and communicating with clients and partners as one of their primary incentives for participating on digital platforms. Literature studies also described how the networking of people on digital labour platforms, like in crowdsourcing, could be beneficial for exchanging ideas, resources and motivating participation in online activities [8, 15]. The result for "ParticipationIntention" resembled that of many studies that use the TAM theory [22].

With regards to the second research question, the regression model, in Table 4, showed that the initial participation in digital labour was observed to have a strongly positive relationship with the average experiential expectations. The qualitative findings did in part reinforce the result for experiential expectations as many of the respondents found their digital labour experience overall to be desirable and had their perceptions of digital labour positively affected. Some respondents however had negative overall experiences and had their perceptions about digital labour adversely affected. The result for experiential expectations partially resembles the idea in certain studies that the experience could have an effect on the use of technology such as an electronic learning system, by individuals [24].

Additionally, for the second research question, the qualitative analysis results indicated that some of the main digital labour aspects described by respondents had some relation with the aspects being investigated in the quantitative analysis and were namely compensation, digital skill, internet costs and access, work opportunities and networking. For most of the qualitative responses, respondents emphasized that compensation was one of the main incentives for participating in digital labour. Also, several felt that there were opportunities to earn wages in the form of foreign currency and guarantee of payment based on the particular digital platform.

Regarding the third research question, from Table 4, the initial participation in digital labour and the experiential expectation of securing a living wage, had a very strong, significant relationship with the continued participation in digital labour. The result for continued participation was reinforced by the qualitative findings, where some respondents suggested that there were numerous opportunities to earn an income based on the digital platform and type of work which would encourage continued participation. Various studies emphasized that the payment received for digital work is a more significant motivator for digital workers than other intrinsic motivators [23]. Also, concerning initial participation, [7] emphasized that constructs that are related to experience and are part of initial use of technology, such as satisfaction and ease of use are crucial in determining the continued use of technology.

7   Conclusion and Recommendation

The research aimed to explore the attitudes and experiences around digital labour in depth. A comprehensive model was proposed that included micro- and macro-environmental variables influencing barriers and initial digital labour expectations. Together with actual experiences, these were found to shape digital labour attitudes.

Attitudes then drive initial and continued digital labour participation, feeding back into future expectations (Fig. 1). This proposed model was substantially validated: it was found that the attitudes and experiences of individuals toward digital labour did correlate significantly with the intention and participation of people in digital labour. Most individuals responded positively toward their experience with digital labour, particularly based on the compensation that they would obtain for their digital work. Also, past digital labour experience was found to correlate notably with the continuation of individuals in digital labour activities, with the compensation in particular being a significant experiential aspect in this regard.

One of the main limitations of this research was the relatively small sample size; offering a more substantial reward for participation could increase the sample size. Additionally, obtaining complete responses for the online questionnaire was a major challenge. Obtaining access to respondents was also a challenge because most digital platforms, such as PeoplePerHour, Upwork, restrict access to contacts and conceal details of users of the platform. As a recommendation for future research, a stronger focus on implementing digital labour in impoverished communities, not just in South Africa but also in other Africa countries, would be of much value to digital labour research. Furthermore, our proposed and tentatively validated model (Fig. 2) would benefit substantially from a larger sample size for further validation and refinement.

References

1. Graham, M., Hjorth, I., Lehdonvirta, V.: Digital labour and development: impacts of global digital labour platforms and the gig economy on worker livelihoods. Transfer Eur. Rev. Labour Res. **23**(2), 135–162 (2017)
2. Heeks, R.: Decent work and the digital gig economy: a developing country perspective on employment impacts and standards in online outsourcing, crowdwork, etc. Development Informatics Working Paper, no. 71 (2017). https://doi.org/10.2139/ssrn.3431033
3. Mbuyisa, B., Leonard, A.: ICT adoption in SMEs for the alleviation of poverty. In: International Association for Management of Technology Conference Proceedings, pp. 1–21 (2015)
4. Cirera, X., Lage, F., Sabetti, L.: ICT use, innovation, and productivity: evidence from Sub-Saharan Africa. World Bank Policy Research Working Paper, no. 7868, pp. 1–53 (2016)
5. Mtsweni, J., Ngassam, E.K., Burge, L.: A profile-aware microtasking approach for improving task assignment in crowdsourcing services. In: IST-Africa Week Conference 2016, pp. 1–10 (2016). https://doi.org/10.1109/ISTAFRICA.2016.7530702
6. Mtsweni, J., Burge, L.: The potential benefits of mobile microwork services in developing nations: research opportunities and challenges. In: IST-Africa Conference Proceedings, pp. 1–10 (2014). https://doi.org/10.1109/istafrica.2014.6880636
7. Rahi, S., Ghani, M.A.: Integration of DeLone and McLean and self-determination theory in internet banking continuance intention context. Int. J. Account. Inf. Manag. **27**(3), 512–528 (2019). https://doi.org/10.1108/IJAIM-07-2018-0077
8. Chuene, D., Mtsweni, J.: The adoption of crowdsourcing platforms in South Africa. In: IST-Africa Conference 2015, pp. 1–9. IEEE (2015). https://doi.org/10.1109/istafrica.2015.7190561
9. Stats SA: General Household Survey (2018). http://www.statssa.gov.za/publications/P0318/P03182018.pdf

10. Asongu, S.A.: The comparative economics of knowledge economy in Africa: policy benchmarks, syndromes, and implications. J. Knowl. Econ. **8**(2), 596–637 (2015). https://doi.org/10.1007/s13132-015-0273-4

11. Luther Osabutey, E., Debrah, Y.A.: Foreign direct investment and technology transfer policies in Africa: a review of the Ghanaian experience. Thunderbird Int. Bus. Rev. **54**(4), 441–456 (2012)

12. Twinomurinzi, H., Phahlamohlaka, J., Byrne, E.: The small group subtlety of using ICT for participatory governance: a South African experience. Gov. Inf. Q. **29**(2), 203–211 (2012)

13. Bornman, E.: Information society and digital divide in South Africa: results of longitudinal surveys. Inf. Commun. Soc. **19**(2), 264–278 (2016)

14. Abrami, P.C., Wade, C.A., Lysenko, L., Marsh, J., Gioko, A.: Using educational technology to develop early literacy skills in Sub-Saharan Africa. Educ. Inf. Technol. **21**(4), 945–964 (2014). https://doi.org/10.1007/s10639-014-9362-4

15. Bott, M., Gigler, B.S., Young, G.: The role of crowdsourcing for better governance in fragile state contexts. In: Closing the Feedback Loop, pp. 107–148 (2014)

16. Onkokame, M., Schoentgen, A., Gillwald, A.: What is the state of microwork in Africa? A view from seven countries. Policy Paper, series no. 5, paper no. 2 (2018)

17. Benghozi, P.J., Paris, T.: The cultural economy in the digital age: a revolution in intermediation? City Cult. Soc. **7**(2), 75–80 (2016)

18. Langley, P., Leyshon, A.: Platform capitalism: the intermediation and capitalisation of digital economic circulation. Finance Soc. **3**(1), 11–31 (2017)

19. Graham, M., et al.: The fairwork foundation: strategies for improving platform work. In: Proceedings of the Weizenbaum Conference 2019, Weizenbaum Conference, Berlin, pp. 1–8 (2019)

20. Dunn, M.: Digital work: new opportunities or lost wages? Am. J. Manag. **17**(4), 10–27 (2017)

21. Khan, I.U., Hameed, Z., Yu, Y., Islam, T., Sheikh, Z., Khan, S.U.: Predicting the acceptance of MOOCs in a developing country: application of task-technology fit model, social motivation, and self-determination theory. Telematics Inform. **35**(4), 964–978 (2018)

22. Nikou, S.A., Economides, A.A.: Mobile-Based Assessment: integrating acceptance and motivational factors into a combined model of Self-Determination Theory and Technology Acceptance. Comput. Hum. Behav. **68**, 83–95 (2017). https://doi.org/10.1016/j.chb.2016.11.020

23. Durward, D., Blohm, I., Leimeister, J.M.: Crowd work. Bus. Inf. Syst. Eng. **58**(4), 281–286 (2016). https://doi.org/10.1007/s12599-016-0438-0

24. Van Doorn, N.: Platform labor: on the gendered and racialized exploitation of low-income service work in the 'on-demand' economy. Inf. Commun. Soc. **20**(6), 898–914 (2017)

Are Ride-Sharing Platforms Good for Indian Drivers? An Investigation of Taxi and Auto-Rickshaw Drivers in Delhi

Anna Fleitoukh[1] and Kentaro Toyama[2(✉)]

[1] Sciences Po Toulouse, 31685 Cedex 6 Toulouse, France
a.fleitoukh@gmail.com
[2] School of Information, University of Michigan, Ann Arbor, MI 48109, USA
toyama@umich.edu

Abstract. It has been several years since ride-sharing platforms such as Ola and Uber have entered the Indian market. As a type of matching service, mainstream economic theory predicts that they will bring economic efficiencies to hired transportation. In this study, we investigate the impact of ride-sharing on drivers of taxi cabs and auto-rickshaws in New Delhi through a mixed-methods study involving 60 drivers. We find mixed outcomes for drivers with little clear evidence of overall benefit. We saw no statistically significant impact of ride-sharing on drivers' average revenue per day, though the data is suggestive of income gains of 7–18% which seem likely to be due to longer hours driven. In contrast to the corporate marketing where driver autonomy and flexibility are oft-cited perks, our participants tended to report less autonomy and control with ride-sharing. And, we find evidence that drivers face greater uncertainty with respect to their income as ride-sharing companies offer intermittent promotional incentives. Our findings are consistent with technological amplification theory. Through ride-sharing platforms, unequal power dynamics between large corporations and low-wage workers are amplified: ride-sharing companies wrest control from drivers while providing little in return.

Keywords: ICT · Sharing economy · Gig economy · Ride-aggregator platforms · Auto-rickshaws · India · Delhi

1 Introduction

Ride-sharing – that part of the so-called "sharing economy" [24, 26] that matches drivers with riders for personal ground transportation through smartphone apps – is now a worldwide phenomenon. In high-income countries, ride-sharing companies such as Lyft and Uber are widely hailed for providing transport services that are convenient, low-cost, widely available, quick to pick up, and good for drivers [9, 10, 23]. On the other hand, critics point out that the platforms bypass local transport regulations, compete with public transportation, and underpay their drivers [9, 18, 23].

In India, the two major ride-sharing companies are Ola, an Indian company, and Uber, the U.S. multinational company. Personal, hired, ground transportation in urban

R. K. Bandi et al. (Eds.): IFIPJWC 2020, IFIP AICT 601, pp. 117–131, 2020.
https://doi.org/10.1007/978-3-030-64697-4_10

India is a different phenomenon compared with much of the developed world. There are vehicle classes other than four-wheeled automobiles, whether it is auto-rickshaws, bicycle rickshaws, or even human-pulled rickshaws. The services are extremely inexpensive, and rides are plentiful and easy to hail [19].

In this paper, we report on a study that focuses on the impact of ride-sharing on drivers of hired transport in India in terms of revenue and driver perceptions. We used a mixed-methods study of 60 drivers in New Delhi, split evenly among three groups: taxi (automobile) drivers who used ride-sharing apps, auto-rickshaw drivers who used ride-sharing apps, and auto-rickshaw drivers who did *not* use ride-sharing apps.

Overall, we find that the impact of ride-sharing on Indian drivers is mixed, with no clear evidence of net benefit. We find no statistically significant impact on drivers' average revenue per day, and even a suggestive (i.e., not statistically significant) 7–18% increase in mean revenue is likely due to drivers working more hours. Qualitatively, we find that many Indian drivers feel pressured into ride-sharing so as not to be "left behind," but there are complaints about a resulting loss of autonomy. Among drivers, ride-sharing appears to exacerbate existing inequalities, with a few high-performing drivers benefiting from the rewards offered by ride-sharing companies while relatively older, smartphone-less drivers who do not own their own vehicles struggle either to participate in ride-sharing or to maintain their levels of income. These findings build on the small literature on ride-sharing in the developing world.

We situate our findings in a critique of capitalism, mediated by technology's amplifying effect [28]. Contrary to claims that the sharing economy represents a departure from capitalism's pathologies that elevates workers by providing new opportunities through individual entrepreneurship, what we suggest is that ride-sharing in urban India is an extreme form of capitalism in which the unequal power dynamics between corporations and workers are amplified, with workers likely losing out as tech titans clash overhead. Thus, while our findings differ in the details, they extend some of the existing criticism of the sharing economy [9, 18, 23].

2 Related Work

2.1 Ride-Sharing and Its Impact on Labor

There is a considerable literature about ride-sharing in developed-world contexts. Some research focuses on the benefit to rider-consumers that includes lower costs compared to local taxi cabs, at least for routine rides [7], as well as shorter wait times and ease of use [8]. Indeed, riders in many cities express delight about ride-sharing, with accompanying complaints about over-priced and outdated taxi services [8]. Riders are even willing to pay the premium when ride-sharing platforms implement "surge pricing" – raising the price of rides during moments of driver scarcity [7].

Other work considers the impact on drivers. One prominent study compared the gross hourly earnings of Uber drivers with those of taxis and chauffeurs across six U.S. cities, and suggested that Uber drivers earn more per h [10]. They found that on average, Uber driver-partners earned $19.19 per h compared to a $16.90 for their counterparts and the authors conclude, "Unless their after-tax costs are more than $6 per h, the net hourly earnings of Uber's driver-partners typically exceed the average hourly wage of employed taxi drivers and chauffeurs."

The same study found that, again in the United States, Uber drivers differ as a group from their taxi-driving counterparts [10]. Among UberX drivers, 19.1% are between 18 and 29 years old, but only 8.5% of taxi drivers are; 21.8% of UberX drivers are between 50 and 64, while 36.6% of taxi drivers. Moreover, "Nearly half of Uber's driver-partners (48%) have a college degree or higher, considerably higher than the corresponding percentage for taxi drivers and chauffeurs (18%)." Uber drivers also often have another job apart from driving, and use driving as a complement to their wage, compared to their taxi-driving counterparts who tend to be drivers full time. Finally, many Uber drivers appear to engage in driving as a temporary option. After a year of driving for Uber, almost half of the drivers quit.

Scholars have also noted that drivers are lured to the platform with promises of high wages for short hours of driving, but Uber intermittently reduces fare rates unilaterally [21]. Another issue is the myth of flexibility that has gradually faded away as the drivers face constant pressure from the platform to drive longer hours, at particular times, and in specific neighborhoods, or rating systems forcing drivers to bear the burden of customer service. Some scholars argue that the algorithms at the center of Uber's system consolidates power fully in the hands of the platform [21]. Unlike a human manager, Uber's system is relentless and uncompromising in its monitoring of drivers' performance and behavior.

A common criticism of the sharing economy overall is that it leads to "casualization of the workforce, informalisation of the formal economy and the so-called 'demutualisation of risk' in modern labour markets" [9]. Ride-sharing companies gain all of the benefits of wage work without the responsibilities through "disguised employment relationships." Indeed, drivers are responsible for their own vehicle maintenance, insurance, and other costs and have neither overtime pay nor sick leave [10, 21]. Critics of ride-sharing tend to agree that the "uberisation of society" exaggerates the problems of capitalism [18, 28]. Moreover, the use of algorithms erodes job quality in the platform economy. The bargaining power of the worker is truncated when operating through a digital tool. The constant monitoring through the process, and rate given when completing the task creates an unfair imbalance [32].

2.2   Ride-Sharing in India

The two major ride-sharing companies in India are Ola and Uber [2, 30, 31]. Ola was founded by an Indian entrepreneur who began with a ride-sharing service for cabs in 2010 and then expanded to auto-rickshaws in 2014, the ubiquitous, covered, three-wheeled vehicles that are common throughout South Asia. Uber, of course, is the U.S.-based multinational [30], entered the market in 2013 and launched the auto-rickshaw option two years later. One scholar, pointing out that ride-sharing is an organization of informal work, suggests that in contexts like India where the informal economy is prevalent, ride-sharing's impact is muted; it is not as disruptive as it is elsewhere [25]. Indeed, "92% of these drivers were driving to earn an income before joining a platform economy company. Only 8% shifted to these companies from different professions" [25].

Another study of drivers in Bengaluru emphasizes how ride-sharing changes the way that drivers operate, often in undesirable ways [12]. "Without Ola, drivers locate passengers by sight, negotiate whether to take them then set off towards their destination… Ola changes the dynamics as drivers must first accept the passenger's request then physically locate them, and do not negotiate with the customer." Customers, however, often cancel, causing drivers to burn fuel without compensation. "Some drivers prefer their regular [i.e., pre-ride-sharing] taxi dispatch systems because they enable seeing and choosing freely between incoming requests," a choice they lose with ride-sharing platforms. Unhappiness with ride-sharing has prompted Indian drivers to strike [31].

Research also highlights the inequalities among drivers that ride-sharing may aggravate. Generally, the drivers using the application are more literate, for example [12]. Such findings are consistent with the literature on the digital divide in developing countries [4, 20, 29], which finds that digitally mediated activities tend to highlight existing inequalities in economic status, social standing, or education.

The research in this paper builds on the above literature through a preliminary attempt to capture the financial impact of ride-sharing on drivers in India, as well as to tease out some of the key differences that Indian drivers experience compared with their developed-world counterparts.

3 Methodology

3.1 Data Collection

We conducted 60 interviews in New Delhi, India, between January and June 2019, each consisting of a questionnaire with questions related to demographics and business as well as a semi-structured portion with open-ended questions. Interviews were conducted with three types of drivers:

- Auto-rickshaw drivers who used Ola or Uber (Abbreviation: RU; 20 interviews)
- Auto-rickshaw drivers who did not use Ola or Uber (Abbreviation: RN; 20 interviews)
- Taxi cab drivers who used Ola or Uber (Abbreviation: TU; 20 interviews)

All interviews were conducted verbally by the first author during hailed (and paid) rides. Interviews were conducted in Hindi through paid interpreters on all rides.

The questionnaire portion asked about their demographic profile as well as the details of the costs and revenues of their driving-related work. The semi-structured portion asked about their perceptions of their job, ride-sharing platforms, and their economic situation in general.

Rides were hailed from well-known ground-transportation hubs in South Delhi (e.g., Hauz Khas Metro Station, Nehru Place), Central Delhi (e.g., Connaught Place, Central Secretariat) and Old Delhi (e.g., Jama Masjid, Red Fort). Ride-sharing apps were used to recruit participants for the 40 participants on ride-sharing platforms. Regular on-the-spot hailing of rides was used to recruit the other 20 participants. Rides were requested for common destinations, as well, so as to allow a series of interviews to be conducted in a single day.

Rides were requested for destinations typically 4–6 km away. On Delhi's crowded streets, this allowed for recruiting of the participant, obtaining informed consent, and an interview that lasted about 15 min. Drivers were generally very open to being interviewed in this way and tended to be succinct and to-the-point. Interviews quickly came to an end when the destination was reached. In addition to the payment for the ride, we paid tips of 30% of the cost of the ride as a token of our gratitude. Audio recordings were not practical due to engine and traffic noise, so notes were taken by hand as the interviews occurred.

Beyond interviews with drivers, we also met with two Ola Mobility Institute employees who conveyed the specifics of Ola's outreach and interaction with drivers. These interviews provided clarification about some of the drivers' claims about their interaction with Ola (e.g., the specific nature of promotional deals), and also provided a view into the ride-sharing companies' perspectives.

3.2 Data Analysis

Our research involved mixed methods with both quantitative and qualitative data analysis.

All of the demographic and business data were entered into a spreadsheet and cleaned. Though most drivers responded to all of our questionnaire questions, they sometimes varied in the specifics of their responses. In a few cases, we used averages from other drivers to infer specific figures – for example, some drivers reported renting their vehicles; even where we did not have their rental rates, we used average figures based on other respondents. Throughout this paper, we report ARPD as net revenue for the driver in the local currency, the Indian Rupee (Rs). (At the time of the interviews, Rs. 70 was equal to US$1.) Once cleaned, the data was analyzed to determine summary statistics and correlations. For the latter, several regressions were run, using a subset of the following independent variables: age, education, length of time as a driver, use of a ride-sharing app, length of time using an app, number of hours driven per day, type of vehicle, and vehicle ownership. ARPD was cast as the primary dependent variable, but we also tried regressions with vehicle ownership as the primary dependent variable. Both dependent variables, incidentally, were highlighted by drivers as how they assessed their own performance or success. Vehicle acquisition can have long-term benefits for the drivers, separate from ARPD.

For qualitative findings, participants are referred to throughout by codes: RUx for rickshaw drivers who are ride-sharing app users; RNx for non-user rickshaw drivers; TUx for taxi drivers (all of whom were app users).

3.3 Limitations

Though we made an attempt to capture a diverse set of Delhi-area drivers, our sample sizes are not large, and the samples were biased in a number of ways: Geographically, of course, our results do not necessarily hold beyond Delhi. Even within Delhi, there may be selection biases due to where the rides were hailed (generally, in high-traffic areas). All interviews were conducted during the day, and drivers taking early morning or late evening shifts were not represented. However, because our ride-hailing methodology was effectively random, we believe our findings have validity within those times and places.

We also acknowledge potential problems with language and culture. Though we – both authors – have lived in large Indian cities, speak some Hindi, and are personally familiar with rickshaws, taxis, and other forms of urban transportation, there are likely nuances of expression that we may have missed.

4   Findings

4.1   Business Basics

Auto-rickshaws have traditionally operated by taking passengers who hail them on the streets. With the advent of ride-sharing platforms, this situation has changed for some drivers in the last few years, but almost all drivers reported a willingness to pick up passengers on the spot. This scenario, however, is somewhat rarer for cab drivers who have over the last 10–15 years, become accustomed to booking rides through private companies and mobile-phone calls.

Next to the type of vehicle driven, ownership of a vehicle is a key differentiator among drivers. When the vehicle is owned, the driver is himself (all of our drivers were male) liable for gasoline, maintenance, and insurance costs. However, for drivers who rent their vehicles, maintenance and insurance are paid by the owner. (Gasoline is typically paid for by the driver, regardless, though there appears to be some variation.) The business relationship that drivers have with vehicle owners is diverse: some pay a rental fee on a daily or weekly basis; others pay their owners a percentage of their daily earnings; still others earn a fixed wage per month (more frequent among ride-sharing drivers). Drivers often aspire to own their own vehicles, and as below, it does appear that ownership leads to greater net income (Table 1).

4.2   Quantitative Findings

Average Revenue Per Day (ARPD). ARPD varies significantly by vehicle type, use of ride-sharing apps, and vehicle ownership. Rickshaw drivers not using ride-sharing apps earned the least, at an average of Rs. 588 a day. App-using rickshaw drivers earned an average of Rs. 743 per day, and cab drivers earned Rs. 1406 on average (Fig. 1).

Thus overall, cab drivers earned Rs. 647 more per day than auto drivers ($p < 0.01$). In addition, each additional hour driven per day appears correlated with Rs. 60 more in earnings. ($p = 0.037$). On the other hand, ride-sharing app usage did not have a statistically significant correlation with increased revenue ($p = 0.5$), even though there is a suggestive difference of Rs. 99. If we perform regressions only on ride-sharing app users, driving a cab is positively linked with an increase of Rs. 658.64 ($p = 0.0007$), while every additional hour driven correlates with an increase of Rs. 74 ($p = 0.08$).

To conclude, while app usage may be correlated with greater revenue, the difference was not statistically significant with our relatively small sample size, suggesting at the least that the variation among drivers due to other variables outweighs use of the app. If our mean differences hold for larger sample sizes, however, ride-sharing app usage

Table 1. Table of the main qualitative findings.

Criteria/Groups	RN	RU	TU
Percentage of vehicle-owners	47%	71%	55%
Percentage of non- owners	53%	29%	45%
ARPD (whole group in Rs.)	587.93	737.88	1405.75
ARPD of vehicle owners (in Rs.)	750.86	798.48	1516.22
ARPD of non-owners (in Rs.)	425.00	620.00	1231.19
Average age in years	40.48	35.10	31.85
Average grade completed	8.50	10.54	9.55
Average time being a professional driver	15.82	13.05	7.71
Average number of hours driven per day	10.97	10.88	12.21
Rate of drivers who have tried to use a ride-aggregating app	11%	–	–
Rate of drivers who have tried the other app	–	65%	25%
Average time using an app in years	–	2.03	2.03

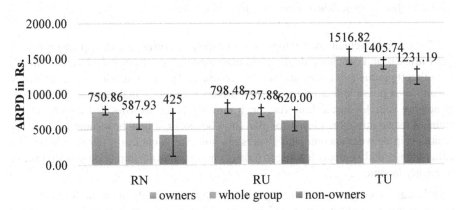

Fig. 1. ARPDs by type of vehicle, vehicle ownership, and app usage. Owners and app-user drivers are likely to earn more than non-owners and non-user drivers. Error bars represent standard errors.

may account for an additional 7–18% in net revenue. However, there does seem to be an advantage to being a cab driver over a being a rickshaw driver, and for rickshaw drivers to be vehicle owners, though we caution that these are correlations, not confirmations of causality. Finally, we confirm, unsurprisingly, that across the board, additional hours driven correlates with greater revenue.

Ownership of the Vehicle. The ownership rate was the highest among rickshaw drivers ride-sharing app users at 71% compared to 47% for non-user rickshaw drivers, and 55% for cab drivers. Group averages suggest that ownership rates are linked to education level, with higher educational levels correlated with higher ownership rates. Whether ownership causes an increase in revenue, or revenue enables ownership is not clear from the data (Fig. 2).

When taking all drivers together, both education (p = 0.0033) and revenue (p = 0.0052) are statistically significant in explaining the likelihood of vehicle ownership. On the whole, our participant cab drivers were less educated than rickshaw drivers using ride-sharing apps (who tended to have the higher ownership rate). The same trend is visible whether rickshaw, cab drivers or app users were considered on their own.

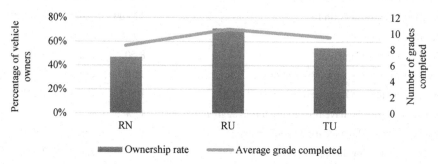

Fig. 2. Rates of vehicle ownership by group plotted alongside level of education. Educational level is likely a direct or indirect cause of vehicle ownership.

To conclude, vehicle ownership does not appear to correlate with app usage, though daily revenue and education do. It seems reasonable to conclude that education directly or indirectly influences ownership (not the contrary). What is unclear is the exact mechanism – it is possible that more educated drivers earn more, making it easier for them to acquire vehicles in the long run; or, it may be that more educated drivers see the value of ownership more clearly, or plan for it better; or, it may be something else. The relationship between income and ownership, however is unclear – our data allows for either greater daily income leading to greater chance of ownership or ownership leading to greater income.

App Usage. Average time of driving with the app was exactly the same for both auto-rickshaw drivers and cab drivers at 2.03 years. First quartile, median and third quartiles are also very similar for both categories: respectively 0.54, 2 and 3 years for rickshaw drivers and 0.56, 2.25 and 3 years for cab drivers.

Volatility of app use among cab drivers is slightly higher because 75% of them have tried both apps, while only 54% of rickshaw drivers report this. 2.03 years of app use on average is quite low compared to the number of years the apps are on the market (since 2013 so, or over 5 years at the time of the interviews). That suggests that our drivers joined recently and the ride-sharing phenomenon is intensifying. Drivers may feel the need to join because they would lose customers otherwise, or because they perceive that ride-sharing apps are advantageous. Of our 20 rickshaw drivers who were not using ride-sharing at the time of the interview, only two had previous experience with Ola or Uber.

Age and Education. On average, rickshaw drivers not using apps are 5.38 years older than their peers using the apps. Similarly, cab drivers using the apps are 3.25 younger than rickshaw drivers using the apps, and thus 8.63 years younger than auto drivers not using them (Fig. 3).

A single-variable regression of age against app usage for all drivers together suggests that age influences whether the driver is likely to use an app or not: for every 10 years of age, the likelihood of using a ride-sharing app drops by 15% (p = 0.04). Rickshaw drivers using the apps are also more educated than drivers not using the apps on average: they completed 8.5 and 10.5 years of formal education, respectively. Cab drivers are not more educated than auto-rickshaw drivers using the app: on average they have completed 9.6 years of education. However, we found no statistically significant link between education and app usage.

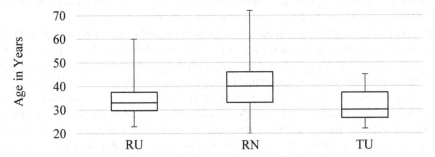

Fig. 3. Boxplots showing the drivers' age scope in years. The age range is wider for RN drivers. TU drivers are consistently younger that RU or RN drivers.

4.3 Qualitative Findings

Overall Views on Ride-Sharing. All of our participants were familiar with both Ola and Uber, regardless of whether they were app users, or whether they used only one of the two ride-sharing platforms.

Many drivers perceived ride-sharing as a new trend that they could not afford to neglect. TU3 said, "Every cab driver came to know about the apps when they entered the market, and I started driving for them because I predicted the market to shift. So, I have used Uber since the beginning." For these cases, it appears that Uber and Ola were not seen as advantages necessarily, but as necessities to begin or to remain in business. Indeed, non-user rickshaw drivers saw themselves to be at a distinct disadvantage: RN4 said, "I am disadvantaged because of Ola and Uber because I get less passengers and thus I earn less". However, it is not clear, especially in light of our quantitative results above, how much these sentiments were based on reality. In fact, some non-user drivers perceived no disadvantage. RN7 said that he did not feel threatened by the apps because "Auto-rickshaws on the apps are not very popular. Indeed, the fares for booking a cab are close to the ones for an auto, so people tend to prefer booking a cab because it is more convenient."

With respect to revenue, reports were mixed. For some, there are clear advantages to ride-sharing, though often, these are based on promotional rewards that do not apply to all drivers. TU18 said, "Uber chose the 100 best drivers in Delhi and I was one of them. I was thus invited in Gurugram for a party, and I was offered an incentive of Rs. 5'700." A commonly cited reward was one attached to a bonus for making, e.g., 44 rides over 4 days. Such schemes are common for both apps.

Others, however, questioned the financial value of ride-sharing. RU4 said, "I do not see much difference between using the app or not." RU10 – an app-user – confessed, "The margins are better when I get customers from the street." And, many have noticed that promotional incentives have decreased in monetary amounts and frequency over time. TU3 said, "I am not very happy with the incentives because they are much lower than before." TU5, who has 3 years of experience with Uber, was specific about the decline in his average revenue: "My wage used to be higher when I joined the company, at about Rs. 80,000 to 90,000 per month the first year. Then, it decreased to Rs. 60,000 to 70,000 the second year. And, now I am left with Rs. 30,000 to 40,000 per month." Several drivers began driving based on rumors of high income, and now they felt trapped. TU20 regretted, "I have no real choice if I want to change my job because I only know driving and nothing else." RU9 said, "I am not happy with the app. The oil prices have increased during the past years, but not the number of customers and incentives are decreasing."

Between Ola and Uber, the participants expressed relative pros and cons to each, though Uber appeared to be the favorite overall. Ola was said to care better for drivers and to have better incentives. Uber was said to bring more customers and to lead to greater revenue. TU6 said, "The incentives are better with Ola, but there are more rides and more customers through Uber." RU11 said, "I prefer the way Ola is done, but I would like to switch to Uber because I could get more money. Ola is also easier to use and Uber is very demanding with the everyday selfies that have to be sent to the platform for identity check." Overall, the majority of our participants (75%) used Uber, which is consistent with anecdotal reports of Uber's dominance in Delhi.

Among drivers using the apps, only three of our cab-driver participants were not professional drivers before they began; the availability of the ride-sharing apps likely lowered barriers to entry for driving taxis. All of our rickshaw-driving participants, however, were drivers prior to using the ride-sharing apps.

Obstacles to Becoming a Ride-Sharing Driver. Some of our participants mentioned problems with technology access, digital literacy, or general education as obstacles to effective use of the ride-sharing platforms. It also emerged that ride-sharing is spread along social networks.

Several participants, mostly non-users of ride-sharing apps, mentioned smartphone ownership as a hard requirement. RN14 said, "Look, I have a very simple phone! I cannot use the apps." Similarly, RN19 was a previous Ola driver who had lost his smartphone.

Others noted lack of education as a barrier: RN14 suggested that even had he owned a smartphone, "I am not educated enough to use the apps." Taxi drivers also mentioned this. TU20 said, "I have failed 10th grade," suggesting it was difficult for him to use the apps. RU12 said, "I know that the older people are more scared to use the apps because they are not well educated and they prefer driving by themselves.", a sentiment was shared by RU13: "Rickshaw drivers using the apps are only 10 to 15% of the rickshaw drivers in Delhi because most of them are scared." Meanwhile, app users affirm that their own education allowed them to take advantage of ride-sharing. RU10 said, "I did not need a training, because I was educated enough to understand the app."

Some mentioned that vehicle ownership was critical. TU13 said, "Using an app is beneficial when the auto is owned." TU4 emphasized, "Owning the auto is what makes the real difference for earnings.", even though ownership was not a hard requirement.

Finally, responses to questions about drivers' colleagues exhibited a trend where ride-sharing habits tended to cluster within drivers' social networks. RU11, an Ola user, said, "My friends are also using Ola over Uber because they had a bad experience in the past." Similarly, non-users of ride-sharing tended to know many other non-users. RN3 said, "I know other drivers, they also do not use the apps.", and some also told us that some of their family members were also drivers. A few interviewees declared they have taken part in protests organized by the auto-rickshaw union, and RN9 also expressed the peer-pressure he felt in the community: "I do observe the strikes because I do not want to be beaten up by other drivers".

The Pressures of Ride-Sharing. Though ride-sharing companies often cite benefits for drivers such as independence and flexible work hours, most of our participants expressed dissatisfaction about longer work hours, inability to choose drivers, inconvenience with pick up (relative to on-street hailing).

Several times, drivers told us that they have to drive longer hours to benefit from ride-sharing. TU12 said, "Before, it was more relaxing to work for my own company because I had only 2 to 3 rides a day." Similarly, in a context of decreasing incentives, TU16 said, "To get the same amount, I used to drive 2 h less every day." Some drivers do not join the companies because they consider that they do not drive sufficient number of hours per day. RN18 said, "I cannot drive for long hours because of health problems, so I have never tried the apps for this reason."

A number of participants mentioned that arranging and finding pick-up locations through ride-sharing apps was less convenient than picking up people hailing rides on the streets. RN9, who had used Ola in the past, said, "I prefer getting customers from the streets because I do not have to spend time to pick them up. The pick-up locations can be hard to find and some drivers go round and round to find a way to get to the location." But, this feeling was not universally shared. RU13 mentioned the convenience of not having to bargain: "It is easier with the app, because I do not have to bargain, but only wait for customers."

One of the major issues that a few participants raised was ride cancellations, when the customer cancels at the last minute. RU14 said, "It is not always fair, because we sometimes have to go towards the pick-up point and it is costly, especially if the customer cancels the trip while we are on the way."

Depending on the ride-sharing app, drivers also have less freedom to decline passengers. RN11 revealed that he did not like Uber's system because "the driver has to accept all requests, while with Ola, I can just ignore [a ride] because other drivers around will be sent the notice." Ride-sharing or not, licensed drivers are not legally allowed to refuse rides for the most part [14], but regulatory enforcement is weak.

Relationship with Ride-Sharing Companies. While most of our participants felt that both apps were generally good companies, some mentioned that they felt poorly treated. TU1 noted pointedly, "I have the feeling that Uber and Ola want to make the passenger happier than the drivers." RU17 added that "Apps are good for customers, but [the companies] do not always listen to the drivers." A common frustration was having ride-sharing accounts suspended because of customer complaints. RN13 said, "My Uber account was blocked a few years back because of a customer complaint.", an experience also shared by RU11. Reactivation typically requires a visit to the corporate office, which can cost drivers a day of work.

Upskilling of the Drivers. Many reported being trained by the company representatives on the spot to learn about the different features of the app, and how to use it, "Uber people told me how to use the app, and how to register" told us RU3. It seems that when going online, the drivers have acquired a set of digital skills. Beyond the ride-sharing app itself, drivers become familiar with bank accounts and digital payments, both of which may have other benefits related to financial inclusion, a point that was raised in our interviews with Ola employees.

5 Discussions

Overall, our findings suggest that the value of ride-sharing for drivers is mixed, with little evidence of clear positive value. We find that much the same phenomenon identified with Uber in North America [21] occurs in India, as well, with minor differences.

While ride-sharing may enable a new income opportunity for some taxi drivers, for others, the benefits seem not to outweigh the inconveniences. Ride-sharing apps appear to push Delhi drivers to work harder for less revenue per kilometer, all while distorting a pre-existing market and reducing overall driver autonomy. First, we did not find a statistically significant increase in revenue for drivers who use ride-sharing. Second, ride-sharing introduces a host of controls for app-using drivers, which reduce real and perceived autonomy; for non-user drivers, the ride-sharing increases fears of being left behind. Third, it seems evident that ride-sharing companies are distorting the market for drivers in unpredictable ways, causing some novices to enter a market and experience difficulties as incentives decrease over time.

These findings extend and qualify previous findings about ride-sharing. Compared with developed-world contexts [10, 23], both the financial and non-financial benefits (e.g., ability to choose one's working hours) to ride-sharing drivers seem muted.

In developed countries, drivers tend to be from the middle-class, with driving often being a supplementary second job; meanwhile, low-income individuals find it difficult to enter the market as ride-sharing drivers [15]. While they share some challenges with their developed-world counterparts [15], they seem better able to engage with the platforms. We suspect this is because the apps have adapted to Indian drivers in the race to recruit them, but also because of the way labour was organized among drivers prior to the existence of the apps. Our findings in Delhi are also similar to many of the qualitative findings from Bangalore [12]. Our work adds evidence to the suggestion [12] that under ride-sharing, drivers are having to drive more, for little or no increase in revenue.

A key novel contribution of our work is a report on the impact of recruiting promotions and incentives on drivers. Many take up ride-sharing because of the promises of bonuses. However, such promotions are temporary and, at least at the time of our research, declining. We predict that reports of drivers going into debt as a result will begin surfacing. Meanwhile, the duopoly structure of the market in the Indian case is likely to lead to more rate-cuts in the future.

All of our findings are ultimately consistent with an amplification theory of digital technology [21, 28]. While technology may enable new activities, benefiting some while harming others, overall, its effect is to amplify underlying human forces. In the case of ride-sharing in India, those human forces are the routine, sometimes pathological forces of global capitalism, as other critiques of the sharing economy have noted [18, 23, 24], but further compounded by the inequalities of the developing world. Among drivers, too, ride-sharing amplifies existing inequalities: Vehicle owners benefit more than non-owners. And, more educated drivers who can afford smartphones are better able to take advantage. Ultimately, the technology that manages ride-sharing is owned by corporations setting the rules unilaterally. This disproportionate share of power echoes and amplifies classical Marxist literature, which highlights the exploitation of workers who own little of the "means of production" [16]. Neo-Marxist theories that incorporate modern digital phenomena are particularly relevant in our case [10, 32]. Our findings suggest that while some drivers benefited from new livelihood opportunities from the apps, most drivers – even those who use the platforms – are not benefiting greatly. If anything, ride-sharing drivers feel pressured to drive longer hours for smaller margins, and non-user drivers begin to feel they are at a disadvantage – all of this is enforced by the technology. Moreover, our participants were conscious that they were at the bottom of the totem pole, with the companies concerned more about customers than drivers. Meanwhile, intense competition between Ola and Uber causes market distortions and collateral damage from powerful entities in conflict is amplified.

There might be a different evolution of the market in the future: First, auto-rickshaw drivers may be able to retain their historical working paradigm, as Uber and Ola remain relatively lightly used among rickshaw drivers. Second, Indian drivers seem to have a measure of community (formal and informal) that might allow them to collectively resist the power of ride-sharing companies. They meet at traffic hotspots, and a vast majority of them have a family member also driving, and friends in the sector; in some cities, there are labour organizers coordinating drivers (including strikes). Whether this collective potential is fully actualized remains to be seen. As result, short of significant policy interventions to protect drivers and their interests, we suspect that over time, benefits to drivers will be shaved down to just the bare minimum to keep enough of them within the fold of ride-sharing companies.

6   Conclusion

This paper presented an exploratory study that sheds light on the effects of ride-sharing on drivers in New Delhi. We find that there are a number of differences in the reported experiences of drivers in India as compared with those in developed countries, with a tendency for ride-sharing's problems to be further exacerbated. For one, the financial benefit of participating in ride-sharing is much less clear in India than in, for example, the United States. We found no statistically significant economic benefit for drivers to participate in ride-sharing, and many reported that they feel less autonomy with ride-sharing, as they feel they must work longer hours and the apps direct almost all of their activity. Overall, ride-sharing appears to exacerbate the potential for low-wage workers to be exploited by large corporations in the developing world.

References

1. Auto-rickshaw fares in Delhi hiked by over 18%. In: India Times (2019, March, 08). https://economictimes.indiatimes.com. Accessed 17 May 2020
2. Bhattacharya, A.: Ola vs Uber: The latest score in the great Indian taxi-app game. In: Quartz India. (2019, February, 12). https://qz.com/india/. Accessed 13 May 2020
3. Goswami, S.: Ola, Uber strike hits Delhi commuters, drivers say bigger protest on Monday. In: Hindustan Times (2017, February, 13). https://www.hindustantimes.com. Accessed 14 Aug 2020
4. Cecchini, S., Scott, C.: Can information and communication technology applications contribute to poverty reduction? lessons from rural india. Inform. Technol. Dev. **10**(2), 73–84 (2003)
5. Circular for the replacement of TSR under section-83 of the Motor Vehicles Act – 1988. Transport Department of NCT of Delhi (2012). http://transport.delhi.gov.in/. Accessed 10 June 2019
6. Circular to grant registration/fitness and permit of new TSRs. Transport Department of Government of NCT of Delhi (2012). http://transport.delhi.gov.in/. Accessed 10 June 2019
7. Cohen, P., Hahn, R., Hall, J., Levitt, S., Metcalfe, R.: Using big data to estimate consumer surplus: the case of Uber. In: National Bureau of Economic Research. Working paper No. 22627, September 2016
8. Cramer, J., Krueger, A.: Disruptive change in the taxi business: the case of uber. Am. Econ. Rev. **106**(5), 177–182 (2016)
9. De Stefano, V.: The rise of the just-in-time workforce: on-demand work, crowd work and labour protection in the Gig-Economy. Comp. Lab. L. Policy J. Forthcoming; Bocconi Leg. Stud. Res. Paper No. 2682602, **37**, 471 (2015)
10. Fuchs, C.: Rereading Marx in the Age of Digital Capitalism. Pluto Press, London (2019)
11. Hall, J., Krueger, A.: An analysis of the labor market for Uber's Driver-Partners in the United States. In: National Bureau of Economic Research. Working Paper Series No. 22843 (2016)
12. Isthiaque, A.S., et al.: Peer-to-peer in the workplace: a view from the road. In: Association for Computing Machinery (eds) CHI'16. Proceedings of the 2016 CHI Conference on Human Factors in Computing Systems. New York: ACM, pp. 5063–5075 (2016)
13. Job quality in the platform economy. International Labour Organization. Global Commission on Future of Work. Issue Brief 5 (2018). https://www.ilo.org/. Accessed 13 May 2020
14. Kejriwal allows auto drivers to refuse customers while returning home, announces fare revision. In: Times of India (2015, May, 17). http://timesofindia.indiatimes.com/. Accessed 13 May 2020
15. Malone, A., Dillahunt, T.: The promise of the sharing economy among disadvantaged communities. https://doi.org/10.1145/2702123.2702189 (2015)
16. Marx, K.: Capital: A Critique of Political Economy. Progress Publishers, Moscow (1995)
17. Meelen, T., Frenken, K.: Stop Saying Uber is Part of the Sharing Economy. In: Fast Company (2015, January, 14). https://www.fastcompany.com/. Accessed 13 May 2020
18. Morozov, E.: Résister à l'ubérisation du monde. In: Le Monde Diplomatique (2015, September). https://www.monde-diplomatique.fr/. Accessed 13 May 2020
19. Number of registered vehicles in Delhi crosses 1 crore mark. In: The Tribune India (2017, June, 04). https://www.tribuneindia.com/. Accessed 13 May 2020

20. OECD. Understanding the Digital Divide. Organization for Economic Co-operation and Development (2001). http://www.oecd.org/. Working Paper on digital economy No. 49
21. Rosenblat, A.: Uberland: How Algorithms are Rewriting the Rules of Work. University of California Press, Oakland (2018)
22. Schor, J.: Debating the sharing economy. J. Self-Governance Manag. Econ. **4**(3), 7–22 (2016)
23. Slee, T.: What's Yours is Mine, Against the Sharing Economy. OR Books, New York (2015)
24. Sundararajan, A.: The 'gig economy' is coming. What will it mean for work. In: The Guardian (2015, July, 26). https://www.theguardian.com/. Accessed 13 May 2020
25. Surie, A., Koduganti, J.: The emerging nature of work in platform economy companies in Bengaluru, India: the case of Uber and Ola Cab Drivers. E-J. Int. Comp. Labour Stud. **5**(3) (2016)
26. The People Who Share Blog. http://thepeoewhoshare.com/blog/. Accessed 13 May 2020
27. Thomas, A.: How Ola is riding the future of mobility in India. In: India Times (2017, August, 25). economictimes.indiatimes.com. Accessed 17 May 2020
28. Toyama, K.: Fair Share? The Sharing Economy Goes Global. World Politics Review (2015). https://www.worldpoliticsreview.com/articles/16166/fair-share-the-sharing-economy-goes-global
29. Toyama, K.: Geek Heresy: Rescuing Social Change from the Cult of Technology. Public Affairs, New York (2015)
30. Uber Wants to Rule the World. First It Must Conquer India. In: The New York Times (2017, April, 14). https://www.nytimes.com/. Accessed 13 May 2020
31. Uber, Ola drivers strike in India, demanding higher fares. In: Business Insider (2018, October, 22). https://businessinsider.com/. Accessed 10 June 2019
32. Wood, A.J., Graham, M., Lehdonvirta, V., Hjorth, I.: Good gig, bad gig: autonomy and algorithmic control in the global gig economy. Work Employ Soc. **33**(1), 56–75 (2019)

Spatiotemporal (In)justice in Digital Platforms: An Analysis of Food-Delivery Platforms in South India

Shyam Krishna[✉]

Royal Holloway, University of London, London, UK
shyamkrishna.r@gmail.com, shyam.K.2014@live.rhul.ac.uk

Abstract. With on-demand labour and location-based services becoming increasingly common, this paper explores the complex social justice impact of spatial and temporal elements of digital platforms. A conceptual framing of 'spatiotemporal justice' is proposed to explore the consequences of algorithmic control of space and time experienced by workers. An interpretive case-study is built focusing on work practices of food-delivery platforms in the south Indian city of Chennai. The qualitative methods used include semi-structured interviews of food-delivery workers and an autoethnographic study by the author as a worker on digital platforms. The empirical analysis demonstrates that (in)justice is involved with the workers' negotiation of multiple micro-spatiotemporalities in their daily work practice. The impacts include workers being forced to balance spatiotemporal risk and stress against the benefits of employment. This is contextualised by inequities propagated due to imperfect digital representation of, and the asymmetrical information on spatiality and temporality within the platform. The workers are further affected adversely in their spatiotemporally subordinated power relationship with other groups of digital platform's stakeholders. Spatiotemporal justice as conceptualised here has direct implications in how future of work is defined, governed and how digital platforms are held accountable – particularly in the global South.

Keywords: Gig economy · Social justice · Digital labour · Spatiotemporality

1 Introduction

The recent conditions of COVID-19 globally have brought into focus the growing reliance on food-delivery digital platforms and the physical, health and economic risks faced by its workers. 'Gig-work' as a mode of flexible and temporary task-based employment using a digital platform is a result of the advances in spatial technology such as smartphone mapping, location-based services, and global positioning systems. A core tenet of gig-work platforms is the on-demand labour or 'just-in-time' customer service [19]. In scrutinizing these platforms centering their digitally mediated spatial and temporal practices, this paper analyses the social justice impacts using an empirical case-study of food-delivery workers in south India.

This paper contributes to critical studies of gig-work and the wider gig-economy, which emanate from fields such as information systems (IS), ICT4D, human geography and surveillance studies. Scholars studying digital platforms globally show evidence of inequities arising due to the changing nature of work and the precarity associated with it [2–4]. Perspectives from Graham et al. [5] and Heeks [6] focus on the developmental impact questioning what 'decent' gig work would and should look like. In a similar vein Graham and Woodcock [7] highlight the need to understand 'fairness' of work in factors such as income, working conditions and risks under digital platforms. Critical analysis of gig-work also hints at inequities arising from the core spatial and temporal characteristics of technologies. Works such as Shapiro [8] and Woodcock [9] reflect on workers negotiating between spatial and temporal autonomy - provided by the promise of flexibility to the workers, and control – brough about by the platform's management of workers tasks through algorithmic manipulation of location and time.

Two gaps in research have been identified, which the paper addresses. First, a focused spatiotemporal angle with a detailed study of digital spatial and temporal elements in gig-work remains largely unexplored. A recent exception to this in IS research is Wu and Zheng [10] who strongly argue for a spatiotemporal perspective as a valid means to understand gig-work practices. Secondly, as protests unfold in south India within the food-delivery sector [11], there is growing interest for research on the workers experiences. The wider body of critical research on gig-work in India largely do engage with the various practices of spatial and temporal control as a main point of discussion. But most of such research are limited to studying cab-hailing platforms [4, 12], with food delivery services under studied. Moreover, this paper takes a step further to query the implications through the minutia of the spatial and temporal features of gig-work. Through this, the paper seeks an insight into how data and algorithms related to routine management of time and space of the workers impact their claims to fairness and equity.

To answer this, the paper uses the lens of 'social justice'. This would encompass issues such as fairness and equity within the work and livelihood of the gig-workers. Various interpretations of social justice have been connected to the study of digital technology such as Heeks and Shekar [13] and Dencik et al. [14]. But such literature does not address the specifics of spatial and temporal aspects, their inter-relationship and their (in)justice impacts. Much as Dencik et al. [14] considers the lens of justice works to identify an 'ethical path' through the critical and complex issues surrounding technology use. Encapsulating these ideas this paper proposes 'spatiotemporal (in)justice' to interrogate practices and peculiarities from global South and question whether the spatial and temporal elements, and their entwinement impact gig-workers in a fair and equitable way.

Given this context this paper seeks to answer the question: *'What are the social justice impacts of the spatiotemporal characteristics of digital platforms?'*.

The rest of the paper is structured as follows. First the theoretical concepts surrounding space, time and social justice are introduced. Then the paper presents the case study background and the methodological basis of the research. Finally, the findings are presented with a discussion and concluding thoughts on the empirical case study.

2 Spatiality, Temporality and Justice

Multiple perspectives of justice have been connected to spatiality and temporality that become relevant to a construct of 'spatiotemporal (in)justice'. Social justice and its intersection with digital platform have been used to understand the (un)fairness of the use of data and (in)equity among the users of technology [14]. The use of social justice as a research lens also acknowledges that issues of (in)justice as Fraser [15] presents emanate from underlying complex cultural, economic or political factors that may not be outrightly evident. It follows then that 'spatiotemporal (in)justice' as this paper proposes would zero-in on how elements of 'space', 'time', their entwinement, and their corresponding digital representations affect issues of (un)fairness and (in)equity within platform mediated work practices. Querying social justice then will involve understanding how management of time or space results in issues such as (un)equal distribution of economic value or resources, (un)fair conditions of work and (im)balance in power within the working environment. These notions can be explored within existing theorisation of spatiality, temporality, and their overlap to construct the conceptual basis for this paper.

'Spatial justice' as presented by Soja [16] seeks fair distribution 'in space, of socially valued resources and opportunities to use them'. As a key interpretation of spatial justice Soja [16] invokes the 'right to the city' notion of Lefebvre [17]. He presented that spatiality is socially produced and reproduced through practices and daily routines, and that explicit 'representations' of space determine the various ways it is experienced. This has intersections with how technology control representations and access to space and spatial resources. Other researchers have picked on this thread. Akbari [18] for instance presents 'spatial data justice' derived from social justice theorisation of Fraser [15] and Soja [16]. She argues that spatial issues in digital context is a matter of intersectional claim for justice. This touches also on what Bissett-Scott et al. [19] term 'spatiality of injustice' and 'injustice of spatiality' in relation to digital technologies. This encompasses impact of digital technology distributed spatially and created by digital interpretations of spatiality.

Exploring 'temporal justice' would serve to understand digitally mediated time and its impacts. Goodin [20] interprets temporal justice directly in relation to labour using language of 'distributive justice' – of fairness in the form of 'discretionary time' available for the worker as a remainder after allowing for time at work and time for worker's personal needs. Three other notions of temporal justice are discussed by Henckel and Thomaier [21]. They argue temporal justice: is dependent on structural, material, and spatial factors among others, is relative depending on cultural and economic context, and that temporal inefficiencies experienced are also a cause of temporal injustices. Sharma [22] advances a similar concept of 'temporal worth' – the notion that workers experience time differently and are varyingly compensated for their time, depending on how they are positioned and valued in a temporally dictated economy. This view is acknowledged by Wajcman and Dodd [23] who say that temporalities are experienced in 'differential and inequitable ways'.

Picking on the above ideas and to engage with (un)fairness and (in)equity surrounding the dual concepts of spatiality and temporality this paper acknowledges first the co-constitution of space and time [24, 25]. That manifestations of space and time are interdependent and socially impact each other. This as 'spatiotemporality' is summed up by what Olmstead [26] presents. They refer to the seminal work of Massey [24] to declare that 'unique spatiotemporal topographies' exist across different platform (in mostly urban) contexts and call for exploring these in research.

Research on IS largely consider temporal constructs as reviewed by O Riordan [27] and Shen et al. [28]. Prominently Orlikowski and Yates [29] argued that temporal structures are shaped by and shape the daily 'recurrent practices' of worker's organizational space. A similar perspective is provided by Díaz Andrade and Doolin [30] how temporal practices in the social lives are entwined with their use of technologies (using a case study of refugees' experience). Within studies of digital platforms and gig-work the interleaving of spatiality and temporality become directly relevant. As Graham and Woodcock [3] argue platforms bring timely supply of and demand for labour together using location-based apps in a 'geographically sticky' manner. Once location is captured and the gig is assigned, the temporal elements such as scheduling or task management take over, providing on-demand, 'just-in-time' labour from spatially close gig-workers [1]. Graham [31] summarises this as platforms solving 'space-time' problems of consumers by approximating the world digitally – through maps, location-data, timestamps and related other data and algorithm. There is further evidence given by Baiyere et al. [32], Manriquez [33] and Moisander et al. [34] of the way digitally mediated spatiality and temporality work.

Many existing research studies focus on space and time with cues on issues of fairness and equity. But a gap can be still seen in addressing the intimate relationship between spatiality and temporality within the specific practices of gig-work and as experienced by workers. For instance, spatiotemporal ideas of (in)justice are found in Chen's [2] work where the varying temporal experiences under algorithmic control of time interleaves with the inequities that Chinese taxi drivers face when they move spatially through the city. Similarly Sharma [35] researches on taxi-cab drivers, showing that power flows spatially and temporally – by workers providing their time as labour and in the act of physically moving the passenger around the city An idea on spatiotemporal imbalance has been discussed by Kitchin [36]. He considers that gig-work practices result in 'space–time movements being commodified' and 'leveraged for the benefit of some at the expense of others'. All these reflects albeit indirectly on ideas of (in)equity and (un)fairness as a result of digital representations of space and time.

A very strong cue for studying spatiotemporal (in)equities comes from Wu and Zheng [10] who take an important 'sociomaterial' perspective using a case study of Chinese food-delivery workers. They theorise that the 'reconfiguration' of space and time as the basis of, and that which shapes digital platforms. They argue for a spatiotemporal perspective in conducting a critical analysis of platforms and the power structures that these platforms embody. A similar hint on this issue is from Greenhill and Wilson [37] taking an IS perspective to consider that gendered nature of spatiotemporal flexibility in work as being driven by 'perceived benefits to the employer, rather than issues of social justice'. Similarly, Graham and Anwar [3] mention that an understanding of 'the spatialities and temporalities' of digital labour market is needed to better shape them and hopefully provide the gig-workers a fairer future. In global South context Firmino et al. [38] relevantly present that there is an inherent spatiotemporal algorithmic logic followed by digital platforms rooted in global North assumptions. They call for exploration of local contexts of workers in studying the commodification of their space and time echoing Kitchin [36].

Deriving from the above discussed notions spatiotemporal (in)justice then encapsulates various aspects within the work practices of gig-work. Much as Massey [24] considers every space and also its digital representations are governed by the rhythms of how time acts within it and in turn time is influenced by the space it is enacted within. This forms the basis of how spatiotemporality is queried in this paper - both in digital and its corresponding physical sense. These would involve analysing notions such as the (un)fairness in algorithmic sense resulting in management of workers space and time, discriminatory potential of spatiotemporal data, the adverse impact of users due to spatiotemporal inefficiencies and (in)equity faced by users though spatiotemporal elements. These ideas direct the empirical discussion and analysis that follows in the next few sections.

3   Research Background and Methods

The app-based food-delivery market in India 2019/20 services 500 cities [39]. Of these, this research was conducted in the south Indian coastal city of Chennai (the capital of Tamil Nadu state). The research focuses on analysis of labour and business practices across Swiggy, Ola and Uber Eats – the 3 major digital food-delivery platforms. Customers using smartphone apps receive nearby list of food-delivery establishments like take-away places or restaurants. These orders are then algorithmically queued for the restaurant who use a separate app and the order is assigned to nearby rider who is available to pick-up food and deliver. Orders can be 'batched' together (or called 'multi-orders') with more than one order picked up from same restaurant and delivered to multiple customer delivery locations.

An approach of interpretive case-study has been used in this research [40, 41], with data collection done between December 2019 and February 2020. First, qualitative semi-structured interviews were conducted with riders across the 3 main platforms who were identified using snowball sampling initiated through personal contacts. The author also conducted auto-ethnography by working as a part-time rider over 6 weeks. Over all 27 semi structured interviews were conducted with varying lengths between 30 min to 2 h. These interviews took place either at the rest spaces (usually on the side of the roads and in front of restaurants where the riders congregate in between their order runs) or was conducted in public places such as cafes and the beach. Further observations were done visiting all 3 major platforms' support centres as a potential rider (5 visits in total) and when author attended a strike action & a protest planning meeting (both done as a researcher and not as a rider). Interviews were also conducted at these locations. The author was part of two rider Whatsapp groups (one mandated by the platform and the other setup by local riders). Majority of the interactions were all conducted in Tamil language of which the author is a native speaker.

The methodological basis for studying the author's own use of digital platforms was under what has been presented as the paradigm of 'self-tracking' [42] and is acknowledged as a digital ethnographic method [43]. This entailed the author's observation and engagement with the data and accessible traces of algorithmic elements generated during the personal use of apps as a rider and as a customer. These include use of screenshots and screen video grabs of the smartphone. Data from apps were collected with due anonymisation and only accessed by the author who was the sole user of the apps [44]. The author also collected autoethnographic photos, video, and audio data during the process of daily work as a rider, memo audio and written notes as a form of research diary. The author has been sensitive to balance own experiences as a rider and interviewees' experience by using the autoethnographic engagement with apps, its data and algorithm mostly to substantiate and bracket data gathered from interviewees' direct experiences. A clear distinction is made while referring to these experiences in the paper mentioning the source of data. To contextualise the collected data, textual sources in form of technical blogs and public documents published by platforms and media articles were used where appropriate. All data were originally in or are translated into English, transcribed where appropriate and thematically coded.

Coding through 'template analysis' [45] resulted in themes and codes. First level themes were broadly categorised in relation to customers, workers and restaurants. This guided the analysis and reflects the structuring used during data collection covering the whole cycle of gig-work. The analysis and the patterns emerging from the data were sensitised by theory. Iterative rounds of data-driven coding were used to further probe the data with emerging sub-themes on spatial and temporal elements which formed the imperative for this paper.

4   Analysis

This section presents the analysis of the case-study describing the details of digitally mediated spatiality and temporality that govern work and livelihood for the gig-workers. The section is structured based on the 3 major themes under spatiotemporal injustice identified: trade-offs, representations, and asymmetries.

4.1   Trade-Offs Between Temporal Stress and Spatial Risks

A common denominator across the three platforms studied are the task-level temporal and spatial controls experienced by gig-workers. Multiple points of digitally mediated spatiotemporal interventions at play were observed by the author's in their own experience and garnered thorough interviews. This can be seen in the simplest flow of tasks during a gig in Fig. 1 below.

The work begins with riders marking their spatial location and availability, followed by waiting time until a gig is assigned. A timed alert follows (30 s to 1-min - some instances were lower) to accept assigned order. The platforms design choice also does not reveal location of the restaurant until order is accepted (or customer address in case of food being picked up). After this route maps are displayed for the worker to navigate to pick-up the food. Here a spatiotemporal balancing act is forced where temporal stress is used to control and institute competition forcing riders on longer distance of travel and speedy actions, as riders point out:

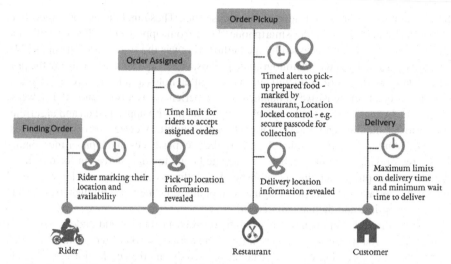

Fig. 1. Multiple spatial and temporal interventions in a standard food-delivery process.

I am pretty fast in accepting orders and press as soon as it buzzes. It's not like I have time to relax and see what is written in there. If I don't [accept the order] someone surely is ready to do it – why waste an opportunity?

...

Even if it is a long drive for the order, I will only know after I press the button [to accept the order]. I cannot decide that fast.

At a specific location such as a pickup point, spatial and temporal elements complement each other to create similar stresses using temporal triggers. For instance as experienced the author, time-limited action or a timed alert is complemented by a location-based spatial control. In one instance a securely generated passcode is needed to confirm pickup of food and is made available to the rider when their smartphone location is within 100 metres of the restaurant. These as 'micro-spatiotemporalities' of control is seen by riders as expectation to travel faster when they are farther away even if they can't act immediately during the ride:

As soon as [the restaurant] marks 'food prepared' the app will say there is only 2 or 3 min. I will be 2 or 3 kms away. I cannot do anything until I reach the restaurant.

Such temporal triggers or prompts linked to proximity of a location nudge the worker to be more efficient using haptic and audio-visual alerts. The larger impact is that the loud alarms and continuous vibration on the smartphone increase risk on road. As one rider recalls:

I will be in heavy traffic and will be focusing on not hitting the bike in front of me. My phone will go brrr... brrr.. woo... woo... Its irritating. But I still need to click on it soon and not miss the order.

In the author's own experience riders endure a rather panic driven work environment where 'alarms' cannot be silenced and need to be responded irrespective of spatial conditions and risk. The multiple intervening spatiotemporal stresses as part of the platform and app design push for speed of actions leaving risks solely as an issue of the worker.

Similar spatiotemporal trade-off of balancing longer worker hours against reaching distance-based targets are inherent to the payment structure set by platforms. For instance, meeting a daily minimum target of 20 location visits with 10 h login time would pay a total of 900 rupees. It sets a target of having to physically travel to a new location (to a restaurant or a customer) every 30 min. But the cumulative weekly target stretches the expectation for moving to a new location averaging every 18 min (230 locations in 70 h). These targets impose an elastic spatiotemporal control of work but with diminishing income returns across the week by commodifying and decoupling spatial and temporal targets. A rider choosing 10 h per working weekday (total 5 days) would need to put in herculean effort to travel to a new location every 9 min working 20 h over weekend to earn maximise weekly income. With delays, additional tasks and controls in play during a workday this can become next to impossible for many:

I keep note of how close I am to daily and weekly target. But some weeks the effort I need to put in gets out of hand. Even if do achieve good targets the weekly targets will force me to put in more and more hours. There is no end and it just becomes really impossible sometimes.

Even those who manage to meet the targets can end up spending close to 16 h per day. This forces the riders to take decisions to trade-off spatial risk for temporal flexibility by front loading their weekly work to 'catch' as many orders – meaning some riders ride around widely earlier in the week, hoping remain time in the week can be more under their own discretion. But there are further complexities such as multi-orders, customer disputes or technology failure. These can trigger a payment condition that revokes their progress towards weekly target or even completely disqualifies them that week. Such unfair formulation means the rider can only try to start another similar spatiotemporal balancing act the next week. Ultimately the workers are put in a position to either take up longer hours or face greater risk on road without which the income target is mostly unachievable.

4.2 Issues in Digital Representations of Spatiotemporalities

Platforms impose some assumptions of certainty in digital representations of locations and time. When reality does not match the digital representation, it forces the workers to step in as a sort of subjective human interpreters - of what the datafied processes intended to achieve. The platforms rely on mapping mostly in English. With Tamil and transliterated vernacular naming of location, places and routes critical spatiotemporal elements come regularly into question. There is clear need for interpretations and error corrections. This means restaurant and customer locations on maps, delivery routes and the estimated time for delivery are presented as objective information in many cases even if it may not be so. In the quote below a rider recalls an experience in delivering in Chennai's 'IT Corridor' – the hub for information technology offices alongside a busy highway with fast moving traffic. This inevitably forms a major area of activity with active presence of customers and restaurants within food delivery platforms:

It is a wide 6 lane highway and there is no place to take U-turn. Restaurant location is marked on the wrong side. I know this by experience... If we go depending on the map, that's it! Another 2 km fuel waste for sure.

Every spatiotemporal negotiation is related to such financial or other costs, and even at work risk for the riders. The rider is this case would either risk by crossing the highway on foot or use their local knowledge to ignore the platform's mapping advice.

The riders also tackle commonly found problems of mapping, customer data literacy, or language issues by voice calls. They try to work around by relying on own local knowledge or by consulting fellow riders over Whatsapp groups – and support is almost always given immediately. In the author's own experience even while riding around in the city, riders help each other, irrespective of the platform they work on – including a case where a rider rode ahead showing the exact path to the author. The actual digital spatial controls and algorithmic rigidity means riders are forced to overcome platform erected barriers while achieving these workarounds. A case in point from author's experience is when a timed task must be done within 100 m of a restaurant – but the actual location is marked incorrectly by the restaurant managers. This situation can easily escalate leaving the rider exposed to income reducing algorithmic triggers such as customer 'disputes' even as they work akin to a 'customer service' personnel to solve issues. Riders report that such disputes can see slow resolution or even an absence of one.

Underlying shortcomings of technologies tend not to account for real-world vagaries such as traffic and road conditions especially those which would be used by scooters. This increases inefficiencies for the rider as it takes away their ability to respond with practical solutions to the reality on road:

When we get second order [in multi order] it would be good if I can decide where to go... [The app] will ask me to go via [a main road] over the flyover and come back another way. But I will never go on the flyover. If I can change and go to second delivery first it will be a easier ride and avoid the flyover.

Platforms also reinterpret spatial representations such as multiple pickups or drop offs as one action in a multiple or batched order creating possibility of rider income reduction. Every order picked up or dropped adds more time, effort, and costs to the rider, but these efforts will not be counted towards income calculation. The platforms can and do change frequently the income calculations involving measurements of distance and time. These changes have made income per delivery and total incentive pay to steadily decrease (despite the initial promises of a high income).

The spatiotemporal elements further affect riders adversely when customers are presented with algorithmic estimations. When inevitable delays occur - like when rider solve errors in location - impatient customers who go by estimated time can intervene by calling up while the rider is negotiating traffic and adding to the risk on road. In an idealised delivery process the estimated time taken to pickup food (from the point of order being assigned to the rider) will be the same as the food preparation time at the restaurant (so would result in no waiting for the rider at the restaurant). But to account for demand at the restaurants the platforms algorithmically forecast preparation (specific to restaurant and the food ordered). In one of the known and complex models the platform can pre-assign a second order O2 to a rider (R1) when the delivery of the first order (O1) is ongoing. But the notification of the second order (O2) may be delayed algorithmically to account for a different rider (R2) emerging spatially closer to second orders' (O2) pickup point. Estimation errors in this affect not one but two income opportunities of rider (R1). The temporal deadzone when rider may be assigned an order and not notified is a point of multiple micro-spatiotemporal unpaid efforts - such as using their local knowledge to go near a popular restaurant and involving fuel costs. These efforts may be overruled by new order (O2) being notified to require moving to a different place. Moreover, platforms misrepresent the process of assignment and a myth of predictability is presented in a bid to spur a rider's near constant availability. Riders across all platforms are consistently told (as experienced by the author in onboarding training sessions) to go near to 'busy restaurants' and essentially chase or hunt orders, though the algorithms can overrule this.

4.3 Spatiotemporal Information and Power Asymmetries

The specific aspects of how digital platforms manage spatial and temporal elements impose asymmetry in power and information that works against riders. Given local power dynamics with restaurants or customers as income entities do not undergo as much spatiotemporal control as the rider. Riders with their clearly visible role (with brightly colored uniforms) face subordination at their gig-work spaces where they occupy a lower rung of socio-economic position. Much as in other situations of entrenched subordination along caste or class lines visible within informal and precarious workspaces, riders are open to expectations of servility. They become answerable to restaurant workers and managers - and with the customers being at the top rung of an imposed hierarchy. This aspect of worker subordination is also strongly evident when a necessary 'deferential' attitude towards customers and restaurants is inculcated through formal trainings at platforms' offices. An equivalence in protection or efforts for dignity of labour is not assured for the riders, making them undertake unpaid tasks rather than being able to challenge local power structures. A rider recalls the expectation for unpaid labour:

We do everything from time to time. From parcelling food, picking spoons for the order, and cleaning the package if it spills... There is this [specific restaurant]. The manager their shouts at us to pack and move fast. That is not my job... But why risk offending him and get a complaint? He doesn't have the customer calling them. That is only my problem.

An explanation can be found in the acontextual dematerialisation of a space as a mere 'location' on a map. Every point on a map that the rider travels to puts them into micro-spatiotemporal negotiation as a worker - done both digitally and in real world. This complexity is not captured in the digital food delivery process. As this rider explains:

If I go to a specific location on the map it's not as if the work is done by itself. It's not as simple as giving the parcel to someone. There are multiple steps on the app. We have to call the customer and be nice. There is a gate, a security guard, parking issues... In office buildings it's even worse, after that its either lift or stairs...

Something unexpected happening, such as when a food inventory runs out automatically means the rider is expected to resolve it given their subordinated position in an asymmetrical power relation. As recalled by a rider:

If the restaurant runs out of food, [the restaurant] need to mark it as not available properly or give something else. What can I do? They ask me to call the customer and check. Can't they call? It is their customer too.

None of these tasks are part of the calculation used for payments. But these extra efforts increase total time taken and rider's costs – and reduces times available for paid tasks.

An asymmetry in availability of information such as ratings also impact the work practices within digital platforms. Customers can have near constant visibility of the riders through location, ratings, and profile-based surveillance from the point when order is assigned until delivery. A rider mentions that such issues leave them to face intense scrutiny on the time taken and even the route taken to the customer address:

We know how long the ride takes. I ride here every-day. Wont I know what will happen? The customers see me on their app and they get some information. The app [estimates] it wrong... Many customers won't bother but one or two may make it a problem and call and instruct constantly – turn left, take a U-turn...

In author's own experience majority of the customers call the rider and expect calls as part of the service by the rider even while on road to follow up on the orders. But platforms actively discourage calling including by extra prompts on apps. The riders encounter this unpaid labour which again eats into the time available for paid work.

This is further bolstered by an unequal ratings and feedback process. The riders are expected to give star ratings to restaurants and customers for the pickup and delivery experience and answer a set of questions. Customers and restaurants can give similar ratings to both restaurant and delivery riders. But the information that these 'stars' represents only affect the riders in the form of performance and tips (some platforms give extra payment of 5 or 10 Rupees for a 5-star delivery). Even though ratings and survey data collected from riders about information like parking availability, road conditions, and correctness of GPS location do formally enhance the spatial data held by the digital platform, riders themselves do not get to see the qualitative information on restaurants or customers. Resolving pickup and delivery issues mostly becomes contextualised by informal knowledge that riders share among themselves over WhatsApp groups.

5 Discussion

This paper furthers the understanding of (un)fairness and (in)equity within the context of data, algorithms, and digital platforms by proposing the construct of 'spatiotemporal justice'. The case study analysing food-delivery practices of gig-workers show three major ways in which spatiotemporality is imbricated with social justice – of spatiotemporal trade-offs between risk and stress, issues of digital representations, and asymmetry of power and information. The spatiotemporal design choices of platforms and algorithmic control show that many practices begin with an unfair burden on workers to balance temporal stress against spatial risk on the job. Further, as platforms seek to digitise physical food delivery practices, it is evident that errors and imperfect digital representations of spatial and temporal elements can bring up issues of (in)justice - such as the unpaid labour faced by the workers in performing platforms' promise of service to the customer. It is also seen that the spatiotemporal dematerialisation can extend and even add to unfair practices in physical food-delivery process. By privileging power and information to customer and restaurants, the platforms use the workers to negotiate difficult physical conditions. This happens under the close control and manipulation of workers' space and time. An ability performed by the platforms through data and algorithms.

This paper contributes a detailed analysis of the consequences of gig-work in south India. This is a valuable addition given the prevalence of similar research stemming from the global North. In this the paper's centering of spatiotemporalities in making claims for justice answers the call of Dencik et al. [14] for a new ontology of social justice. In doing so the research provides insight on the local conditions in the global South amidst the related issues of the uncertainty under COVID-19 for workers in India and the ongoing protests and strikes for fair pay among food-deliver workers in Chennai [46]. In such ongoing debates the workers consistently voice their issues using language and terms which highlights the manipulation of spatiotemporal elements of their daily work. This paper has picked up this strand to provide valuable auto/ethnographic accounts of gig-work. The findings show the intimate and individual spatiotemporal machinations inherent to gig-work, unpicks the local global South specificities and above all allows exploration of the mostly opaque nature of platforms and algorithms.

Spatiotemporal justice also has congruence with the strand of IS research on ethics. Chiasson et al. [47] recently position a need for IS research to study ethics of Big Data, in a way that helps to theorise not only the extractive nature of data-driven 'surveillance capitalism' [48], but to include study of social actors beyond the management layers and understand complex consequences. This paper's co-positioning of spatiotemporality and justice helps us query practices beyond the notions of spatial and temporal at organizational level of the digital platforms. Gig-work is characterized by the capture and measurement of fleeting spatiotemporal elements such as worker location, distance driven, waiting times and timed alerts. By understanding the negotiation of these – what is termed here as 'micro-spatiotemporalities' – show that micro-politics is at play in the daily work practices of digital platforms. So, echoing Graham [31], it is this 'ephemeral' digital duplicate of the spatiotemporalities within the platform that becomes the arena for seeking justice and even resistance. Every task done by a gig-worker is a negotiation of what can be construed as a 'spatiotemporal cost' balanced against possible economic benefit.

The findings here go beyond the conceptualisation of platforms as an 'invisible' manager [49]. Spatiotemporal justice reconciles unfairness in digital representations with the actual impact on daily work practices of gig-workers. Reflecting on what boyd and Crawford [50] argue is an 'aura of truth, objectivity, and accuracy' ascribed to data and algorithms, this paper shows that inefficiencies, erroneous objectivity and unfairness in spatiotemporal representations have a direct impact on workers. Ethical design of algorithms [51] and fair governance of platforms then must consider the impact of their spatiotemporal approximations.

Both practitioners and academics can use the vocabulary presented in this paper of 'spatiotemporal (in)justice' to seek accountability from digital platforms. Spatiotemporal aspects can also help in claims for 'collective justice' given the clear subordination of workers compared to restaurants and customers. Globally as workers movements and struggles foreground 'fair pay' as a claim to economic or redistributive justice, the conception provided here exposes myriad (in)justices beyond the redistributive sense. Spatiotemporal justice then would help establish truly 'fair' practices, standards, and metrics for food delivery gig-workers - as has been done before for workers such as cabdrivers or online freelancers.

Future research can pick up from this point to focus on the efforts of workplace resistance and collective action within gig-work environments and how they take a spatiotemporal dimension. Once instance is the #Logout movements that are taking different forms involving gig-workers and businesses such as restaurants. Moreover, such study can extend valuable insight by conducting global south-south or north-south comparisons of digital platforms and their practices.

A limitation of this research stems from the author's acknowledged positionality as a member of privileged socio-economic class devoid of direct experiences of customary or entrenched forms of labour subordination and servility [52] - as these are rooted strongly in dynamics of caste and status in India. This is a strong line of interdisciplinary inquiry that needs critical and sensitive attention for future researchers to contextualise experiences of gig-workers specific to India.

6 Conclusion

The paper has presented an interpretivist case-study of digital work practices on food-delivery platforms set in south India. The paper contributes 'spatiotemporal justice' as a construct in capturing impact of spatial and temporal control and management which form the core of digital platforms. The analysis demonstrates that (in)justice is involved with workers' being forced to trade-off spatiotemporal risk and stress against benefits of employment. This is contextualised by inequities propagated due to imperfect representation of and asymmetrical information about spatiality and temporality which affect the workers in their subordinated position of power. The paper establishes that micro-spatiotemporal practices and negotiations inherent in digital platforms cause issues for workers such as unpaid labour, unfair income or risky working conditions. Spatiotemporal justice as conceptualised here has direct implications in defining future of work and holding digital platforms accountable by making spatiotemporality a main domain of contestation and claims for justice.

References

1. De Stefano, V.: The rise of the just-in-time workforce: On-demand work, crowdwork, and labor protection in the gig-economy. Comp. Labor Law Policy J. 37(3), 471–501 (2015)
2. Chen, J.Y.: Thrown under the bus and outrunning it! Logic of Didi and taxi drivers' labour and activism in the on-demand economy. New Media Soc. 20(8), 2691–2711 (2018)
3. Graham, M., Anwar, M.: The global gig economy: Towards a planetary labour market? First Monday 24(4), 1–32 (2019)
4. Surie, A., Koduganti, J.: The emerging nature of work in platform economy companies in Bengaluru, India: the case of Uber and Ola Cab DRIVERS. E-J. Int. Comp. Labour Stud. 5(3), 1–29 (2016)

5. Graham, M., Lehdonvirta, V., Wood, A., Barnard, H., Hjorth, I.: Could online gig work drive development in lower-income countries? In: Galperin, H., Alarcon, A. (eds.) The Future of Work in the Global South, pp. 8–11. International Development Research Centre, Ottawa (2018)
6. Heeks, R.: Decent work and the digital gig economy: a developing country perspective on employment impacts and standards in online outsourcing, crowdwork, etc. Development Informatics Working Paper 71, University of Manchester, Manchester, UK (2017). http://hummedia.manchester.ac.uk/institutes/gdi/publications/workingpapers/di/di_wp71.pdf
7. Graham, M., Woodcock, J.: Towards a fairer platform economy: introducing the Fairwork Foundation. Alternate Routes **29**, 1–12 (2018)
8. Shapiro, A.: Between autonomy and control: strategies of arbitrage in the on-demand economy. New Media Society **20**(8), 2954–2971 (2018)
9. Woodcock, J.: The algorithmic Panopticon at Deliveroo: measurement, precarity, and the illusion of control. Ephemera. **21** (2020)
10. Wu, P., Zheng, Y.: Time is of the essence: spatiotemporalities of food-delivery platform work in China. In: Proceedings of Twenty-Eight European Conference on Information Systems (ECIS2020), Marrakesh, Morocco (2020)
11. The Wire.: Swiggy Delivery Executives Strike in Chennai and Hyderabad Over Reduction in Payment. The Wire (2020). https://thewire.in/labour/swiggy-delivery-executives-strike-in-chennai-and-hyderabad-over-reduction-in-payment. Accessed 05 Sept 2020
12. Kashyap, R., Bhatia, A.: Taxi drivers and taxidars: a case study of Uber and Ola in Delhi. J. Dev. Soc. **34**(2), 169–194 (2018)
13. Heeks, R., Shekhar, S.: Datafication, development and marginalised urban communities: an applied framework. Inf. Commun. Soc. **22**(7), 992–1011 (2019)
14. Dencik, L., Jansen, F., Metcalfe, P.: A conceptual framework for approaching social justice in an age of datafication. DATAJUSTICE Project **30,** 1–9 (2018)
15. Fraser, N.: Abnormal justice. Crit. Inq. **34**(3), 393–422 (2008)
16. Soja, E.: The city and spatial justice. Spat. Just. **1**(1), 1–5 (2009)
17. Lefebvre, H.: The Production of Space. Blackwell, Oxford (1991)
18. Akbari, A.: Spatiall data justice: mapping and digitised strolling against moral police in Iran. Development Informatics Working Paper, University of Manchester, UK (76) (2019)
19. Bissett-Scott, J., Odeleye, D., Frame, I.: Spatial justice: towards an ethics of spatial equity. In: Proceedings of the ACM First International Workshop on Understanding the City with Urban Informatics, Melbourne, Australia, pp. 31–34 (2015)
20. Goodin, R.E.: Temporal justice. J. Soc. Policy **39**(1), 1–16 (2010)
21. Henckel, D., Thomaier, S.: Efficiency, temporal justice, and the rhythm of cities. In: Henckel, D., Thomaier, S. (eds.) Space-Time Design of the Public City, pp. 99–117. Springer, Dordrecht (2013). https://doi.org/10.1007/978-94-007-6425-5_8
22. Sharma, S.: In the Meantime: Temporality and Cultural Politics. Duke University, Durham (2014)
23. Wajcman, J., Dodd, N.: The Sociology of Speed: Digital, Organizational, and Social Temporalities. Oxford University Press, Oxford (2017)
24. Massey, D.: For Space. SAGE, Thousand Oaks (2005)
25. Massey, D.: Politics and space/time. New Left Rev., 65–84 (1992)
26. Olmstead, N. A.: Data and temporality in the spectral city. Phil. Technol., 1–21 (2019). https://doi.org/10.1007/s13347-019-00381-8
27. O Riordan, N., Conboy, K., Acton, T.: How soon is now? theorizing temporality in information systems research. In: Proceedings of Thirty Fourth International Conference on Information Systems, Milan (2013)

28. Shen, Z., Lyytinen, K., Yoo, Y.: Time and information technology in teams: a review of empirical research and future research directions. Eur. J. Inf. Syst. **24**(5), 492–518 (2015)
29. Orlikowski, W.J., Yates, J.: It's about time: temporal structuring in organizations. Organ. Sci. **13**(6), 684–700 (2002)
30. Díaz Andrade, A., Doolin, B.: Temporal enactment of resettled refugees' ICT-mediated information practices. Inf. Syst. J. **29**(1), 145–174 (2019)
31. Graham, M.: Regulate, replicate, and resist–the conjunctural geographies of platform urbanism. Urban Geogr. **41**(3), 453–457 (2020)
32. Baiyere, A., Islam, N., Mäntymäki, M.: Duality of work in sharing economy-insights from Uber. In: Proceedings of AMCSI 2019 Conference, Cancun, Mexico (2019)
33. Manriquez, M.: Work-games in the gig-economy: a case-study of Uber drivers in the city of Monterrey, Mexico. In: Work and Labor in the Digital Age (Research in the Sociology of Work, vol. 33, pp. 165–188 . Emerald Publishing Limited, London (2019)
34. Moisander, J., Groß, C., Eräranta, K.: Mechanisms of biopower and neoliberal governmentality in precarious work: mobilizing the dependent self-employed as independent business owners. Hum. Relat. **71**(3), 375–398 (2018)
35. Sharma, S.: Taxis as media: a temporal materialist reading of the taxi-cab. Soc. Identities **14**(4), 457–464 (2008)
36. Kitchin, R.: The timescape of smart cities. Ann. Am. Assoc. Geogr. **109**(3), 775–790 (2019)
37. Greenhill, A., Wilson, M.: Haven or hell? telework, flexibility and family in the e-society: a marxist analysis. Eur. J. Inf. Syst. **15**(4), 379–388 (2006)
38. Firmino, R.J., de Vasconcelos Cardoso, B., Evangelista, R.: Hyperconnectivity and (Im) mobility: Uber and surveillance capitalism by the Global South. Surveill. Soc. **17**(1/2), 205–212 (2019)
39. Livemint: Indian online food-delivery market to hit $8 bn by 2022: Report. Livemint (2020). https://www.livemint.com/technology/tech-news/indian-online-food-del ivery-market-to-hit-8-bn-by-2022-report-11580214173293.html. Accessed 05 Sept 2020
40. Barrett, M., Walsham, G.: Making contributions from interpretive case studies: examining processes of construction and use. In: Kaplan, B., Truex, D.P., Wastell, D., Wood-Harper, A.T., DeGross, J.I. (eds.) Information Systems Research. IIFIP, vol. 143, pp. 293–312. Springer, Boston, MA (2004). https://doi.org/10.1007/1-4020-8095-6_17
41. Walsham, G.: Interpretive case studies in IS research: nature and method. Eur. J. Inf. Syst. **4**(2), 74–81 (1995)
42. Lupton, D.: The Quantified Self. Polity, Cambridge (2016)
43. Hjorth, L., Horst, H., Galloway, A., Bell, G. (eds.): The Routledge Companion to Digital Ethnography. Routledge, New York (2017)
44. Rogers, R.: Digital Methods. The MIT press, Cambridge (2013)
45. King, N.: Doing template analysis. Qual. Organ. Res. Core Methods Curr. Chall. **426**, 77–101 (2012)
46. NDTV.: Serving 100% Of Chennai: Swiggy Says Striking Delivery Partners Back. NDTV (2020). https://www.ndtv.com/chennai-news/swiggy-strike-chennai-back-to-serving-chennai-says-swiggy-on-delivery-executive-strike-over-low-pay-2282983. Accessed 05 Sept 2020
47. Chiasson, M., Davidson, E., Winter, J.: Philosophical foundations for informing the future(S) through IS research. Eur. J. Inf. Syst. **27**(3), 367–379 (2018)
48. Zuboff, S.: The Age of Surveillance Capitalism: The Fight for a Human Future at the New Frontier of Power. Profile Books, London (2019)
49. Gandini, A.: Labour process theory and the gig economy. Hum. Relat. **72**(6), 1039–1056 (2019)
50. Boyd, D., Crawford, K.: Critical questions for big data: provocations for a cultural, technological, and scholarly phenomenon. Inf. Commun. Soc. **15**(5), 662–679 (2012)

51. Martin, K.: Designing ethical algorithms. MIS Q. Executive **18**(2), 129–142 (2019)
52. Gooptu, N.: Servile sentinels of the city: private security guards, organized informality, and labour in interactive services in globalized India. Int. Rev. Soc. Hist. **58**(1), 9–38 (2013)

Understanding Platform Ecosystems for Development: Enabling Innovation in Digital Global Public Goods Software Platforms

Scott Russpatrick[✉]

University of Oslo, 0555 Oslo, Norway
scott@dhis2.org

Abstract. *Purpose* - While the potential of digital platforms for socio economic development is recognized, limited knowledge exists on the development of these platforms beyond the literature that is focused on commercial for-profit business models in the Global North. Platforms that host application ecosystems have the most potential for value creation for the platform owner and all users. However, little is understood about how public-sector platform owners can enable the creation of application ecosystems where traditional economic incentives for 3rd party, generic application development are not so explicit. Drawing on case study data drawn from the recent proliferation of third-party applications in the district health information software (DHIS2) digital platform, the authors propose themes influencing the innovation by 3rd party application developers for a digital global public goods (DGPG).

Design/methodology/approach - The paper draws on a study of the DHIS2 that is implemented in over 80 countries globally. The platform operates a free and open source (FOSS) philosophy, has a core application that can be downloaded for free, and an app hub containing supplementary, generic 3rd party developed applications. The platform core is supported by University of Oslo and major international donor organizations to support its implementation in contrast to the business models of commercial digital platforms that require explicit monetization. Following a thematic analysis case study methodology, this paper investigates the motivators of complementors to create innovative apps thus creating a virtuous cycle of value generation for the platform.

Findings - The data reveal that there are three themes that exist in the decisions by 3rd-party developers to produce generic applications within the DHIS2 platform; boundary resources, networks for innovation, and enlightened self-interest. Working in concert, these themes influence the complementor to create a generic application that can be applied across thousands of DHIS2 databases and generate value for the platform and all users equitably.

Originality/value - This paper offers a new theoretical perspective to illuminate the motivators for contributors to digital innovation platforms for development. In parallel, it draws practical implications for public-sector and DGPG platform owners seeking to develop application economies.

Keywords: Application ecosystems · Innovation · Platforms · Global digital public goods · Development · Low and middle-income countries

© IFIP International Federation for Information Processing 2020
Published by Springer Nature Switzerland AG 2020
R. K. Bandi et al. (Eds.): IFIPJWC 2020, IFIP AICT 601, pp. 148–162, 2020.
https://doi.org/10.1007/978-3-030-64697-4_12

1   Introduction

Digital innovation platforms provide the foundational elements for innovation in the form of applications or components that can be built upon [1]. The essential challenge for platform providers is to continuously maintain and nurture an innovative ecosystem around the platform [2]. A classic example is the Android operating system, where a stable core is maintained that allows for periphery applications to be supported. This "application ecosystem" enables many innovators to develop complementary applications or services within the digital platform ecosystem [3]. Applications can be highly specific to a single end-user or generic to a broad range of end-users. Innovation platforms have the unique ability to create extensive platform ecosystems while also enabling 3rd party application developers, complementors, to address local challenges [4].

Digital Platforms have three key properties: they are enabled by technology, facility interactions between users and user groups, and allow users to perform certain actions [3, 5]. Jacobides and colleges [6], point out that the key goal of a platform is to facilitate interactions between platform participants. Platform owners have the challenge of developing and maintaining an innovative ecosystem which can utilize the expertise and ingenuity of a diverse developer community [2]. An open platform ecosystem enables both core and third-party developers or complementors to co-create new applications to address the requirements of an every growing and increasingly varied community of users [7]. However, complementors must see sufficient incentives and value, while being able to overcome technical and knowledge boundaries, to contribute to innovation within the platform ecosystem [8]. An application ecosystem built around a common platform core that does present sufficient value to complementors while minimizing barriers is best positioned for growth and adoption [6].

From a technical perspective, a platform must possess a "layered" architecture with a modular design [4]. Architecture refers to structure of the inner system, the components and how they perform [9]. Typically, these would commonly be referred to as the "back-end", "front-end", the application programming interface (API), and/or standard application kit (SDK). A layered architecture is defined by generic core components with a low degree of variability, complementary or periphery applications with higher variability, and an interface between the two [10]. The modular design of the platform refers to the development of small, reusable components with a well-defined user interface [10–12].

Innovation platforms provide the foundation for which applications or components can be built upon. Again, a classic example is the Android operating system, where a stable core is maintained that allows for periphery application to be supported. Mandel [13] describes this as application economies, or "a collection of interlocking innovative ecosystems where each ecosystem consists of a core ecosystem, which creates and maintains a platform and an app marketplace." In the application economy multiple individuals, groups and organizations – e.g. developers, companies, or governments- are able to create, launch, and maintain their own applications. Innovation platforms enable a large number of innovators to develop complementary applications or services within the platform ecosystem by providing technical foundational elements [3]. Applications can be highly specific to a single end-user, such as an application that aids community health workers in Zambia in diagnosing Malaria, or highly generic to a broad range of end-users, such as Whatsapp [4].

Global Digitcal Public Goods (GDPG) – Specifically, in the context of low and middle-income countries, innovation platforms can lend to the creation of application economies and the development of tools to address local challenges [14]. In the winter of 2017, a consortium of development multilaterals and donors aligned on digital investment principals to ensure continued investment in platforms operating in developing countries. These platforms must meet the criteria of a GDPG to be eligible for donor support. According to Digital Investment Principles [15],

> "Global Goods are digital health tools that are adaptable to different countries and contexts. Mature digital health global good software is software that is (usually) Free and Open Source Software (FOSS), is supported by a strong community, has a clear governance structure, is funded by multiple sources, has been deployed at significant scale, is used across multiple countries, has demonstrated effectiveness, is designed to be interoperable, and is an emergent standard application"

Although the merit of GDPGs is acknowledged, Smith [15] contends that there is no commercial incentive to create them. National government, donor, and multilateral agency provision of public goods is provided through taxation and licensing, and their very nature means that market-based mechanisms of competition, profit, and selectivity cannot be applied. Hippel and Krogh [17] explore potential motivators for developers to make contributions to FOSS public goods. They point out that the cost of losing property rights to innovation must be outweighed by the benefit of diffusion of the innovation. Contributors need to face "low rivalry conditions" meaning the diversity of the contributors diffuses a rivalrous nature. They also report that contributors to FOSS develop a sense of ownership and control over their product that is not typically the case in more commercial products. This research in many ways is a test of these assertions by Hippel and Krogh.

Much has been written on the market-orientation, competition, pricing strategies, and mechanisms of platforms that enable complementor application development [18]. Digital platform owners must create a business model in which complementors see clear incentives to create, distribute, and sustain platform innovations [1]; however, where traditional market incentives are lacking, creating incentives has proven to be particularly difficult. This becomes an inherent challenge for public sector digital innovation platforms [17, 19]. For platforms where profit is not the main goal, the challenge is for the platform owner to be able to align the self-interest of the complementors to the health and mission of the platform ecosystem [17, 20]. There is a paucity of research into what these incentives may be, and in response to this gap, the objective of this paper is to identify themes in the creation of complementor applications for public sector digital global public good innovation platforms.

In order to do this, we examine the recent proliferation of generic, complementor applications in the free and open source District Health Information System 2 (DHIS2) innovation platform in its role as a national health management information system (HMIS). Some 67 mainly low- and middle-income countries have adopted DHIS2 as their central digital platform for their health system [21]. DHIS2 has a core database and application programing interface (API) developed and maintained by the Health Information System Project (HISP) headquartered at the University of Oslo. Beyond the core is a continuously increasing number of third-party developed applications that are developed with little or no involvement from the core development team in Oslo. These periphery, generic applications are by nature more reusable across countries and contexts and increase the value of the platform as a whole to all users [14].

Research Question: What are the themes that emerge in the principal considerations by complementors who decide to develop generic, publicly available applications for a FOSS, public good platform?

In what follows we define our methods of identifying leading third-party, generic applications in the DHIS2 ecosystem, and we follow that with the identification and justification of the themes that exist in generic complementor application development.

2   Methods

This paper employs a qualitative thematic analysis to detect and identify principal considerations that influence behaviors, actions and thoughts of the platform complementors [22, 23]. Thematic analysis is a method for identifying, analyzing, and reporting patterns (themes) within a data set [24]. Thematic analysis allows for the description of implicit and explicit ideas via a coding and data reduction process that links raw data with concepts. The various concepts are then linked to broader themes via an inductive (derived from the data) approach as well as a priori approach stemming from the investigator's prior theoretical understanding of the phenomenon under study [25].

We initially identified five suitable case studies from the 3rd party applications that were submitted to the "Application of The Year" competition at the 2019 DHIS2 Annual Conference. The DAC is the largest annual gathering of leading DHIS2 implementers and developers with dozens of use-cases and user stories, innovation highlights, technical sessions, networking events, micro-trainings, and feedback sessions over the course of four days. Of the18 application submitted, three were selected as finalists based upon their impact, accessibility, and quality. The five applications presented in this research include the three finalist and two additional applications. These five were selected based on three criteria. First, each of the applications were publicly available, meaning the application was published in the DHIS2 application repository, freely available to all, and the source code was open and accessible. Second, the primary author of this research has had long-term involvement and access with the application developers to be able to produce rich, contextual data. Third, these case studies match with Gerring's [26] classification of an "extreme case" or a case that is, "considered to be prototypical or paradigmatic of some phenomenon of interest." By focusing on "extreme," idealized case rather than representative case selection we are better able to apply the findings to the generation of theoretical concepts such as themes [27–29].

2.1   Data Collection

Data was collected through document analysis, presentation analysis, interviews, and survey analysis. First, we conducted a review of the submitted material for the "App of the Year Competition." This included a video tutorial of using the application itself and a short description of why the application was developed, who uses the application, and what its impact has been. Next, we conducted a written survey of the applications principally to assess the motivations and expectations for making the application. Finally, we conducted ten follow-up interviews, five with the lead application developers themselves, and five more with the manager of the organization that created the application. All participants in the research gave verbal and written acknowledgement of willingness to use their responses in this research.

2.2 Data Analysis

A three phase data reduction process was utilized to identify the prevailing themes presented in this research. First, after collection, the data was tabulated so that it could be coherently analyzed. For example, as each interviewee was asked the same questions those questions were collated together so that variation across answers could be discerned. The second phase involved highlighting key excerpts from the text that contribute to the study's question [30]. The third stage creates a reasonable and logical chain of evidence through data coding to derive concepts (see Fig. 1) upon which a-priori theory is applied to deduce the final themes [24]. This process is an inductive approach in that collection starts with precise content then applies broader generalization and ultimately leading to theory generation. This process largely safeguards that the themes are linked to the data [31].

3   Case Description

District Health Information Systems (DHIS2) - Here we use the example of the free and open source DHIS2 as an innovation platform in its role as a national health management information system (HMIS). DHIS2 has a core database and API developed and maintained by the Health Information System Project (HISP) headquartered at the University of Oslo. The core development team also develop and maintain a suit of "core" generic applications that are the minimal tools necessary for an HMIS. These are: data capture applications, analytics applications, such as dashboards, pivot tables, charts, and maps, and social analytics and messaging applications which enable users to directly communicate with each other enabling commentary around the data analytics. There are also data quality application as well as meta-data configuration and user management applications. These applications reuse common components and exist on top of a stable application programing interface (API) forming a layered, modular architecture. Beyond the core is a proliferation of locally developed applications that are developed with little or no involvement from the core development team [14]. These periphery applications can be generic and, thus, more reusable across countries and contexts or highly specialized for a specific end-user or function [14]. In the case of DHIS2, while the core development does receive long-term support from a consortium of international aid donors and multilaterals, the generic applications that are developed outside of the core by platform complementors do not receive the same level and duration of financial support. Often these periphery applications are developed with time bound project funding. In essence, by making a generic application that can be installed in any DHIS2 instance, the developers are pledging to support the application (improvements and bug fixing) indefinitely without any guarantee of continued funding.

Building on the DHIS2 case-study, one can begin to form linkages between digital platforms and the concept of global public goods. DHIS2 being a free and open source platform means that there is a non-rivalrous nature. In other words, the use of the platforms by one individual does not prevent that of another. Likewise, no single institution or person can be excluded from the use of the platform. "Free", in this case, does not only mean no cost to obtain, but also the broader sense of freedoms such as choice or freedom of speech [32]. These notions touch on another element of public goods in that they are often centered in basic human rights such as the right to health care or the right to education. The "global" element comes into play in several regards. First, is the scale of adoption with the tools and services in DHIS2 now covering approximately 2.28 billion people globally [21]. The second is the degree of country ownership. Some 67 countries have deployed DHIS2 as their central digital platform for their health system. DHIS2 is also global in terms of its development. While a relatively small core team is in Oslo, there exists a vast distribution of developers implementing core application and creating complementary, peripheral applications. Finally, the last element of global is the global network of the implementation community. DHIS2 maintains a central, web-based community of practice (CoP) where implementers across the globe can ask question, find answers, and share resources and best practices.

This research further focuses on five "extreme" cases of generic, publicly available applications that have been made for the DHIS2 platform ecosystem:

Interactive dashboards – In late 2016, HISP Tanzania, based in Dar es Salaam developed the Interactive Dashboard application. This dashboard application was in response to specific requests from the Tanzanian Ministry of Health for a more flexible dashboard application than the core dashboard application produced by UiO. The Interactive dashboard application allows users to "bookmark" dashboards, toggle between different visualization types and dimensions, and user messaging is tied to single dashboard items. The application was developed utilizing the same API endpoints and resources as the core dashboard, and it was posted to the DHIS2 App Hub making it freely available. The interactive dashboard also formed the foundation for the 2018 rewrite of the core, UiO produced Dashboard application.

D2D – Starting in 2017 the Ministry of Health in Mozambique began capturing daily morbidity and mortality data against individual patient in DHIS2. This frequency and granularity are critical in disease control and prevention. However, the data is also required to be aggregated to a monthly dataset in a separate instance of DHIS2. In the health facilities this meant that data had to be captured twice, which was overly burdensome. Saudigitas, a Mozambique DHIS2 implementation and development company, in response to this inconvenience to the users, developed the D2D application in 2018 which enables administrators to pull individual data from one instance of DHIS2 into aggregated data in another. This eliminates the need for data to be entered by the clinician in two separate instances. The application utilizes core code libraries and user interface (UI) templates to produce a generic solution that can be downloaded and installed by the DHIS2 community without any intervention or support from Saudigitus.

DHIS2 Data Import Wizard – In 2018 a team based in at the NGO HISP Uganda developed the DHIS2 Data Import Wizard. This application was developed to enable intuitive excel, csv, or API imports of data into DHIS2. While this is a functionality covered in core applications, the core application has long been understood to be poor performing and difficult to use by community and core developers. Yet, the roadmap for core development has required development resources to be put in other applications and functionalities. Appreciating this gap and in a need to address their own issues with importing data from several projects, HISP Uganda over the course of 18 months developed a generic application for user-friendly and intuitive data import. In-fact this application won the application of the year popular vote during the 2019 DHIS2 Annual Conference.

DHIS2 Web Excel Importer – In 2017 HISP India faced the same issues with routine importing data from excel into DHIS2 as HISP Uganda. They developed the DHIS2 Web Excel Importer to address this problem. The application automatically reads the column header in excel and aligns this with the proper DHIS2 import format. Much like the DHIS2 Data Import Wizard application, this functionality represents a dramatic improvement over the core, HISP UiO produced Data Import Application. This a generic application which can be used to import data to any DHIS2 aggregate systems and can be easily downloaded and configured by another country or project without the direct involvement by the original developers. The application utilizes core API endpoints and data stores and is publicly available on the DHIS2 App Hub.

Advanced Metadata Export Application--The University of Catalonia in 2018 developed The Advanced Metadata Export app which allows users to share and exchange metadata with other DHIS2 instances, gathering all necessary dependencies (e.g., global DHIS2 instance with many different metadata and local, country instances specialized only in particular disease). In addition, the app also allows packaging specific metadata for migrating them between different instances in the same organization (e.g., pushing metadata from development to production instance). This application introduces completely new functionality to DHIS2 while utilizing core code and user-interface libraries.

4   Thematic Analysis

Table 1 shows the identified themes, their description, and component concepts. These themes were identified via an inductive, a priori approach and mapped to the underlying data in Fig. 1.

Boundary Resources
The data analysis revealed the existence of key platform owner provided resources as necessary for developing generic innovative applications in the DHIS2 platform ecosystem. These boundary resources are both technical and social in nature and allow for periphery applications to extend the functionalities of the platform beyond what is perceived or possible to be done by the platform owner [33]. These boundary resources operate not as isolated elements, but as an integral part of the platform infrastructure maintained by the platform owner [34].

Table 1. Themes

Theme	Description	Concepts
Boundary Resources	Complementors are attracted and enabled to utilize platform owner provided resources to more easily innovate within the platform application ecosystem	• *Technology boundary resources*: Platform owner provided easily assessable and implementable boundary resources such as APIs, code libraries, and use of common programing languages. These can make it easier for complementors to produce generic applications that can be utilized globally over customized, client specific applications • *Knowledge boundary resources*: A clear short and long-term core development roadmap and timeline developed by the platform owner enables complementors to know what and when a new application is necessary
Networks for Innovation	Complementors extend their generic innovations across their known networks and beyond into new networks	• *Indirect network effects* develop as the number of user groups increase enabling multiple user groups to contribute to the development and refinement of the same application • *Communities of practice*, maintained by platform owners, serves as a stage for complementors to promote their innovations beyond their known networks. This increases adoption globally and thusly more indirect network effects
Enlightened Self Interest	Complementors innovate with an aim to increasing the overall value of the platform for all users	• *Global platform perspectives* by complementors prompts generic innovation with the intent of increasing the value of the platform as a whole. As platform providers, this subsequently increases their value/services they can provide to their clients by being able to utilize their own and innovations supplied from other complementors

Technology boundary resources, provided by the platform owner, give the ability for platform complementors to create new applications via accessible technical resources. These exist as open platform resources (APIs, SDKs, code libraries, user interface standards and templates, app stores, etc.) which form the platform technical boundaries that define the degree to which complementors are able to co-create and innovate within the platform ecosystem [35, 36].

Knowledge boundary resources are resources that furtherer regulating the ability of complementors to innovate and create value within the platform ecosystem [37]. Knowledge boundary resources seek to provide the practical knowledge and understanding necessary for complementors to access and utilize the technical boundary resources [37, 38]. More difficult to scale than technical boundary resources, knowledge boundary resources can be guidelines, programming tutorials, information portals, online courses, workshops and co-innovation projects. Platform owners who adopt open development standards such as common programing languages, code libraries, and methods which often already have third-party developed wikis, courses, and books can lower the barriers for complementors to co-create with the platform and minimize the number of platform specific knowledge boundary resources [37].

Networks for Innovation
The data exposed that social networks for promoting, sharing, and even refining innovations are a key theme in complementors' decisions to develop generic applications. The networks are engaged through platform owner provided physical events, conferences, and digital communities of practice as well as across complementor own internal networks.

Network effects are a unique property of digital platforms where increasing the number of users increases the platform's value to the platform owner and all users. Essentially, the more users the larger the user networks and often the number of complementary innovations. New network effects appear as a third-party complementors make new connections with an increasing distributed group of users. These connections encourage third-party firms to create complementary innovations. These innovations thus attract more users to the platform which prompts more innovation from complementors, and a virtuous cycle of value creation emerges and continues, ideally, indefinitely [1]. Network effects can be direct or indirect. Direct network effects form when a technology benefits a user by enabling them to connect to many other users and complementors. The potential benefit of the platform to the user increases as the number of users and complementors increase in the platform [39]. Indirect network effects form when one group of users tangentially effects a different group of users in a positive way. This is essentially when the number of users grow in one group the benefit and number of users can grow in a different group [39, 40].

Communities of practice (COP) are defined by Wegner et al. [41] as, "…groups of people who share a concern, a set of problems, or a passion about a topic, and who deepen their knowledge and expertise in this area by interacting on an ongoing basis." The roles of individual COP members are not set, they are fluid and informal in which users should feel no risk in contributing, and much like a platform in general, the more members and contributors to a COP the more value that is generated for all users [42]. Wenger and Snyder [43] argue that a community of practice to be most successful must be guided by strategic objectives that are defined by the central sponsor. In the case of DHIS2, the University of Oslo sponsors both virtual and physical communities of practice.

Enlightened self-interest is an ethical philosophy which proposes that a person who acts to serve the collective interests of others or the interests of groups that they belong are, in essence, serving their own interests. Enlightened self-interest is a response to

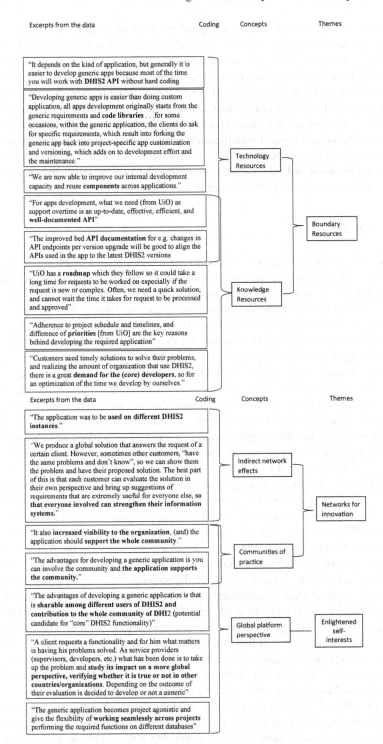

Fig. 1. Data reduction: mapping of themes to the data

the classical economic premise that acting solely on an individual's self-interest is the best way to maximize profits and generate value [44]. It also differs from altruism in that it does not compel one to pursue the interests of others at the expense of their own interests [45]. In the seminal work on contributors' motivations for open-source software development, Hippel and Krogh [17] reveal that along with producing a software product, open-source contributors also generate collective resources such as knowledge, networks, relationships, goals, and even ideologies. These collective resources over time become a reward and motivator unto themselves and contributors stop regarding participation as costly, but rather beneficial [46]. Contributors get benefits from increasing the value of the platform and subsequently increasing the value/services they can provide to their clients—a repeated theme we see in the data.

5   Discussion

The importance and enabling of the technology boundary resources played a prominent role in the responses from application developers. In the case of Interactive Dashboard and the DHIS2 Data Import Wizard application, the developers utilized and built on top of pre-existing APIs and reusable components while the DHIS2 Web Excel Importer consumed standard code libraries and preexisting applications. In fact, the developers from both the Interactive Dashboard and the DHIS2 Data Import Wizard stated that generic application development is easier to develop than a custom, client specific applications because they can focus their efforts on creating the new functionality while reusing existing resources for functionality shared across other applications. The DHIS2 Web Excel Importer developers voiced concerns that when client requirements become more specific, the application becomes more custom and ultimately harder to develop and maintain. There is then an appreciation that reuse of technology resources not only makes the initial development easier, but also make the application more able to be sustainably maintained over time.

When asked, "what kind of support you expect to receive to maintain the applications", again, technology boundary resources (specifically the API) is clearly a principal concern for enabling development of applications. All case-studies interacted directly with the API and were completely dependent on its stability and continued maintenance by the platform owners. Therefore, any changes or errors in the API would have cascading negative effects on the functionality and performance of their applications.

UiO product managers produce a core application development roadmap that outlies the short- and longer-term development priorities and timeline for development. The roadmap is driven by community needs and allows for open community submissions, voting, and feedback. The product management team selects from the community submission those features that will have the most impact to the greatest number of users, considers votes/popularity, and technical feasibility. However, on average community submissions are nearly twice that of what core developers can address, and new submission, if approved for development, will take at least 6 months, but more likely a year or more to be released. Because the roadmap is open and the priorities for core development are communicated publicly, 3rd-party application developers have the knowledge necessary to determine if there is a need to develop a new application. In this way, a clear roadmap and development timeline drives how and when complementors develop new innovative applications. Three of the case studies expressed that the knowledge of the roadmap and its inherent priorities and timeline where major deciding factors in the appreciation that they would need to develop their own application.

As described in the methods section, at the 2019 DHIS2 Annual Conference (DAC), UiO introduced an Annual Application Competition. The finalists presented/demoed their application in a plenary session and the community members at the DAC voted for their favorite application which was named the "DHIS2 Application of the Year." When asked what the benefits to your organization are in making a generic application Charles Olupot, from HISP Uganda, and the winner of the application competition responded, *"It also increased visibility to the organization, (and) the application should support the whole community."*

Certainly, presenting in front of over 400 DAC participants and winning the popular vote elevated the perception of HISP Uganda. The community of practice present at the DAC prompted this but the effects lingered on in the web-based COP. This COP includes the digital space community.dhis2.org (launched by UiO in 2018) which hosts many topical forums, Q&A and support channels, a 'marketplace' with job and project postings, and announcements from the core development team. The application competition finalists and winner were immediately posted to community.dhis2.org after the DAC. Within one day, 587 additional community members had viewed the post and a conversation thread developed where several organizations requested use of the applications. Interestingly, a bug and new suggestion for improvement were made for Olupot's application as well. In this example, we can see the COP (both physical and digital) enabling many indirect network effects for application developers. It serves as a stage for them to promote their innovations beyond their known networks, and it encourages application developers to produce high quality, generic applications that can be utilized and refined by a larger user base.

In all the case studies, the application developed was to be used by different DHIS2 instances/data bases. While these databases did not connect, the users of each directly benefited by the existence of each other, forming indirect network effects. The initial intent for the applications were, for them, to be deployed to only the instances that each organization supported. However, by making the application generic and publicly available it has formed additional network effects with platform users that have no connection to the instances for which the application was developed.

The situation described by the developers of the D2D application also highlights the role of indirect network effects that a platform can enable multiple user groups to contribute to the development and refinement of the same application. While each individual client's use of the application is independent, each benefit from the existence of the other by contributing functional design requirements that the application developer *disembeds* into generic functionality that address the collective needs. A client may not even appreciate the existence of a certain need while others already have. This need can be addressed, and the application redistributed to all clients. Consequently, this has the potential to preemptively address an issue for several clients based upon the experiences of one—in effect developing a generic solution to fit all users.

In our case study evaluation, we saw a repeated theme of independent contributors voicing an intrinsic need to develop a product that may be applicable far beyond their own use-cases. We called this concept a ***global platform perspective***. As evident in the data, the developers of all the applications in the case studies made deliberate decisions to make the applications generic and publicly available because they appreciated that the application could present a global solution. There were subtle nuances to this perspective, however; for example, the developers of the Advanced Metadata Export Application hoped that by increasing the global user-base of the application HISP UiO would consider taking up the long-term support of the application. Additionally, the developers of the D2D and the DHIS2 Web Excel Importer both expressed that by solving global problems they were increasing the utility of DHIS2. With their business tied to the utility of larger DHIS2 platform, and acting in good faith, they benefit both from presenting global applications as well as using applications in their own projects developed by other complementors also acting in good faith. This phenomena unto itself is some sort of new network effect derived not from personal connections but from shared benefit from expanding the platform utility. Here we see a culture of openness, concern for the global good, and sharing propagated around the platform where individual contributors do not regard developing global solutions as overly costly.

These use-cases represent ideal scenarios. Many motivators and influences in the decisions by other complementors have not been analyzed or appreciated. Certainly, powerful forces exist that create tensions between creating an open, generic application or a project specific, closed application. This research is relatively one-sided, focusing on the motivators for generic, open application development. These tensions are not explicitly described here in detail, but further research could be able to present a more wholistic picture.

6 Conclusion

This paper presents the perspective of complementors to a FOSS, GDPG platform who decide to develop generic, openly available applications. The many considerations that go into the complementor's decision to develop these applications can be distilled down to clear concepts and themes. This research does partially address the dearth of research on innovation drivers (economic, social, technological, etc.) of GDPGs. As GDPGs continue to grow in number, scale, and scope, additional research will be necessary to describe their unique properties. We also see these GDPGs receiving increasing focus as every country around the world responds to the global Covid-19 outbreak. GDPGs offer many countries, especially low and middle income, out-of-the-box solutions to monitoring and containing these kinds of outbreaks. This increasing focus and implementation will surely drive additional innovation and virtuous value generation within the platforms.

References

1. Gawer, A., Cusumano, M.A.: Industry platforms and ecosystem innovation. J. Prod. Innov. Manag. **31**(3), 417–433 (2014)

2. Cusumano, M.A., Gawer, A.: The elements of platform leadership. MIT Sloan Manag. Rev. **43**(3), 51 (2002)
3. Evans, P.C., Gawer, A.: The rise of the platform enterprise: A global survey (2016)
4. Yoo, Y., Henfridsson, O., Lyytinen, K.: Research commentary-the new organizing logic of digital innovation: an agenda for information systems research. Inf. Syst. Res. **21**(4), 724–735 (2010)
5. de Reuver, M., Sørensen, C., Basole, R.C.: The digital platform: a research agenda. J. Inf. Technol. **33**(2), 124–135 (2018)
6. Jacobides, M.G., Cennamo, C., Gawer, A.: Towards a theory of ecosystems. Strateg. Manag. J. **39**(8), 2255–2276 (2018)
7. Ceccagnoli, M., Forman, C., Huang, P., Wu, D.J.: Co-creation of value in a platform ecosystem: the case of enterprise software. MIS Q. **36**, 263–290 (2012)
8. Benlian, A., Hilkert, D., Hess, T.: How open is this platform? The meaning and measurement of platform openness from the complementers' perspective. J. Inf. Technol. **30**(3), 209–228 (2015)
9. Van Schewick, B.: Internet Architecture and Innovation. MIT Press, Cambridge (2012)
10. Baldwin, C.Y., Woodard, C.J.: The architecture of platforms: a unified view. In: Platforms, Markets and Innovation, pp. 131–162. Edward Elgar Publishing Limited (2009)
11. Maccormack, A., Rusnak, J., Baldwin, C.Y.: Exploring the structure of complex software designs: an empirical study of open source and proprietary code. Manage. Sci. **52**(7), 1015–1030 (2006). https://doi.org/10.1287/mnsc.1060.0552
12. Baldwin, C.Y., Clark, K.B.: Design Rules: The Power of Modularity, vol. 1. MIT press, Cambridge (2000)
13. Mandel, M.: Where the jors are: the app economy. In: Techent, M.M.B., Huberman, M.A.(eds.) Qualitative Data Analysis: an Expanded Sourcebook. Sage 1994 (2012)
14. Roland, L.K., Sanner, T.A., Sæbø, J.I., Monteiro, E.: P for platform. architectures of large-scale participatory design. Scand. J. Inf. Syst. **29**(2), Article 1 (2017)
15. The Principles of Donor Alignment for Digital Health (2019). Accessed 05 Apr 2020. https://digitalinvestmentprinciples.org/
16. Smith, R., Beaglehole, R., Woodward, D., Drager, N. (eds): Global Public Goods for Health. Oxford University Press, Oxford (2003)
17. Hippel, E.V., Georg, V.K.: Open source software and the 'private-collective' innovation model: issues for organization science. Organ. Sci. **14**(2), 209–223 (2003). https://doi.org/10.1287/orsc.14.2.209.14992
18. Boudreau, K., Hagiu, A.: Platform rules: multi-sided platforms as regulators. In Platforms, Markets and Innovation (2009)
19. Janssen, M., Estevez, E.: Lean government and platform-based governance—doing more with less. Gover. Inf. Q. **30**, S1–S8 (2013)
20. Boudreau, K.J.: Let a thousand flowers bloom? An early look at large numbers of software app developers and patterns of innovation. Organ. Sci. **23**(5), 1409–1427 (2012)
21. Collect, Manage, Visualize and Explore your Data. (n.d.). http://www.dhis2.org/
22. Hatch, J.A.: Doing Qualitative Research in Education Settings. SUNY Press, Albany (2002)
23. Creswell, J.W.: Research Design: Qualitative, Quantitative, and Mixed Method Approaches. Sage, Thousand Oaks (2003)
24. Braun, V., Clarke, V.: Using thematic analysis in psychology. Qual. Res. Psychol. **3**(2), 77–101 (2006)
25. Ryan, G.W., Bernard, H.R.: Techniques to identify themes. Field Methods **15**(1), 85–109 (2003)
26. Gerring, J.: Case Study Research: Principles and Practices. Cambridge University Press, New York (2007)

S. Russpatrick

27. Weber, M.: The Methodology of the Social Sciences. Free Press, Glencoe (1949)
28. Lopreato, J., Alston, L.: Ideal types and the idealization strategy. Am. Sociol. Rev. **35**(1), 88–96 (1970)
29. Ohlsson, S., Lehtinen, E.: Abstraction and the acquisition of complex ideas. Int. J. Educ. Res. **27**(1), 37–48 (1997). https://doi.org/10.1016/s0883-0355(97)88442-x
30. Alhojilan, M.: Thematic analysis: a critical review of its process and evaluation. West East J. Soc. Sci. **1**(1), 39–47 (2012)
31. Patton, M.Q.: Qualitative Research and Evaluation Methods, 3rd edn. SAGE, Thousands Oaks (2002)
32. Nicholson, B., Nielsen, P., Saebo, J., Sahay, S.: Exploring tensions of global public good platforms for development: the case of DHIS2. In: Nielsen, P., Kimaro, H.C. (eds.) ICT4D 2019. IAICT, vol. 551, pp. 207–217. Springer, Cham (2019). https://doi.org/10.1007/978-3-030-18400-1_17
33. Ghazawneh, A., Henfridsson, O.: Balancing platform control and external contribution in third-party development: The boundary resources model. Inf. Syst. J. **23**(2), 173–192 (2013)
34. Hanseth, O., Lyytinen, K.: Design theory for dynamic complexity in information infrastructures: the case of building internet. J. Inf. Technol. **25**(1), 1–19 (2010). https://doi.org/10.1057/jit.2009.19
35. Parker, G., Van Alstyne, M.W., Jiang, X.: Platform ecosystems: how developers invert the firm. Boston University Questrom School of Business Research Paper, 2861574 (2016)
36. Kallinikos, J., et al.: The ambivalent ontology of digital artifacts. MIS Q. **37**(2), 357–370 (2013). https://doi.org/10.25300/misq/2013/37.2.02
37. Foerderer, J., Kude, T., Schuetz, S.W., Heinzl, A.: Knowledge boundaries in enterprise software platform development: antecedents and consequences for platform governance. Inf. Syst. J. **29**(1), 119–144 (2019)
38. Nambisan, S., Sawhney, M.: Orchestration processes in network-centric innovation: evidence from the field. Acad. Manag. Perspect. **25**(3), 40–57 (2011)
39. Gawer, A.: Bridging differing perspectives on technological platforms: toward an integrative framework. Res. Policy **43**(7), 1239–1249 (2014)
40. Hagiu, A., Wright, J.: Multi-Sided platforms. SSRN Electron. J. (2015). https://doi.org/10.2139/ssrn.2794582
41. Wenger, E., McDermott, R.A., et al.: Cultivating Communities of Practice: A Guide to Managing Knowledge. Harvard Business School Press, Boston (2002)
42. Probst, G., Borzillo, S.: Why communities of practice succeed and why they fail. Eur. Manag. J. **26**(5), 335–347 (2008). https://doi.org/10.1016/j.emj.2008.05.003
43. Wenger, E., Snyder, W.M.: Communities of practice: the organizational frontier. Harvard Bus. Rev. **78**, 139–145 (2000)
44. Ikerd, J.: Organization for Competitive Markets. University of Missouri, Organization for Competitive Markets (1999). http://web.missouri.edu/ikerdj/papers/Rethinking.html
45. D'Souza, J.F., Adams, C.K.: On unenlightened altruism. J. Hum. Values **20**(2), 183–191 (2014). https://doi.org/10.1177/0971685814539416
46. Elster, J.: Social norms and economic theory. J. Econ. Perspect. **3**(4), 99–117 (1989)

Transforming Healthcare

Power, Technology and Empowerment

A Case Study of Community Health Workers in India

Priyanka Pandey[✉] and Yingqin Zheng

Royal Holloway, University of London, Egham, UK
priyanka.pandey.2017@live.rhul.ac.uk, Yingqin.Zheng@rhul.ac.uk

Abstract. This paper addresses the importance of using a power perspective to understand the social impact of technology in society. We use the Foucauldian concept of technologies-of-the-self to highlight the dialectical relationship between dominating structures of power and the individual capabilities of human actors, as mediated through technology, within a given context. This is done by studying the use of an mHealth intervention by health workers within a PHC (primary health care) centre in India. The study generates theoretical implications for understanding the processes of empowerment through technology within a developing country context.

Keywords: mHealth · Power · Self · Empowerment · Foucault

1 Introduction

Community health workers (CHWs) in developing countries build bridges between the formal health systems and rural communities, working to improve the relevance, acceptability, and accessibility of formal health services. Functions of CHWs include conducting home visits, assessment and preventive treatment of disease, data collection and reporting, education and counselling and referrals for further care [1, 3]. By directly visiting households, CHWs increase access to healthcare for groups which are particularly difficult to reach, such as secluded women, the extremely poor, or the lowest classes of society subject to stigmatization [3].

The introduction of information and communication technologies (ICTs) to rural CHWs has been shown to bridge lacunae in their work environment resulting from under-capacitated facilities, constrained access to information and delayed responses to emergencies [1, 3]. From a health systems and practitioner's point of view, mHealth research focuses more on problematizing the existing inefficiencies of the health system and sees technology as a solution to improve the workflow of the CHWs which could lead to an improvement in health outcomes [1, 3, 4, 17, 27].

Such studies have shown that health workers could easily learn how to use mobile phones and apps and, once trained, found the tools available via a mobile to be useful in relation to reinforcing and improving the services they already offer [1]. Some other studies reported that the use of mobile technologies improved CHW motivation and

© IFIP International Federation for Information Processing 2020
Published by Springer Nature Switzerland AG 2020
R. K. Bandi et al. (Eds.): IFIPJWC 2020, IFIP AICT 601, pp. 165–179, 2020.
https://doi.org/10.1007/978-3-030-64697-4_13

improved their credibility in the community [5, 11, 21]. In contrast, ICT4D research on mHealth often focuses on the failure of technology's ability to deliver its outcomes and becoming largely a medium of control and surveillance for the CHWs [18, 21, 26].

In this paper we seek to explore these contradictory effects of mHealth through a case study of health workers in a public-private partnership managed primary health care (PHC) centre in Karnataka, India. The study focuses on the perspective of CHWs [5, 11, 21] and how technology shapes their relations with the health system and their sense of the self. Using the Foucauldian concept of *technologies of the self*, we will be explicating the complex relationship between technology and empowerment of individual health workers, or the lack thereof, as situated in existing power structures. We argue that *technology simultaneously shapes the individual sense of self of CHWs and the structural reproduction of power, while mediating the dialectic relations between the two.*

In the rest of the paper, we will first review existing research on CHWs and mHealth, then introduce Foucault's concept of *technologies of the self* as our theoretical perspective, before presenting the case study and discussion.

2   Community Health Workers in India

In India, the foundation of the rural health system is grounded in the network of PHC (primary health care) centres and is also the main link to India's CHW programs [9, 27]. The CHW program includes 3 cadres of health workers. The ANM or the *Auxiliary nurse midwife* is the first cadre of health workers and provides care at the sub-centre level (housed under the PHC level). Their main responsibilities include providing preventive, curative care to beneficiaries in the villages she visits, collecting beneficiary information from the field and reporting it to the PHC centre [21, 27]. The second is the *Anganwadi* Workers (AWW), who work solely at the village level and focus on the provision of health education and nutritional supplementation to young children, adolescent girls, and lactating women [11, 21, 27]. The most recently created cadre is the *Accredited Social Health Activist* (ASHA), who also work at the village/community level. ASHA workers are given performance-based incentives and aid in facilitating institutional birth deliveries, immunizations, provision of basic medicines, referral of patients to the sub-centre and assisting the ANMs/AWWs whenever required [27].

Today many aspects plague the ANM and ASHA workflow processes [4, 9, 11, 18, 27, 29]. A systematic review done on the ASHA program [9] looked at the various individual, environmental (health systems), and community level factors that affected CHW workers. At an individual level and community level, what motivated CHWs were the aspects of altruism and social responsibility of their job role. Being able to participate in community meetings, receiving peer support and receiving recognition of their work in the eyes of the community. At the level of the health systems however, CHWs appeared to be demotivated due to increases in workload, changing and overlapping health programs, limited autonomy to move around and execution of responsibilities, poor training and incentivization [1, 9, 11]. For instance, the unavailability of drugs at the sub-centre due to the stockout and long replenishment times grounded in the poor communication between the ASHAs and ANMs and their supervisor at the PHC centre, would lead for community members/beneficiaries to resort to informal private health care providers. Then poor training and supportive supervision would render the CHWs having inadequate level of knowledge. Being asked to constantly attend refresher trainings at health centres to remote areas took away their personal time, making them feel overburdened. This also led to them having a sense of limited autonomy at work to perform their social responsibilities beyond the specified guidelines [4, 9]. Subsequent studies across India have consistently found similar issues and have called for reforming the CHW program to enhance their motivation and capability to contribute to PHC system's performance [11, 20, 27, 29, 30]. As Som [30] points out, "one of the more salient of these was exemplified by the thwarting effect that public blaming and shaming and reprimands have upon CHWs' motivation and job (dis)satisfaction. Over the years, CHWs have ended up as the last link in the health workforce" [30].

Consequently, CHWs are undermined in their ability and credibility to represent the community, while being expected to meet the targets and demands of the health system [29]. For rural women becoming an ASHA/ANM/AWW is seen as an opportunity for empowerment – individually, socially and to some extent financially. Yet because they are placed at the nexus of the health care delivery system and their community, existing problems from both sides affect their efficacy [4, 9, 11, 27]. Meanwhile, many studies show that the involvement of locally based NGOs and community-based organizations to aid state governments through public-private partnerships have been a complimentary mechanism to support and empower CHWs [1, 9, 11, 27], and external norms such as rewards, incentives, and positive feedback, among others, can also improve health worker motivation [1, 27].

3   Community Health Workers and mHealth

In the Indian context, many PHC and district centres through public-private partnerships have prevailed, wherein NGOs with/and external funding agencies or private companies in partnership with the respective state health governments intervene with mHealth interventions to provide support for health workers in their workflow processes. Some examples include ICTCCS in Bihar [4] mSakhi in Maharashtra [23], ImTecho In Gujarat [17], ReMind in UP [24], CPHM in Karnataka [19] and MfM in Jharkhand [11].

The ICTCCS [4] mHealth application in Bihar was used to increase the coverage, quality, and coordination of maternal, child and reproductive health services. The use of the mHealth application did improve certain behaviors amongst the beneficiaries in terms of prenatal and antenatal care registrations and follow ups. But, while for the ASHAs the mHealth application became a medium of increased knowledge and increase in self-confidence, however due to the equalizing of the roles in the process of task shifting as brought by the technology, the AWWs felt less confident and the need for more training. This had a direct effect on the reinforcement of existing coordination problems between the ASHAs and AWWs. Another aspect that led to the weak reception of the mHealth application was the parallel continuation of the paper-based system which lead to an increase in burden of the workflow for the CHWs [4].

While there are some improvements in the workflow processes and an increase in self-efficacy cited by CHWs using mHealth interventions, they are also plagued with several social and infrastructural constraints [4, 11, 17–19, 24, 26]. Infrastructural barriers include poor electricity, lack of mobile connectivity, faulty hardware, lack of charging points, theft, security, poor roads, poor PHC facilities. Social barriers include the existing lack of trust in the public health care system by communities, prevalence of traditional and religious beliefs/practices of giving birth at home, poor credibility of CHWs due to lack of knowledge, training, and poor communication with their PHC supervisors leading to data discrepancies in the PHC system [1, 3, 11, 19, 21, 27].

Similar findings were established through the Mobile for Mothers (MfM) project [11]. The mHealth application was conceptualized by two NGOs in collaboration with the state of Jharkhand for use by CHWs to improve the delivery of maternal services and the health awareness regarding maternal knowledge. Low literacy levels, technical and infrastructural problems affected the effectiveness of the MfM application. On the other hand, the app also facilitated improvement in sharing of health knowledge between CHWs and community members [11].

Existing infrastructural and local health system level problems can be both limiting or enabling factors to mHealth intervention effectiveness [10, 18, 30]. Overall, these factors point to the complexity of introducing mHealth technology within the Indian public health care system. We will be using the Foucauldian concept of technologies of the self, to bring to light, the dialectical interplay between the individual capability of health workers and the health system that governs their role.

4   Technologies of the Self

Studies conducted on power within IS and ICT4D, emphasize firstly, on how technology further reinforces the status quo and solidifies institutional structures of overt power [2, 6]. Secondly, they make visible the struggles and politics amongst the users, designers and the senior management or people in positions of power, when in theory these technologies were meant to empower the workforce or the underprivileged by the so called enlightened leaders [2, 6, 18, 26, 31]. While the above studies explain how technology becomes a medium of control and reinforcement of power, they do not delve deeply into the subtleties of the power processes that arise at the individual level. Technology is developed, implemented, and used within the prevailing rationale [6]. Human actors constantly find themselves being further subjected to dominating rules and norms of the organization they are a part of, while using technology [2] – yet many studies also show unintended consequences arising from technology use [22]. What requires more attention then, is to unearth the various subjectivities a human actor enacts, during technology use. On the one hand an individual is subjected to reproduction of power, ascribing technology use to the norms and rules of the dominant rationale. On the other hand, technology can be perceived and used in an unanticipated manner due to various social factors or interpretive flexibility at an individual level [2, 6, 31]. It becomes imperative then to also explicate this dialectical relationship between structural reinforcement of power and individual capability during technology use to understand organizational/institutional change.

Foucault's theory of relational power is a useful starting point to study technologies-of-the-self, as the *self* is embedded in relations of power, of everyday practices [14, 16]. For Foucault 'human subjectivity' is constituted within and through social practices.

Here, subjectivity is taken to be something that varies according to, more or less, what one might call a social role [13]. Where human actors in different contextual situations act in accordance with the role they imbibe as embedded in social and power relationships. However, this does not mean that every time there is a change in a situation, human actors transform into a different constitution of themselves [16]. "We acquire our practices, and so they are habitual; thus, even though subjectivity is relative to social practices, since practices are themselves repeated habitually over time, this implies the continuity in subjectivity" [13].

By *technologies of the self*, Foucault [7] does not really refer to technological arte-facts but *techniques* or processes, i.e. relationships. He stipulates that the human actor operates simultaneously in two terrains: the inside and the outside. Dimensions located 'outside' of the human subject are those that revolve around how knowledge and power are subjected on human actors and how human subjects act upon each other [7, 14, 16]. However, in his later work he focuses more on the 'inside' terrain i.e. relationship which human actors have with themselves - how the 'ethical' and 'moral' relationship with oneself can be derived from power and knowledge without being dependent on them [13, 16]. Foucault conceptualizes this relationship as the 'double' which is the interiorization of the outside, doubling of one's own relations with others, termed as 'subjectactivation' [13].

He advocates subjectactivation involves ethical self-care, aesthetic self-stylization, and critical self-awareness [7, 13, 16]. The ethical self reflects the aesthetic concern in which individuals hold the 'will to live a beautiful life' by applying certain values, reproducing certain examples, and depicting a virtuosity in their lives [13]. He then defines morality as encompassing a moral code and the behavior in relation to that code, between which there are varying degrees of compliance in practice [13, 16]. Moral codes act as guiding principles that shape the individual's self-assessment on how they should go about their lives and conduct themselves [7]. "It is through the practices of these moral codes that individuals become ethical agents and in such ethical work, subjectivity is approached" [14]. For Foucault, the need for ethics today is not to develop a tool to gain mastery over others, but for something that would help human actors to obtain their own freedom. He argues that freedom from governmentality of individualization can take place through an everyday aesthetic stylization of the self: "a constant reinvention of the self at the level of the micro-physics of existence" [16]. Foucault emphasizes that only through a critical awareness of the limitations of the self in one's cultural conditions can the outside be folded into the inside to create change [7, 13].

While Foucault's earlier work has been critiqued for ignoring the human actor's ability to resist practices of domination i.e. the exercise of agency [31], his work on technologies-of-the-self does try to address change arising from the human actor's ability. As Foucault [16] focuses more on the local, intimate operations of power, it is possible to examine how everyday reproduction of power can affect capabilities of human actors [16, 31], and provide a useful lens to study contestation of the subjectivity at an individual level. Through this lens researchers can study how the individual becomes a subject of power within the dominant discourse of the organization while also having some individual capacity at the level of the ethical/moral self.

When it comes to linking Foucault with technology use, Bloomfield [2] stresses that in seeing "reality as materially heterogeneous and relational, it becomes valuable to employ Foucault's relational notion of power. This is because technology increasingly mediates how power circulates, is exercised and what it produces".

5   Methodology

5.1   Research Site

The PHC (primary health care) centre where this study was conducted is located at the foothills of the Biligirirangana (BR) hills in the Yelandur taluk within the Chamrajnagar district of the southern state of Karnataka, India. It has a relatively high population of indigenous people and is one of the worse-off districts with respect to health and development [12, 28]. Most of the indigenous people in this district live in and around thickly forested and hilly areas, that are not typical of the most other regions in Karnataka. The hills are also a home to the Soliga tribal population of 23,000 individuals that have dwelled in the forests of BR hills for centuries [28].

The PHC centre there is managed through a public private partnership model, where the state government of Karnataka in collaboration with a local NGO is responsible for the provision of the required human resource and logistics to deliver preventive, promotive, curative, and rehabilitative health care services to the Soliga tribal population, within the National Health Mission guidelines [12]. The NGO employs health workers, namely ANMs, ASHAs and AWWS, to go on field visits, perform ante-natal care (ANC) and pre-natal (PNC) registration, educate expectant mothers about maternal health and children on hygiene, follow up each patient throughout their pregnancy until delivery and follow up on child immunization [12]. The PHC centre consists of medical rooms, one medical officer, one administrator, one dentist, one block health education officer, four staff nurses, one pharmacist, one laboratory technician, a supervisor, five ANMs, and two male health workers (MHWs) [12].

Despite the integration of the PHC system, much of the rural population still suffered from acute chronic diseases and did not primarily depend on the PHC due to their existing faith in traditional medicine and practices. Even with involvement of the health workers who are chosen from the community, much of the population found it 'inconvenient' to travel to the PHC center. It would cost 30 rupees (0.03 GBP) to go from the BR hills to the foothills, which is where the PHC centre is located, to get medical treatment or advice. Hence health workers become pivotal in providing this population with preventive services and for linking them with the PHC centre. In 2015, an mHealth intervention i.e. an android tablet was launched to assist and streamline the health worker's workflow which was plagued with issues (discussed in detail in the findings). The tablet is mainly used by the ANMs and few ASHAs who assist them and is mostly centered around maternal and child health services. It houses a plethora of specialized features relating to ante-natal care registration, post-natal care registration, child-birth registration, child immunization record maintenance, record maintenance on follow-up care, treatments and tests of maternal beneficiaries and beneficiary ID records. The tablet contains features of storability and retrievability of information, smoother interface to feed in and view the data, the aspect of connectivity and syncing of the data from the tablet to the computer systems in the PHC centre, automatic collation of data through the inbuilt software, GPS functionality and a reminder system. The ANMs were also provided with training on how to use the tablet by the engineers. Even today the ANMs continue to have monthly sessions with the engineers for training and provide feedback on the tablet use [12].

5.2 Data Collection and Analysis

Data collection centered specifically, around the use of the mHealth intervention by the ANMs and few ASHAs and by the PHC staff and was done during the implementation phase of the mHealth app. Data collection methods included semi-structured interviews and field observation [25]. Field observation was used to shadow health workers and observe what a typical routine day looked like for them. This helped as an indirect guide to develop the interview topic guide, as the observation gave an understanding of the points at which the interaction with the tablet by the ANMs was the deepest. Visual aids in the form of photographs, video and audio recordings were taken during the interview and observation process, which later assisted in creating iteration in the thematic coding process. Secondary material was also collected in the form of paper health records that the health workers used as an original template to compare and match up the electronic data.

Interviews were conducted, whilst the ANMs and ASHAs were conducting their routine day to day duties. The staff at the PHC centre were interviewed separately whilst the health workers were not around. The interviews have been organized in a semi-structured way, for the health workers to develop their own recounts of how they felt about the use of the tablet in their existing work processes. Field observation was used to cross-reference and helped understand the link between the health worker's account with the accounts given by the PHC staff. Thematic coding was performed to visualize patterns. Patterns regarding health workers correlated along codes such as 'self-confidence' 'happiness' 'burden' 'workload' whereas patterns regarding the PHC staff's account correlated along keywords such as 'trust' 'accountability' 'improvement' 'tracking' 'timely'. Codes were created, and later categorized into broader themes. Similar or repetitive codes were merged. The analysis process was informed by an inductive approach, wherein the researcher was able to identify certain emerging patterns and themes based on the answers by the interviewees and link it to the appropriate constructs of power.

Please note that the focus of this study is purely around the use of the mHealth android tablet by the ANMs, few ASHAs and the PHC staff. While the data from the tablet is synced into the MCTS (HIS) platform, through the PHC centre, that is not the focus of this study. Next, as this mHealth intervention is implemented only in this particular PHC centre, it is not representative of other mHealth interventions or PHC centres in India. The actual name of the tablet has been anonymized, but it has been acknowledged that all the data collected and stored in the tablet is fed into the MCTS (governmental HIS) platform via the PHC centre computer systems once a month. The data for this study was collected during the implementation phase of the mHealth app.

6 Findings

The original method of data collection and reporting on maternal and child health such as: ante and post-natal care registration, childbirth and immunization registrations and follow up on treatments and care, would entail the health workers (ANMs) to manually write and record data in paper-based registers. Each health worker would be allotted a set of household visits to conduct within their given radius. The health worker during these house visits, would have discussions with the beneficiaries about their health, ongoing treatments, registration and follow ups. She would then manually fill the required health information in the register. Sometimes the health worker would conduct 20-30 household visits in a day and the data would be filled in 25-30 registers. This would then be reported to the PHC centre at the end of the week. This process of manually filling up registers and collating the data, alongside doing the house visits, and then reporting to the PHC centre (which was based at the foothills) was time consuming and cumbersome. This was also, many times, impossible for a one ANM to do at a single time, so other junior health workers (ASHAs) would assist them. The pressure of collecting data from many households and reporting it on time often lead to errors in the data. There would also be a time lag in the reporting process. The lag and error in data would especially prove to be problematic during emergency cases, when the PHC centre would be unequipped to provide the right kind of treatment or care, and there would be delayed response times, sometimes even resulting in patient mortality. This inadequacy would be attributed to the health workers, thereby damaging their credibility both from the PHC staff's and communities' perspective.

6.1 Psychological Empowerment of CHWs

Streamlining of Data Collection and Reporting
The introduction of the tablet has considerably streamlined the above processes. The tablet affords the aspect of portability, automatic data collation, ease of data retrievability, storability and an easier interface to view the data. The tablet comes with an inbuilt software that contains various features to assist the health worker in filling out data systematically. It contains different categories and sections for different kinds of (pre-natal, post-natal and child immunization) registrations, symptoms, and follow up. This aspect of the tablet made it easier for the health worker to fill in the correct information in the right section, which was then automatically collated by the in-built software. Just like the registers, the tablets are also amenable to being physically carried to different households. They are easy to carry and store all the information in just one tablet instead of multiple registers. These process changes inadvertently affected the relationship between the health workers and the PHC staff. Their supervisor at the PHC centre was noted saying:

"although we always trusted the judgment of the health workers as they are the ones who directly interact with the community, but due to the poor data quality it was difficult to take their judgment on the patients seriously…the data was of poor quality because of them… the registers reported to us would be filled with mistakes and delays.

But today they are the primary users of the tablet itself and are also the ones who put the data in it which is then reported to us. This improvement in reporting has increased our trust on them, the data has less errors and as soon as the tablet catches connectivity it syncs the data collected by them into the PHC computer system"

Aiding in High Risk Cases

The automatic collation feature of the tablet has helped in improving the response time for tending to high-risk pregnancies. In the former case, a high-risk patient would not get the immediate attention or care, due to the delayed response time caused by the delayed and errored data reporting. This would render the PHC staff unequipped to provide the correct treatment to the patients. But the in-built feature of the tablet, automatically collates the data and starts beeping red in front the beneficiary name, who might need immediate assistance. This notifies the health worker who then notifies the PHC staff by calling them from their mobile phone. And, if there is good internet connectivity in the region then the tablet automatically syncs this information into the PHC system as well. This aspect of streamlining the process of providing care in emergency cases, has made some health workers feel acknowledged for the work they do for the community today, one of the ANMs was noted saying: *"We feel motivated to do our job now. Before, even the community members would blame us for not being able to deal with emergency situations. But today we have more confidence when it comes to dealing with emergency cases. We feel happy to be able to serve our community and get recognized for it".*

Health Workers were noted saying that they felt *happiness (khushi)* with this change in perception by their PHC staff. Today they feel that they are relied on for their feedback, as they are the ones who feed the data in the tablet. They feel important in the community and are taken more seriously – *"We feel more valued by the community for what we do today. The PHC staff take us more seriously now and sometimes the PHC staff now even ask for our opinion, especially when it comes to certain serious cases. They ask our opinion when they are going through the beneficiary information that has been put by us in the tablet".* Here we see that the aspect of 'faulting' the health workers, for the inefficiency in the data reporting and collecting process, as being reduced. This is leading to a change of their own self-perception. They feel they are better perceived by their community and the PHC staff for what they do.

6.2   Infrastructural and Structural Constraints

Mobile Connectivity and Charging Issues

However, there are also several concerns that prevail surrounding the use of the tablet. For instance, mobile connectivity is a key aspect that is required to enable the data from the tablet to be synced to the PHC centre systems. Another important aspect is the tablet having enough battery charge throughout the process of the data collection by the health worker. Every time the tablet would run out of battery charge or the internet data pack, the ANMs would have to return to the PHC centre. As Chamrajnagar is a rural and tribal area, electricity issues are prevalent. The ANMs would have to constantly make an effort to make trips to the PHC centre, which is all the way at the foothills and far off from the beneficiary houses, to sync the data or charge the tablet. As noted by one of the ANMs, *"during busy period, it becomes quite tiring to go all the way back to the PHC centre to sync the data or charge the tablet as there is better connectivity and electricity there, especially when I am in the middle of collecting beneficiary information. Sometimes the tablet would have to be left there (PHC centre) overnight for charging which means I would have to travel all the way to the PHC centre again to pick up the tablet".*

Increase in Workload

The ANMs were also asked to collect beneficiary identification (ID) information to have a digital repository of the IDs of the members of the village. One of them was recorded saying *"You see in the beginning of using the tablet, we were also going from one house to another to collect their identification information. So now if someone loses their ID card or forgets to get it to the PHC or sub-centre, they can still come and get treated as their identification information is digitally recorded."* However, ANMs were also noted that this process of collecting ID information in addition to their existing responsibilities was time consuming and cumbersome. Especially as many community members were reluctant to give their personal or family information.

Then the aspect of using registers and the tablet simultaneously, was also creating issues of duplication of data and dual entry of data. Health workers feared that they might be asked to show the registers by the district officers or PHC staff, or that the tablet might undergo a hardware issue. While health workers preferred using the tablet as it is easier to carry and automatically collates the information, they complained about feeling overburdened: *"initially we had to only fill in registers the information we collected in our routine visits. But now since the use of the tablet we had to take all the already existing information from the registers and put it in the tablet and also collect the beneficiary identification information, while doing our routine visits!".* The health workers felt overburdened with the duplicity of the work.

Monitoring and Surveillance

Lastly, the aspect of the reminder feature and the implementation of an electronic dashboard at the PHC centre would entail that the health workers could be monitored. If a health worker forgets or is running behind her schedule of conducting a follow-up or house visit, the tablet would send her a reminder. The aspect of there being a probable dashboard would also help the PHC staff to keep an eye on the progress of health worker's workflow from the centre. Upon asking the health workers about these aspects, we received a twofold answer, some health workers were noted as saying that the reminder feature greatly helped them in remembering certain visits if they forgot, like immunization visits etc. However, some others showed disgruntlement on being monitored during their routine work processes and wanted the space and freedom to do their tasks at their own pace, time, and suitability.

7 Discussion

In this section we will use *technologies of the self* as a sensitizing lens to explain the inside and outside terrain of the health worker.

Outside Terrain

According to Foucault [14], every individual is caught in a network of power relations through which they are constituted as a subject. "Power both subjugates and makes subject to as it applies itself to immediate everyday life which categorizes the individual, marks him by his own individuality, attaches himself to his identity, imposes a law of truth on him which he must recognize and which others have to recognize in him. It is a form of power which makes individual subjects" [14]. In our case, the social role or identity of the health worker is defined by the country's National Rural Health Program where they are historically seen as a link between the community and formal health services [27, 30].

However, over the years the role of CHWs has morphed more into one of a 'health data/information collector from the field' [3]. Technology in such a scenario, is only implicated in the existing norms and rules surrounding the health workers, so technology intervenes as a medium to assist the health worker in collecting information from the field. The various features of technology such as storability, retrievability, reminder facility, mobile connectivity, simpler user interface, and automatic data collation then become a medium of domination over the health worker. Structurally and institutionally, the 'health worker role' does not permit them to question the legitimacy of the use of the technology or its features. Therefore, they become docile users of technology and does what it tells them to do, even if they find certain aspects of it inconvenient for themselves. For instance, the health worker is compelled to conduct a house visit when the tablet reminds her, or visit the PHC centre when the tablet runs out of the internet data pack or battery, conscious of the fact that her activities might be monitored by the PHC centre through the electronic dashboard. Even when overburdened with the extra workload, she normalizes it as part of the work routine rather than to resist it. It short, while technology helped address the accountability of the health workers from PHC center's perspective, it also constituted a *disciplinary power* over them. Technology as implicated in existing rules and norms becomes a *technique of domination and discipline* governing the conduct/role of the health workers which produces their subjectivity.

Inside Terrain

However, community healthcare work also has a *moral dimension* to it [10]. Existing CHW studies have highlighted the value that health workers attribute to their role and responsibilities [8–10, 15]. For instance, in Nepal [8], CHWs apparently resisted financial rewards, which they believed would undermine their social standing and detract from the purity of their altruistic motivation towards their work. In India, CHWs similarly felt a sense of pride and moral worth from their work [9]. Such institutional rhetoric arguably then "shapes CHWs' own political subjectivities, motivations, and capacities" [10]. Therefore, health workers imbibe more than one subjectivity towards their role. There is an aspect of selflessness and care of providing health care to their community. On the other hand, their role and duties are also subjected upon them by the broader health care policy norms and rules. In many countries, CHWs programs appear to be largely politicized and so CHWs are generally at pains to truly emphasize their 'passion' and desire to 'serve the people' [10, 15].

The use of technology thus mediates the production of multiple subjectivities of CHWs. The relationships they have with other health workers, the PHC staff and the community also shape their perception and enactment of the technology. For instance, the decrease in data errors and improved syncing of data, inadvertently reduced the blame that the PHC centre landed on the health workers and this then (inadvertently) had a positive psychological effect on them. Health workers felt an increase in their self-efficacy; in being recognized for their work. There is a double inadvertence here and this is where the *subjectactivation* of the health worker emerges. The use of technology by the health worker is inscribed in the rules, norms and guidelines as stipulated by the state, designers, and national health policy rationale, giving them little or no space to ask for a change. However, even in this subjugated use of technology, the health workers find spaces of psychological empowerment, i.e. an increase in their self-efficacy and their moral sense of self arising from improved perceptions of them, by the PHC staff and community members.

While describing technologies of the self, Foucault [7] explains the relevance of the moral/ethical and aesthetic self and critical self-awareness. We focus only on the aspect of the moral self where the health workers by feeling an increase in their self-efficacy, attune to their altruistic and selfless aspect of their health worker role. They feel good in doing something for their community and in being appreciated for it, rather than being blamed for the inefficiencies. Here the emergence of the moral self does not necessarily give rise to a new or invented practice, but it is essentially the folding of the everyday existing practices to also recognize an *'other version'* of the self. While feminist literature talks about the relevance of the technologies-of-self lens as a way to counter structures of oppressive power, in our case, the lens reveals how technology mediates the reconciliation and tension between individual efficacy (capability) and the domination of power, where health workers feel a degree of psychological empowerment through the moral self, albeit situated within the larger reproduction of structural power. The technology artefact while perceived as a 'technology of domination' also helps negotiate new meanings for the job role of the health worker, who is placed at the crux of the contradiction between the two.

Foucault [13] states the aspect of 'subjectactivation' should be derived from existing power and knowledge, but without being dependent on them. However, in asymmetrical power relations [16] such as the one which the health worker has with the health system, the possibility of the formation of another ethical, moral or aesthetic self is unlikely to happen without drawing upon the very power that objectifies them. The sense of self is largely derived from the very political, cultural, and institutional structures holding the individual in its place [16], which is also then inscribed into the technology artefact.

8 Conclusion

The point of this paper is not to state that the mHealth intervention was a success or failure but to highlight the subtle localized nuances of power that come into play at the individual level during technology use. Our findings align with many of the other mHealth and CHW studies done in India and other developing countries [1, 3–5, 11, 19, 20, 24]. However, our theoretical lens brings a new perspective to understanding the impact of technology on health workers during their routine workflow. Through our study, we were able to see how health workers felt psychologically empowering changes at the individual level, but as grounded within the larger structural reproduction of power of the health system, both of which were mediated by technology. Foucault's concept of technologies of the self, becomes important in addressing how technology mediates the dialectical interplay between the individual self and structures of domination. Even within the everyday relational flows of power, technology can assist human actors to ascribe to a, other (version) self of themselves. However, it is also important to note that recognition of the ethical or moral self, itself does not challenge existing structures of power, or transform one's position within the dominant discourse [16]. According to Foucault [7, 14] only severe critical reflection about the paradoxes of one's life achieved through the moral and ethical self, in conjunction with other human actors can create resistance to challenge structures of oppression or transform practices. Thus, our theoretical insight can form a useful starting point to critically understand the processes of empowerment and its link with technology. Empirically it highlights the importance of recognizing the power and technology interplay in the digitization of community health work processes in developing countries like India.

While our study was conducted over one month, for future research it would be even more beneficial if a longitudinal study would be conducted. That would help map out the processes of transformative change as mediated through technology e.g. if the health workers now are informally or formally included in decision-making at the PHC level or if policy changes around health worker's roles have been institutionally made.

References

1. Agarwal, S., Perry, H., Long, L., Labrique, A.: Evidence on feasibility and effective use of mHealth strategies by frontline health workers in developing countries: systematic review. Tropical Med. Int. Health **20**, 1003–1014 (2015)
2. Bloomfield, B.: Power, machines and social relations: delegating to information technology in the national health service. Organization **2**, 489–518 (1995)
3. Braun, R., Catalani, C., Wimbush, J., Israelski, D.: Community health workers and mobile technology: a systematic review of the literature. PLoS ONE **8**, e65772 (2013)
4. Carmichael, S., et al.: Use of mobile technology by frontline health workers to promote reproductive, maternal, newborn and child health and nutrition: a cluster randomized controlled Trial in Bihar, India. J. Glob. Health **9**, 0204249 (2019)
5. Chib, A., Lwin, M., Ang, J., Lin, H., Santoso, F.: Midwives and mobiles: using ICTs to improve healthcare in Aceh Besar, Indonesia. Asian J. Commun. **18**, 348–364 (2008)
6. Doolin, B.: Information technology as disciplinary technology: being critical in interpretive research on information systems. J. Inf. Technol. **13**, 301–311 (1998)
7. Fornet-betancourt, R., Becker, H., Gomez-Müller, A., Gauthier, J.: The ethic of care for the self as a practice of freedom. Phil. Soc. Criticism **12**, 112–131 (1987)
8. Glenton, C., Scheel, I., Pradhan, S., Lewin, S., Hodgins, S., Shrestha, V.: The female community health volunteer programme in Nepal: decision makers' perceptions of volunteerism, payment and other incentives. Soc. Sci. Med. **70**, 1920–1927 (2010)
9. Gopalan, S., Mohanty, S., Das, A.: Assessing community health workers' performance motivation: a mixed-methods approach on India's Accredited Social Health Activists (ASHA) programme (2012)

10. Hampshire, K., et al.: Who bears the cost of 'informal mhealth'? Health-workers' mobile phone practices and associated political-moral economies of care in Ghana and Malawi. Health Policy Plan. **32**(1), 34–42 (2017)
11. Ilozumba, O., Dieleman, M., Kraamwinkel, N., Van Belle, S., Chaudoury, M., Broerse, J.: "I am not telling. The mobile is telling": factors influencing the outcomes of a community health worker mHealth intervention in India. PLOS ONE **13**, e0194927 (2018)
12. Trust, K.: Karuna Trust Annual Report. Karuna Trust, Bangalore (2020)
13. Kelly, M.: Foucault, subjectivity, and technologies of the Self. In: Falzon, C., O'Leary, T., Sawicki, J. (eds.) A Companion to Foucault, pp. 510–525. Blackwell Publishing Limited (2013)
14. Kemp, P., Dreyfus, H., Rabinow, P., Foucault, M.: Michel Foucault. Beyond Structuralism and Hermeneutics. History and Theory, vol. 23, p. 84 (1984)
15. Maes, K.: "Volunteers are not paid because they are priceless": community health worker capacities and values in an aids treatment intervention in urban ethiopia. Med. Anthropol. Q. **29**, 97–115 (2014)
16. Markula, P.: The technologies of the self: sport, feminism, and foucault. Sociol. Sport J. **20**, 87–107 (2003)
17. Modi, D., et al.: Cluster randomized trial of a mHealth intervention "ImTeCHO" to improve delivery of proven maternal, neonatal, and child care interventions through community-based Accredited Social Health Activists (ASHAs) by enhancing their motivation and strengthening supervision in tribal areas of Gujarat, India: study protocol for a randomized controlled trial. Trials **18** (2017)
18. Mukherjee, A.: Understanding empowerment through technology driven power structures: Case from mother and child tracking system in India. In: International Federation of Information Processing (IFIP) 9.4, Proceedings of the 13th International Conference on Social Implications of Computers in Developing Countries, Negembo (2015)
19. Naik, P., Shilpa, D., Shewade, H., Sudarshan, H.: Assessing the implementation of a mobile App-based electronic health record: a mixed-method study from South India. J. Educ. Health Prom. **9**, 102 (2020)
20. Nimmagadda, S., et al.: Effects of an mHealth intervention for community health workers on maternal and child nutrition and health service delivery in India: protocol for a quasi-experimental mixed-methods evaluation. BMJ Open **9**, e025774 (2019)
21. Nyemba-Mudenda, M., Chigona, W.: mHealth outcomes for pregnant mothers in Malawi: a capability perspective. Inf. Technol. Dev. **24**, 245–278 (2017)
22. Orlikowski, W.: Using technology and constituting structures: a practice lens for studying technology in organizations. Organ. Sci. **11**, 404–428 (2000)
23. Patel, A., et al.: M-SAKHI—mobile health solutions to help community providers promote maternal and infant nutrition and health using a community-based cluster randomized controlled trial in rural India: a study protocol. Maternal Child Nutr. **15**, e1285 (2019)
24. Prinja, S., Gupta, A., Bahuguna, P., Nimesh, R.: Cost analysis of implementing mHealth intervention for maternal, newborn & child health care through community health workers: assessment of ReMIND program in Uttar Pradesh, India. BMC Preg. Childbirth **18**, 390 (2018)
25. Ritchie, J., Lewis, J., McNaughton Nicholls, C., Ormston, R.: Qualitative Research Practice: A Guide for Social Science Students and Researchers. Sage Publications, London (2013)
26. Sahay, S.: Are we building a better world with ICTs? empirically examining this question in the domain of public health in India. Inf. Technol. Dev. **22**, 168–176 (2014)
27. Scott, K., George, A., Ved, R.: Taking stock of 10 years of published research on the ASHA programme: examining India's national community health worker programme from a health systems perspective. Health Res. Policy Syst. **17**, 29 (2019)

28. Seshadri, T., Madegowda, C., Babu, G., Nuggehalli, S.P.: Implementation research with the soliga indigenous community in Southern India for local action on improving maternal health services. SSRN Electron. J. (2019)
29. SOCHARA: An external evaluative study of the State Health Resource Centre (SHRC) and the Mitanin Programme. Society for Community Health Awareness, Research and Action, Bangalore (2005)
30. Som, M.: Volunteerism to incentivisation: changing priorities of mitanins work in Chhattisgarh. Ind. J. Gend. Stud. **23**, 26–42 (2016)
31. Willcocks, L.: Foucault, power/knowledge, and information systems: reconstructing the present. In: Willcocks, L., Mingers, J. (eds.) Social Theory and Philo sophy for Information Systems, pp. 238–296. Wiley Publishing, Chichester (2004)

Practical Affordance: EMR Use Within Outpatient Consulting on Women's Health

Ayushi Tandon[✉]

Indian Institute of Management Ahmedabad, Ahmedabad 380015, India
ayushitandon@iima.ac.in

Abstract. We have seen increased adoption of electronic medical records (EMR) to facilitate the monitoring and recording patient trajectories. Information systems and allied discipline researchers have argued that paper persistence post EMR implementation is pervasive because: limitations in the system design and institutional policies lack an understanding of the clinical workflow. I question the doctor focused and clinical workflow-oriented understanding of medical record-keeping that ideates EMR as having a role only within the hospital boundaries. By providing empirical data from two settings: a rural secondary care hospital, and a metropolitan multinational hospital, I unpack situations when patients' healthcare needs were central to the doctor's work, instead of using information technologies, i.e., EMR. The projection of EMRs as artefact limited to the hospital setting and only for clinical purposes discounts the role of patients' life world in clinical interactions, and runs the risk of devaluing the experiential and affective knowledge of both patients and doctors. EMR, I argue, cannot support doctors' work unless the patient's role is recognized. I propose that EMR systems be flexible, situated in the patient's practical context, rather than administrative and clinical work-oriented only.

Keywords: Electronic Medical Record · Affordance · Women health · Consultation · Health Information Technology

1 Introduction

"The scan shows Polycystic Ovary, so I advised her lifestyle changes for the weight reduction. I told her that she could do exercise and yoga, she should avoid junk food and drink plenty of liquids. This thing I will write [on print out] and give it to her." - Interview excerpt Dr Savitri (Corporate hospital, Metropolitan City)

"No naturally, this is will not go in the computer, something are kept verbal, most of these things are general instructions. Like, she should not sit down on the ground multiple times, she cannot do much work at home. ... If you write these things on the computer what they will understand." - Interview excerpt Dr Rita, (Secondary care hospital, Rural district)

© IFIP International Federation for Information Processing 2020
Published by Springer Nature Switzerland AG 2020
R. K. Bandi et al. (Eds.): IFIPJWC 2020, IFIP AICT 601, pp. 180–193, 2020.
https://doi.org/10.1007/978-3-030-64697-4_14

These are excerpts from the interview of two senior doctors specialized in obstetrics and gynecology (OB/GYN), working in two different hospitals. Electronic Medical Record (EMR) system used by Dr Savitri had templates specifically designed for OB/GYN consultation note taking. In the above excerpt, Dr Savitri describes patient as unmarried with chief complaint being "irregular periods (menstrual cycle)". The patient was carrying diagnostic reports and it indicated Polycystic Ovary Syndrome[1](PCOS). PCOS diagnosis provides probable explanation of infertility in women. Doctor Savitri was having understanding about stigma associated with PCOS label, especially for unmarried women, so she avoided keeping EMR. She explained patient verbally and noted instructions like "avoid junk food" on the print out of consultation notes. In another excerpt, Dr Rita shares about consultation session of a pregnant woman. The patient was working as informal manual worker (farming) and was not functionally literate. Dr Rita explained her to avoid physical exertion but nothing about this interaction was noted as part of EMR. Likewise, I encountered many instances where doctors embraced alternative ways, often called as "informal means" or "workarounds" instead of using functionalities available via EMR systems. In this article, I investigate similar situations where doctors justified their *differential use of EMR as part of ensuring practicality of interactions for women coming for consultation on sexual and reproductive health.*

Patient record is a collection of clinical information, compiled by physicians, nurses, and other health care professionals as part of the investigation and treatment trajectory of the patient [1]. The electronic versions of patient's records within an institution are called as EMR. Depending upon the information systems deployed to manage and record patient transactions, EMR may be partially or entirely realized [2]. Hospitals are investing in health information systems with special focus on having EMR systems to improve efficiency and quality of health care. Fundamental understanding of quality healthcare informing EMR design is, "managing patients' trajectories: doing investigations, monitoring, intervening and re-intervening in order to at least temporarily cure or palliate patients' problems [3]. The fields are provided in EMR systems to record clinically relevant details of patients' trajectories in standardized format for use in future. We could see similar approach towards role of medical records in providing quality care for women leading to suggestions on EMR functionality for obstetrics and gynecology consultation [4]. On the other hand, studies show that "paper persistence" post EMR implementation is pervasive in hospitals. To address this, suggestions are made to upgrade EMR features allowing for hybrid systems: digital and paper-based medical records, integrating dictations tools or appointing support staff [5, 6], or separately documenting information related to patients for which definitive pieces of evidences are not possible [7–9]. The underlying approach towards EMR in these studies is limiting as it considers EMR as document relevant only for coordinating and communication between doctors (or healthcare workers) or within clinical interactions with same doctor (follow-up visits).

Patients play critical role in coordinating and communication actions, and EMRs are also made available to patients either as physical copy (copied, print out) or digital

---

[1] Polycystic ovary syndrome (PCOS) affects 5–20% of women of reproductive age worldwide. This is stigmatized condition in India and two readings helpful in understanding its meaning in Indian context are https://feminisminindia.com/2019/06/12/pcos-women-health/ and https://www.epw.in/engage/article/how-flawed-understanding-pcos-robs-women-their.

copy (email, mobile application). EMR systems are not designed with the understanding of experiences of patients, thus excluding clinical and non-clinical complexities part of patient's life [10]. In this study, I show the implication of this exclusion on use of EMR systems by doctors within consultations. The empirical data used in this paper is part of longer project. The project involved data collection of eight doctors (and their teams) working in four diverse settings. Each setting had (some form of) electronic medical record keeping of OB/GYN outpatient consultation. Details of project are available in already published peer reviewed study [11]. In this paper, I introduce the concept of "practical affordances" by empirically engaging with affordances for whom and where not only what is affordance [12, 13].

2 Related Work

In the last two decades, EMR has emerged as a potent subject of research across information systems and allied disciplines like human computer interaction (HCI) and computer supported cooperative work (CSCW). Work practice related studies have shown that EMR systems are not standalone technologies and paper, whiteboard, post-it notes, "shadow charts" and "parallel charts" [14] are used by health care providers in place or along with EMR system functionalities. Extant literature in Information Systems area largely has 'technology deterministic' approach; researchers hold a static view of contextual realities in investigating features of EMR like problem list, clinical notes, referral notes, diagnostic order, etc. as standalone components used for coordinating and communicating clinical interventions required [5, 15]. Taking functional approach towards EMR studies shows that patient's care does not align with action (im)possibilities because of EMR design [16]. These studies limit the scope and action possibilities by healthcare providers (doctors) within the boundaries of professional work (workflow of consultation as linear) and recommend additional features that incorporate affordances of paper-based records like viewing, reviewing, annotating and amending data [17]. Research shows that health records (EMR) act as a boundary object between doctor and patient, use pattern of doctor have implications for the patient and vice versa [18]. Use of EMR benefit patients by enabling access to quality healthcare [19] and improved self-care by providing them access their medical records. Defining the scope and purpose of EMR as coordination among doctors only is limiting.

In majority of research studying EMR boils down to examining actions available to a healthcare provider (doctor), who is executing a healthcare routine. Scholars have often turned to the concept of affordances as a theoretical lens of choice [20, 21]. The concept of affordance first emerged within ecological psychology as Gibson suggested that objects have inherent capabilities because of fundamental properties determining how object can be used or interacted with. Norman extended the understanding of affordances by focusing on 'functional' or dispositional nature of affordance, as intended by designers and embedded in the objects. Markus and Silver (2008) defined affordance as "...the possibilities for goal-oriented action afforded to specified user groups by technical objects" [22]. Affordance is an interdisciplinary construct and there are many debates within the affordance literature on its definition, usage and conceptualization [23]. Kaptelinin and Nardi [24] suggest to include social and cultural aspects of human interactions by considering local/situated activities mediated by cultural tools, like technology. Prior most research on EMR has focused on affordance as "emerging" and "actualizing", broadly referring to the affordance as range of functions and constraints that EMR system provides for i.e. designed and potential affordance [25]. The critique by Davis and Chouinard [13] of these conceptualizations as "failure to account for diverse subjects and circumstances" resonated with themes I used to describe my findings.

3 Method and Sites Description

I collected data around multiple cases of EMR use within OB/GYN outpatient consultation. These cases (doctors) are located at various sites and are part of larger project. Details of project are available in already published peer reviewed study [11]. The study design was approved by institution's ethical review board and each participant (pseudonyms used) was briefed about the purpose of study before they signed the consent form. In case of functionally illiterate participants, mostly at Hospital_R, audio consent was recorded after briefing purpose of study. In some situations doctors also stepped in and took permission for me, allowing me to sit thorough the consultation sessions from patients and people accompanying them. Before starting the field work, I attended educational seminars related to medical technologies used by gynecologists and obstetricians (OB/GYN). This was used for developing an understanding of medical terminologies, and preparing initial interview protocols for doctor and patient. This paper includes data from field work done at two hospitals: One is large corporate hospitals (Hospital_U, where Dr Savitri was practicing), and another is secondary hospital in the rural part of India (Hospital_R where Dr Rita was practising). Both doctors had (some form of) electronic medical record keeping of gynecology/obstetric outpatient consultation.

The field work involved interviewing doctors in their consultation rooms (or a room chosen by interviewee located in hospital premise) and interview of patients in the hospital premise (like hospital lobby or porch or cafeteria/canteen). I conducted unstructured and conversational interviews [26] spread over duration of access granted at each research site. I also asked scenario based questions from doctors around their earlier consultation sessions, documented in my field notes. With these questions I mostly enquired about the specifics of the sessions and records related to it. Field notes and interviews were used to corroborate one another during the data analysis. All audio recordings were transcribed (including translation of interviews conducted in Hindi at Hospital_R) and, brief handwritten field notes and details of informal discussions scribbled on diary were digitalized. All the data was imported to Atlast.ti 8.0 software which was used for data management and doing structured memo writing. Principles of grounded approach [27] are applied as tool while analysing data. I have arranged my findings thematically, where "theme captures something important about the data in relation to the research question" [28]. In findings sections, I explicate the themes and show how the diverse situations resulted in differential use of computers by doctors and to maintain EMR of women as patients.

The data used in this paper are from Hospital_U (Dr Savitri) having EMR with detailed module for OB/GYN consultation and, Hospital_R (Dr Rita) EMR having basic module designed for general physician's consultation. In next Sect. 1 provide brief of both sites, followed by thematically arranged findings [28]. I followed suggestion by Stern and Pyles [29] and tried to use concept of affordance described in previous studies on EMR to tell my story (analysis); But as it did not neatly fit my work, I conceptualized "practical affordance" to describe how functionalities available via EMR systems were put to use by doctors in order to support women patients. I have also included one episodic instance from Hospital_R, reconstructed as vignettes using field notes and interview data in the hope of evoking empathy towards participants of this study [11]. Vignette allows reader to engage with situation arising in the field and supports my argument that we need to take into account practical implications of EMR features (where and when is affordances) for patients.

3.1 Dr Savitri's Context: The Urban Setting

Hospital_U was located in city identified as the' fastest growing tech hub' of India. Hospital was marketed as suitable for working couples (professionals) who were busy with their demanding and stressful careers, often involving long hours of work and travel. Most patients who came for consulting in Hospital_U were either working in multinational companies or government employees, covered under health insurance provided by their employers. Keeping medical records of patient on computer was mandatory and printed consultation notes (on A4 Sheet with hospital name on top and digitized signature of consulting doctor at bottom) were given to patient.

3.2 Dr Rita's Context: The Rural Setting

Hospital_R was located in the rural district of eastern India and patients from many neighbouring gram panchayat areas used to visit this hospital. Patients told during field work that they had to use van, bus, or auto to reach this hospital. Most people visiting Hospital_R for consultation were illiterate, some of them (mostly men) were "tenth (equivalent to high school) appeared but failed." Dr Rita was senior (more than 15 years of experience) OB/GYN consultant, assisted by Junior doctors. Patients were not given any printed consultation notes except a slip of paper (around 5 cm × 7 cm) on which their registration number, blood pressure, weight was noted using pen. Most of the patients were not able to read paper slips or records about them on computer.

4 Findings

4.1 Valuing Life World in Assessment and in Patient's Record

Doctors mentioned that they had to listen to women, their experiences and descriptions of illness. Dr Rita mentioned during interview that computers distracted her and interfered with her assessment of patients.

> *"When I see the patient, when we see a patient right from the time the patient walks in my attention goes to the patient to see it how she walks in, my diagnosis begins.*

When she comes and sits down and when I talk to her and then I understand her and by the time I examine her I take history, I go and examine her, I have some diagnosis in my mind already." - Dr Rita

Dr Savirti used to take time while interacting with patients and taking down notes on computer, she was able to spend around fifteen minutes with each patient, sometimes listening to patient and confirming previous records, updating or adding details about them on their electronic or physical files.

"First, I will understand everything, let them talk what they want to talk, let them say, you have to listen, listening, listening is important listening will give them the confidence and ok mam is hearing my problem so they feel so good. I hear so many patients tell .. .. I thought of telling my personal problem but I couldn't, I was not able to tell her because she was just talking all the medical things and she just sent me off, just like that, I wanted to talk." – Dr Savitri

Dr Savitri and Dr Rita both sourced information about health of women in dialogue with them and their care givers or person accompanying. Doctors involved people accompanying women in conversations to understand their signs, symptoms and experiences. They also ensured that people accompanying understood clinical care and health related needs of women outside hospital. This was applicable in both the hospital (U and R) however, women coming for consultation with Dr Rita were not able to answer all the questions about family income, daily household chores, convenient time to come for follow up and many other details. They were hesitant in speaking about their husband and in-laws. In all these situations, Dr Rita preferred talking to the person accompanying the women to understand the condition of the family and she used to explain them care required by the patient. Most families in India, young women are supposed to cook for the entire family (comprising of many generations living together in rural areas) besides helping in the fields and taking care of animals. Women consulting with Dr Savitri were mostly working professionals but this does not mean that they were not required to do household chores (some of them mentioned having domestic helpers). While consulting women having weakness and other related symptoms indicating high physical stress, doctors had to explicitly mention to husbands or parents (in laws) that, they should support and care for women.

The written accounts of interactions with patients and their conditions were focused on clinical narrative of patient's experiences. These records were created to support the monitoring symptoms and response towards treatment. The information was processed and presented in a manner facilitated by the EMR, interactions with and about family (support system) are often obliterated from EMR. This tells that clinical narrative recorded is not the complete picture, as next quotes show that doctors do attend to the experiences of patients, their fears and recognize them as social beings.

"All this is all small-small things we cannot write, we have to explain it to the patient, if you write these things on the computer what they will understand." Dr Rita

"So the patient will come and a lady like a mother will come. We understand all these things, our mentality and our sensitivity. So it is for our information, so that some things we cannot write here, we should not write. We should not write something which is very personal the personal thing should be in person." – Dr Savitri

Doctor Savitri summarized about the life worlds of women in records using medical taxonomy, but she also mentioned about being sensitive towards potential harm of having all details in EMR. Dr Savitri mentioned in interview that consultation is not only about writing the clinical treatment, so if she has to write some personal instructions, she preferred writing on print outs and not recording on the computer. During my field work at Hospital_U, I observed that support staff (managing the gynaecology lobby) used to give print outs of consultation records for some patients, in the middle of ongoing consultation with Dr Savitri. In some cases, the treatment also required psychiatric counselling but she either advised patient verbally to go to a counsellor or herself discussed their concerns. However, neither "non-clinical" treatments nor the details on psychiatric counselling required by the patient was recorded in EMR by Dr Savitri.

"It's like giving something a boost mentally we have to give something the counselling should be there, nothing I wrote on the system whatever happened all those things everything is lady relations emotional heart to heart, never on the back of some paper or the system." – Dr Savitri

The excerpt given in the start of paper highlights that Dr Savitri did not document in EMR about patient having PCOS, doctor only mentioned that she had been counselled on "lifestyle modification". Dr Savitri believed that if some information could be documented on computer privately, it would be useful during follow up visits. If patient was counselled about anything during consultation, hardly it was elaborated in the EMR, unless doctors considered it very critical for ongoing care with possibility of patient visiting multiple hospitals (like infertility treatment, elderly and complicated[2] pregnancy). Sometimes doctors used to write sensitive details on EMR (like in Hospital_R here), especially if they could restrict access to records within hospital and need not give any copy to patients. Dr Rita was mostly dealing with functionally illiterate patients and since records were kept for hospital use only, she summarized about interactions in EMRs after explaining patients along with their care givers verbally.

Dr Rita - Those things also we write, we are not showing them what we are writing so we just write, yes we write that this is a family problem or there is another problem

Dr Rita used EMR fields more flexibly as she made detailed notes about hygiene related conditions causing disease, or even mentioned about patient experiencing domestic violence in records. While the record of consultation (small hand written slip) given

---

[2] Doctors I had interacted with, labelled pregnant women having age more than 30 years as elderly pregnancy and women with comorbidities like diabetes, thyroid and/or blood pressure were labelled as having complicated pregnancy.

to patient hardly mentioned anything except follow up date, vitals and very rarely names of medicine.

4.2 Exceptions in Relation to EMR Use

Records Involved in Outside Hospital Coordination and Communication

Sometimes doctors had to augment patients' experiences while taking notes on computer for ensuring that EMRs were usable for them. This was done to support practicality of clinical delivery of care. Dr Savitri believed in explaining treatment, understanding patients' concerns, and responding accordingly before prescribing anything along with alternative treatment possibilities, their pros-cons, etc. For explaining she used paper, computer screen. She preferred using paper for explaining which patients could easily take away with them; keep safely or discard depending upon their situation. The explanation was done to give patient choices, discuss choice with care givers, family members and letting them decide which treatment was best for them and sometimes clarifying the doubts which patient developed after reading online.

"I will listen and then I will explain everything because now not only in the system I will explain them on the papers, everywhere." – Dr Savitri

Dr Savitri narrated during interview situations where compliance in treatment was necessary, i.e., patients were expected to take medicine daily and introduce changes in their routines, explanations were required for not only patient but also to people living with her or because of relationship with patients living with her. She also believed that if she could make patients understand their clinical conditions, they were more careful in adhering to treatment and took better care of their bodies. Sometimes she used to write about food and additional diet related changes or instructions for people with whom woman was living or care givers at home. Dr Savitri was consulting in hospital in metropolitan city, and patients coming for consultation were mostly educated, and comfortable with the English language. Despite their education background, Dr Savitri pointed out that she had to explain the functioning of the female reproductive system as they lacked understanding about the female sexual and reproductive organs. She used to draw on paper or show images and videos on computer screen before prescribing treatment or advising additional care like diet, exercise.

"This is what and you know once you tell this to patient you explain with the diagrams with the photos the patient will understand much and they will be comfortable." - Dr Savitri

Fields in EMR or paper (print outs) were used flexibly to support women and also ensuring that it remained relevant in future consultation with doctors. This was slightly different for patient coming from the rural area and consulting Dr Rita, as they were not asking explanations from her about treatment and their condition. They were more concerned about avoiding repeat visits to the hospital. One patient whose consultation session I observed had C-section few weeks before. She was visiting for follow up. She asked the doctor about post-surgery hygiene and when she could take a bath. Dr Rita after consultation was over shared that she had experience of dealing with patients who wanted the doctor to intervene and explain their family against some customs like not cleaning body after surgery, eating fatty food and ghee during pregnancy. These patient sometimes belonged to the community where such customs were followed. The local culture and customs were imposed upon the patients to follow, so patients shared their concerns with doctors. Depending upon the time and situation doctor either counselled the caregivers or advised patients to avoid some customs and household chores which could impact their health and wellbeing. Sometimes she explained husband, like in this consultation session that I observed. Dr Rita used to call mother in law or any other person accompanying the patient inside her consultation room and explain the care required by the patient. She often noted on the computer one-line summary about this interaction, presumably to serve as a reminder for follow-up sessions. In situations where, patients were visiting the hospital with husband (but living in joint family), Dr Rita shared with me that counselling husband was of no use. Customs were mandated by elders in the family, whom doctors had no way of reaching and counselling. Giving printed records or writing instructions for the caregivers of the patient in English was also not useful for her patients as most of them were not able to read English. Dr Rita used to sometimes write in Hindi on small sheet of paper given to patient, or ask them to come with their mother in laws for follow up visit.

Within Hospital Coordination and Communication Using EMR

Vignette: Making Exceptions or to Design Considering Exceptions

It was post lunch time and I was sitting in outpatient consultation room with Dr Suresh (Hospital_R). He was consulting OB/GYN patients that day, as Dr Rita was busy in surgery. Dr Suresh was sitting and working on computer. He was typing something and looking at the papers fixed on the examination board. The papers were pink, yellow and white in colour. One woman entered consultation room and she was wearing bright purple saree, having beaded embroidery and silver colour border. I requested both of them permission to sit through consultation and they both nodded their head giving permission, but along with it they gave me a confused look. Dr Suresh looked at me and said, *"This patient is registered in the name of the Dr Rita, but she is not here right now. So we have this privilege with this software here, that anyone can see the patient who is assigned to any (other) doctor and anyone can handle the patient. This privilege was not there previously in the software but this was added specifically for us (Hospital_R). Because here everyone is able to consult all types the patient and we all care for patient, care for each other, and the senior doctors are surgeon so they do surgery also. So if they (senior doctors) are busy in some surgery in the operation theatre and some patient is waiting in the OPD, so initially we were not able to open and consult the patient and then they have to wait for 2 to 3 h, now that is not the case. Since most of the patient are coming from low socioeconomic background this (waiting) was not good."*

Dr Suresh turned towards the woman and asked her some questions. He typed something on computer and then told them room numbers they were supposed to go to make payment for diagnosis and medicine ordered using EMR. The woman and her husband came back with staff nurse after 5 min and nurse told doctor that they were having 1000 rupees only and all investigation were costing around 1600 rupees. Only doctors were having permission to edit order placed using EMR. Doctor edited few investigations and then confirmed, if they had enough money for commute and for meals during the day. The total of investigation, after editing was coming to be 1010 INR, which bothered husband, since he calculated that he would be left with exact amount left required by them to return back after paying 1000 INR and paying 10 rupees (INR) extra would make things difficult for them. Dr Suresh told him not to worry and go and make the payment of 1000 INR only. As I was sitting inside the room, I saw that Dr Suresh called payment counter and requested them to make an exception of 10 rupees (INR), which he added could be adjusted later from his account.

5 Limitations

I acknowledge that I do not know native language of Dr Savitri and my dialect of Hindi differs from the dialect of junior doctors working in Hospital_R. Second, I had not talked about caste and religion informing interactions and experiences and it would be wrong for me to say that it did not operate. Rather I believe that I did not see some social categories that are discriminating (particularly caste and religion) and inform experiences of people, this only means that I am privileged enough to not see it. This limits my interpretations and analysis.

6 Discussion

Majority of research (as summarized in related work section) on practice around EMR use boils down to examining actions available to a healthcare provider (doctor), who is executing a healthcare routine [30]. Activities considered as part of healthcare routine are rooted in individual and disembodied notion of patient. This understanding has been challenged by my findings. First, I discuss what mechanism operate in relation to doctor as subject. Next, I discuss that variations in affordance is related to conditions: and it is pertinent that we consider situation while describing what, when and where of the affordance; elaborated as practical affordance. I present my findings with the help of Davis and Chouinard's [13] conceptualization of affordance as, taking it as starting point.

6.1 Functional Affordance for Doctors

Work done by doctor from clinical perspective is supported (mediated) by functionalities in EMR. Functional affordance emerge in relation to doctor's mandate of keeping medical record, i.e. EMR mechanisms demanding set of actions and refusing certain actions. This is related to functionalities and features available in EMR that are identified as set of affordances in previous studies. Doctors share the understanding of these functionalities from their professional training of record keeping and when realized in action it constituted visible affordances [25]. These affordances operate through gradations and are non-uniform [31]. Thus functionality in the EMR like fields to enter data, order diagnostics and write prescription etc. values clinical expert perspective i.e. of doctor [22], thus requesting and encouraging certain actions, but not requiring it i.e. allowing variations.

These mechanism are designed by focusing on 'functional' or dispositional nature of affordance, which builds on assumption that doctors take note of clinical diagnosis of patient's, in order to make it accessible for clinical usage by medical professional (within organization) in future. Faraj and Azad [32] criticized the feature centric approach towards information systems since it leaves little possibility for questioning taken-for granted features. They stressed on looking at both functional affordance in the sense of enabling and constraining action of the technology, and relational affordance that varies with the changing meanings in the context of use. Findings of this study show that depending upon the situation doctors documented and engaged with EMR differently; like writing on printed notes or verbally explaining. Within consultation doctors leveraged artifacts available like paper, computer, online content and explained patients considering them as layperson, translating information recorded about them so that they could act on medical advice. There were instances where doctors have to resort to use of paper or verbal communication with care-givers also while explaining patients, due to lack of language flexibility or modes of communicating information available in EMR. Thus we need to look at the gradation in affordances in relation to situations and actors (human and non-human both) part of it.

6.2 Practical Affordance Within Situations

We have seen that once materialized in action artefacts of medical records (printed or written records) become part of other relations; it is important to note that there is no breaking point, its flux and that is why in relation. With the changing medical or cultural discursive framings i.e. conditions the meanings around these artefacts keep changing as new meanings emerge. For instance, bed rest advice written in records of pregnant women enabled them to get support and care at home. This also communicated other doctors that patient had difficult pregnancy. In Hospital_R EMR if had details about patient's life world, it helped doctor in explaining patient better, but details on EMR or on printed notes in English were of no direct relevance for patient. These affordances are results of creative co-construction within interactions among actors (human and non-human both), giving rise to meanings in relation to materialities [33]. By seeing affordances as emerging in specific situations we could foreground the practical experiences and emotions of stakeholders.

Women's health and their life worlds are intertwined not only with the disease but also with values and interests coming from society, family they live with, their life partners. Doctors besides having knowledge about their medical field applied cultural understanding about patient while using EMR or interacting with them within consultation. Doctors while treating women considered them as a person and, not mere symptoms or numbers in the records. They were using computer system and EMR for ensuring care, creating records of patient according to their life worlds (like relationship with and support from paternal family, partner, husband, mother in law and socio economic background). My findings make visible the additional work that doctors have to do in these interactions around medical records that are part of consulting process. EMR because of rigid mechanisms lack support for such interactions, making practical affordance limited to certain situations and adding more responsibilities to doctors or patients (including care givers).

My theorization of "practical affordances" is drawing on finding and taking Davis and Chouinard's [13] conceptualization. They demarcate the mechanisms of affordance as artefact—request, demand, allow, encourage, discourage, and refuse subject. We have seen similar mechanism in discussion on functional affordance as summarized above. These mechanisms operate in relation to not just doctor but also patient and their care givers. Thus they are part of context and as per Davis and Chouinard [13] contextual variations in affordance is related to conditions: perception, dexterity, and cultural and institutional legitimacy. Based on my findings, I make some recommendations to the conditions as defined by Davis and Chouinard. Dexterity instead of being limited to physical and cognitive competencies also includes economic aspects; perception is informed by social approval and cultural norms gaining relevance in situation i.e. when we see affordance; cultural and institutional legitimacy is not limited to hospital or medical institutions but social institutions like family (having roles ascribed to women) or society (having norms about women bodies like mothering). These conditions may change with space and time thus there is spatial and temporal aspect to affordance conceptualization, which I am calling as practical affordance.

7 Conclusion

Doctors when see patient as being living and navigating society, they try to make living with disease or condition more liveable and EMR becomes part of the process. Electronic record keeping systems as designed and mandated in use is indicative of cultural values of individualized, disembodied, systemic and decontextualized understanding of patient. My analysis shows that a system introduced to improve medical record keeping and with this notion of patient in clinical care actually marginalizes the experiences and understanding of patients, especially women. In other words, there is an essential 'tension' between the clinical care valuing efficiency and care involving seeing patient as "living being". Thus I argue that richness and nuances of the medical records, requiring the ability to deal with ambiguous and complex experiences part of living as women, can in no way be replaced with 'structured data' without compromising patient care in practical sense.

References

1. Bansler, J.P., Havn, E.C., Schmidt, K., Mønsted, T., Petersen, H.H., Svendsen, J.H.: Cooperative epistemic work in medical practice: an analysis of physicians' clinical notes. Comput. Support. Coop. Work (CSCW) 25(6), 503–546 (2016). https://doi.org/10.1007/s10606-016-9261-x
2. Kohli, R., Tan, S.S.L.: Electronic health records: how can is researchers contribute to transforming healthcare? MIS Q Manage Inf. Syst. 40, 553–573 (2016). https://doi.org/10.25300/MISQ/2016/40.3.02
3. Berg, M.: Patient care information systems and health care work: a sociotechnical approach. Int. J. Med. Inform. 55, 87–101 (1999). https://doi.org/10.1016/S1386-5056(99)00011-8
4. McCoy, M.J., Diamond, A.M., Strunk, A.L.: Special requirements of electronic medical record systems in obstetrics and gynecology. Obstet. Gynecol. 116, 140–143 (2010). https://doi.org/10.1097/AOG.0b013e3181e1328c

5. Mørck, P., Langhoff, T.O., Christophersen, M., Møller, A.K., Bjørn, P.: Variations in oncology consultations: how dictation allows variations to be documented in standardized ways. Comput. Supported Cooperative Work (CSCW) **27**(3), 539–568 (2018). https://doi.org/10.1007/s10606-018-9332-2

6. Bardram, J.E., Houben, S.: Collaborative Affordances of Medical Records. Comput. Support. Coop. Work (CSCW) **27**(1), 1–36 (2017). https://doi.org/10.1007/s10606-017-9298-5

7. Chen, Y., Tang, C., Zhou, X., et al.: Beyond formality: informal communication in health practices. In: Proceedings of ACM Conference Computer Support Cooperative Work CSCW, pp. 307–311 (2013). https://doi.org/10.1145/2441955.2442030

8. Zhou, X., Ackerman, M.S., Zheng, K.: Doctors and psychosocial information: records and reuse in inpatient care. In: Conference Human Factors Computing System – Proceedings, vol. 3, pp. 1767–1776. https://doi.org/10.1145/1753326.1753592

9. Murphy, A.R., Reddy, M.C.: Ambiguous accountability: the challenges of identifying and managing patient-related information problems in collaborative patient-care teams. In: Proceedings ACM Conference Computer Support Cooperative Work CSCW, pp. 1646–1660 (2017). https://doi.org/10.1145/2998181.2998315

10. Pearl, R.M.: What health systems, hospitals, and physicians need to know about implementing electronic health records. Harvard Business Review, 15 June 2017. https://hbr.org/2017/06/what-health-systems-hospitals-andphysicians-need-to-know-about-implementing-electronic-healthrecords. Accessed: 13 Aug 2020

11. Tandon, A., Kandathil, G., Deodhar, S., Mathur, N.: Electronic records of obstetrics and gynecology encounter: beyond professional logics of health care. In: ACM International Conference Proceeding Series, Article no. 3, pp. 1–14 (2019). https://doi.org/10.1145/3364183.3364196

12. Bloomfield, B.P., Latham, Y., Vurdubakis, T.: Bodies, technologies and action possibilities: when is an affordance? Sociology **44**, 415–433 (2010). https://doi.org/10.1177/0038038510362469

13. Davis, J.L., Chouinard, J.B.: Theorizing affordances: from request to refuse. Bull. Sci. Technol. Soc. **36**, 241–248 (2016). https://doi.org/10.1177/0270467617714944

14. Flanagan, M.E., Saleem, J.J., Millitello, L.G., Russ, A.L., Doebbeling, B.N.: Paper and computer-based workarounds to electronic health record use at three benchmark institutions. J. Am. Med. Inform. Assoc. **20**(e1), e59–e66 (2013)

15. Bossen, C., Jensen, L.G., Udsen, F.W.: Boundary-object trimming: on the invisibility of medical secretaries' care of records in healthcare infrastructures. Computer Supported Cooperative Work (CSCW) **23**(1), 75–110 (2013). https://doi.org/10.1007/s10606-013-9195-5

16. Pine, K., Mazmanian, M.: Institutional logics of the EMR and the problem of "perfect" but inaccurate accounts. In: Proceedings of the ACM Conference on Computer Supported Cooperative Work, CSCW, pp 283–293 (2014)

17. Bossen, C., Jensen, L.G.: How physicians "achieve overview." In: Proceedings of the 17th ACM Conference on Computer Supported Cooperative Work & Social Computing - CSCW 2014. ACM Press, New York, USA, pp 257–268 (2014)

18. George, J.F., Kohnke, E.: Personal health record systems as boundary objects. Commun. Assoc. Inf. Syst. **42**, 21–50 (2018). https://doi.org/10.17705/1CAIS.04202

19. Hausvik, G.I., Thapa, D.: 'What you see is not what you get' - challenges in actualization of EHR affordances. In: Proceedings of the 38th International Conference of Information Systems (ICIS), Seoul, South Korea (2017)

20. Goh, J.M., Gao, G., Agarwal, R.: Evolving work routines: adaptive routinization of information technology in healthcare. Inf. Syst. Res. **22**, 565–585 (2011). https://doi.org/10.1287/isre.1110.0365

21. Strong, D.M., Volkoff, O., Johnson, S.A., et al.: A theory of organization-EHR affordance actualization. J. Assoc. Inf. Syst. 15, 53–85 (2014). https://doi.org/10.17705/1jais.00353

22. Markus, M.L., Silver, M.: A foundation for the study of IT effects: a new look at DeSanctis and Poole's concepts of structural features and spirit. J. Assoc. Inf. Syst. **9**, 609–632 (2008). https://doi.org/10.17705/1jais.00176
23. Klecun, E., Hibberd, R., Lichtner, V.: Affordance theory perspectives on IT and healthcare organization. In: 2016 International Conference on Information Systems, ICIS 2016 (2016)
24. Kaptelinin, V., Nardi, B.: Affordances in HCI: toward a mediated action perspective. In: Conference on Human Factors Computing System – Proceedings, pp. 967–976 (2012). https://doi.org/10.1145/2207676.2208541
25. Lanamäki, A., Thapa, D., Stendal, K.: When is an affordance? Outlining four stances. In: Introna, L., Kavanagh, D., Kelly, S., Orlikowski, W., Scott, S. (eds.) IS&O 2016. IAICT, vol. 489, pp. 125–139. Springer, Cham (2016). https://doi.org/10.1007/978-3-319-49733-4_8
26. Rubin, H., Rubin, I.: Qualitative Interviewing (2nd ed.): The Art of Hearing Data. Qual Interviewing (2nd ed) Art Hear Data, pp. 71–92 (2012). https://doi.org/10.4135/9781452226651
27. Glaser, B.G., Strauss, A.L.: Discovery of Grounded Theory: Strategies for Qualitative Research. Routledge, New York (2017)
28. Braun, V., Clarke, V.: Using thematic analysis in psychology. Qual. Res. Psychol. **3**, 77–101 (2006). https://doi.org/10.1191/1478088706qp063oa
29. Stern, P.N., Pyles, S.H.: Using grounded theory methodology to study women's culturally based decisions about health. Health Care Women Int. **6**(1–3), 1–24 (1985). https://doi.org/10.1080/07399338509515680
30. Lienhard, K., Job, O., Bachmann, L., Bodmer, N., Legner, C.: A framework to advance electronic health record system use in routine patient care. In: European Conference of Information Systems, Guimaraes, Portugal, pp. 1114–1128 (2017)
31. Evans, S.K., Pearce, K.E., Vitak, J., Treem, J.W.: Explicating affordances: a conceptual framework for understanding affordances in communication research. J. Comput. Commun. **22**, 35–52 (2017). https://doi.org/10.1111/jcc4.12180
32. Faraj, S., Azad, B.: The Materiality of technology: an affordance perspective. In: Materiality and Organizing, pp. 237–258. Oxford University Press (2012)
33. Leonardi, P.M.: When flexible routines meet flexible technologies: affordance, constraint, and the imbrication of human and material agencies. MIS Q. Manage. Inf. Syst. **35**, 147–167 (2011). https://doi.org/10.2307/23043493

Sustainability Qualifiers of Health Management Information Systems Implementation: Case Study of DHIS2 in India

Jyotsna Sahay[1], Sundeep Sahay[2(✉)], and Arunima Sehgal Mukherjee[1,2]

[1] HISP India, Noida, India
[2] Department of Informatics, Universitetet i Oslo, Oslo, Norway
sundeeps@ifi.uio.no

Abstract. This paper reports on a rare story of sustainability success of a HMIS implementation in a low and middle income country context of India. The narrative is set in the Indian state of Odisha, where the DHIS2 is being implemented for the state Health Management Information System since 2008. The authors of this paper have been engaged both in research and practice supporting the implementation since the start, and draw upon this rich and longitudinal data source to analyze from the perspective of the state government "the challenges they faced with respect to sustainability, and how have they overcome them". Three sets of sustainability qualifiers were identified-benefits/continued benefits, institutionalisation/ routinisation and development - which have been key in enabling sustainability. However, going forward, the authors identify the need for additional qualifiers to strengthen the aspect of data use, which till date remains weak as compared to data quality management.

Keywords: Sustainability · HIS · LMICs

1 Introduction: Importance of HMIS to Strengthen Health Systems Performance

There has been a growing awareness that improving population health is significant for development of a society, particularly for low and middle-income countries (LMICs), who are typically under resourced and fragile. The World Health Organisation (WHO) identifies Health Information Systems (HIS) as one of the core building blocks to strengthen health systems. India, like many other LMICs have made concerted efforts to reform and integrate its systems, with the routine Health Management Information System (HMIS) being the springboard for reform. Rationalisation of the existing data management system and related practices and transition from legacy paper-based system to ICT enabled ones are at the core of the reform.

Our paper focuses on the sustainability of the HMIS, which provides the foundation of the national health information system (HIS), spanning from the lowest level of the community through the district and state levels to the national and global. The

Published by Springer Nature Switzerland AG 2020
R. K. Bandi et al. (Eds.): IFIPJWC 2020, IFIP AICT 601, pp. 194–206, 2020.
https://doi.org/10.1007/978-3-030-64697-4_15

HMIS provides data for both strengthening local level care processes and also for state and national level programme management and policy making processes. By the fact that the HMIS contains data from all public health facilities in the country, it becomes the foundation for providing effective health services to the whole population, particularly the rural and marginalized populations who cannot afford privately delivered care services.

Given that the HMIS spans the country, it is inherently complex and houses multiple competing interests, and thus challenging to successfully implement. IT. Efforts globally to strengthen HMIS through computerisation have resulted in large-scale failures [1] and the potential of technology remains largely unrealised. A key enduring challenge thus is of sustainability, implying the capability of the HMIS to endure over time and space, with-out external support. The dual challenge of achieving sustainability is of how systems can be deeply institutionalised within governmental systems so best serves the needs of the state, while yet being flexible and adaptable to evolve with the evolving informational needs and priorities of the government. A key challenge in the analysis of sustainability is the dominant focus on the "supply side" (provision of computers, mobile phones, internet etc.), which ignores an understanding of the "demand side" dynamics (such as user needs and their capacities). This paper seeks to address this bias, by understanding the HMIS sustainability challenge, as seen from the perspective of a state government in India. The following research question is addressed:

What challenges of HMIS sustainability does a state government in a LMIC context experience, and how can they best overcome these challenges?

We approach this research question through an analysis of a ten-year experience of a HMIS based on the free and open source digital platform (DHIS2- District Health Information System – see dhis2.org) implementation in the Indian state of Odisha. This analysis conducted within a temporal perspective, provides rich insights into how a state government could strive to address the various socio-technical sustainability challenges encountered, with the aim of improving their health system performance.

The paper is organised as follows. In Sect. 2, we discuss conceptually the challenge of sustainability. Section 3 details the methods followed in the case study narrated in Sect. 4. Our case study analysis, with a focus on sustainability is presented in Sect. 5, which is followed by discussions and conclusions in Sect. 6.

2   The Enduring Challenge of Building Sustainability

This section comprises of three main parts. In the first, we discuss some key sustainability challenges to HMIS as reported in literature. In the next, we discuss some conceptual approaches to study sustainability, and their respective strengths and weaknesses. Finally, we present our conceptual framework to guide the analysis.

2.1   Challenges to HMIS Sustainability

Traditionally computerization of HMIS in LMICs have followed technical trajectories representing a "supply side push." Sustainability tends to get equated with establishing required digital infrastructure and mitigating risks threatening the long-term viability of

IT [2]. This approach ignores the socio-technical nature of the challenges, such as how to deal with legacy systems and their institutionally embedded practices. Computerization efforts cannot start from scratch, as history is important with both enabling and constraining influences on new initiatives [3, 4].

Another implementation challenge concerns the centralized nature of initiatives, which marginalize supporting care processes responsive to community needs [5]. This strong predisposition of national health programmes to be vertically structured, often supported by different donors for specific programme needs, have led to a proliferation of fragmented and compartmentalized systems, that are not able to sustain since they are not nurtured within a state unified framework. Reform efforts thus often miss out on an organized and unified central data resource and requisite infrastructure required to build integrated health information architecture [6].

Another impediment to sustainability concerns the weak governance and stewardship of national HMIS, which limit the use of health data standards and clearly defines the roles and responsibilities of different stakeholders towards the HMIS. While many LMICs, including India, have come out with policy announcements to support free software and open standards, in practice this does not happen in an effective manner, and governmental procurement systems continue to support proprietary systems [7].

The raison d'etre of a HMIS is to support "data use for action". Research abounds on stories of data not being used for action but primarily only to support upward bureaucratic reporting. Various reasons contribute to this including capacity, infrastructure, high existing workloads and weak culture of using data for action. Weak data use implies poor demand for data, and increasingly less attention being paid to providing quality data. This leads to a vicious cycle of data not being used leading to poorer quality data and more non-use. The end outcome of this vicious cycle is that the HMIS does not sustain over time [8].

In summary, multiple conditions impede the realization of sustainable HMIS. We next discuss how these can be conceptually understood.

2.2 Conceptually Understanding Sustainability

The Information Systems research perspective offers different perspectives to understand sustainability. We discuss some of them, along with their strengths and weaknesses.

The *diffusionist perspective* inspired by Roger's model [9] traces the trajectory of an innovation and its adoption over time conceptualized as an "S" curve. This diffusion approach focuses primarily on the supply side of an innovation, assuming that it takes birth at the "centre" and then gradually is adopted at the "peripheral" levels. Attributes such as donor funding and system usability and perceived usefulness qualify sustainability concerns. We believe this approach is limited in its understanding of sustainability as it does not actively consider the demand side of user practices which emerge within an embedded social and institutional context. It primarily represents a top-down approach focusing on preserving the technical fidelity of the interventions [10], ignoring local user needs [2, 11, 12] and ignoring that local processes are dynamic, non-linear, full of unexpected events, and rife with probability of 'sustainability failure' [13]. Nhampossa [14] has argued against the efficacy of the diffusionist perspective in the context of Mozambique. He writes that such an approach is limited as it assumes that knowledge and innovation will only emanate from the centre, and the periphery is incapable of building anything new. He advocates instead to adopt a "translation" approach, where the movement of technology is not seen as one giant leap from point A to B, but a series of small steps or translations, where at each steps new forms of socio-technical networks emerge, which shape the process of evolution and also the contents of the technology.

To address challenges inherent in techno-centric and top-down approaches, the *socio-technical* philosophy has been drawn upon by IS researchers. This perspective conceptualizes technology as a "socio-technical network" [12] wherein boundaries between the social and technical are blurred and organisational actors enact distinct technology-in-practices based on their cognitive schemas and the social contexts they are embedded in [15]. Participatory design based approaches become important in shaping the technology based practices. Understanding the interplay of contextual dynamics and actors' rationality, stakeholders and their interests, and the logic of their negotiations [6] are central to these approaches [16] and to identify the design-reality gaps and build sustainability [17].

Braa et al. [17] advocate the networks of action approach to address the HMIS sustainability challenge in LMICs. This action research approach seeks to enable learning in collectives rather than in isolated instances, to enable sharing of experiences and resources, and avoid "reinventing the wheel of mistakes". Learning amongst peers fundamentally challenges the top-down diffusionist thinking, and the action in this approach is to enable the sharing of resources, ideas and experiences across the different actors in the action network. This approach has been key in the sustainability of HISP (Health Information Systems Programme) network over 80 countries through two decades. Enduring the test of time and scale, is an active proof of sustainability.

The practice based approaches operate at a more micro and pragmatic level, on the assumption that systems become sustainable manner only when it is routinely used institutionalized in the everyday work of the organization. This includes stakeholders engaging in joint activities, insightful discussions, and experience & knowledge sharing, as a key means of addressing recurring problems [18, 19]. The practice based approaches has been combined with the institutional work perspective to understand how practices are shaped by and also shape institutional influences [20].While helpful in grasping the key requisite of sustainability – institutionalisation, these approaches leave unaddressed the challenge of how to translate the requisite into practice, and how systems respond are to change. To address this gap, Fleiszer and others [21] discuss the "qualifiers of sustainability", which we now discuss.

Analytical Perspective based on "Sustainability Qualifiers"
Fleiszer et al. [11] enumerate the following qualifiers of sustainability:

a) *Benefits, continued benefits.* Sustainability is typically equated with the persistence of the innovation-related benefits. [22–24]. Effective innovations are sustainable if they continue to provide benefits [25] with respect to the objectives of the innovation for clients [23, 26] and system providers [27]. This involves the continued maintenance of resolution to problems and their enhancement [23, 28]. While achievement of objectives is central to sustainability, equally important is how benefits are perceived, beyond what is documented by formal evaluation [28].

b) *Routinisation/institutionalisation.* This refers to the embedding of structures and processes around an innovation into habitual practices of individuals, organisations and systems [13, 22, 29, 30]. This involves a process of 'mutual adjustment' between an innovation and its context, such that the innovation eventually 'loses its separate identity' [22 p. 94] [28] and becomes standard 'business as usual' [31 p. 261]. While routinisation implies cycles of repeated action in a social structure, institutionalisation implies the concretisation of organisational infrastructure (e.g. established committees, dedicated budgets, embedded data management technologies) around the routines [32].

c) *Development.* Fleiszer et al. [21] identify two inter-connected perspectives around development. One, one which addresses the evolution of the innovation and another that draws attention to the emerging changes in stakeholder needs and how the innovation adapts to them. Development then represents additional or ongoing innovation [30, 33]. While a management-focused approach focuses on performance improvements, a stakeholder centric approach focuses on 'ongoing development' of an innovation [34] in response to evolving circumstances [33, 35]. From this perspective, sustainability represents the continual enhancement of users' abilities and resources to maintain an innovation and associated changes [22, 24, 26, 28].

In summary, our analytical perspective is built around the identification of sustainability qualifiers, focusing on user-based practices and their shaping by the institutional context. Such a perspective helps place the focus primarily on the demand side of the innovation, as contrasted to the typical supply side bias that underpins many sustainability analysis.

3 Empirical Approach and Methods

3.1 Research Setting

The empirical component of our analysis is the eastern Indian state of Odisha with a population size of 47 million. Odisha has a high degree of geographic inaccessibility of health services, a significant tribal population, a heavy reliance on informal health providers, and affected periodically by natural disasters such as floods and typhoons. Despite these odds, the state has made remarkable progress on strengthening and sustaining their HMIS, which makes it an interesting case for us to analyze on how this has been achieved from the perspective of the state.

Our empirical work involves two forms of engagement of practice and situated research. In terms of practice, the authors of this paper have been engaged with national and state level HMIS reform efforts through their design and implementation since 2008 till today. This engagement has emerged through a local NGO called Health Information Systems Programme, India (HISP India) which has supported Odisha in their HMIS strengthening since 2008. This engagement has provided rich insights into the context, including various centre-state tensions. In terms of research, we have conducted in 2019 a detailed empirical analysis of selected districts in the state, to understand how the HMIS has evolved over a 10-year period. Our focus has been on understanding the implementation trajectory of the HMIS, and what are the sustainability qualifiers and how they have been achieved.

Data Collection

Mode of Practical Engagement: In 2008, the National Rural Health Mission (NRHM), Ministry of Health, started a process of health systems reform for strength-ening public systems. The aim was to bring architectural corrections, including in the HMIS by making it more decentralized, standardized and evidence based. The authors were integrally engaged in this reform process, and its subsequent implementation in states, including Odisha. As a part of this process, we visited Odisha 3–4 times, and had discussions and presentations with the state on how they wanted to adopt the reform, including the new formats and software system. As a part of the reform process, the national level designated a centralised web-portal built on a proprietary platform, for all states to report their HMIS data. Odisha adopted the DHIS2 open source platform, as the state portal, and to also comply with their national reporting requirements.

This national level process continued till 2012, after which Odisha made a bilateral arrangement with a NGO, HISP India, to support their DHIS2 based HMIS, which continues till today. This long term engagement of HISP India, of which the authors are members off, has yielded immense data in terms of technical reports, presentations, correspondence with the state and contracts. This data has been systematically compiled, key events mapped, and the implementation trajectory identified.

Mode of Situated Empirical Assessment: A second source of data was through in person interaction with DHIS2 users and related stakeholders at the state and sub-state (district and block) levels. The district constitutes the middle layer of linking the state to the block which is responsible for service delivery. The fieldwork was carried out in two phases over a period of four months. (March – July 2019). Six of the thirty districts in the state were covered, and in each, three blocks were visited. Some sub-block level interactions were also carried out.

Phase 1. This was over a week and carried out by a team of four members with multi-disciplinary expertise. The team focused on identifying key practices around data collection, reporting, analysis and use practices, including how the DHIS2 supported or not these practices. At the state, the researchers met the IT and M&E team responsible for the HMIS upkeep and use. The district and sub-district visits then followed, to meet the data and programme managers.

Phase 2. Here, interactions at the district level M&E team formed the starting point, followed by block and sub block level visits. The focus was on primarily understanding the field-level practices around the collection, reporting and use of data for local action. In addition to speaking to users, various paper-based data records and reports, both formal and informal, were studied to understand how DHIS2 was being used.

Data Analysis

The focus was to interpretively understand the unfolding of the implementation trajec-tory, comprising of the interplay of contextual contingencies, stakeholders' interests and the mediation of technology. At the end of each day, each researcher made their field visit notes, which summarized the discussions, key observations and learnings. This was followed by joint discussions as sense-making sessions of the implementation trajectory and the underlying sustainability qualifiers. Prior to moving to the next district, the notes were revisited, and comparative experiences were also discussed. Slowly, an overall picture of the implementation trajectory was pieced together and mapped against the data collected through the mode of practical engagement.

4 Case Study

DHIS2 was introduced in Odisha as a state portal to support facility level reporting and analysis while enabling export of required data to the national portal. Being open source and designed with user-friendliness and flexibility in mind, the State saw DHIS2 as an effective tool to support their decentralisation agenda. The implementation trajectory is outlined over three phases.

Phase I. Initiation (2008–2010): A situation analysis conducted as a part of the national reform process, also included Odisha state. In addition to the national mandated data standards, HISP India was part of a state specific process to identify the local data needs, which necessarily did not need to be reported to the national level. Through the flexibility offered by DHIS2, these state requirements were incorporated into the database, and its deployment was supported by a series of workshops, orientation and training sessions. The software and technical support was provided free to the state, supported by a national budget, a process, which continued till 2012.

Phase II. Transition to DHIS2 based systems (2010–2012): This phase involved complete transition from the paper based HMIS to DHIS2. The platform adaptation, capacity building and handholding support were major activities carried out in this period, working closely with the state and district level teams. Customizations were primarily about incorporating state specific requirements not addressed by the national process. In addition, trouble shooting and bug fixing issues were addressed on a continuous basis, particularly focused on strengthening work practices around data quality management and data use.

Phase III. (2012 – ongoing) In 2012, national level support to states was withdrawn, and Odisha was advised to develop bilateral relationships with HISP India to continue support for the DHIS2 implementation process, if they so chose. By this time, the state HMIS team had gained adequate understanding of DHIS2 and were seeing its value in practice of it being able to support their local needs. They found that DHIS2 could rapidly support their evolving needs at a low cost, without having to build systems from scratch. They thus decided to continue the HISP India relationship, something which continues till today.

4.1 Understanding the Outcomes of the Implementation Process

Three key outcomes of the implementation process were identified: i) significant improvements in data coverage; ii) significant improvements in data quality; and, iii) a steady progression towards an "integrated state data warehouse" based on DHIS2. These three value-adding processes are now discussed.

Improved Processes of Data Coverage. These benefits arose through the transition from a paper-based to a web-based free and open source digital platform – DHIS2.

This transition address historical challenges related to redundant and inconsistent data formats, inconsistences in data recording and reporting practices, errors resulting from manual data processing and lack of timeliness in reporting. While the earlier system was geared only towards upward reporting, the DHIS2 allowed for the first time for local levels to see their own data, and address problems of inflated reporting. Now even the block level users could directly do data entry into the web-based system, and slowly the state achieved 100% data coverage. A district user commented on the value of increased visibility of data:

"Increasing numbers of data elements means more data to be presented in monthly meetings. It becomes possible to focus on poor performers. Increasing data quality and reporting rate has also been seen in the district. Urban areas with many private facilities are currently the focus as they have lower reporting rates and poorer data quality".

Data Quality Management. Well-defined institutional protocols for data quality management were defined around data reporting and evolved through regular use. These protocols took into account the existing practices related to data collection reviewing, confirmation and submission, and built upon aim. The aim was not to eliminate the legacy practices but to build upon it, make them more stringent and visible through digitization. To support digitization, explicit guidelines, responsibilities and resources were agreed, such as analysis of data validation errors generated by the system. Through data rationalization, the amount of data to be collected was significantly reduced, enabling improvements in data quality. The DHIS2 allowed for easy identification of facilities that did not report data, enabled correctness checks at the very point of data entry, could lock the data once confirmed to prevent late changes in data, run data validation checks, and implement functionalities such as role based user authorizations.

These technical improvements were only made possible through the establishment of institutional processes. Validation committees at each level of the reporting hierarchy (state, district and block) were setup to routinely review data quality and to provide support for making corrections. The validation committees did not seek to change the authority structure but to enhance the visibility and accountability of the information function. Conversations around data of the committees and data providers helped increasing awareness about the value of data and to build a sense of pride around its upkeep. With increasing maturity in data quality, there was a shift from data use for performance evaluation and control to corrective action to strengthen service delivery. With this, increasingly more stakeholders got involved in the conversations around data. A block level functionary noted:

"... 2006 there was a big booklet of around 25 + pages that he had to fill. Each data element was disaggregated by Schedule Caste, Schedule Tribe and Others, further broken by male and female. Data was entered in Excel to be aggregated, which generated a lot of mistakes. District level only had block level data and could not drill down... Now, we are getting directly contact with the lowest level, we can look at their data and call them if something is wrong. Even state level is in contact with the lower levels now as they can see their data. State level is also contacting SCs"... In 2006, only one programme was included in HMIS. Now they have integrated multiple programme to make reporting easier ..."

Gradual Progress Towards an Integrated State Data Warehouse. Driven by the initial agenda of the implementation, the early focus was on strengthening data coverage and quality, primarily for the national level programmes. Over time, requirements emerged for addition of both national and state specific programmes, which were incorporated in the DHIS2. As many as ten programmes have now been integrated, and the DHIS2 is evolving into a state data warehouse, as a repository of all health data. However not all the integrations have been well embedded into routine use, and uptake has been variable. The focus now is on building the use of the data, and creating a more integrated perspective in terms of use and policy making.

5   Case Analysis: Identifying Sustainability Qualifiers

Our analytical framework identified three key sustainability qualifiers: i) benefits, continued benefits; ii) routinization and institutionalization; and iii) development. We discuss here how these qualifiers were achieved in the empirical case, from the perspectives of the data providers, the M&E and IT teams.

Benefits, Continued Benefits: For the data providers, data rationalization reduced their workload, and DHIS2 enabled a transition from the manual and time taking work to something more easy, accessible and more efficient. Achieving 100% coverage, meant data providers could avoid the threat of reprimand for non or late reporting. For the M&E team, all data in one database, enhanced visibility of the health status, and their ability to drill down to the lowest level to identify events and their causes. This greatly strengthened their analytical abilities to conduct monitoring and evaluation. For the IT team, there was firstly the opportunity to work with a state-of-the-art digital platform, and in collaboration with the responsive HISP India technical support team, also build their capacities and strengthen local ownership. This was self-motivating.

Routinization, Institutionalization: The process of routinization and institutionalization is well illustrated through the data management function. An explicitly defined protocol for data quality management, was established by the state, imparting it the necessary legitimacy and became routinely used across the state. The protocol took was based on legacy data management practices, rather than creating something radically new, and were thus not perceived as a threat. Mechanisms such as data review meetings and Validation Committees provided the structure to ensure compliance of the designed practices and processes, thus leading to a deep institutionalization of practices.

Development: Key to the sustainability process was the continuous development taking place both technically and institutionally. For example, the guidelines for data quality management was continuously improved with due discussions and clarifications with relevant stakeholders and disseminated at regular intervals. Various technical improvements were introduced, such as multi-level data quality checks, self-validation of data, supervisory approvals prior to report submission, and integrated reports at block level which were used for review meetings. Supporting these development processes was a stable and visionary governance structure, who realized the need to have a strong and low-cost technical partner in HISP India. Whenever new features were required or modifications and troubleshooting, HISP India would quickly respond leading to an ongoing evolution of systems. These developments were of course enabled through the flexibility and customizability offered by DHIS2, and that it was not locked through proprietary licenses. Some areas of development have proved to be tricky, such as the scaling of a malaria surveillance system, because of national level priorities being different. In some development exercises, the legacy practices were deeply embedded and thus challenging to deinstutionalize.

In the following summary table, we highlight the key sustainability qualifiers (Table 1).

Table 1. Sustainability qualifiers shaping Odisha HMIS implementation trajectory

Sustainability qualifiers	Supporting practices	Institutional shaping of practices
Benefits, continued benefits	*Data providers:* reduced data load; easier access to entry; improved quality *M&E team:* Increased visibility of data; improved visualization and analytics *IT team:* Working on state of art technology with responsive HISP India support team	Establishing *validation committees* to have monthly conversations around data *Monthly review meetings* based on HMIS data Ongoing *support agreements* with HISP India continued over 10 years
Routinization, institutionalization	Routines of review meetings, data quality checks, data analysis and use were clearly established, and imparted necessary legitimacy to be institutionalized, such as through budgets and human resources	District and block level structures created for data quality review and use; at state level, dedicated IT team and data center identified; state M&E team enhanced the demand for quality data, putting pressure on the supply side
Development	Demand for new functionalities and modules rapidly incorporated; regular capacity building to build awareness and use	State promoted the progressive policy of building an integrated data warehouse based on DHIS2

6   Discussion and Conclusions

The paper presents a rare example of a HMIS in a LMIC that has endured and continues to thrive even after 12 years. This has been despite various pressures such as varying national priorities on software and many other competing systems. In an environment where there are frequent changes in state government administration, the Odisha governance structure has been consistent in supporting DHIS2 and the technical team – HISP India – behind it. The state approach and actions highlight their acknowledgement that system implementation is a matter of years and not months and the importance of supporting both continuity and innovation.

The paper contributes to understand sustainability and how it can be achieved from the perspective of the state government. The notion of sustainability qualifiers seen as user practices and their institutional shaping, provides a framework to understand key determinants of sustainability. All these qualifiers are seen within a temporal and not a snapshot perspective – how benefits are continued, how routines are institutionalized over time, and how developments continue with ongoing innovation and support.

While the state can indeed be proud of their continued sustainability of their HMIS, some qualifiers are identified for enabling continued evolution. While great progress has been made in establishing systems and processes for higher quality and coverage of data, the same progress cannot be noted on data use. Good quality data can be seen as a necessary but not sufficient condition for enhancing data use. This requires additional qualifiers such as institutional incentives, dissemination of successful case studies and stories, and the foregrounding of data use champions. Further, the process could benefit by expanding the network of stakeholders who depend on the data beyond the health sector, such as the local politicians and district administrators. This expansion will help to strengthen the demand side, and create champions on data use, which can serve as self-reinforcing mechanisms to attract other users and made innovations.

While our empirical case is focused on Odisha and the DHIS2 platform, there are some general principles which we believe can be relevant to other contexts and systems. One, to focus on sustainability from the perspective of the state and the owning institution. Two, to understand sustainability from a temporal perspective. The three qualifiers have helped to identify key determinants of sustainability. Four, qualifiers are best understood through the lens of user practices and how they are institutionally shaped.

References

1. Heeks, R.: Information systems and developing countries: failure, success, and local improvisation. Inform. Soc. **18**(2), 101–112 (2002). https://doi.org/10.1080/01972240290075039
2. Korpela, M., Soriyan, H., Olufokunbi, K., Mursu, A.: Blueprint for an African systems development methodology: an action research project in the health sector. In: Avgerou, C. (ed) Implementation and Evaluation of Information Systems in Developing Countries. Proceedings of the Fifth International Working Conference of IFIP WG 9.4, Bangkok, Thailand, pp. 273–285 (1998)
3. Aanestad, M.: Cultivating Networks: Implementing Surgical Telemedicine. Department of Informatics, University of Oslo (2002). https://www.researchgate.net/publication/242383259_IMPLEMENTING_SURGICAL_TELEMEDICINE
4. Callon, M.: The sociology of an actor-network: the case of the electric vehicle. In: Callon, M., Law, J., Rip, A. (eds.) Mapping the Dynamics of Science and Technology, pp. 19–34. Macmillan Press, London (1986). https://doi.org/10.1007/978-1-349-07408-2_2
5. Mukherjee, A.: Empowerment: The invisible element in ICT4D projects? The case of public health information systems in India and Kenya. Department of Informatics, University of Oslo, Norway (2017). https://www.mn.uio.no/ifi/english/research/networks/hisp/research-library/thesis/mukherjee2017empowerment.pdf
6. Braa, J., Sahay, S.: Integrated Health Information Architecture: Power for the Users: Design Development and Use. Matrix Publishing, New Delhi (2012)

7. Sahay, S.: Free and open source software as global public goods? what are the distortions and how do we address them? Electron. J. Inform. Syst. Dev. Countries **85**, e12080 (2019). https://doi.org/10.1002/isd2.12080

8. Misund, G., Høiberg, J.: Sustainable information technology for global sustainability. Digital Earth - Information Resources for Global Sustainability Symposium Brno, Czech Republic, pp. 21–259 (2003). http://wwwia.hiof.no/~gunnarmi/omd/dig_earth_03/

9. Rogers, E.: Diffusion of Innovations, 5th edn. Simon & Schuster, New York (2003)

10. Carroll, C., Patterson, M., Wood, S., Booth, A., Rick, J., Balain, S.: Conceptual framework for implementation fidelity. Implementation Sci. **2**, 40 (2007). https://doi.org/10.1186/1748-5908-2-40

11. Venkatesh, V., Morris, M., Davis, G., Davis, F.: User acceptance of information technology: toward a unified view. MIS Q. **27**(3), 425–478 (2003). https://doi.org/10.2307/30036540

12. Kling, R., McKim, G., King, A.: A bit more to it: scholarly communication forums as socio-technical interaction networks. J. Am. Soc. Inform. Sci. Technol. **54**(1), 47–67 (2003). https://doi.org/10.1002/asi.10154

13. Best, M., Kumar, R.: Sustainability failures of rural telecenters: challenges from the sustainable access in rural India (SARI) project. Inform. Technol. Int. Dev. **4**(4), 31–45 (2008). https://doi.org/10.1162/itid.2008.00025

14. Nhampossa, J.: Re-thinking technology transfer as technology translation: a case study of health information systems in Mozambique. Department of Informatics, University of Oslo, Norway (2005). https://www.mn.uio.no/ifi/english/research/networks/hisp/research-library/thesis/nhampossa2006.pdf

15. Orlikowski, W.: Using technology and constituting structures: a practice lens for studying technology in organisations. Organ. Sci. **11**(4), 404–428 (2000). https://doi.org/10.1287/orsc.11.4.404.14600

16. Walsham, G., Symons, V., Waema, T.: Information systems as social systems: implications for developing countries. Inform. Technol. Dev. **3**(3), 189–204 (1988). https://doi.org/10.1080/02681102.1988.9627126

17. Braa, J., Monteiro, E., Sahay, S.: Networks of action: sustainable health information systems across developing countries. MIS Q. **28**(3), 337–362 (2004). https://doi.org/10.2307/2514864

18. Yahya, H., Braa, K.: Mobilising local networks of implementers to address health information systems sustainability. Electron. J. Inform. Syst. Dev. Countries **48**(6), 1–21 (2011). https://doi.org/10.1002/j.1681-4835.2011.tb00342.x

19. Li, L., Grimshaw, J., Nielsen, C., Judd, M., Coyte, P., Graham, I.: Evolution of Wenger's concept of community of practice. Implementation Sci. **4**, 11 (2009). https://doi.org/10.1186/1748-5908-4-11

20. Orlikowski, W., Barley, S.: Technology and institutions: what can research on information technology and research on organisations learn from each other. MIS Q. **25**(2), 145–165 (2001). https://doi.org/10.2307/3250927

21. Fleiszer, A., Semenic, S., Ritchie, J., Richer, M., Denis, J.: The sustainability of healthcare innovations: a concept analysis. J. Adv. Nurs. **71**(7), 1484–1498 (2015). https://doi.org/10.1111/jan.12633

22. Shediac-Rizkallah, M., Bone, L.: Planning for the sustainability of community-based health programs: conceptual frameworks and future directions for research, practice and policy. Health Educ. Res. **13**(1), 87–108 (1998). https://doi.org/10.1093/her/13.1.87

23. Scheirer, M., Hartling, G., Hagerman, D.: Defining sustainability outcomes of health programs: illustrations from an on-line survey. Eval. Program Plann. **31**(4), 335–346 (2008). https://doi.org/10.1016/j.evalprogplan.2008.08.004

24. Greenhalgh, T., Robert, G., Bate, P., Kyriakidou, O., Macfarlane, F., Peacock, R.: How to spread good ideas: a systematic review of the literature on diffusion, dissemination and sustainability of innovations. In: Health Technical report: National Co-ordinating Centre for NHS Service Delivery and Organisation R & D (NCCSDO) (2004)

25. Racine, D.: Reliable effectiveness: a theory on sustaining and replicating worthwhile innovations. Adm. Policy Ment. Health 33(3), 356–387 (2006). https://doi.org/10.1007/s10488-006-0047-1

26. Scheirer, M., Dearing, J.: An agenda for research on the sustainability of public health programs. Am. J. Publ. Health 101(11), 2059–2067 (2011). https://doi.org/10.2105/AJPH.2011.300193

27. Stirman, S., Kimberly, J., Cook, N., Calloway, A., Castro, F., Charns, M.: The sustainability of new programs and innovations: a review of the empirical literature and recommendations for future research. Implementation Sci. 7, 17 (2012). https://doi.org/10.1186/1748-5908-7-17

28. Scheirer, M.: Is sustainability possible? A review and commentary on empirical studies of program sustainability. Am. J. Eval. 26(3), 320–347 (2005). https://doi.org/10.1177/109821 4005278752

29. Becker, M., Lazaric, N., Nelson, R., Winter, S.: Applying organisational routines in understanding organisational change. Ind. Corp. Change 14(5), 775–791 (2005). https://doi.org/10.1093/icc/dth071

30. Gruen, R., et al.: Sustainability science: an integrated approach for health programme planning. Lancet 372(9649), 1579–1589 (2008). https://doi.org/10.1016/S0140-6736(08)616 59-1

31. Slaghuis, S., Starting, M., Bal, R., Nieboer, A.: A framework and a measurement instrument for sustainability of work practices in long-term care. BMC Health Serv. Res. 1(1), 314 (2011). https://doi.org/10.1186/1472-6963-11-314

32. Trottier, L., Denis, J., Villeneuve, M.: Anchoring and Sustaining Change in Healthcare Organisations. CHSRF/CIHR GETOS Chair & CIHR/AnEIS Program, Montreal (2007)

33. Davies, B., Edwards, N.: Sustaining knowledge use. In: Straus, SE., Tetroe, J., Graham, I.D (eds) Knowledge Translation in Health Care: Moving from Evidence to Practice. John Wiley & Sons, Sussex, UK, pp. 237–248 (2013)

34. Buchanan, D., Fitzgerald, L., Ketley, D.: The Sustainability and Spread of Organisational Change: Modernising Healthcare. Routledge, London (2007)

35. Fixsen, D., Naoom, S., Blase, K., Friedman, R., Wallace, F.: Implementation Research: A Synthesis of the Literature. University of South Florida, Tampa (2005)

Patients' Trust in Public Health System Mediated by Hospital Information Systems in Context of LMIC

Harleen Kaur[1], Sundeep Sahay[2(⊠)], and Arunima Mukherjee[3]

[1] University of Delhi, New Delhi, India
harleenkaur@ms.du.ac.in
[2] University of Oslo, Oslo, Norway
sundeeps@ifi.uio.no
[3] HISP, Noida, India

Abstract. Public health information systems in LMICs have an been studied in the context of primary health care while systems in district hospitals have not attracted the required attention. This is a sad neglect, given that district hospitals in LMICs cater to a high proportion of the population in a district and also provide life-saving healthcare services. ICTs have played a significant role in improving social trust in LMICs and we explore this in context of public health in India. While getting hospital information systems to work in district settings is a non-trivial and expensive challenge, it becomes imperative to understand what benefits citizens experience with the introduction of such systems. Drawing from an empirical base of a successful 10-year implementation of a hospital information system across a network of 20+ district hospitals in the state of Himachal Pradesh, India, the authors use the conceptual perspective of institutional and interpersonal trusts to analyze the perceived benefits seen for patients, and how this has helped shape patient trust towards the technological intervention and the hospital from where they avail services.

Keywords: Public health · Hospital information system · Patient trust · India

1 Introduction

Trust represents "an instantiated informal norm that promotes co-operation between two or more individuals" [1]. Studies have also argued that trust in society is related to economic and human development [2, 3]. Özcan and Blørnskov [4] conducted an empirical analysis of the relationship between trust and human development across 86 countries and found that while there are high levels of trust in Scandinavian countries, there are significantly lower levels in Rwanda, Brasil and Trinidad and Tobago. We find this analysis intriguing to further explore, particularly in the context of ICT4D research, to understand the role that ICTs may play in enhancing or undermining trust. We explore this in the context of public health in India.

© IFIP International Federation for Information Processing 2020
Published by Springer Nature Switzerland AG 2020
R. K. Bandi et al. (Eds.): IFIPJWC 2020, IFIP AICT 601, pp. 207–221, 2020.
https://doi.org/10.1007/978-3-030-64697-4_16

Having experienced health care systems in both Scandinavia and in India, we can reflect on a lay understanding of the role of trust. In Scandinavia, when one takes an appointment with a doctor, you are sure to meet the doctor, get 15 min of a good hearing, and receive the medicines prescribed. In India, these certainties are not a given, particularly for those living in rural areas, who may make a long trek to the public health facility to find that the doctor or the prescribed medicines not available. From the perspective of citizens, in Scandinavia, the health system can be trusted, which encourages citizens to avail the facilities and care, while the same is not the case in India. Improved access to health services, undoubtedly strengthens development processes, which explains Scandinavia's high levels of trust scores [4].

An interesting question from the perspective of ICT4D research is how does ICTs influence the growth or not of trust in a public health context in a LMIC? For example, it could be possible that ICTs may help citizens to pre-book their appointments to ensure they can meet their doctor on the scheduled time. ICT enabled electronic medical record (EMR) systems can potentially provide longitudinal records of a patient, which can help strengthen individual clinical care. Arguably then, understanding how ICTs shape trust processes becomes crucial in how they can both improve health care and broader development processes. The research question this paper addresses is: "How do patients perceive their healthcare experience with public hospitals with the introduction of technology, and what implications does that have on their trust in the public health system?"

The empirical basis to analyze this question is a state level hospital information system in an Indian state. After this brief introduction, in the next section, we provide a brief overview of the public health context in India relevant to our analysis. We then present our conceptual perspective around trust and ICTs. This is followed by a discussion on the methods and then the case study narrative. The case analysis and discussion sections then follow.

1.1 The Context of Public Health in India

The Indian economy in the past decade has shown immense growth, that has also resulted in further widening of disparity among rich and poor. Growing socio-economic disparity has also led to worsening of health outcomes [5] as incomes, do not by themselves, ensure the health and well-being of people [6]. The right to live is conferred by constitution of India upon its citizens, consequently the government is required to guarantee right to health for all [1]. India's budgetary allocation (approximately 1.28% of GDP in 2017–2018) for health has always been inadequate given its population size and the health challenges it faces. While the Indian government has been reasonably successful in building the digital infrastructure at district levels, the availability of adequate healthcare professionals remains a big challenge [7], with more than 50% specialist positions not filled in district hospitals [8].

Applications of ICTs are a central part of health reform in most LMICs. However, in India, as in many other LMICs, the focus has been on strengthening primary health care systems. Efforts to strengthen the hospital sector with ICTs has remained limited, and so also is research in this domain. This is a significant lack, given that a large proportion of health care to citizens is provided through the hospital sector. Braa and Sahay [9] point out that the hospital sector has tended to be neglected by the donor community because hospitals represent complex organization where it is far more difficult to show results than in the primary care sector.

2 Trust – Basis for the Conceptual Framework

Trust can cause patients to be more receptive to pre-treatment counseling, encourage relevant medical disclosures, enable exchange of medical information and patient participation in decision making around their health issues [10]. Patient satisfaction with greater trust in the health system will potentially better clinical outcomes [11]. Prior studies, primarily in rich countries, have analyzed trust with a key focus on data sharing issues [12]. In LMICs, the priority is to ensure cost-effective healthcare to large populations. Since trust can be an important resource in improving outcomes of scarce resources. ICT reform efforts should seek to enhance trust.

Trust exists in a situation of vulnerability of a trustor who is confident that the trustee will take care of his/her interests with due importance [13–15]. This suggests the inseparability of trust with vulnerability, and that trust is not needed in a situation where trustor is not vulnerable. Vulnerability is inevitable and unavoidable in medical settings given the power and knowledge asymmetries between the doctor and the patient. Trust tends to be voluntary and cannot be coerced into any relationship [16], representing a "judgment in a situation of risk that the trustee will act in the best interests of the trustor, or at least in ways that will not be harmful to the trustor" [17]. In practice, trust plays a massive role in the choice a patient makes towards selecting a doctor or visiting a facility for conducting diagnostic or imaging tests. In India, doctors have the status of gods leading to blind trust of patients in them, and the doctor's recommendations is taken as the "truth" [18].

Research has emphasized both institutional [19] and interpersonal forms of trust [20]. Institutional trust represents a form of public trust indicating the structural aspects of the healthcare system [21]. Giddens [22] has argued that interpersonal trust is built upon institutional trust, which takes place at interaction sites or 'access points', involving 'facework' or 'faceless' commitments depending on whether a physical representative is involved [22]. Facework commitment is reflected by personality related facets, such as professionalism, communication, general mannerisms and caring attitude, exhibited by a system representative [23]. On the other hand, faceless commitment is created by legitimacy and technical expertise, leading to higher quality services [22, 24].

In a medical setting, both interpersonal and institutional trust are relevant in conjunction [25]. Assessment of institutional or public trust is necessary as it has implications on interpersonal trust between patient and the health system [21, 26]. We next discuss how ICTs may mediate these trust related processes.

2.1 Trust and ICTs

Trust has been studied in the context of Electronic Health Records (EHRs) [27, 28], primarily in rich countries. Institutional trust and technical reliability are intimately intertwined [29], and studies have focused on their implications on improving technological outcomes [30]. While trust may be enhanced if the ICT helps the patient to spend reduced time in the hospital, the opposite may happen if there are frequent system breakdowns resulting in the patient having a worse experience in the hospital than before.

Trust is a process which builds gradually based on several interactions between the trustee and trustor [14]. Offe [31] argues that institutions must commit to values of truth and justice to build a strong foundation of trust of patients, even if the patient has weaker ability to pay for medical expenditures [32]. Across LMICs, trust in medical relationships has been institutionalized in different ways vis-à-vis "ethical commitments" in Tanzania, "quality of training, and "sufficiency of equipment and medicines" in Sri Lanka, and "accountability for complaints mechanism" in South Africa [33]. Trust has typically been treated as a variable or a construct [34], while others have viewed it as a process comprising of trust creation, development and maintenance [26]. Lee and Choi [35] have focused on discourses around trust, including its initiation and evolution.

2.2 Our Analytical Framework

We propose an analytical framework which combines both institutional and interpersonal forms of trust from a process perspective. Luhmann [19] argues that trust helps individuals to deal with complexity, even though their actions may not appear completely rational. Patients may simplify their choices of the institution in the presence of trust in the care provider. Patient's interpersonal trust may outweigh issues of institutional conditions. A patient is situated in a web of interactions with the hospital staff including doctors, lab technicians, pharmacists, and registration clerks, which span both institutional and interpersonal forms of trust relationships.

Crucial to the shaping of trust, is the patients' knowledge and the flows of information he/she is engaged with. For example, the registration number is crucial for the patient to understand how he/she is remembered by the institution, how safe the data is, and the benefits the ID provides, for example, health insurance. So, how the registration clerk may register or retrieve the ID number shapes both the institutional and interpersonal levels of trust [36]. ICTs bring forth new forms of collecting and representing information, which potentially influences trust relationships over time based on repeated interactions [24]. Our analytical framework seeks to understand how a patient's interaction at the hospital at both the institutional and interpersonal levels is mediated by ICTs, and the implications it has on trust.

3 Research Methodology

3.1 Research Design

The current paper is part of a larger action research initiative to design, build and implement a hospital information system (HospIS) in a network of 20+ While this project has been ongoing for over a decade, we report in this paper on research conducted over May-November 2019, when we made personal visits to a set of five hospitals and interviewed 66 patients to understand their experience in the hospital post the implementation of HospIS.

3.2 Data Collection

Trust in HospIS and public health system was gauged using analysis of qualitative data collected through checklists, in-depth interviews and observational methods on patients and attendants in the hospitals. Guided by theory, checklists were formulated reflecting proxies to understand trust, and finalized in discussion with other members of the research team. These probes in the checklists were in the form of pointed questions such as - whether they felt the system provided them with improved care and what features of HospIS they found relevant [37]. Secondary data from various reports was extracted to develop a deep understanding of current state of affairs at the district hospitals of India.

We contacted Out-Patient Department (OPD) patients at various locations in the hospital, e.g. near registration desk, waiting areas, outside doctor's chambers, imaging labs and pharmacy. In-Patient Department (IPD) patients were not contacted considering issues of hygiene and severity of their medical condition. However, their attendants were generally consulted on relevant issues.

4 Data Analysis

The qualitative data collected was interpreted to identity themes of institutional and interpersonal trust and their interplay. We discuss the interpretations of case narratives about patient trust in the following section which is organized around four key themes illustrating institutional and interpersonal trust, and their interplay.

In the Table 1 below, we show some illustrations of the themes.

Table 1. Themes of trust.

Sl.no	Themes	Interplay of interpersonal and instiutional factors
1	Improving patient experience in hospitals	New system of computer generated tickets in hospitals, which gives clear directions on whom to visit; reduced chaos and orderly queues, with separate queue for senior citizens, and no jostling for personal favors; reduced waiting time; a more positive consultation experience with doctors
2	Improved documentation for patients	New forms of communication, such as sending of lab reports by text SMS; improved possibilities for the retrieval of lost medical records; printed prescriptions and lab test reports, with medical ranges; empowering patients with OPD slips/prescriptions etc., which can provide patients with other opportunities for accessing care
3	Sense of fair treatment	Equal opportunities of treatment to the disadvantaged; Clerks ensure queues are not jumped by privileged class; fee of cost treatment for all
4	Potential linkage of other Public health schemes	Smart card linked health insurance (e.g. PM-JAY); Transparency in distribution of public goods, e.g. drugs

4.1 Improved Patient Experience

Older patients categorically mentioned some changes in the information flows they saw initiated through HospIS. Patients, particularly those with prior experience with the hospital, could see some positive changes, enhancing their sense of trust, and further recommending the provider to others. On the other hand, if patients had an untoward experience, possibly due to system malfunctioning or power failures, causing unnecessary long waits and increased frustration, it created distrust for system and institution.

Patients who had frequent interactions with the system tended to have more positive feelings of trust, which motivated them to make repeat visits to the hospitals and also recommend same to the others. This represents a cyclical process of system experience, institutional and interpersonal trust, and enhanced referrals leading to growing feelings of trust [18]. Some examples of improved patient experiences are given below.

Reduced Chaos and Improved Management of Queues. Patients appreciated greater organization of queues at the OPD due to a unique token ID being issued to them at the registration. Several participants cited reduced physical chaos in the hospital including, less running around, reduced bypassing of the queues, reduced harassment to small children, physically disabled and women. A separate queue provided for senior citizens, were recently introduced reforms which were attributed to the ICT intervention. Everyone who comes to the hospital now knows that they must wait for their turn as represented in their registration slip. *"Earlier the stronger men would push the weaker lot, and get to the queue and doctors first but that cannot happen now"*, as testified by a female patient. Another old patient mentioned *"registration at the hospital is an age-old practice, earlier it used to be done manually which used to be a long and clumsy routine. After computerization, registration is much more organized and faster"*. *"Technology played a hugely important role in streamlining the process of health care delivery"*, quoted another patient. The trust in the healthcare provider breaks if the patients' time is not valued and there is mismanagement in attending to patients by hospital staff. A poor experience with a system representative also affects institutional trust adversely, in the long run. The sense of greater order with the queuing system, an institutional intervention, also helped improve the interpersonal trust between the hospital staff and patients, who would earlier have been the target of patients' anger when the queues were poorly managed.

Improved Efficacy of Hospital Staff. It is the care and motivation to care for the trustor's welfare, emphasizing affective opinions, on which trust is, based [38]. Patients generally reported experiencing cordial behavior of the hospital staff. Only negligible number of participants reported misbehavior by the lab staff or doctors. Mostly, all the patients reported that during consultation, despite heavy load, doctors listened to the patients calmly and conducted a thorough diagnosis of their problem. Reportedly, at least some part of the doctor-patient consultation process is now managed by the system rather effectively, resulting in reduced anarchy at every level. For example, once the patient was registered, his/her record would show up on the doctor's screen which reduced the effort required by the patient to tell his/her history to the doctor. The institutional system thus had positive implications at the interpersonal level. However, since the OPD module was not well utilized by all doctors, the full institutional potential the system provided could not be leveraged.

Patients outside OPDs now patiently wait for their turn as they know no one will bypass the ordered queue. Also, doctors at bigger facilities have support of data entry operators for processing patient information into the system so that prescriptions can be printed. A patient was quoted saying, "*When there is less noise and crowd outside OPD, the doctor is able to focus on consultation and attends to the patients well*".

Further probing about patients' institutional trust, more specifically, their perceptions of competency of the doctors, was done by asking whether the patients recovered from illness following doctor's advice; whether patients took second opinion from outside private facilities; if patients ever felt that doctors were in a hurry to wind up consultations since there was long queue? Surprisingly, to all the questions we got encouraging responses. Patients had enormous trust in the doctors of the surveyed hospitals, particularly in the department of gynecology, surgery and orthopedics. Reportedly, they surrendered themselves to the doctor completely for the treatment and followed their advice diligently, demonstrating both interpersonal and institutional trust. Improved quality of interaction with staff also enhanced interpersonal trust. A patient testified about the altruistic attitude of doctors saying, "*I know there was huge queue waiting outside for this doctor but he never avoided answering repeated questions about his medicine prescription. Had I been at his place I would have definitely given irritated response, really appreciate his service intent*", reinforcing his trust in doctor as well as the health system, representing an interplay of institutional and interpersonal levels of trust.

This improved patient experience, was also seen as a blessing for the non- medical staff. One staff at a OPD said:

> "*Earlier, patients used to jostle with each other to know about their turn and even after repeated requests (to them) for taking seat in the OPD waiting room, it would fall on deaf ears of anxious patients. However, with the computerized token system facilitated by HospIS, they sit patiently for their turn as they already know their order in the queue for a particular OPD*".

> "*It is such a relief for us. Patients (in the past) used to accuse us of favoring some patients over others and sometimes also talked to us in harsh or abusive language. Now the token numbers of patients are called and there are no grudges,*" said one of the attendants at the gynecology ward. Automated token system was crucial in building trust. The older generation was particularly content with the way hospital operates now, as one of them was quoted saying, "*Now there is a separate queue for oldies like us, and we are not pushed back by stronger and younger fellows for the registration slip*"

4.2   Improved Documentation for Patients

Retrieval of medical records from HospIS: There was an old man waiting at the surgery OPD, extremely worried about having forgotten his lab reports at home and had no one accompanying him to fetch the report from his home. Looking at his worrisome state, we approached and informed him that he need not worry if he had an old prescription with his CRR number (HospIS generated unique ID) which would allow retrieval of his record any time. He was much relieved to learn about this feature, which then helped him to have a thorough consultation with the surgeon for his upcoming surgery. Such positive experiences were crucial in building interpersonal trust which helped enhance institutional trust.

Printed Prescriptions and Lab Test Reports. Reduced the probability of medical errors such as wrong prescriptions and diagnosis, often caused by illegible handwriting of the doctor. This supported both interpersonal and institutional trust. In their experience, patients observed that hand-written prescriptions are often illegible, as a result either they remained tied up with the same doctor or end up taking wrong medicines because they had to rely on the ability of the pharmacist to correctly read the hand-written prescription. With the introduction of HospIS at the hospital, also came increased opportunities of choice for the patients. Now, with a printout, they could access the correct medicines either from the hospital or external pharmacies employing interpersonal trust. Furthermore, if the patient wants to opt for a second opinion elsewhere, they could do so with the printed OPD slip, which they previously did not receive. Exercising such a choice helps empower patients [37] and enhances institutional trust.

Text Message Indicating Completed Lab Reports. HospIS also provided patients with an important feature of notifying by SMS when the lab reports are ready. Many patients reported having received a text message on their phone about their lab test report being ready for pick up while a few were apparently unaware of this functionality. Overall patients were found to have benefitted from HospIS, through getting empowered over time citing several examples.

4.3 Sense of Fair Treatment

Prior to HospIS, a patient known to a member of the hospital staff often would take advantage of this to bypass the queues and directly approach the doctor. Such behavior of "jumping the queue" would infuriate the other waiting patients, and potentially negatively influence patients' sense of institutional trust as was not seen as being "fair". The vulnerable and disadvantaged patients were the most affected. HospIS made such behavior a thing of the past since the queues were now operated using registration numbers and consultations with doctors was based on patient's serial number in the queue.

This queuing system also had adverse effects on those who were used to being dispensed with favors in earlier times. We saw the case of a senior government official getting furious at the registration clerk for not allowing him to see the doctor directly and requiring him to register in the system at the registration this. While this was a "fairer" system than before, we were told by some patients that the trend of favoritism still continued in the smaller hospitals:

"The hospital staff doesn't bother following the registration order with villagers like me. I always have to spend the whole day waiting for the treatment while staff members bring their relatives and they get the treatment immediately".

Approximately one third of the patients surveyed at these facilities mentioned that hospital staff favors relatives or friends and gets them registered from a different "staff" queue. Other patients, who had not encountered similar situations, were positive about the computerized system. This difference of opinion could be attributed to the lack of administrative control and monitoring in district hospitals distant from the state capital. Strict controls on hospital staff are required to implement "absolutely no undue favors to any relative or friend" policy to achieve the purpose of equality for all [39], a key determinant of institutional trust.

While, many other patients also mentioned that they got free treatment at the hospital irrespective of whether they knew any staff member or not. Also, registration desk ensured that the allotted serial order is mostly followed. With HospIS managing the patient inflow, they are more confident about transparency and fairness from the hospital staff about medical treatment.

4.4 Potential Building of Linkages to Other Public Health Schemes

Several patients acknowledged available public health schemes, such as free treatment to pregnant woman and children under the age of 5 years. Some respondents were already using smart cards issued under these schemes while others were curious to understand how they could enroll and avail benefits under these different schemes. A pregnant woman told us about the general lack of awareness citizens had about such schemes. She seemed particularly enthusiastic about the digitization at the hospital, as she believed that it could help building awareness and help them to enroll under these schemes. She also suggested that awareness about various zero-bill schemes linked with Aadhar card (universal identity) of the users should be created. Such information dissemination amongst citizens through pamphlets or radio would help enhance greater public trust in the health system. Such schemes, when linked with system, could help ensure the removing of bottlenecks in fair distribution of benefits under them. Broadly, the more the public can take advantage under public health schemes; greater will be their institutional trust in the health system, with positive implications on the building of interpersonal trust with the hospital staff.

5   Discussions

Our case analysis helped us identify some key recommendations for three key stakeholder groups (technology providers, hospital administrators and citizens) on how to build trust at both institutional and interpersonal levels. These are now discussed and briefly presented in Table 2.

5.1 System Design Team

We provide some recommendations for the system design team which we believe could strengthen both interpersonal and institutional level trust.

Table 2. Summarizing recommendations to stakeholders

Factors	Recommen-dations for stakeholders	Interplay of interpersonal and institutional factors
Institutional	System design team Hospital administration Citizens	Electronic bill boards displaying array of information useful to patients, e.g. doctors on leave, tests not available, etc. Online registration from home Enabling transfer of medical files electronically through intra-hospital networking Creating awareness about several system-linked public health schemes Separate queue for patients waiting for lab test Employing more manpower (both medical and non-medical) Surprise visits to hospital for ensuring HospIS being used by staff Being more information demanding, e.g. Printed prescription in smaller facilities also, insisting doctor to check on computer screen past record of patient Getting smart cards made Developing understanding of available public heath schemes
Institutional and Inter-personal factors intertwined	System design team Hospital administration	Pharmacy networked with OPDs so that only available medicines are prescribed by doctors More technology interventions to ensure HospIS implementation at all levels in hospital More awareness on aspect of confidentiality of patient information
	Citizens	Patients should question about serial order of those who are bypassing queues Patients should carry old prescription or CRR number so that they are not registered as a new patient IPD patients may ask for printed discharge summary

Strengthening Easy and Cross-Functional Access to Information A female patient, who had specially taken leave from her workplace to come down to the hospital for consultation with orthopedics, was particularly annoyed because she had to wait a long time in the registration queue for her turn, only to realize that the orthopedics doctor was on leave that day. If she could get this information soon after reaching the hospital, she would have gone back to work to come again some other day. So, she made a useful suggestion after this experience - information which could save patients' time, e.g. doctors on leave, tests and medicines not available and number of beds occupied/available at the emergency section, may be displayed on electronic billboards as extracted from the system. Such simple technology additions can bring in more order and discipline at the hospital, value the time of patients, prevent unnecessary crowd and reduce unnecessary footfall at the registration desk as well as at the OPDs.

Similarly, if the pharmacy is linked with the OPDs through the system, doctors can then prescribe only those medicines that are shown to be available by the system. Such cross-functional and easy access to information will help patients form positive perceptions about the HospIS and thus, develop greater trust in the health system at large. Though this functionally was technically available in the system, it was not being well utilized because of the poor use of the OPD module by the doctors.

Online Registration from Home. A senior government officer who was not too amused to go through registration had suggested for a provision of online registration from home. He suggested that this will not only reduce the burden on registration desk but also be more convenient for patients, thereby saving patients' time, supporting their institutional trusts in the system. Again, we believe building this functionality is not only a technical task but requires an institutional commitment to make such a system work.

Enabling Intra-Hospital Networking. The interactions with patients revealed that in case of transfer to another hospital, their medical details were either handed over to the patient or sent out physically to the referred hospital directly. It will add to the convenience of patients if the medical details are transmitted through HospIS from one hospital to another. This will likely require some process reengineering on the part of administration to create intra-hospital networks within the public health system. Also, systems of data regulation would need to be strengthened to ensure patient privacy is maintained and due consent is taken on use of personal information.

5.2 Hospital Administration

Below, we list some expectations from the hospital administration that came out in our interactions with patients, likely to enhance their institutional trusts in the system.

Technology Interventions for Greater Perceived Fairness. HospIS played a major role in reducing favoritism and bringing in equality of treatment. From the interactions, we inferred that patients look for further technology and administrative interventions such as surprise visits, or CCTV cameras to ensure enhanced fair treatment for all. This will also help patients build institutional trust based on enhanced interpersonal trust delivered through higher levels of staff monitoring [22]. However, we must be sensitive to the fact that enhanced staff monitoring may lead to their resistance and counter-implications.

Programs for Increased Awareness About System and Government Interventions. Many of the patients interacted with were either clueless about how to avail benefits under different government schemes or found the procedure for claiming benefits cumbersome. Greater awareness can help minimize procedural complications and will allow amateur and less literate patients to avail benefits under these schemes with greater confidence, further strengthening institutional trust for them.

On a similar note, most of the patients do not understand the implications of unsecure private medical information. When patients know that no one else will see their medical information except for those authorized, they will also have less hesitation answering taboo questions from the doctor e.g. about HIV infection or family planning, rendering system with better quality data and more confident patients.

Improved Processes for Patient Inflow Management. A patient who only came for getting her ultrasound scan done was miffed to have waited in a long registration queue and suggested for a separate queue for people who have already been diagnosed and prescribed pathology or imaging scan by the doctor. This will both reduce the queue size and value patients' time. Further, several patients perceived that, at every stage, from data entry operators to doctors, increasing the manpower will help improve the efficacy of healthcare delivery. This will also help in collecting large scale and quality data which can then be used to analyse trends and patterns longitudinally for improving health outcomes in the state, thus, enhancing citizen's trust in HospIS.

The implementation of these suggestions will further serve the overarching purpose of providing adequate and superior care to the patients making them content with the treatment and facilities, thus, enhancing their trust in government, public facilities and public healthcare, in specific. The institutional trusts in public health system will positively affect their perceptions about the hospital staff, further improving interpersonal trusts.

5.3 Citizens

The above discussion reflects that the nature of health consumers or patients surveyed under the current study is information demanding. They are more empowered and inquisitive about their interaction with the healthcare provider and treatment being received.

The patients should make demands to doctors for checking their past medical history in the system from their unique CRR number during consultations. They should even demand from doctors to give printed prescriptions at all the hospitals as is done in bigger facilities of the capital. Patients, at the time of discharge from hospital, can ask their doctor to provide a printed summary of the treatment done and tests performed along with their results to facilitate consultations later. Given the fact that the technology intervention has been developed with tax money, patients should be made aware of their rights to demand different types of system generated information.

6 Conclusions

This research provided an understanding of the process of building patient trust in the public health system, especially as mediated by the hospital information system. With several examples cited by surveyed patients, about their care experience at the hospital, the complex role of trust is further validated, especially concerning the issues of justice and equity. A clear distinction between the application of interpersonal and institutional trusts was a challenging task since the process of trust development in any health system involves intertwined patterns of relationships between both forms of trusts. This overlap of trust in certain instances is consistent with prior work [38]. While prior research has focused on ICTs, this research studied this issue in the hospital sector. Studying the implications of ICTs from the perspective of patients is another important contribution.

References

1. Fukuyama, F.: Social capital, civil society and development. Third World Q. **22**, 7–20 (2001). https://doi.org/10.1080/713701144
2. Gunnar, S., Gert, S.: The puzzle of the scandinavian welfare state and social trust. Issues Soc. Sci. **3**(2), 90–99 (2015). https://doi.org/10.5296/iss.v3i2.8597
3. Knack, S., Keefer, P.: Does social capital have an economic pay-off? A cross-country investigation. Q. J. Econ. **112**, 1251–1288 (1997). http://hdl.handle.net/10.1162/003355300555475. Accessed 14 Aug 2020
4. Özcan, B., Bjørnskov, C.: Social trust and human development. J. Soc.-Econ. **40**(6), 753–762 (2011). https://doi.org/10.1016/j.socec.2011.08.007
5. Wilkinson, R.G., Pickett, K.E.: Income inequality and population health: a review and explanation of the evidence. Soc. Sci. Med. **62**, 1768–1784 (2006). https://doi.org/10.1016/j.socscimed.2005.08.036
6. Rao, K.S.: Do We Care? India's Health System, 1st edn. Oxford University Press, New-Delhi (2017)
7. Gupta, I., Bhatia, M.: Indian health care system. In: Mossialos, E. (ed.) et al. International Profiles of Health Care System, The Commonwealth Fund (2017). https://www.commonwealthfund.org/sites/default/files/documents/___media_files_publications_fund_report_2017_may_mossialos_intl_profiles_v5.pdf. Accessed 20 May 2020
8. Kasthuri, A.: Challenges to healthcare in India - the five A's. Indian J Community Med. **43**, 141–143 (2018). http://www.ijcm.org.in/text.asp?2018/43/3/141/241651
9. Braa, J., Sahay, S.: Integrated Health Information Architecture: Power for the Users: Design Development and Use, 1st edn. Matrix Publishing, New Delhi (2012)
10. Gilson, L.: Trust and health care as a social institution. Soc. Sci. Med. **56**, 1452–1468 (2003). https://doi.org/10.1016/s0277-9536(02)00142-9
11. Thom, D.H., Kravitz, R.L., Bell, R.A., Krupat, E., Azari, R.: Patient trust in the physician: relationship to patient requests. Fam. Prac. **19**(5), 476–484 (2002). https://doi.org/10.1093/fampra/19.5.476
12. Platt, J., Kardia, S.: Public trust in health information sharing: implications for biobanking and electronic health record systems. J. Pers. Med. **5**(1), 3–21 (2015). https://doi.org/10.3390/jpm5010003
13. Baier, A.: Trust and antitrust. Ethics **96**, 231–260 (1986). https://doi.org/10.1086/292745
14. Bigley, G.A., Pearce, J.L.: Straining for shared meaning in organizational science: Problems of trust and distrust. Acad. Manag. Rev. **23**, 405–421 (1998). https://doi.org/10.5465/amr.1998.926618
15. Carter, M.A.: Ethical Analysis of Trust in Therapeutic Relationships. University of Michigan Press, Ann Arbor (1989)
16. Misztal, B.A.: Trust in Modern Societies: The Search for the Bases of Moral Order. Polity Press, Cambridge (1996)
17. Goudge, J., Gilson, L.: How can trust be investigated? Drawing lessons from past experience. Soc. Sci. Med. **61**(7), 1439–1451 (2005). https://doi.org/10.1016/j.socscimed.2004.11.071
18. Hall, M.A., et al.: Measuring patients' trust in their primary care providers. Med. Care Res. Rev. **59**, 293–318 (2002). https://doi.org/10.1177/1077558702059003004

19. Luhmann, N.: Familiarity, confidence and trust: problems and alternatives. In: Trust: Making and Breaking Cooperative Relations Basil Blackwell, Great Britain (1988). https://www.nuffield.ox.ac.uk/users/gambetta/Trust_making%20and%20breaking%20cooperative%20relations.pdf

20. Fukuyama, F.: Trust: the Social Virtues and the Creation of Prosperity. Free Press, New York (1995)

21. Peters, D., Youssef, F.F.: Public trust in the healthcare system in a developing country. Int. J. Health Plann. Manage. **31**(2), 227–241 (2016). https://doi.org/10.1002/hpm.2280

22. Giddens, A.: The Consequences of Modernity. Polity Press, Cambridge (1990)

23. Meyer, S.B., Ward, P.: Do your patients trust you?: A sociological understanding of the implications of patient mistrust in healthcare professionals. Australas. Med. J. **1** (2008). http://hdl.handle.net/2328/26516

24. Whitehead, A.N.: Science and the Modern World. CUP, Cambridge (1926)

25. Rhodes, R., Strain, J.: Trust and transforming medical institutions. Cambridge Q. Healthc. Ethics CQ Int. J. Healthc. Ethics Committees **9**, 205–217 (2000). https://doi.org/10.1017/S0963180100090207X

26. Khodyakov, D.: Trust as a process: a three-dimensional approach. Sociology **41**, 115–132 (2007). https://doi.org/10.1177/0038038507072285

27. Mittelstadt, B.D., Floridi, L.: The ethics of big data: current and foreseeable issues in biomedical contexts. Sci. Eng. Ethics **22**(2), 303–341 (2015). https://doi.org/10.1007/s11948-015-9652-2

28. Yusif, S., Soar, J., Hafeez-Baig, A.: Older people, assistive technologies, and the barriers to adoption: a systematic review. Int. J. Med. Inf. **94**, 112–116 (2016). https://doi.org/10.1016/j.ijmedinf.2016.07.004

29. Montague, E., Kleiner, B., Winchester, W.: Empirically understanding trust in medical technology. Int. J. Ind. Ergon. **39**, 1–7 (2009). https://doi.org/10.1016/j.ergon.2009.01.004

30. Adjekum, A., Blasimme, A., Vayena, E.: Elements of trust in digital health systems: scoping review. J. Med. Internet Res. **20**(12) (2018). https://doi.org/10.2196/11254. PMID: 30545807; PMCID: PMC6315261

31. Offe, C.: How Can We Trust Our Fellow Citizens?. In: Warren, M.E. (ed.) Democracy and Trust, pp. 42–87. Cambridge University Press, Cambridge (1999)

32. Russell, S.: Treatment-seeking behavior in urban Sri Lanka: trusting the state, trusting private providers. Soc. Sci. Med. **61**, 1396–1407 (2005). https://doi.org/10.1016/j.socscimed.2004.11.077

33. Gilson, L.: Editorial: building trust and value in health systems in low and middle income countries. Soc. Sci. Med. **61**, 1381–1384 (2005). https://doi.org/10.1016/j.socscimed.2004.11.059

34. Mcknight, D., Choudhury, V., Kacmar, C.: The impact of initial consumer trust on intentions to transact with a web site: a trust building model. J. Strateg. Inf. Syst. **11**, 297–323 (2002). https://doi.org/10.1016/S0963-8687(02)00020-3

35. Lee, J.N., Choi, B.: Effects of initial and ongoing trust in IT outsourcing: a bilateral perspective. Inf. Manage. **48**, 96–105 (2011). https://doi.org/10.1016/j.im.2011.02.001

36. Schilke, O., Cook, K.S.: A cross-level process theory of trust development in interorganizational relationships. Strateg. Organ. **11**(3), 281–303 (2013). https://doi.org/10.1177/1476127012472096

37. Sahay, S., Walsham, G.: Information technology, innovation and human development: hospital information systems in an indian state. J. Human Dev. Capabilities **18**, 1–18 (2017). https://doi.org/10.1080/19452829.2016.1270913

38. Gilson, L.: Trust in health care: theoretical perspectives and research needs. J. Health Organ. Manage. **20**, 359–375 (2006). https://doi.org/10.1108/14777260610701768
39. Ozawa, P.S., Sripad, P.: How do you measure trust in the health system? A systematic review of the literature. Soc. Sci. Med. **91**, 10–14 (2013). https://doi.org/10.1016/j.socscimed.2013.05.005

Building Agility in Health Information Systems to Respond to the COVID-19 Pandemic: The Sri Lankan Experience

Pamod Amarakoon[1,2](✉) [ID], Jørn Braa[3] [ID], Sundeep Sahay[3,4] [ID],
Pandula Siribaddana[1,2] [ID], and Roshan Hewapathirana[2,5] [ID]

[1] Postgraduate Institute of Medicine, University of Colombo, Colombo, Sri Lanka
pamodm@gmail.com
[2] HISP Sri Lanka, Colombo, Sri Lanka
[3] Department of Informatics, University of Oslo, Oslo, Norway
[4] HISP India, New Delhi, India
[5] Faculty of Medicine, University of Colombo, Colombo, Sri Lanka

Abstract. Agile methods have been popular in the software industry particularly in relation to technical innovations. However, agility in terms of providing health information support within a crisis laden pandemic situation such as COVID-19 is less well understood. This paper focused on an ongoing response of design, development, and implementation of a COVID-19 surveillance system based on DHIS2 platform in Sri Lanka. Our analysis aims at understanding; and developing agility.

An interpretive case study approach was adopted where qualitative data were gathered using multiple methods such as participant observation, document analysis, historical accounts, informal interviews and using secondary data. Thematic analysis technique was adopted where themes were identified collectively following multiple iterations of collaborative analysis.

We argue that the flexibility of the software platform, good technical and medical capacity and new modes of collaboration on systems development across institutional borders have contributed to the agility shown in the Sri Lankan context and its success in meeting health information challenges posed by COVID-19.

Keywords: COVID-19 · Agile software development · DHIS2 · Surveillance system · Health Information Systems

1 Introduction

While it has been documented that a crisis helps ignite innovation, we add to that argument that agility is also needed to combat pandemics such as COVID-19. Time is off essence, as there have been reports that countries which moved fast and early in establishing lock downs and social distancing measures (such as Vietnam) were more successful in managing the pandemic than the late starters (such as US and UK). How to best develop

© IFIP International Federation for Information Processing 2020
Published by Springer Nature Switzerland AG 2020
R. K. Bandi et al. (Eds.): IFIPJWC 2020, IFIP AICT 601, pp. 222–236, 2020.
https://doi.org/10.1007/978-3-030-64697-4_17

information systems to respond to health crisis as pandemics and the need for agility is the topic of this article, based on an empirical analysis of the COVID-19 response in Sri Lanka. In building our analysis, we also learn from the information system response to the 2009 H1N1 Swine influenza pandemic in three Asian countries.

Responding to the H1N1 (Swine Flu) pandemic in Japan in 2009, the software team in charge deemed it necessary to apply agile iterative approaches in developing the information system responses, because, as they argue, pandemics bring about unexpected and dynamically changing situations, policies, and requirements, which cannot be handled by traditional 'waterfall' approaches [1]. When the H1N1 (swine flu) hit Japan in 2009, the software team in charge. Analysing the same H1N1 pandemic in Singapore and Taiwan, Lai highlight the need for agility in response, as he sees as the iterative, successive process of adjustment, swift decisions and routine breaking actions needed to address the uncertainties associated with a pandemic [2].

Rigby, et al. [3] argue that agile responses do not typically come from a strategic plan or being driven by top management, but comes as someone, somewhere identifies an urgent need and then breaks through traditionally existing bureaucracies and constraints to find solutions to the problems drawing upon peer-to-peer networks that break down traditional structures.

Agile methods [4] are currently a popular approach in the software industry, a form of rapid prototyping based on short and continuous cycles of software development, release, feedback and improvements, so as to provide continuous value to the customer. However, it can be argued that Agile methods as they are currently practiced, focus primarily on the technical aspects of software design and development, and do not stretch into processes of implementation and use. Further, they focus primarily on the technical process, and do not examine the mutually reinforcing process of how a particular crisis situation may require different modes and forms of agility, and how this agility can help to respond to the crisis.

The COVID-19 crisis represents such a situation, which demands agile responses to building solutions, which should contribute to managing the crisis. We particularly focus on the domain of health information system, which provides the bedrock of a response strategy through its support for surveillance related processes. We will explore how this mutually reinforcing dynamic can be created and the modes by which the health responds to disaster management situations. This issue is particularly interesting to explore in the context of developing countries, which typically are poorly resourced and arguably are shackled by systems of bureaucracy and associated ills of tardiness and corruption, which are obvious bottlenecks to promoting systems and processes of agility. The research questions this paper thus pursues are:

What constitutes agility in the context of health information support for addressing pandemics like COVID-19?

How can agility be promoted within the context of a developing country facing such pandemics?

The paper is developed based on an ongoing response of design, development and implementation of a COVID-19 surveillance system in Sri Lanka. We analyze this successful example in terms of the impetus for its agile development, the process followed, and some of its outcomes in supporting the response. In conclusion, we reflect on the challenges of making this system more relevant for future cases. After this brief introduction, we discuss the methods underlying this empirical investigation, followed by the case study description. We then analyze the contributing conditions to enable agility, and how it may be relevant in the future and how it can be generalized beyond Sri Lanka.

2 Conceptual Framing: Agility in and with Digital Platforms

Our conceptual framing is informed by two key concepts: digital platforms and agility, leading to our conceptualization of the notion of "agility with digital platforms." We draw upon this notion for the analysis of the empirical case, of how multiple institutional actors come together to identify requirements and to develop different apps, modules, features and functionalities within a framework we label digital platforms following approaches of agile development. There is the need for institutional agility given the crisis situation, while digital platforms afford agility in the development methods, which we contribute to "agility in and with digital platforms". We discuss this development within the perspectives of agility and platforms.

2.1 Digital Platforms

Tiwana defines a software platform as a "software-based product or service that serves as a foundation on which outside parties can build complementary products or services" [5]. Tiwana also argues that platforms must be multisided, meaning they bring together two or more actors or groups of platform users, such as end users and app developers. Baldwin and Woodard define platform architecture as consisting of a platform core with a set of stable components, and complementary components that interact with the core through well-defined interfaces [6]. The wider software platform eco-system is therefore composed by software modules, apps, interfaces between them, developers, users and a variety of stakeholders.

Henfridsson and Bygstad suggest that in order to better understand digital platform dynamics, the unit of analysis should not be the core of the platform but its boundary resources [7]. These resources are made up of software tools and regulations facilitating the relationships between platform provider and app developers. In line with such socio-technical perspective on platforms, Gawer proposes to bridge two theoretical perspectives: economics, which see platforms as multiple sided markets that have both demand and supply-side users and with network effects between and within them, and engineering, which sees platforms as technological architecture. This leads Gawer to a new conceptualization of platforms as evolving organisations or meta organisations [8].

The DHIS2 platform discussed in this paper, was initially conceived as a web-based integrated information system and not as a platform. With an increasing number of implementations and use cases, it became increasingly difficult to address the tension between meeting more specialized local requirements and building a generic software which could be used in multiple locations and across different use cases [9]. To address this, the software has over the last few years been gradually re-designed towards a platform architecture, where the generic functionality is in the platform core, and local requirements can be addressed through more specialized apps which can speak to the core through open APIs [9].

2.2 Agility

Lee and Xia define software development agility as a software team's ability to efficiently and effectively respond to user requirement changes in a rapid and evolving manner [10]. More generally agile software development differs from traditional stepwise, structured, plan-driven 'waterfall' like approaches and in many ways similar to rapid cyclic proto-typing [11]. The need for heterogeneous teams with a variety of qualifications are high-lighted as a key characteristic for agile development [12]. Self-organized and empowered teams are better equipped to adjust to changing environments and requirements, fun-damental conditions for acting with flexibility and responsiveness. The Agile Alliance recommends to build projects around motivated people; 'give them the environment and support they need, and trust them to get the job done' [13].

Diverse competencies and perspectives in the team is needed to stimulate learning and innovations and generate more alternative solutions to complex problems [10]. A team with diverse expertise and experience can access a wide range of social networks and professional communities which enabled them to be more capable of handling requirement changes [10].

The term agile software development is often traced to the agile manifesto, which is building on various progressive values [13], emphasizing individuals and interactions over processes and tools, the need for building functional software over comprehensive documentation, collaboration over contractual negotiations and the importance of responding to change over dogmatically following a plan. The manifesto claims that adherence to such agile processes will help promote sustainable development as 'The sponsors, developers and users should be able to maintain a constant pace indefinitely.'

The Agile manifesto is written by a consortium with representatives from agile core software development communities such as Extreme Programming and SCRUM, which differ from the typical development context of a software platform ecosystem as being closer to the core platform. The principles and values, however, are seen to be equally relevant also across areas important in our analysis, such as for agile government [14] and agile governance [15].

2.3 Agility in and with Digital Platforms

The pandemic crisis fundamentally demands for agility in response, including relating to the surveillance support. Our framework helps examine agility in and with digital platforms. Institutional actors, which in normal times may be more tardy, are forced and motivated to be agile, which should break down delay creating traditional bureaucratic structures. Digital platforms are built for promoting innovation through the recombination of different digital components, building integration across systems, all on a free and open source code base, which is not shackled by license encumbrances. The DHIS2, discussed in this paper, we argue, is an example of such a platform where the generic functionality is in the platform core, and local requirements can be addressed through more specialized apps, which can speak to the core through open APIs, and thus supporting agile development practices, and thereby enable agility in and with digital platforms.

3   Methods

We adopted a case study methodology for this paper as it allowed us to examine in-depth both the context and the dynamics associated with the phenomenon – agile development of HIS (Health Information Systems) in a pandemic situation within a LMIC context of Sri Lanka. Such an approach according to Darke et al. is useful in newer and less developed research area such as the phenomenon investigated through this study [16]. In line with the definition of a case study by Yin, our approach was an empirical enquiry investigating a contemporary phenomenon within a real-life context – Sri Lankan health system context [17].

Authors of this paper have been directly or indirectly involved in the Sri Lankan context both prior and during the COVID-19 pandemic. Two of the authors of this paper, senior professors from the University of Oslo (JB & SS), have been involved in Sri Lankan setting from the time the masters programme was established as collaborators of the project, academics contributing to research and development work, supervisors for PhDs from Sri Lanka and as facilitators for DHIS2 implementation in the local context. Two of the other authors are doctoral graduates from the University of Oslo who have been involved in capacity development and research related to HIS in Sri Lanka as senior lecturers, supervisors and project team members (PS & RH). One of the authors was a masters graduate and now an MD trainee in health informatics with expertise in DHIS2 (PA), was directly involved in the development of the DHIS2 based COVID19 surveillance system. All the authors were involved as key resources in the entire cycle of development and implementation of the COVID-19 surveillance system. Those on the ground were involved with stakeholder meetings held in the Ministry of Health (MoH) in identifying the requirements of the surveillance system as well as analysis of the available solutions at the inception of the system. As different phases of the prototype was being developed, the researchers were involved in obtaining feedback from end users and in follow-up meetings in the MoH exploring possible solutions to address them. They were also involved as resource persons in online training programmes in which they identified the effective means of conducting training programmes based on the existing context. The authors also formed the link between global and local communities bridging the path for innovations to take place and its sharing both within and across different countries. Thus, we were able to link between agile development efforts that took place during the pandemic with historical accounts gathered by the authors during the last decade in the Sri Lankan context. This also enabled the authors to be sensitive to the intricate challenges experienced how these were overcome in contrast to pre-COVID era.

As proposed by Yin, the methods of data gathering in this case were multiple [17], spanning socio-technical methods. Some of the authors had lived experiences in the form of narratives of system development efforts. Observations at stakeholder meetings during setting-up of the DHIS2 in the form of memos were also gathered. Secondary data including reports published by public health agencies, documents presented at stakeholder meetings as well as notes generated following informal meetings with stakeholders were also data sources. Furthermore, the historical accounts by the authors themselves in the establishment of the Masters programme, the contribution by the graduates to the digital health ecosystem and the evolution of health informatics in Sri Lanka were also taken into consideration during the analysis. The study also made use of publications related to capacity development in health informatics in Sri Lanka and Masters thesis of graduates of the Bioinformatics program.

During data analysis we constantly engaged in exchanging our experiences and views related to gathered data. As suggested by Braun et al., the case narrative was then constructed collaboratively, and thematic analysis technique was used to identify patterns emerging in the presentation of this paper [18]. The two key themes emerging through the analysis included 'institutional networks of collaboration' and 'agile development of software solutions in the platform'. The collaborative approach to analysis helped to bring in multiple perspectives, making the narrative richer and more holistic.

4   Case Study

This case study section is divided into two parts. In the first, we outline the HIS context in the country, with a key focus on the BMI Masters programme on health informatics and how this has helped strengthened the national HIS. In the second, we outline the development process of the COVID-19 surveillance App, focusing on the innovations involved and the rapid cycles in which they have evolved.

4.1   The Context of HIS in Sri Lanka: The Role of the Masters Programme

In Sri Lanka, the MoH provides full funding for the medical officers to pursue postgraduate studies to become medical specialists, including in health informatics, at the Postgraduate Institute of Medicine of University of Colombo.

In 2009, the Masters in Biomedical Informatics degree programme was established with financial and technical support from the University of Oslo, Norway. This programme had a futuristic vision of producing medical specialists with a background of biomedical informatics who will work towards strengthening national HIS, and thus reducing dependence of external entities such as foreign experts and private sector. The students in this programme undergo extensive education on modern methods of informatics supplemented by a long-term thesis project where they work on real implementation topics. The relation with Oslo has enabled the use of DHIS2 as a training tool for the students, which they use in courses, thesis work, and many of them blossom to develop and nurture full-blown systems in different units of the MoH.

On completion of the programme, the graduates are reverted back to the MoH where they assume duties as 'Medical Officer in Health Informatics', with a wide range of responsibilities including health policy, design, development and implementation of HIS, training programmes and much more. Thus, these graduates, with rare hybrid skills of medicine and informatics, become crucial technical and administrative experts in driving the national HIS forward.

These graduates have been fundamental in the evolution of the Sri Lankan national HIS over the last decade and through their duties in various health departments in the MoH, the situation of strengthening national HIS has considerably improved. The DHIS2 platform, from its early days of use in 2013, has evolved into the de-facto national system, and more than 10 institutes in the preventive health sector, such as Reproductive,

Maternal, Newborn, Child Health (RMNCH) services, Tuberculosis, Malaria, Nutrition, Quarantine sector, and non-communicable diseases (NCDs), have based their systems on DHIS2. Experience, expertise, knowledge and trust in the DHIS2 platform have been important prerequisites for building the agile responses to the COVID-19 pandemic, which we describe in the next section.

4.2   Narrative on COVID-19 Implementation in Sri Lanka

This narrative is around the core components of the COVID-19 surveillance App development, as described in the timeframe of how it evolved (Fig. 1).

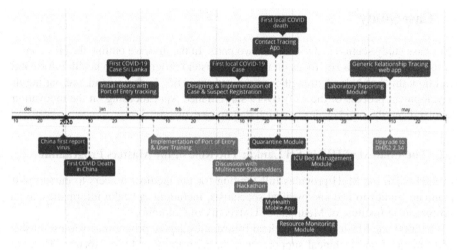

Fig. 1. Timeline of events related to development of information system for COVID-19 in Sri Lanka

Initial Development of Port of Entry Module: Jan 20–27, 2020

Initial discussions between the MoH and HISP Sri Lanka around setting up a COVID-19 application system happened around the third week of January 2020, as there was a rise in cases in South Asia and there was high likelihood of the disease entering Sri Lanka carried through the high inflow of tourist traffic to the country. Sri Lanka did not have an outbreak management HIS, which was integrated with curative healthcare and preventive health sectors and other necessary entry points related to COVID-19. Given the urgent impending threat, the MoH was keen to build this system from a platform and with existing resources rather than designing from scratch based on a platform, which was already in use in the country and was familiar to the health staff. At this stage HISP Sri Lanka explored the possibility of adopting DHIS2 for this purpose. A priority requirement of the MoH was to focus on tracking suspected passengers entering the country.

The design process created with the workflow of initial registration at the port of entry, which was to be continued with follow-up visits while the passengers were in the community. The system needed to capture sociodemographic information of arriving passengers, their recent travel information and symptoms present on arrival. This information should then be accessible to the community health staff to follow up that particular passenger in the community, and to establish whether the patient displayed positive symptoms. The first version of the system was thus focused on the port of entry component and was presented and approved by the Director General of Health Services in the fourth week of January just prior to the country reporting its first case of coronavirus on 27th January. Rapid training was conducted for users to use this functionality and the system went live. During use, it was seen that due to high passenger load, the data operators preferred to enter data into Google Sheets. Training programmes continued till 20 February, and then for reasons of scale and rapidity, training was done over Zoom.

Building of Clinical Management Component - From March 10th
Sri Lanka reported its first indigenous case in the second week of March 2020, catalyzing the MoH shift in focus to clinical management information of confirmed cases, including data on sociodemographic factors, symptoms, daily clinical updates, laboratory information and outcomes. The HISP team could rapidly build this functionality using the DHIS2 Tracker module on which they had prior competence, and later extend this to also include suspect cases tracking.

In the process of this development, various gaps in the DHIS2 core modules were identified, which constrained the meeting of some of MoH's priority requirements. This included restrictions in changing the enrolment organisation unit, automation of transmission of information and certain required visualisations such as contact mapping. To rapidly deal with addressing these limitations, a collaborative meeting was held around 14th March between the ICT agency of Sri Lanka, MoH staff, academics from the BMI programme of the University of Colombo, HISP Sri Lanka, and the Immigration Department. The ICT agency offered its cloud hosting services to deploy the DHIS2, thus enabling rapid country-wide diffusion.

As an outcome of these discussions, a hackathon was organized by the ICT Agency, which attracted volunteer developers from around the world representing public-private players including local developers, putting into practice agile development methods. The Hackathon helped created various outputs such as the contact tracing web application, ICU bed management application, tracing location through mobile towers and integration functionality with the immigration department system. The University of Oslo also joined hands providing mentoring support and creating changes in the core where needed. These diverse resources working together helped create rapid innovations in weeks which otherwise would have taken months or even years to build. Another product of the hackathon was the myHealth mobile application which enabled public messaging and to alert citizens of potential contacts with infected cases.

Integrations and Innovations Through Multi Sectoral Collaborations - March 14th Onwards
A DHIS2 web application was next built to analyze relationships and contact tracing, building upon one of the outputs of the hackathon. This functionality was aimed at enabling epidemiological research based on the cohort of confirmed patients. The DHIS2 relationship model provided the functionality to link internally the registered patients

but it lacked the visualisation component to analyze the transmission process. The HISP team wanted to build this functionality within DHIS2 to enable it subsequently becoming a core generic feature. Therefore, a DHIS2 web application was developed for contact visualization by a volunteer developer under guidance of the a DHIS2 core developer. Another requirement highlighted by the MoH was to capture patient locations over the past two weeks which might not have been divulged by a person due to various reasons. For this, with permission of the regulatory authorities, the mobile tower location data was shared with the ministry. A middleware component was developed linking the contact tracing application with the tower location, further extending the core functionality. The end users complained of data entry being very time consuming, and to minimize this an integration functionality was designed to enable data transfer directly from the immigration information system to the DHIS2 to avoid re-entry of data except relating to clinical updates and travel information history.

Tracking of Imported Cases March 26th Onwards
From the second week of March, it was noted that most Sri Lankans living in high burden countries like Italy and South Korea started returning home, resulting in a sudden surge of cases towards the third week of March. This led to a change in approach from community follow-up of suspected passengers to compulsory quarantine at government run facilities. The DHIS2 could quickly support this new demand, simply by adding on a new tracker programme.

Utilization of Platform for Resource Management: April 7th Onwards
The MoH was responsible for the distribution of PPE resources to all hospitals in Sri Lanka and tracking the logistics to monitor impending shortages. Therefore, the MoH requested for a functionality be created to support these requirements. An aggregate data set was designed to capture the requirements, and dashboards designed to monitor the stock status. With the inclusion of this aggregate module, the number of users accessing the system significantly increased given the challenge of providing co-located training. End user manuals were designed and rapidly disseminated to enable scale. The use of this system was driven by a MoH mandate making use of this system mandatory. Users were motivated to move from their earlier use of Google Sheets because the DHIS2 provided rich analytical dashboards, using also the existing predictor module functionality.

The ICU Care Functionality – April 5th Onwards
In the first week of April, with the increasing number of patients requiring ICU care, the MoH requested for a critical care module which could be accessed by clinicians from all hospitals to help locate the nearest ICU bed. The current ICU system of the MoH was non-functional since a few years, a new module was required which could be integrated with the surveillance. The development team then quickly created to track ICU beds nationally with custom interfaces and an in-app dashboard was designed.

Globalization of Local Innovations: April 25–May 15
The initial version of the contact tracing application developed by the HISP Sri Lanka was shared in the DHIS2 community, who started to work on making this application more generic. The application was made available to the global HISP community and

a rapid process of eliciting global requirements was initiated to identify requirements for a generic contact tracing visualization app. Further developments in Sri Lanka were also now guided by the global team to ensure developments took on a generic character. With the inputs of global DHIS2 experts, it was possible to release the first version of the generic application by the second week of May. Following the official release of the contact tracing application, a dedicated post on the app was made available in the DHIS2 community, which encouraged the global community to use the app and provide feedback which was to be incorporated to refine the app further.

The MoH also requested the local team to incorporate an aggregate reporting component, which could be utilised by the COVID testing laboratories in Sri Lanka to report daily summaries of tests that were performed related to COVID from each of the laboratory. This was designed in the latter part of April as an aggregate data set with access to all national laboratories.

Current Focus on Self-Reporting Module - May 10th Onwards

One component which was lacking in the entire ecosystem was the provision for citizens to self-report and monitor their health. A third-party mobile application was developed to monitor the status of health and to educate those who were on self-quarantine. The MoH wanted to incorporate information from such persons for monitoring and public health intervention purposes. Therefore, the HISP Sri Lanka team has initiated the development of this functionality.

The MOH of health was promoting use of the DHIS2 dashboards for the health administrators, focusing on as real time data as possible - representing the time interval between data entry and analytics process execution in DHIS2. The initial interval was set at 15 min and now the MoH is requesting for a smaller interval. The DHIS2 version 2.34 was equipped with real-time analytics which made the task of having updated dashboards with real-time data possible, and so the HISP team upgraded the version of DHIS2 to 2.34 on second week of May, about 10 days after its release.

5   Discussion

We discuss the case along the following perspectives; the agility of the pandemic creates new modes of collaboration across organisational barriers; and, agile and innovative development of the platform.

5.1   Pandemic Creating New Institutional Networks of Collaboration

We take Rigby, et al. as point of departure in who argue that agile responses are situational, not part of top-down planning, triggered by urgent needs and are drawing on new peer-to-peer structures breaking with traditional bureaucracies [19]. In the case of the COVID-19 outbreak we see that all these issues are valid as the first action taken is only days after the spread of the disease outside China is confirmed. Traditionally in Sri Lanka, the different health programs, public health and ICT department are not actively collaborating on systems development across their organizational boundaries. For example, in 2017, the team identified more than 20 DHIS2 installations operational as each program maintained their own instances with little collaboration across. More integration has happened since then. In this case, however, we see that new constellations of institutions and people collaborating on developing responses are being formed. With new developments in the situation on a weekly and even daily frequency, there is no time to wait and bureaucratic structures are broken down and give place for new and more agile ways to develop organisational responses.

The hackathon was initiated by the ministry with the agenda to bring together different actors such as the ICT department, private open source company and the HISP Sri Lanka team in order to optimize available expertise and to create a new constellation across organisational borders. Creating teams with such heterogeneity and diversity also is generally seen to be beneficial when addressing rapidly changing requirements as well as be better able to provide alternative solutions to complex problems such as those experienced during the COVID-19 pandemic, where, as documented in the case, new and changing requirements appeared constantly [10]. While the team that developed the COVID-19 information response has a variety of competences within health, ICT, app development and the DHIS2 software platform, its heterogeneity of members from multiple institutions means it could reach out to and learn from a variety of communities and sectors, which is important in responding to the COVID-19.

In the new agile organizational situation, the software adoption and implementation approval process has changed. Normally, for a software system to be adopted it may need approval from the director of the institute, deputy director general level etc. This process will typically take some time. Further, if the software and information system is spanning across domains of multiple institutes, the process multiplies by number of hierarchies involved, and typically will drag on over time. Now, in the agile organizational setting, multiple institutes provide inputs and system is approved by DGHS level with deputy director general level informed, in a very short time. In the case study, we have documented 8 major system interventions that have been specified, developed and managed through the acceptance process during the exceptionally short time of 2–3 months.

5.2 Agile Development of Software Solutions in the Platform

Very early in the COVID-19 pandemic, the global DHIS2 team had developed the COVID-19 DHIS2 response package and made it available as a configuration package for DHIS2 which can easily be downloaded and adapted to meet individual country needs. This package has been continuously extended and updated since the first version of early March 2020 (https://www.dhis2.org/covid-19) [20]. Currently more than 30 countries have been implementing the packages or are in the process of implementing them. Important in this context is that this global development started and was inspired by the first development in Sri Lanka and, as documented in the case, the Sri Lanka DHIS2 team has been actively involved in the further development of the global DHIS2 platform COVID-19 'package'. Generally, in a software platform, the core platform is seen as stable while agile development is free to happen as e.g. app development on the top of the platform or as new or modified functionalities at the fringes. Contrary to this, in our case we have seen agile core platform development based on development in the periphery, in Sri Lanka. The agile platform development process has consisted of four steps; 1) the Sri Lanka team develop a custom app configured for the local context, as was the case of contact tracing and network analysis app; 2) the case and visual example are shared in the DHIS2 community; 3) several countries express interest for a similar app; 4) the Sri Lanka team 'gets assigned a dedicated global core developer' and together they specify the new generic app which is then developed as a core app in DHIS2 and becomes available for all countries. Agile responses were observed in various phases of development in each of the modules in the surveillance system.

Table 1. Agile response in development of modules.

Module	Agile response
Port of entry	• Need to work with multiple stakeholders • Needed to establish an information system from the scratch within short span of time • Needed optimize system to minimize data entry burden to ensure compliance from end users
Quarantine Persons Tracking	• Government policy changed towards mid-march from tracking tourists in community to mandatory quarantine at government quarantine centres • Information on persons held on mandatory quarantine
Case Management	• The need arises only when case load surged towards latter part of March when they wanted to track disease progression and socio-demographic factors
Contacts visualization	• In a context with minimal community spread, ministry of health required to understand disease progression and epidemiological context of the disease • The feature of contact mapping not supported in DHIS2, but required to incorporate the feature as a highly requested business requirement
ICU Bed Tracking	• Required to track the nearest ICU bed available for critical COVID-19 patients • However, minimal time available to train intensive care unit staff on workflows of DHIS2. • Required to develop a module within existing system with simple interfaces and workflows
Health sector resource Monitoring	• It was noted in late March that routine logistics management system in ministry of health was too slow to track logistics/resources requirements related to COVID-19 • Simple aggregate form was customized in the system which was utilized by all hospitals in Sri Lanka

Interesting is also that the contact tracing app was one of the results from the hackathon which included participants from multiple institutions, and from many countries, online and offline. Hackathon is a primary example of agile software development methodology [21], which in our case resulted in new functionalities, modules and apps as described in the case. We have seen that the platform enables agile application development. Core modules like port of entry tracking and case management are easy to configure, as are dashboards, which can be designed together with users. All this makes it possible to break out from Google sheets and Excel sheets as reporting tools. At the same time we see that features, which are not there can be added by the team in collaboration with the core developers, as for example the tricky issue of being allowed to enroll patients – or clients – when you are located in an immigration office and not in a health facility. The large number of solutions that developed to respond to a variety of problems have been enabled by the free and open source nature of the software platform. The open API, for example, made it possible to integrate with the immigration system and thereby save a lot of double entry work (Table 1).

While the new situation of social distancing following the pandemic has made it difficult to conduct on-site training, zoom and other online meeting tools have made it possible to roll out the system and the frequent updates with new functionalities and use cases and train the increasing number of users in an agile manner.

In sum, a combination of agile and horizontally driven organizational processes, coupled with the platform features combined in conditions of a crisis to develop agile innovations in and with digital platforms.

6   Conclusion

The case of the digital health COVID-19 response in Sri Lanka represents an impressive example and illustration of agile development and tangible results. Over the first 2-3 months of the pandemic 8 modules have been developed, passed through the official acceptance bureaucracy and been implemented, and also made available to the global community. The rapid steps of system development, including collaboration between local and global teams, managed to keep up with the pace of the pandemic and is by itself a proof of the advantage and necessity of agile development, when the requirements are constantly changing in an emerging crisis. Solutions first developed in Sri Lanka have been made generic through collaboration with the global team and are now being part of the general DHIS2 COVID-19 package and used by many countries We argue that the flexibility of the software platform, and the good technical and medical capacity represented by the Medical Officers in Health Informatics employed throughout the programs and services within the Ministry of Health, have been key reasons for the success. These cadres have been educated through the Biomedical Masters in Informatics, which is another important factor. The new modes of collaboration on systems development across institutional and national borders have also been important. Given this background, we may conceptualize platforms such as the DHIS2 as being of socio-technical nature and in significant ways being formed through strong network effects between and within supply-side users (Developers in local and global teams) and demand-side users (responding to COVID-19 in Sri Lanka and other countries), in line with Gawer's concept [8] of platforms as evolving organisations The important question, however, is how this process can become sustainable. Here we can revert to the agile manifesto [13]:

'Agile processes promote sustainable development. The sponsors, developers, and users should be able to maintain a constant pace indefinitely.'

The local MoH and the Sri Lanka team must institutionally reflect on the lessons learnt through this experience and how the practices can become part of national policies towards HIS development.

References

1. Murota, T., Kato, A., Okumura, T.: Emergency management for information systems in public health a case study of the 2009 pandemic-flu response in Japan. In: 8th IEEE International Conference on Pervasive Computing and Communications Workshops (PERCOM Workshops), Mannheim, pp. 394–399. IEEE (2010)
2. Lai, A.Y.-H.: Agility amid uncertainties: evidence from 2009 A/H1N1 pandemics in Singapore and Taiwan. Policy Soc. **37**(4), 459–472 (2010)
3. Rigby, D.K., Elk, S., Berez, S.: Develop agility that outlasts the pandemic. https://hbr.org/2020/05/develop-agility-that-outlasts-the-pandemic. Accessed 5 Aug 2020
4. Hamed, A.M.M., Abushama, H.: Popular agile approaches in software development: review and analysis. In: 2013 International Conference on Computing, Electrical and Electronic Engineering (ICCEEE), Khartoum, pp. 160–166. IEEE (2013)
5. Tiwana, A.: Platform Ecosystems: Aligning Architecture, Governance, and Strategy. Morgan Kaufmann, Amsterdam, Waltham (2014)
6. Baldwin, C.Y., Woodard, C.J.: The architecture of platforms: a unified view. SSRN Electron J. **24**(3), 373–390 (2008)
7. Henfridsson, O., Bygstad, B.: The generative mechanisms of digital infrastructure evolution. MIS Q. **37**(3), 907–931 (2013)
8. Gawer, A.: Bridging differing perspectives on technological platforms: toward an integrative framework. Res. Policy **43**(7), 1239–1249 (2014)
9. Roland, L.K.: Designing architectural patterns for distributed flexibility in health information systems (2018). https://www.duo.uio.no/handle/10852/61595. Accessed 25 May 2020
10. Lee, G., Xia, W.: Toward agile: an integrated analysis of quantitative and qualitative field data on software development agility. MIS Q. **34**(1), 87–114 (2010)
11. Kapyaho, M., Kauppinen, M.: Agile requirements engineering with prototyping: a case study. In: 2015 IEEE 23rd International Requirements. Engineering Conference, Ottawa, pp. 394–399. IEEE (2015)
12. Cockburn, A.: Agile Software Development: the Cooperative Game, 2nd edn. Addison-Wesley, Harlow (2007)
13. Agile Alliance: Manifesto for Agile software development (2001). https://agilemanifesto.org. Accessed 25 May 2020
14. Mergel, I., Gong, Y., Bertot, J.: Agile government: systematic literature review and future research. Gov. Inf. Q. **35**(2), 291–298 (2018)
15. Luna, D., Almerares, A., Mayan, J.C., Bernaldo de Quirós, F.G., Otero, C.: Health informatics in developing countries: going beyond pilot practices to sustainable implementations: a review of the current challenges. Healthc. Inform. Res. **20**(1), 3–10 (2014)
16. Darke, P., Shanks, G., Broadbent, M.: Successfully completing case study research: combining rigour, relevance and pragmatism. Inf. Syst. J. **8**(4), 273–289 (1998)
17. Yin, R.K.: Case Study Research: Design and Methods. Sage, Los Angeles (2014)
18. Braun, V., Clarke, V.: What can "thematic analysis" offer health and wellbeing researchers?. Int. J. Qual. Stud. Health Well-being (2014). https://doi.org/10.3402/qhw.v9.26152
19. Rigby, D.K., Berez, S., Caimi, G., Noble, A.: Agile Innovation. Bain & Company, Inc. (2015)

20. COVID-19 Surveillance Digital Data Package|DHIS2. https://www.dhis2.org/covid-19. Accessed 25 May 2020
21. Alkema, J.P., Levitt, P.S., Chen J.Y.J.: Agile and hackathons: a case study of emergent practices at the FNB codefest. In: ACM International Conference Proceeding Series, pp 1–10. Association for Computing Machinery, New York (2017)

Rapid Systems Response to COVID-19: Standards Disseminated as Digital Health Packages

Olav Poppe[1]([✉]), Zeferino Saugene[2], Edem Kossi[3], Johan Ivar Sæbø[1], and Jørn Braa[1]

[1] University of Oslo, Oslo, Norway
olavpo@ifi.uio.no
[2] HISP Mozambique, Maputo, Mozambique
[3] HISP West and Central Africa, Lomé, Togo

Abstract. The COVID-19 pandemic has highlighted the need for good quality data. The World Health Organization (WHO) has published recommended data standards for managing information about the pandemic, and in this paper we study an initiative to rapidly disseminate and implement these standards at the national level. A common challenge in standardisation initiatives is the tension between global, "universal" standards and the local. We contribute to the body of knowledge around this tension, through our case that concerns the diffusion of a global standard for management of COVID-19 information using a digital platform. A defining feature of the platform architecture is how it consists of a relatively stable platform core, which can be extended with variable complements. We show how this characteristic can facilitate the dissemination of standards, by allowing implementors of the standards to adapt the standard through innovative complements, thus easing the tension between the "universal" aspects of the standard and the local reality.

Keywords: Health information systems · Digital platforms · Standards

1 Introduction

The COVID-19 pandemic has highlighted the need for rapid responses at health services and policy levels, which are dependent on good quality data. The World Health Organization (WHO) has developed and published recommended data standards for use by countries in managing information about the pandemic, however, these standards have little impact unless implemented in functioning information systems. Diffusion of standards in the developing world has been highlighted as an area in which current research is limited [1]. Furthermore, a common challenge that has been brought up in standardisation literature is the issue of flexibility of standards, and the tension that emerges when implementing global, "universal" standards locally [2–4]. We seek to contribute to the body of knowledge concerning this tension, through our case that concerns the diffusion of a global standard for management of COVID-19 information using a digital

© IFIP International Federation for Information Processing 2020
Published by Springer Nature Switzerland AG 2020
R. K. Bandi et al. (Eds.): IFIPJWC 2020, IFIP AICT 601, pp. 237–250, 2020.
https://doi.org/10.1007/978-3-030-64697-4_18

platform. A defining feature of the platform architecture is how it consists of a relatively stable platform core, which can be extended with variable complements [5]. Such an architecture is seen as a way to manage large and complex information systems in a way that allows these systems to be dynamic and evolvable, through the flexibility that the variable complements afford. In this paper, we aim to improve our understanding of how digital platforms can be used to disseminate standards and help address the tension between the "global" and the "local" in standardisation processes.

Empirically, this paper is about the dissemination of a digital health package for COVID-19, which builds upon on a project initiated by WHO in 2014. The digital health packages consist of data standards, guidance on data analysis and specifications for analytical dashboards and data collection tools. This content is itself software agnostic, but the digital health packages also include an implementation of these standards for the DHIS2 software platform. The DHIS2 platform is used by Ministries of Health on a national scale in 59 countries, primarily in Sub-Saharan Africa and South Asia, and is *de facto* a technical standards in this part of the world.[1] By May 2020, over 50 countries in the global south have implemented or are in the process of implementing the digital health package for COVID-19.[2] We describe and discuss the development of the digital health package for COVID-19 and its dissemination to 10 Lusophone and Francophone countries in Africa. While still early, the experiences of the development and dissemination of the COVID-19 package is already providing important learning on various aspects of the digital health package approach to disseminating health data standards.

The platform discussed here, DHIS2, is an open source, web-based software for collection, management and analysis of health information. While the software is web based, each implementing organization hosts their own separate instance of DHIS2 that they own and manage. A community of DHIS2 experts, organised in different groups under the Health Information Systems Programme (HISP) umbrella, support Ministries of Health and other organisations using DHIS2 through capacity building and technical support.

2   Related Literature

The case of the COVID-19 digital health package will be discussed and analysed by drawing from literature on standards and software platforms, which we present below.

2.1   Standards

Standards can be seen as something that makes comparisons possible over space and time, and that is shared across more than one community of practice [3, 6]. Standardisation, then, is a process where standards are used to create uniformity over time and space, often backed up by some form of external organisation or body [7, 8].

Global standards are voluntary and will thus only be implemented if organisations make a decision to use them. One reason for using such global standards is that the

---

[1] https://www.dhis2.org/inaction.

[2] https://www.dhis2.org/covid-19.

standards themselves are seen as beneficial and have the potential of improving the performance of the adopting organization [9]. Another important reason is the legitimacy that the adoption of a standard infers on the organisation adopting it [8]. This role of legitimacy is particularly important when existing legitimacy is questioned or when existing practices are delegitimised and leading to "legitimacy crisis" [10]. Organizations acquire legitimacy by proving that they conform to norms or standards or adopt widely used and accepted practices [11]. When standards are adopted for legitimising purposes, they may be implemented rhetorically or on paper only, without resulting in any actual change in practices [8]. Referring specifically to the context of developing countries, which is our empirical focus, Perez-Aleman [1] highlights the limitations of current research on the diffusion of standards and note also that the role of technology in standards dissemination is not well understood or researched.

Standards are in different ways adapted to the local context and use when implemented, and they thus change [7, 8]. For example, the International Classification of Diseases (ICD) is designed so that local adaptations and additions are possible [7]. Thus, while standards may be thought of as "universal", they are rather "local universals" that are continuously adapted to the local context through negotiations, adaptations and reinterpretations [3, 12, 13].

Arguably, standards that are less explicit are more difficult to implement than those that are vague and abstract [9]. At the same time, if standards are too vague and too flexible, they become useless [8]. Finding the right amount of flexibility for a standard is thus important to ensure that it allows the necessary flexibility for it to be adapted and implemented, but not making it so flexible that it loses its purpose: to achieve some level of uniformity. This is a topic that has previously been discussed in general [4], but also related to standards for health data [7], and to the digital platform used for disseminating the standards in our case [14, 15].

2.2 Digital Platforms

Just as the issue of flexibility is a topic in the area of standards and standardisation, the tension between stability and flexibility has also been a topic of research within the information systems field for many years - and digital platforms have been proposed as having the potential to address this issue [2, 16, 17]. Despite their increasing prominence as objects of study in recent years, there is not one clear and agreed-upon definition of digital platforms. Baldwin and Woodard [5] define platform architecture as consisting of a platform core with a set of stable components, and complementary components that interact with the core through well-defined interfaces. Tiwana, referring specifically to a software platform, defines this as "a software-based product or service that serves as a foundation on which outside parties can build complementary products or services" [18, p. 5]. Tiwana also argues that platforms must be multisided, meaning they bring together two or more actors or groups of platform users, such as end users and app developers.

Koskinen et al. [19] categorises platforms into innovation platforms, transaction platforms and integrated platforms. Innovation platforms serve primarily as core codebases on top of which complements or apps can be developed, for example iOS, SAP or DHIS2. Transaction platforms, exemplified by WhatsApp, Skype or Uber, are marketplace platforms whose primary purpose is to connect different groups of users, i.e. they are multi-sided and thus more in line with Tiwana's [18] definition. Integration platforms are platforms that functions both as innovation and transaction platforms.

The platform ecosystem includes both the platform core, the complementary components, and the organisations associated with these, such as third-party developers [18]. Within a developmental context, Msiska and Nielsen studied how innovation can happen at the fringes of platform ecosystems [20]. Introducing the concept of "socio-technical generativity", they emphasise how innovation within a platform ecosystem requires both generative technology and social relationships within the ecosystem. More broadly, the structure and dynamics of platform ecosystems has been highlighted as an area that is under-researched [17].

3 Methods

The methodology applied for this study is case study, retrospectively drawing on strong elements of active participation in the events described. It thus fits the label of participative case study [21].

The data presented and discussed in this paper stems from the authors' participation in activities related to the development, implementation and use of the DHIS2 software platform, including the development and implementation of digital health packages in collaboration with WHO since 2014. Three of the authors are based at the University from which development of both the DHIS2 software and the DHIS2-related aspects of the digital health packages are developed. Two of the authors are based in the two main HISP groups that support Ministries of Health in the Lusophone and Francophone countries of Sub-Saharan Africa respectively with DHIS2-related activities, including with the implementation of the digital health packages.

All five authors have to varying degrees been involved in the discussion taking place around the design, development and implementation of the COVID-19 digital health package. We have participated in several online seminars organised around use of DHIS2 for management of data related to COVID-19 pandemic, where the digital health package has been presented and countries have shared their experiences. Two of the authors have been closely involved in the activities that have taken place in the 10 countries presented here.

In these pandemic times, with the authors residing in three different countries, data analysis was carried out online through much the same means as the support that was given to implementing Ministries of Health; through virtual meetings, chat programs, and email. Data was analysed iteratively, where the themes emerged from comparing experiences in the different countries. Concretely we asked ourselves how the key issues identified in the literature for dissemination of standards, such as legitimacy and local adaptations, were relevant for each country in question. The initial analysis pointed to differences in the role of local politics, for instance, tied to the perceived legitimacy of DHIS2 with different actors even within countries. This deductive process continued with a more inductive process analysing the role of the software platform, the fact that it represents a near global installed base in the region, and the role of the local support teams.

4   Case

In order to better understand the country-level process of adopting (or not) the COVID-19 digital health package, we present here the experiences from 5 Lusophone and 4 Francophone countries in Africa. Most countries in Sub-Saharan Africa use DHIS2 as their national health information systems, typically organized under the Health Management Information System (HMIS) unit or directorate. Surveillance of communicable diseases such as measles, cholera - and COVID-19 - will typically be organised by disease surveillance units, separately from the HMIS unit. These are thus key stakeholders in the discussions around use of the COVID-19 digital health package in countries. During the COVID-19 pandemic, as was the case for the Ebola Virus Disease, many countries have also established high level COVID-19 committees which are also responsible for the "digital" COVID-19 responses.

First, however, we give a brief introduction to the digital health package initiative, and the process of developing the digital health package for COVID-19.

4.1   Digital Health Packages for DHIS2

The development of digital health packages began within WHO in 2014, aiming to provide digital standards and content for data collection and use. The DHIS2 platform was used as a vehicle for these packages, since it was and is a *de facto* standard for routine facility data in a large proportion of the countries in the global south for which the content was primarily being developed. There now exist packages for several health programmes, such as HIV, malaria, immunisation and tuberculosis, and a range of countries have adopted and adapted at least one of these in their national health management information system. A key point has been that flexibility in these standard packages is both wanted and needed. Wanted, because countries have peculiarities that should be accommodated to increase utility, and needed because legacy systems and data (even if running on the same software) dictate the space for change [15].

4.2   The Digital Health Package for COVID-19

The development infrastructure and experience accrued over the last few years with work on the digital health packages was put to use with the ongoing COVID-19 pandemic. In about a month, a digital health package for COVID-19 was developed, based on WHO guidelines but not directly involving them in the process, with components for registration of cases, contact tracing, reporting daily and weekly summaries and more. This was released on March 11, available as a configuration package for DHIS2 which can easily be downloaded and adapted to meet individual country needs.

The development of the package has drawn on the experiences from Sri Lanka, which set up a DHIS2 module for port-of-entry COVID-19 screening and tracking already in early February 2020. As will be shown below, there have been many examples already of local improvements and innovations around the COVID-19 packages that have been taken up by the global development team and made publicly available. Currently (September 2020), more than 50 countries have implemented or are in the process of implementing one or more component of the COVID-19 digital health package. To raise awareness of the packages, a series of online demonstrations has been organized for francophone, lusophone and anglophone countries. The package has also been presented in webinars organised by the WHO-led Health Data Collaborative (HDC) and CDC Africa with several hundred participants in both English and French.

We use the support network for Lusophone and Francophone countries in Africa to illustrate how the implementation is playing out in practice in countries and how the rapid dissemination is made possible.

4.3   COVID-19 DHIS2 Implementation in Lusophone Africa

The five Lusophone countries in Africa, Angola, Mozambique, Cape Verde, Guinea Bissau and São Tome all use DHIS2 as national health information management systems, supported by the HISP group based in Mozambique (HISP Mozambique). At the beginning of the pandemic, HISP Mozambique suggested to the countries to take advantage of their existing infrastructure and knowledge and adapt and implement the COVID-19 digital health package. They therefore took the initiative to translate the first version of the COVID-19 package to Portuguese and demonstrated this to the Ministries of Health. Following this, Angola, Cape Verde and Guinea-Bissau requested support to implement the package. The Portuguese translation created by HISP Mozambique was subsequently shared with the global team publishing the COVID-19 package and included in the next release of the package.

Technically, the implementation of the package in countries was done in a separate database from the main platform instance, to speed up the deployment and reduce the risk of interfering with the existing system. However, different resources were still re-used from the existing system, such as server infrastructure and health facility lists.

Due to the COVID-19 travel restrictions all installation and further adaption and development of the different national implementations was done online. The countries, and provinces in Mozambique, were trained online using online video platforms. The facilitators, based in Maputo, were able to access the different national databases and use those through screen sharing for training in system administration, data entry and data analysis.

Angola. The Ministry of Health of Angola was first introduced to DHIS2 in 2015, and currently uses it in the management of several programs including Malaria, HIV, TB, Immunization and disease surveillance. The COVID-19 package was installed and customized to suit the needs of the Ministry of Health Management Information System (HMIS) and IT units. The customization included adjustment to the content of the package, as well as the server infrastructure and domain server specifications. However, when a high-level COVID-19 committee reporting to the cabinet of the President of the Republic was created, it was decided to use a system developed by the National Institute of Statistics for management of COVID-19-related information instead. The Ministry of Health HMIS and IT units now envision making this system interoperable with the previously configured COVID-19 package.

Guinea Bissau. The country has been using DHIS2 for HMIS and disease surveillance since 2011. HMIS and Surveillance from the very beginning of the adoption of the

DHIS2 COVID-19 package decide to involve its traditional partner including UNDP and WHO. These players and others such as UNICEF, UN Migration also played several roles during the COVID-19 pandemic response. Guinea-Bissau did not have paper forms designed specifically for COVID-19 response before the package was presented. The country designed its paper tools by mimicking the forms from the global package. As the system gained visibility and recognition, partners started to request changes and add new variables and features into the package. For example, collaboration with the WHO country office led to the development of 1) Infection Prevention and Control (IPC) for COVID-19 assessment tool; 2) a tool for the assessment of risk factors for COVID-19 in health workers; and 3) an inpatient case management tool. Collaboration with the COVID-19 high commission led to the development of several new apps, to meet local requirements. This includes a mobile app for self-registration of travellers at points of entry, a self-reporting/lab request app, and an app for accessing and printing lab results.

Mozambique. DHIS2 was adopted by the country in 2013, but only in 2016 the system was in use by all district health officers. The COVID-19 package was presented to the HMIS team through an email sent to all Lusophone DHIS2 and data managers. However, it was only when the number of cases started to increase and several departments within the Ministry of Health started to put pressure on the HMIS unit for lacking a functioning information system for COVID-19 data management that they responded. The HMIS unit request HISP Mozambique for a demo, and subsequent customization of the package based on the paper forms for COVID-19 reporting that had been made available by the disease surveillance unit to all facilities, districts and provinces. At this time COVID-19 data was being collected using the Survey123 tool introduced by the WHO country team. Since Survey123 was introduced without consent from the HMIS unit, and agreement between HMIS and the surveillance unit was demanded. In the discussions between the two units it was decided that Survey123 would be used until DHIS2 with the COVID-19 package was customised and introduced to the reporting sites. Survey123 and the DHIS2 COVID-19 package coexisted for quite a long time, and at one point, the possibility of interoperating Survey123 and DHIS2 with the COVID-19 package was on the table. However, once the HMIS unit realised that the COVID-19 package was more widely used than Survey123, the decided to direct its all effort on strengthening its DHIS2 implementation rather than connecting it to another system.

Cape Verde. The adoption of DHIS2 for HMIS in Cape Verde started in 2018, although the disease surveillance unit has been introduced to DHIS2 as a West African regional data sharing platform since 2014. Prior to COVID-19 pandemic, DHIS2 was used for immunization, disease surveillance and reproductive health data management. With support from HISP Mozambique, the country has implemented the DHIS2 COVID-19 package. As part of the implementation, the package was adjusted to align with the paper reporting tools used. A contact tracing app developed based on requirements from Angola and installed in Guinea-Bissau and Mozambique systems was also adopted by Cape Verde. Just like Mozambique, Angola and Guinea-Bissau, the country also adopted DHIS2 web as well as DHIS2 android as data capturing mechanisms.

São Tomé and Principe. São Tomé and Principe has been using DHIS2 since 2019. Even though disease surveillance data is being collected by DHIS2, the system is used mainly for HMIS. In São Tomé demonstrations of the COVID-19 package were made several times to country teams including HMIS, the Minister of Health, and the disease surveillance director. A decision on whether or not to adopt the COVID-19 package took time, and in the meantime HISP Mozambique learned that Facebook, PDF-files and static web portal was used to share COVID-19 information. HISP Mozambique decided to develop an interactive public web portal, which could automatically extract data from DHIS2 on a daily basis and present it to the public in a visually more pleasant way. The portal was demonstrated to the Ministry of Health HMIS team, which consequently decided to adopt the COVID-19 package without further changes, and to officially launch the portal to the media and the public.

4.4   COVID-19 DHIS2 in Some Francophone African Countries

Here we outline the efforts to implement the COVID-19 digital health package in four Francophone African countries, and the organisational politics involved.

Togo. DHIS2 is used in the country mainly for HMIS. The disease surveillance information system is fragmented, although stakeholders are working toward integration with DHIS2. As in the other countries, a COVID-19 committee has been created at a very high level and reports to the cabinet of the President of the Republic. This has led to the side-lining of the traditional health information and IT actors in the HMIS directorate, who no longer have a say in what system to use despite their expertise and established network of actors ranging from health facilities up to central level. This caused a deadlock with no consensus around management of COVID-19 information, and growing frustration around the inability to coordinate data management. Data has been collected with Excel sheets sent from the various districts. The COVID-19 package has been installed and customised according to local requirements and is ready for use, and a consensus was finally reached to use it after lengthy meetings and demonstrations. However, in the end a decision came from the higher levels of the government to impose another completely new system.

Mali. The country has been using DHIS2 as a HMIS and for disease surveillance since 2016. Despite the creation of a COVID-19 committee at a high level, key stakeholders agreed to collaborate on strengthening the existing system, and to let traditional players such as the HMIS and disease surveillance units continue to play their traditional roles, with WHO and Global Fund as partners. Although the role of coordinating disease surveillance reporting was unexpectedly handed to the regional health office of the capital, stakeholders were able to adjust to that new reality. The National Health Directorate is well aware that the regional office could never be a threat and key players simultaneously see the COVID-19 package as beneficial to the country and a way to further strengthen their own position. Subsequently, they all contributed to funding the implementation of the COVID-19 package. HISP WCA provided remote support to the national HMIS technical team to adapt the package to the Malian requirements. After a series of demonstrations and tests, the system was validated by stakeholders and rolled out. Since then it has been in use in the country.

Burkina Faso. The country has been using DHIS2 for HMIS since 2013, but not for disease surveillance, for which a locally developed system is being used. With the COVID-19 pandemic, however, the IT department took advantage of DHIS2's flexibility to quickly design a system for COVID-19 case management from scratch, even before the release of the COVID-19 package. This solution became the official COVID-19 system in the country, endorsed by the high level COVID-19 committee, thus leaving no room to the traditional disease surveillance stakeholder to contest the choice of the system. Burkina Faso thus uses DHIS2 for COVID-19 data management, but not the COVID-19 package. However, the COVID-19 package was later used as an inspiration when improving the analytical outputs of the locally developed system. By going for solutions developed by the IT unit, the tradition of disease surveillance data management is broken. This leaves open the question of its sustainability after the pandemic.

Senegal. Senegal has used DHIS2 as a national health information system since 2015. As one of the first countries in Africa to report a COVID-19 case, the disease quickly attracted attention in the country. Given the good collaboration between the disease surveillance and the HMIS units, they quickly agreed on using the COVID-19 package, which was published just at the right time for Senegal. With some limited help from HISP WCA, the COVID-19 package was installed and adapted by the inclusion of two local data collection forms. However, after the adaptation and validation of the system, the HMIS team was faced with the challenge of deploying the system across the country with a limited number of staff and travelling restrictions in place. The solution was to set up online training and support sessions for end users. Despite the high stake of the pandemic and the creation of a COVID-19 committee, the HMIS and disease surveillance units were not side-lined in the process of establishing a COVID-19 reporting system. Based on the collaboration around COVID-19, the two units are now discussing how to develop and implement an integrated system for disease surveillance across diseases using DHIS2. A digital health package for integrated disease surveillance is scheduled to be released in the coming months and will be one of the options considered in Senegal.

5   Discussion

"A pandemic is the worldwide spread of a new disease" (WHO)[3]. Consequently, global standards developed to help fight a pandemic should be usable worldwide. This points to a challenge that has been brought up frequently in the literature on standardisation, namely the tensions that emerge when implementing global, "universal" standards in diverse, localised settings [2–4]. Furthermore, during a pandemic, the speed at which these standards can be diffused and, critically, implemented is important. In the previous section, we presented an initiative to develop standards, in the form of digital health packages, for countering the ongoing COVID-19 pandemic. We also presented experiences from a handful of African countries that use or have considered using these standards, to understand the local dissemination and implementation processes.

---

[3] https://www.who.int/csr/disease/swineflu/frequently_asked_questions/pandemic/en/.

We argue that the rapid development and deployment of the COVID-19 digital health package in over 30 countries is an example of the successful dissemination of a global standard. This has been possible primarily for three reasons. First, that the digital health package was perceived both as potentially useful, and also as having legitimacy. Second, the DHIS2 platform itself, that is an infrastructure available in over 70 countries with an architecture that allows simultaneously the use of global tools and the development of local complements. Third, the ecosystem *around* the DHIS2 platform, including Ministries of Health, the regional HISP groups, the core DHIS2 development team and other actors that support and maintain the DHIS2 platform around the world. Each of these factors will be discussed below, drawing on and contributing to the literature around standardisation as well as digital platforms.

5.1 Adoption of the COVID-19 Digital Health Package

Despite being developed in a somewhat different way than previous digital health packages, with less direct involvement from WHO, we argue that the COVID-19 digital health package can be seen as an example of a global standard. It is based on WHO content standards and developed and published by the organisation behind the software platform that is a *de facto* standard in low income countries. Perez-Aleman [1] argues that the diffusion of standards in low income countries is not well understood, in particular the role of technology. Standards, including global standards, are adopted for different reasons. The perhaps most obvious reason is that they are perceived by the adopting organisation as beneficial or useful [9]. Given the rapid adoption of the COVID-19 package worldwide and through discussions with the countries presented here, we believe it can be assumed that it was generally seen as potentially useful by the Ministries of Health.

However, as several of the Francophone country examples show, other alternatives were in many cases considered and, in some cases (like Togo and Angola), the alternatives were preferred. In these discussions, the perceived legitimacy of COVID-19 standard can be of relevance, both directly and through the legitimacy it infers to those adopting it [8], who are then seen to conform to the prevailing norms and standards [11].

While addressing the adoption of IT innovations rather than standards, Wang and Swanson also point to how the authority and reputation of the organisations behind the promulgation of an innovation is important to its legitimacy [22]. Within the context of our case, the organisations behind the COVID-19 package was also developers of the DHIS2 platform itself and were thus authorities with regards to the technical aspects. The content is based on standards from WHO, which is an authority on health standards. Furthermore, the package has been presented through webinars organised by both the Health Data Collaborative and CDC Africa with several hundred participants in both English and French. All this has been important for the legitimacy of the COVID-19 package, which has in turn been an important discursive mechanism for being accepted in countries. The examples in particular from Francophone Africa indicate that the extreme impact of the pandemic, not the least to the economy, has led to a considerable battle over what system to select, and the decision making has been lifted to the political level of the cabinet of the president in many countries.

5.2   A Platform for Standard Dissemination

While the perceived usefulness as well as the legitimacy of the COVID-19 digital health package has contributed to its rapid adoption, the large installed base and the architecture of the DHIS2 platform have also been important.

The installed base of DHIS2, being used as a national health information system in 59 countries[4], has been an important factor in enabling the rapid dissemination of the COVID-19 digital health package. In these countries, which includes the 9 francophone and lusophone countries we have described above, there was already trust in the system and its network of support, and an installed base in place which could be leveraged. This includes, for example, servers, computers and phones, end users and administrators familiar with the system, and digital resources such as lists of health facilities. In addition, there was the network of HISP groups that could support Ministries of Health in making use of these resources, the role of which we discuss in the next section.

While DHIS2 was already used in the countries described here, the COVID-19 package was not installed directly in the existing DHIS2 systems. Instead, a separate instance or database of DHIS2 was established specifically for COVID-19, re-using relevant components such as health facility lists. This is a potential sustainability issue but was done to facilitate the rapid implementation of the COVID-19 package without risking any disruptions in the existing system. Longer term, the COVID-19 package should be integrated with the routine disease surveillance system.

In addition to serving as an infrastructure or installed base for the COVID-19 digital health package, the platform *architecture* of DHIS2 was important for the dissemination and implementation. DHIS2 can be seen, at least primarily, as an innovation platform, i.e. a core codebase with interfaces that can be used to build apps or complements [19], and to configure data collection formats and analytical outputs. This allowed HISP groups supporting Ministries of Health in implementing the COVID-19 digital health package to customise and adapt their implementations with tailor-made apps, filling gaps in functionality, what Msiska and Nielsen refer to as "innovation at the fringes". These apps help address the challenges that arise when implementing global standards in diverse, local settings [4, 7]. We saw an example of this in the case of Angola and Mozambique. There was a need for the system to produce a list of COVID-19 positive cases and contacts based on residential address, per health facility, to support the health workers doing contact tracing. HISP Mozambique developed an app for this purpose, extending the functionality of the digital health package. In Burkina Faso customized the data collection formats themselves before the COVID-19 package was disseminated, but later learned from the package and adapted its analytical outputs.

It could be argued that those local solutions and adaptations are related to the *flexibility* or *customizability* of the software in general, and not attributable to the software architecture. For example, Braa *et al.* [14] emphasised the importance of the flexibility of an earlier version of DHIS software, before it was re-architected as a platform, in supporting flexible standards and local adaptations through customisations. However, by enabling developers to leverage existing functionality and resources in the platform core, the platform architecture allows far more substantial adaptations and customisations, including creation of completely new user interfaces, which would not otherwise

---

[4] https://www.dhis2.org/inaction.

be possible. And critically during a fast-moving pandemic, these apps can be developed at a fast pace.

5.3 The Platform Ecosystem

A third important factor that has enabled the rapid dissemination of the COVID-19 digital health package is the ecosystem around the DHIS2 platform. While the existing DHIS2 infrastructure has been important, as discussed in the previous section, most countries have needed some level of assistance in setting up new servers, configuring and adapting the COVID-19 package within their infrastructure, customising additional data collection formats, training users and so on. The ecosystem around the DHIS2 platform, where the various regional and national HISP organisations play a key role, has been critical in supporting countries in adopting and adapting the COVID-19 digital health package. For the 9 countries discussed here, HISP Mozambique and HISP WCA have played an instrumental role in this regard.

This role of the participants in this ecosystem goes beyond training and support, however. It is within this ecosystem that innovations are shared, and feedback and requirements related to the COVID-19 package has reached the global team who can make adjustments in new versions. A case in point is how the initial initiative for the COVID-19 digital health package in fact started on the basis of the development and implementation of a port of entry module in Sri Lanka by the HISP team there. The work done in Sri Lanka triggered the work on the development of a global digital health package for COVID-19.

Similar sharing of new tools and innovations has happened in the countries and regions discussed here as well. For example, when HISP Mozambique had translated the package into Portuguese in order to demonstrate it to the Lusophone countries in Africa, these translations were shared so that they were included in the next global release of the package and became available for Lusophone countries elsewhere. Another example is the app for listing positive cases by residential address described in the previous section, which was developed by HISP Mozambique based on requests from Angola and Mozambique. This app is now also being made generic and made available to others within the ecosystem.

These examples illustrate the importance of the ecosystem, and the potential benefits from connections between organisations within the ecosystem. Msiska and Nielsen [20] argued that innovation within a platform ecosystem requires both generative technology *and* social relationships within the ecosystem. These social relationships have been important in our case as well, both in supporting the dissemination of the COVID-19 package, and to facilitate the sharing of new tools and innovations.

6 Conclusion

We have presented a successful example of the rapid dissemination of a global standard. A challenge highlighted in the standardisation literature is the tension between "universal" standards, and the differences in the local contexts in which they are to be used. This challenge is also present with the standard discussed here, a digital health package for

COVID-19. However, we have shown how the platform architecture of the software in which the standard is deployed has made it possible to address this challenge through the development of local platform complements. Three additional factors have also been important in enabling the rapid diffusion of the COVID-19 digital health package. First, the existing infrastructure that the DHIS2 software platform represents, as a *de facto* standard for health information management in low income countries. Second, the ecosystem around the software platform, which is what has made it possible to leverage the flexibility and evolvability that the software architecture affords. Finally, underlying it all is the perceived legitimacy and usefulness of the standard itself.

COVID-19 represents unknown terrain also for health standard makers, as we see that key use cases in Africa include for example point of entry registration, tracking of truck drivers crossing several countries and support of call centre activities. The software discussed here, to a large extent by nature of its platform architecture, has enabled a number of innovations in the form of new features and apps supporting a range of workflows and use cases that go well beyond the health data standards that could have been defined *a priori*.

References

1. Perez-Aleman, P.: Collective learning in global diffusion: spreading quality standards in a developing country cluster. Organ. Sci. **22**(1), 173–189 (2011)
2. Hanseth, O., Monteiro, E., Hatling, M.: Developing information infrastructure: the tension between standardization and flexibility. Sci. Technol. Human Values **21**(4), 407–426 (1996)
3. Timmermans, S., Berg, M.: Standardization in action: achieving local universality through medical protocols. Soc. Stud. Sci. **27**(2), 273–305 (1997)
4. Rolland, K.H., Monteiro, E.: Balancing the local and the global in infrastructural information systems. Inf. Soc. **18**, 87–100 (2002)
5. Baldwin, C.Y., Woodard, C.J.: The architecture of platforms - a unified view. In: Gawer, A. (ed.) Platforms, Markets and Innovation: An Introduction. Edward Elgar, Cheltenham (2009)
6. Bowker, G.C., Star, S.L.: Sorting Things Out: Classification and Its Consequences. MIT Press, Cambridge (1999)
7. Bowker, G., Star, S.L.: Situations vs. standards in long-term, wide-scale decision-making: the case of the international classification of diseases. In: Proceedings of the Twenty-Fourth Annual Hawaii International Conference on System Sciences, vol. 4, pp. 73–81 (1991)
8. Timmermans, S., Epstein, S.: A world of standards but not a standard world: toward a sociology of standards and standardization. Ann. Rev. Sociol. **36**(1), 69–89 (2010)
9. Wiegand, N.M., et al.: All talk, no action? Am. J. Phys. Med. Rehabil. **91**(7), 550–560 (2012)
10. Nelson, P., Lawrence, T.B., Hardy, C.: Discourse and institutions. Acad. Manag. Rev. **29**(4), 635–652 (2004)
11. Suchman, M.C.: Managing legitimacy: strategic and institutional approaches. Acad. Manag. Rev. **20**(3), 571–610 (1995)
12. Hanseth, O., Braa, K.: Who's in control: designers, managers - or technology? Infrastructures at Norsk Hydro. In: Ciborra, C., Cordella, A., Braa, K. (eds.) From Control to Drift. Oxford University Press, Oxford (2001)
13. Sahay, S.: Global software alliances: the challenge of "standardization". Scand. J. Inf. Syst. **15**(1), 11 (2003)
14. Braa, J., et al.: Developing health information systems in developing countries: the flexible standards strategy. Manag. Inf. Syst. Q. **31**, 381–402 (2007)

15. Poppe, O., Sæbø, J.I., Braa, J.: Strategies for standardizing health information analysis. In: Nielsen, P., Kimaro, H.C. (eds.) ICT4D 2019. IAICT, vol. 551, pp. 260–271. Springer, Cham (2019). https://doi.org/10.1007/978-3-030-18400-1_21

16. Tilson, D., Lyytinen, K., Sørensen, C.: Digital infrastructures: the missing is research agenda. Inf. Syst. Res. **21**(4), 748–759 (2010)

17. de Reuver, M., Sørensen, C., Basole, R.C.: The digital platform: a research agenda. J. Inf. Technol. **33**(2), 124–135 (2018)

18. Tiwana, A.: Platform Ecosystems. Morgan Kaufmann, Boston (2013)

19. Koskinen, K., Bonina, C., Eaton, B.: Digital platforms in the global south: foundations and research agenda. In: Nielsen, P., Kimaro, H.C. (eds.) ICT4D 2019. IAICT, vol. 551, pp. 319–330. Springer, Cham (2019). https://doi.org/10.1007/978-3-030-18400-1_26

20. Msiska, B., Nielsen, P.: Innovation in the fringes of software ecosystems: the role of socio-technical generativity. Inf. Technol. Dev. **24**(2), 398–421 (2017)

21. Baskerville, R.L.: Distinguishing action research from participative case studies. J. Syst. Inf. Technol. **1**(1), 24–43 (1997)

22. Wang, P., Swanson, E.B.: Launching professional services automation: institutional entrepreneurship for information technology innovations. Inf. Organ. **17**(2), 59–88 (2007)

Designing for Scale: Strengthening Surveillance of Antimicrobial Resistance in Low Resource Settings

Sundeep Sahay[1]([⊠]), Gitika Arora[2], Yogita Thakral[1,2], Ernst Kristian Rødland[1,3], and Arunima Sehgal Mukherjee[1,2]

[1] Department of Informatics, Universitetet i Oslo, Oslo, Norway
{sundeeps,arunimam}@ifi.uio.no
[2] HISP India, New Delhi, India
[3] Norwegian Institute of Public Health, Oslo, Norway

Abstract. This paper reports on the process of designing an Antimicrobial Resistance (AMR) surveillance platform based on expertise from multidisciplinary approach involving informatics, infectious diseases and global health. Conceptualizing the surveillance platform as an Information Infrastructure (II), we draw upon design principles for its development based on the free and open source digital platform - DHIS2. We describe the scaling process over three action research cycles, with the learning from each cycle feeds into the other both practically and conceptually. The first two cycles are based in India, the first at the regional level of surveillance and the second at a hospital facility level. The third cycle concerns efforts to build global networks to facilitate scaling efforts. The paper builds learning around the design and development process, with a particular focus on functional and geographical scaling, contributing to building the information systems response to address a very urgent and fast rising global health challenge of AMR.

Keywords: Surveillance · Antimicrobial resistance · Information system · Information Infrastructure · India

1 Introduction

Antimicrobial resistance (AMR) is a grand challenge of our times, and knowledge of the problem in different sectors is incomplete affecting multiple levels of society. As the former secretary general of the World Health Organization (WHO), M. Chan has said, this "slow moving tsunami" threatens us with "the end of modern medicine as we know it" [1]. The consequences of rising rates of AMR for human and animal health, for economies and for the environment seem dire, endangering the future of societies at large [2].

Since the late nineties, a number of global declarations and research publications have emphasized the need to strengthen interventions to combat AMR. Some examples

© IFIP International Federation for Information Processing 2020
Published by Springer Nature Switzerland AG 2020
R. K. Bandi et al. (Eds.): IFIPJWC 2020, IFIP AICT 601, pp. 251–264, 2020.
https://doi.org/10.1007/978-3-030-64697-4_19

of these global efforts include the World Health Assembly (WHA) Resolution of 1998 and the WHO Global Strategy for Containment of Antimicrobial Resistance published in 2001. In May 2015, the 68th WHA adopted the global action plan on AMR, and all member states were urged to implement National Action Plans (NAPs) by 2017. At present many countries have in place these plans, but what's next? How these action plans get implemented in practice, particularly in health facilities in low- and middle-income countries (LMICs), which are at the forefront in engaging with the AMR challenge.

A key recommendation in the global and national action plans has been on ***strengthening the knowledge and evidence base through surveillance and research.*** However, along with high AMR burdens, LMICs continue to suffer from having the weakest surveillance systems. O'neill, [2] leading to a cycle of inadequate knowledge of AMR followed by poorly designed interventions without a scientific evidence base. Emergence and spread of AMR are the consequences. An important adverse consequence of this is the misuse of antibiotics. In India for example, one of the countries with highest prevalence of resistant microorganisms, consumption of antibiotics increased by more than 100% over the period from 2000 to 2015 [3]. Information and communications technology (ICTs) play a key role in surveillance systems for making improvements at both the policy and clinical levels. At the policy level, surveillance can help in making better estimates of the location and volume of AMR, which can guide decisions related to resource allocation and building of regulatory frameworks. At the clinical level, effective surveillance is needed for targeted treatment, to help strengthen infection control practices, and to develop guidelines for antibiotic prescription practices. How do we break this vicious cycle and follow the science which emphatically has argued for strengthening surveillance in combating AMR? How can LMICs seek to be better prepared?

AMR represents a unique challenge concerning scale and dimensions. First is the geographical dimension, since AMR represents a national and global problem without any geographical constraints. Then the functional dimension since AMR surveillance is grounded within a One Health (OH) approach which acknowledges the interconnectedness of humans, animals, and the environment [4]. The AMR platform thus being used to develop surveillance for human domain, needs to be scalable to other domains of veterinary medicine and the environment.

This paper addresses the following research question:

What are approaches to design AMR surveillance systems for supporting geographical and functional scale?

In the next section, we discuss the AMR surveillance challenge, followed by a description of the methods and care study. The analysis and discussion section then follows. Finally, we present the conclusions.

2 The AMR Surveillance Design Challenge

As one of the largest contemporary global health threats, AMR is estimated to contribute to annually 10 million deaths and a cost of 100 Trillion USD by 2050 [5]. The threat is aggravated by a 65% global increase in human antibiotic consumption during 2000–2015 and an 80% rise in the use of antibiotics in the animal sector [3].

While LMICs like India are considered global AMR hotspots, the magnitude of the problem is largely unknown because of the poor surveillance systems. The potential spread of AMR from such hotspots also represents a risk to low AMR prevalence countries like for example Norway. This threat arises from intensification of globalization processes exemplified by movements of more than 1 billion people across borders annually [6], and a high number of tourists to the tropics being colonized by resistant microbes [7]. This require collaboration between physicians, veterinarians, informaticians and other related disciplines. Given the global and inter-connected nature of AMR, it becomes important to design AMR surveillance with scale in mind, to expand use across geographical regions and different domains.

A recent study demonstrated that LMICs have weak surveillance systems [8], making their strengthening an urgent development priority. In 2014, five of the 11 South East Asian Region Office (SEARO) countries (India, Bangladesh, Indonesia, Maldives, and East Timor) could not generate AMR data. Only Thailand and Nepal showed capacity to collect and collate data from more than five laboratory sites [9]. As a result, governments' possibilities are limited in establishing the epidemiological linkages between rampant use of antibiotics and AMR. There are two basic approaches to control AMR: technological solutions and curtailing consumption. Much attention has been given to efforts to produce technology, like novel antibiotics or rapid diagnostic tests. However, there is limited focus on strengthening surveillance systems, leading to minimal quality data on consumption and use.

While the importance of surveillance in the fight against AMR is universally acknowledged, less is discussed on how effective systems can be designed, implemented and scaled. This issue is particularly relevant in LMICs which often face a weak, if not absent, system of systematic reporting. It is a double burden, with countries who need AMR surveillance most are those who have the weakest systems. While this is the case for surveillance in human medicine, systems are even more limited and weak in the domains of animals and the environment. Integration of data across these domains is still only a far-away dream

Our work is grounded in India, where the challenge of scale is particularly acute, given the numbers of health facilities, the high population figures, and the high AMR prevalence. Many millions of people still lack access to relevant health services such as to effective antimicrobials and diagnostic facilities, and risk becoming impoverished because of health spending [4]. Rural communities in India, which typically are the source of emerging infectious diseases, are not able to access adequate diagnostics as microbiology testing facilities are available only in tertiary care facilities [9]. Samples from district hospitals (more than 800 in India) would need to be sent to the tertiary hospitals, representing a huge logistics challenge. Further, India suffers from drastic misuse and overuse of antibiotics, allowed to flourish in the absence of a regulatory frameworks and antibiotics usage guidelines [10]. Data reporting from private facilities to national systems is minimal, and very little is known about domains of agriculture and veterinary medicine [1].

Designing an AMR surveillance system for scale – across geographical and functional boundaries – represents a wicked problem in India and also globally. In this paper, we discuss how we are approaching this problem, even though we are at a very early stage in this process. To guide our design thinking, we are inspired by the Information Infrastructure theoretical perspective.

3   Conceptualizing the Design Challenge: An Information Infrastructure (II) Perspective

Our design approach is guided by Information Infrastructure (II) theory, which helps understand the design and evolution strategies of large-scale, complex and distributed systems like the Internet and national health surveillance systems. IIs represent interconnected technical and institutional elements, without finite start and end dates, which are forever evolving. IIs are shared, and no one entity controls the whole infrastructure. The nature of heterogenous interconnections and their dynamic nature, make them complex, and tackled differently from traditional stand-alone systems [11, 12]. IIs involve multiple and heterogeneous stakeholders with asymmetric power relations, conflicting goals, requiring diverse and novel design approaches [13, 14].

An AMR surveillance platform within an OH framework needs to be conceptualized as an II, as it requires to manage data from multiple domains each with their own subsystems. These different components need to technically and institutionally work together, which is complex since each component is owned by different departments or entities (such as health or animal husbandry). II theory emphasizes the cross-boundary and disciplinary knowledge to "force unity from diversity, centralization in the face of pluralisms, and coherence from chaos" [15]. The analysis of the Internet based on II theory identified two fundamental challenges of bootstrapping and adaptability. Bootstrapping refers to the early phase of an II evolution when there are limited users, thus providing limited value in attracting new users, which constrain growth. The adaptability problem arises when an II grows into a large installed base, which constrains its adaptability to new situations, thus constraining the II evolution.

To deal with these two problems, [14]. proposed five design principles (DPs) which can serve as broad guidelines to approach II development, and help "formulate in concrete terms how to generate and select desired system features as to achieve stated system goals" (ibid, p. 5). DP 1 is to design for direct usefulness by offering useful functionalities for a small group and without much a need of a large installed base. DP 2 is to build upon existing installed base by leveraging on existing functionalities to create added values. DP 3 is to expand installed base by persuasive tactics to enrol new uses and users to generate momentum. To address the adaptability problem, DP 4 is to make the II as simple as possible, and DP 5 is to modularize the II, minimizing tightly coupled dependencies, and build buffers to minimize risks of full breakdowns when one part of the II malfunctions.

We will use these DPs as our initial guidelines, which we will customize, adapt and extend given the particularities of AMR surveillance and the specificities for the human domain, and its subsequent scaling to other contexts. In the course of applying these principles within an ongoing initiative we will identify different challenges experienced, and how we have tried to address them.

4 Research Methods

Methodologically, we draw upon an action research approach to the AMR platform design involving two levels of use: i) regional level, including a set of 27 facilities pan India reporting data into a surveillance platform; and ii) at the level of a public health facility, catering to the facility and lab specific requirements.

Specifically, we draw upon the Canonical Action Research approach [16]. which has the following characteristics: i) the research process takes place in collaboration with the research team and the organization (called client-system infrastructure) to solve a problem which the organization recognizes as significant; ii) the research process involves iterative action research cycles of problem definition, diagnosis and design of interventions, followed by implementation and assessment; iii) the research will be guided by a theory of change, in our case drawing from II, specifically relating to how to design and evolve IIs. The overall aim of the research initiative is to generate new theoretical (around design strategies) and practical (capacities to use the new system) knowledge with each action research cycle which helps improve the subsequent one.

We describe our research in the form of three broad action research cycles: 1) designing and field testing the regional level surveillance platform; 2) adapting and extending the same platform suitable for a hospital facility; 3) building global networks to enable scaling across multiple contexts. As is common in action research, learnings from each cycle feed to improve subsequent cycles.

In the table below we summarize the timelines and data collection methods for the action research cycles (Table 1).

Table 1. Timelines and data collection systems for the action research cycles.

Action research cycles	Timelines (for Human domain)	Key aim	Data collection methods	Data analysis methods
AR1: Regional level	July,18 – April, 19	Design of system for research and surveillance which aids in assessing severity of AMR at a macro level	Using the existing system as a design reference to build the same system on a new platform; study of user manuals of existing system, focus group discussions, global/national workshops, discussions with AMR experts	Guided by interpretive approach; identification of design related themes; relating these themes to Design Principles drawn from II

(continued)

Table 1. (*continued*)

Action research cycles	Timelines (for Human domain)	Key aim	Data collection methods	Data analysis methods
AR2: Facility level	March 19 – October, 19	Design of the surveillance system which support workflow of the microbiology lab in recording and reporting daily cultures done, enabling physicians to make evidence-based decisions while prescribing antibiotics and conducting infection control activities	Interviews and discussions with end users, namely the microbiologists, doctors and hospital administrators, and study of existing work flows and data collection forms	Guided by interpretive approach; identification of design related themes; relating these themes to Design Principles drawn from II
AR3: Scaling strategies	Nov 19-ongoing	Building for scale to enable taking the platform to other locations in India and also globally	Study of technical documents; interaction with expert groups from WHO and Norwegian Institute of Public Health to gain understanding of scaling requirements	Guided by prototyping approaches in interaction with expert groups; building scaling design frameworks

5   Case Study

The case study narrative concerns the building and scaling of the AMR surveillance platform on the free and open source DHIS2 platform. The DHIS2 is available to all without licensing encumbrances, thus positively enabling scaling efforts. The DHIS2 currently has high global legitimacy as a defacto standard for health information system (HIS) development [17], expressed through support of multiple global partnerships including WHO, Global Fund, UNICEF, NORAD and others, as a digital global public good (DGPG) to enable free and unencumbered access to countries. Given that DHIS2 finds wide-spread use in 80+ countries, it has a large installed base of supporting resources of capacity and infrastructure, which in the long run can be leveraged upon to strengthen

AMR platform scaling. We now describe how the DHIS2 was developed upon across the three cycles.

Action Research Cycle 1 – the Regional Level: A national level research organization (anonymized as InMo) had since 2016 established an AMR surveillance network comprising of 27 specialty hospitals and private sector laboratories across India. The platform had been built in-house, and soon experienced functional scaling challenges, particularly related to analytics. InMo were already aware of DHIS2, and they decided to replicate their existing platform on DHIS2. InMo approached an Indian NGO (HISP India) to undertake this project, as they had long standing DHIS2 expertise and agreed to do the development without cost.

The NGO took an incremental design approach, by first replicating the existing data entry module in DHIS2, followed by the output module. Requirements were elicited through the study of the existing design documents, discussions with the developers and seeing system demos. The initial requirements were shared in the form of Excel sheets extracted from application's database. Data was organized in the form of masters in the database with different tables for organisms, antibiotics, breakpoints, sample and test types. Antibiotic panel masters were designed representing a combination of the logics to define what antibiotics to test for a particular organism.

A big challenge in our research was the inability of the system developers to meet the end users in the 27 network hospitals. InMo believed, since they had engaged with the users in building the first system, they were on top of the requirements, and HISP India only needed to interact with them. We found this thinking problematic, as we never heard the voices of the users and arguably many things were lost in translation. The prototypes which were replicated represented requirements of speciality hospitals and private sector labs. InMO made various requests to add or remove functionalities, and the planning was very adhoc causing frustration to the development team. For example, there was a demand to enable data sharing between the existing AMR surveillance platform WHONET used in multiple Indian facilities, and the platform we were developing. When we were told that the functionality developed initially did not fully support the data transfer process, we wanted to talk to the end user to understand the problem. This access was not granted, making it challenging and adding extra time to the development process. To enable a degree of standardization of the nomenclature, we used the standard libraries available in WHONET for terminology/nomenclature for organisms, antibiotics, test types and results.

InMo would assure us that after a certain set of functionalities were completed, field testing would start. However, as the prototype was completed, the research team would ask for more functionalities to be added before commencing field testing. For example, integration with WHONET was one request and then there was a demand for a isolate transfer module to track samples from one lab to another for quality testing. This functionality followed the specific workflow that was imitated within the network, requiring a batch of samples sent each quarter from regional labs to the respective nodal lab for quality testing and reporting test results to the regional lab. These functionalities were not simple replications, but represented quite new requirements, which were difficult to understand and build, within very aggressive timeframes, and in the absence of direct interaction with the users and where In MO themselves were unclear of the requirements.

In summary, this action research cycle can be seen as a "top-down" approach where the end user voices were invisible. A key learning from this was understanding the limits of a top down model to system scaling. On the practical side, HISP India learnt about the AMR surveillance domain on which they had limited prior experience. Another key learning was the experience of extending the DHIS2 platform to use in the hitherto uncharted area of AMR surveillance. Even through the platform developed did not find active use amongst the existing 27 hospitals, but that does not discount the potential for future use here or in similar regional kind of settings.

Action Research Cycle 2 – the Health Facility Level: The rich experience gained in the first cycle was motivating to the NGO to approach a state government hospital facility to build an AMR surveillance platform for local use. Since the NGO had already been working in that particular state building hospital information systems, they carried the trust of the state who granted them ready access to design and implement the platform in one medical college facility. For the NGO, a starting point to this process was to develop a detailed understanding of the work and information flows on how AMR testing was carried out, and how data was collected, reported and used.

The initial idea was to design the system prototype based on the user requirements at the microbiology laboratory. During this process, the microbiologist and lab staff realized that in absence of protocols and experience of AMR data collection and reporting, articulating requirements was difficult. Hence, they suggested to start working on the prototype created in the first action research cycle, and in this process learn about the specific facility requirements and simultaneously enhance the platform. The prototype from the first cycle was demonstrated to the lab staff at the hospital facility but was found inadequate to their needs. While the concept behind reporting the information was similar to the regional system, it was not sufficient in supporting the clinical and laboratory work. The test results must enable the physician to optimize the treatment of the patient, while in the earlier system the aggregated data was to be used primarily to form a picture of the degree of AMR in the population at large. With this vision, development of the application at a facility level was started in collaboration with microbiology lab technical staff and has been going on for over a year now.

The hospital has now assigned two data entry operators to the microbiology department, who are responsible for entering data on a daily basis from Mondays to Saturdays. The data entry operators usually follow a weekly roster where specific days of the week are assigned to them. With the COVID-19 outbreak, data entry work was suspended from March for a few months, but now has regained full momentum since mid-July. About 20–25 records are being entered every day. As regular use has progressed, the hospital has made some requests for enhancing the application ranging from minor changes to the dashboards to major changes in the functionalities itself. Some of these changes include: i) fitting the list of organisms, antibiotics, phenotypic test types and organism groups (such as Streptococcus) to match their local needs; ii) adding location details (e.g. OPD, IPD etc.) to the existing tables in the dashboards; iii) changing the graphs and the tables from being organism-specific to sample specific; iv) addition of some missing species in organism group list like pseudomonas spp. in NFGNB; and v) reconfiguring the data entry App which was earlier organism-specific to patient-centric by adding a patient reporting form that captures details like the name, age, gender and state.

Work is ongoing to generate patient-specific output reports containing sample details and RIS(Resistant Intermediate Susceptible) graphs.

The table below summarizes some differences in requirements from the first to the second action research cycles (Table 2).

Table 2. Requirements for an AMR surveillance system for research and clinical perspective.

AMR Surveillance system requirements	
Regional level	Hospital facility level
Application focused on a few groups of microorganisms	Would need to report on all microorganisms isolated in the laboratory
Specific antibiotics listed/tested for an organism species	A flexible list of antibiotics was required to reflect current usage
Specific organism groups were pre-defined	Organism regrouping was required based on laboratory requirements
Antibiotic specific susceptibility tests results were analysed	Analysis was based on class of antibiotics required Segregation of oral and injectable drugs was required Segregation and analysis of antibiotics based on the department they are used in the hospital was required A combined report for all the above categories is required for a monthly analysis
Application did not include other hospital/lab specific modules	Sample collection, transfer to other labs and sending test results to physician electronically was essential
Data validation at various levels was required	Data validation/approval process not essential
Isolate transfer module was required to track sample transfer	This module was not required

After few rounds of continuous interactions with the lab users, the module has been periodically updated, and the platform is now under routine use in the facility.

Action Research Cycle 3 - Building Global Networks to Enable Scale: As the platform has got stabilized with continuous use and system upgrades, there has been interest expressed by three global groups on the use of the platform, which has provided further impetus to enhance scale. The firs concerns the WHO AMR group in HQ, who were interested to see the potential of the platform being able to share data with their global system called Global Antimicrobial Resistance Surveillance System (GLASS). The second concerned a research group from Germany who were interested in seeing how this platform could be adapted and made relevant for 6 hospital facilities across 5 Sub-Saharan African countries. The third was the Norwegian Institute of Public Health who are exploring the possibility of using the platform at two levels of a hospital laboratory and at the regional level. In analysing these different requirements, we saw that our system may be too "India specific" and needs to be made more generic. This has led to designing for scale through creating a number of enhancements, and by separating out the "core or essential" requirements, with that of the enhancements which different sites could use.

The first enhancement was the integration of the platform with WHONET, which is globally the most popularly used AMR system running in nearly 3000 facilities. By doing this integration, the users are given the choice of either using their existing WHONET platform and transfer the data to the DHIS2 platform for strengthening analytics and dissemination. However, completely changing from WHONET to the DHIS2, is also an option. The second was the integration with the WHO GLASS system, which would allow countries to report their national data to the global system. The third was to enhance the use of standards, which was carried out through the use of data standards from WHONET and also through the incorporation of the ICD11 standards.

To meet the requirements from the German research group, the NGO sought to improve their documentation, by clearly describing the "Baseline AMR surveillance system", listing down the core and must-have functionalities required in a base system. This way, contexts who wanted to just use the essential features, could appropriately select. Secondly, the document also included the additional functionalities, which could be used by those who needed them. Thirdly, the document detailed the core functionalities of DHIS2, which could be further drawn upon to build new modules and functionalities (such as Android reporting). This document then provides a strategic approach to scale both functionally (more features) and also geographically (additional use contexts). Based on this strategic approach, the German research group has initiated a project to implement this platform in six hospitals spanning different countries in Sub-Saharan Africa. This effort will also be conducted in an action research mode, and the cycles of learning and improvements will continue in the future. With the Norwegian Institute of Public Health, the platform has been evaluated, and a research proposal has been formulated involving two levels of use, one, at the level of a hospital lab facility to collect lab data and transfer into another instance of the platform to enable regional and national level reporting.

All three streams of effort are in process, and should lead to further scaling as the systems get implemented on the ground.

6 Case Analysis

The case study analysis is informed by the II theory's DPs, which is drawn upon to examine the challenges and approaches used in our development approach across the three AR cycles.

DP1: Design for Direct Usefulness
This DP was difficult to apply in the regional system as we had no access to end users and our understanding of requirements was mediated through the InMo. While we did try to work around this problem by extensive study of documents and discussions with

InMo, our understanding remained inadequate. As a result, we could not provide adequate functionalities at the initial level, which meant that we could not enrol new users. However, in the second cycle, we worked closely with users, understanding what was directly useful for them enabling us to provide for identified needs with requisite functionalities. In the third cycle, we had two key end users. One, was the WHO HQ, who were primarily keen to enable the integration with GLASS, which we could provide. The next steps are at present under consideration.

The other end user was the German research group, who have seen the relevance of the system for their project in Africa and are planning to proceed with the implementation. Based on the ongoing discussions and feedback from the AMR team at WHO HQ, the system will be developed for it to be able to follow global standards and terminologies like SNOMED CT. Country specific data reporting and analysis is essential to understand the regional and global AMR picture. The system will be designed to allow countries to report different pathogens and include their list of antibiotics being tested for respective pathogens.

In the Indian context, the plan is to scale the application currently implemented at one facility to all 4 teaching hospitals of the state. To facilitate standardization, a baseline AMR instance has been developed with basic features and requirements to report, monitor, and analyze AMR data. Specific requirements from any facilities will be added on top of the baseline instance. Having the data reported on the same parameters, this will promote a standard usage of the data elements and provide a clear picture of the AMR situation in the state.

DP2: Build Upon Existing Installed Base

II theory guides us on the importance of the existing installed base and its both enabling and constraining influences. In the first cycle, the existing regional system represented the installed base, and it clearly had constraining influences on the development process. As the project mandate was clearly to replicate the existing system, we were forced to incorporate the existing design, including its inefficiencies. In the absence of our access to end users, we were not able to add improvements. In the second cycle, the installed base was the existing manual processes and the absence of a digital infrastructure. This base proved enabling, as we could provide value in improving the existing manual processes. The users saw this as being positive, and they increasingly showed more support and motivation to expand the project. In the third cycle, the existing GLASS system represented the installed base, and providing a data sharing mechanism represented a relatively structured and executable task, and potentially an enabling influence.

DP3: Expand Installed Base by Persuasive Tactics to Enrol New Uses and Users to Generate Momentum

As discussed under DP1, our inability to access users in the regional system meant we could not enrol the end users to generate momentum for scaling. Under action research cycle 2, we have focussed primarily in the microbiology lab and have enrolled the microbiologists and technicians in the lab. There are at least two higher levels of users to be enrolled. One, is at the hospital level, so that the systems could also be made relevant for other departments like OPD, IPD, surgeries etc. Two, is at the state level, where systems developed and tested in this hospital could be shown to authorities to convince them to implement it in other hospitals. We have not achieved this level yet, but that is clearly the ambition. In the action research cycle 3, we are collaborating with WHO and expecting them to use their position of legitimacy and expertise to persuade country level users to explore this platform. The collaboration with the German group follows the same principle of drawing upon the legitimacy and expertise of an external partner to persuade end users and build momentum.

DP4: Make the II as Simple as Possible

The design process was both constrained and enabled by the DHIS2 core architecture, which places boundaries on what can be done or not. However, in the regional case, since the task was of replication rather than designing from scratch, we could not consciously design for simplicity. In the hospital facility case, keeping simplicity was a guiding principle and we tried to implement this by replicating the existing forms and workflows of the lab technicians, so that they did not feel they are dealing with something alien. In the scaling phase, we have tried to separate out the "simple" system through describing the baseline and detailing how it can be incrementally expanded based on needs.

DP5: Modularize the II

The DHIS2 has a modular structure, which was enabling in creating a modular AMR surveillance system. Further, we created separate Apps for data entry, outputs, isolate transfer, WHONET and GLASS integration etc., to implement this modular structure. Applications for interoperability with other laboratory information systems have been developed.

7 Discussions and Conclusions

Design Principles provided by II theory have been applied to analyse the design challenges relating to the scaling of an AMR platform. We had started with describing the scaling challenge to play out under the two dimensions of functionality and geography. The functional dimension has played out with different design requirements at the different levels of the regional and global facilities. Technically, these challenges have not been unsurmountable, and the DHIS2 platform, with its open source and modular architecture, allows for this functional scaling to be enabled. However, the organizational level conditions which limited access to end users greatly impeded the adoption and scaling process. So, scaling can never be seen as merely as a technical exercise, but needs to be considered in a holistic perspective.

We have realized the importance of creating a standardized approach to the collection, analysis, and sharing of AMR data at the country global level is essential to facilitate scaling. The current application follows WHO standards and uses the same codes for pathogens, antibiotics, and samples which makes it easier for integration with other applications and has a comprehensive list of pathogens and antibiotics that can be filtered out based on specific country requirements, thus allowing scalability for different pathogenicity. WHO encourages and facilitates the standardization of data in countries to get a whole picture of the AMR in a country. This country-specific information is imported to a global platform WHO GLASS, a platform for global data sharing on antimicrobial resistance (AMR which facilitates the AMR data analysis at a global level. To standardize the AMR data being collected, unique functionality of interoperability with WHONET, a free Windows-based database software developed for the management and analysis of microbiology laboratory data with a special focus on the analysis of antimicrobial susceptibility test results (the current WHO supported system) has been developed. This interoperability enables the potential for scaling across sites currently using WHONET. The development of a web-based utility for the integration of DHIS2 with GLASS is ongoing. This will enable the facilities using DHIS2 to submit data to GLASS which allows to shift from only reporting data from individual isolates towards including epidemiological, clinical, and population-level data. To promote standardization ICD 11 diagnostic codes for AMR have been configured in the application to improve decision-making and drive national, regional, and global actions.

References

1. Chan, M.: WHO Director-General briefs UN on antimicrobial resistance: WHO (2016)
2. O'neill, J.: Tackling drug-resistant infections globally: an overview of our work. The review on antimicrobial resistance. Wellcome Trust, London (2016)
3. Essack, S.Y., Desta, A.T., Abotsi, R.E., Agoba, E.E.: Antimicrobial resistance in the WHO African region: current status and roadmap for action. J. Public Health **39**(1), 8–13 (2017)
4. Heudorf, U., Krackhardt, B., Karathana, M., Kleinkauf, N., Zinn, C.: Multidrug-resistant bacteria in unaccompanied refugee minors arriving in Frankfurt am Main, Germany, October to November 2015. Eurosurveillance **21**(2), 30109 (2016). https://doi.org/10.2807/1560-7917. ES.2016.21.2.30109
5. Klein, E.Y., et al.: Global increase and geographic convergence in antibiotic consumption between 2000 and 2015. Proc. Natl. Acad. Sci. **115**(15), E3463–E3470 (2018)
6. The World Bank.: Drug-Resistant Infections: A Threat to Our Economic Future (2017)
7. de Smalen, A., Ghorab, H., Ghany, M., Hill-Cawthorne, G.: Refugees and antimicrobial resistance: a systematic review. Travel Med. Infect. Dis. **15** (2016). https://doi.org/10.1016/j. tmaid.2016.12.001
8. Singh, P.K.: A universal good: how increased health coverage can help beat back antimicrobial resistance. World Health Organization, Regional Office for South-East Asia (2017)
9. World Health Organization: Tracking universal health coverage: 2017 global monitoring report. World Health Organization and International Bank for Reconstruction and Development/The World Bank, Geneva (2017). http://pubdocs.worldbank.org/en/193371513169 798347/2017-global-monitoring-report.pdf
10. World Health Organization: A vision for primary health care in the 21st century: towards universal health coverage and the Sustainable Development Goals (No. WHO/HIS/SDS/2018.15). World Health Organization (2018)
11. Ciborra, C.U., et al.: From Control to Drift: The Dynamics of Corporate Information Infrastructures. Oxford University Press, Inc., New York (2000)
12. Hanseth, O.: Who's in control: designers, managers or technology?: Infrastructures at Norsk Hydro. From Control to Drift: The Dynamics of Corporate Information Infrastructures (2000)
13. Sahay, S., Monteiro, E., Aanestad, M.: Toward a political perspective of integration in information systems research: the case of health information systems in India. Inf. Technol. Dev. **15**(2), 83–94 (2009)
14. Hanseth, O., Lyytinen, K.: Theorizing about the design of Information Infrastructures: design kernel theories and principles, vol. 4 (2003)

The Dark Side of Digitalisation

Digital Technology for Unmasking Labour Exploitation in Supply Chains

Hannah Thinyane[(✉)] and Francisca Sassetti

United Nations University Institute in Macau, Casa Silva Mendes, Estrada do Engenheiro Trigo no 4, Macao SAR, China
hannah@unu.edu, franciscasassetti2@gmail.com

Abstract. This paper aims to understand how digital technology can support businesses in unmasking labour exploitation in supply chains towards more effective remediation. It presents a case study using empirical evidence collected through expert interviews, document analysis, and a survey. Our findings illustrate that digital technology has the potential to support businesses in identifying cases of labour exploitation in supply chains during social compliance audits if tools are used within enabling environments. This research constitutes an original analysis of the intersection between corporate social responsibility and social compliance auditing, digital technology, and the critical issue of labour exploitation in supply chains. It identifies a flawed logic in expecting workers to use technology to report on exploitation without providing necessary scaffolding or support structures. We identify the role of intermediaries or surrogate accountability as critical in assisting workers and transforming working conditions.

Keywords: Digital technology · Labour exploitation · Social compliance audits · Supply chains · Worker reporting

1 Introduction

Global supply chains are complex networks of suppliers and manufacturers, that together produce goods for sale to consumers. As an example, the supply chain for a pair of running shoes would consist of multiple components that have been harvested (Tier 4 supplier: e.g. cotton farming, leather hide), processed (Tier 3 supplier: e.g. cotton weaving, leather tanning; Tier 2 supplier: e.g. textile embroidery) and manufactured (Tier 1 supplier: shoe lace, rubber sole, leather upper factories) across different countries and regions. From an economic standpoint, these global supply chains "take advantage of the best available human or physical resources in different countries, with a view of maintaining their competitiveness by augmenting productivity and minimizing costs" [1, p. 1]. Large corporations do business with hundreds or thousands of first-tier suppliers, and tens of thousands of higher-tiered suppliers. For policymakers in developing countries, global supply chains offer potential for "employment, improvement in technology and skills, productive capacity upgrading and export diversification into more

R. K. Bandi et al. (Eds.): IFIPJWC 2020, IFIP AICT 601, pp. 267–280, 2020.
https://doi.org/10.1007/978-3-030-64697-4_20

value added… [which in turn] would increase their attractiveness for more foreign direct investment" [1, p. 1].

With the passing of the California Transparency in Supply Chains Act (2010), UK's Modern Slavery Act (2015), France's Duty of Vigilance Law (2017) and Australian Modern Slavery Bill (2018), businesses are being forced to be accountable for labour abuses that occur not only in the first tier, but across their extended supply chains. Grant and Keohane characterise accountability as consisting of three elements: standards; information; and sanctions. The term accountability "implies that some actors have the right to hold other actors to a set of *standards*, to judge whether they have fulfilled their responsibilities in light of these standards, and to impose *sanctions* if they determine that these responsibilities have not been met" [2, p. 29]. The third element, *information*, refers to the collection of evidence to enable those holding actors to account to justify any sanctions that are imposed.

A primary tool for accountability within global supply chains is the social compliance audit. This tool is used to monitor labour conditions and health and safety standards within corporations' supply chains. Social compliance audits are varied in form, with some corporations using a self-regulatory approach, complete with self-declarations; to private regulatory systems with third party certification (refer to Sect. 2.3 for more details).

We position this research against this backdrop, and in this paper describe our case study of the current practices of private auditors in Asia-Pacific within the garment, toy and retail manufacturing sectors of large multinational corporations. Our aim was to understand current social compliance auditing practices, and to identify the key enablers and constraints to their practice. In particular we aimed to understand how digital transformation has impacted and could potentially impact the ability to support auditors to proactively and consistently collect standards-aligned worker feedback in a way that could be used to develop an evidence base to inform remedy and other actions.

2 Background

This work builds on the understanding that labour exploitation can be mapped onto a spectrum, ranging from what the International Labour Organization (ILO) refers to as 'decent work' at one end, through various labour and criminal law violations, to extreme exploitation or 'forced labour' at the other [3]. An experience of exploitation does not sit statically on the continuum: changes in personal factors (e.g. age, health), situational factors (e.g. migration status) and circumstantial factors (e.g. unemployment) make a worker more (or less) vulnerable to exploitation [4]. In this way, we can see that work situations that begin as consensual and mutually beneficial, can transform to oppressive and exploitative environments.

Studies in the fields of supply chain management and auditing often characterize factory owners and multinational corporations as 'power wielders' who in some cases violate laws and regulations, forcing workers into situations of labour exploitation. Workers or 'accountability holders' are hampered in their ability to prevent these breaches by structural factors including poverty, lack of education, prohibition from organizing, being seen as an easily replaceable workforce, and a lack of alternative forms of employment. It is worth noting that factories themselves suffer from power asymmetries too, with respect to large multinational buyers. While factories are more powerful than the workers themselves, they are often far less powerful than the buyers. Rubenstein notes that the power asymmetry is "exacerbated by the absence of domestic and international institutions that make sanctioning powerful actors (especially transnational actors) easier" [5, p. 617]. Ultimately, the solution for this asymmetry is to reduce the inequality between workers and their employers, and in turn employers and buyers, but this is a long term, complex (and some may say idealistic) goal. As a 'second-best', Rubenstein points to the need for 'surrogate accountability' in countries marked by weak institutions, high levels of corruption, and the inability of governments to enforce and implement regulations [5]. Surrogates involve an actor who substitutes for an accountability holder in one or more phases of 'setting standards, finding and interpreting information, and most importantly sanctioning the power wielder if it fails to live up to the relevant standards [5, p. 618]. This section now turns to the three elements of accountability, mapping them to the context of social compliance auditing within global supply chains.

2.1 Standards and Sanctions

There are a number of state-based, private and transnational trends in governance/regulation of labour and human rights standards for businesses. From a state-based perspective and stemming from the definition of labour exploitation as a violation of criminal or labour law, a key standard and list of sanctions can be found in state-based legal frameworks. In countries with weak laws and low state capacity (or motivation) to sanction exploitation, middle tiered buyers often require sellers to be audited by private bodies. The Accord for Fire and Building Safety in Bangladesh (The Accord) is a prime example of a cross-sector, private industry response to regulate conditions of work. As a results of a number of highly publicized workplace tragedies in Bangladesh in 2012 and 2013, public outcry from consumers influenced multinational buyers to pressure Bangladeshi suppliers with respect to building safety compliance [6]. As a direct response to this pressure, The Accord was developed, committing factories to maintain minimum building safety standards. This framework included independent safety inspection of signatory factories, with corrective action plans required to address violations before factories would receive orders from signatory brands.

From an international perspective, the UN Protect, Respect and Remedy Framework for Business and Human Rights (referred to as the Ruggie Framework) was passed in 2008, recognizing: the state's duty to protect workers against human rights abuses from third parties (including from multinational corporations); the corporate responsibility to respect human rights of workers; and the rights of victims to access remedy (both through formal and informal channels) [7]. Bilchitz critiques this framework, calling for corporates to be obliged not only to include obligation to avoid harm ('respect human rights'), but to "contribute actively to the realization of fundamental rights" [8].

Building on this framework, Wettstein argues for a capability-based approach to remedial action, based on an actor's capability to remediate human rights abuses within their domain, instead of human rights-based approaches that delegate that responsibility to governments alone [9]. Wettstein's approach places responsibility on businesses to protect and respect human rights, and to address the root causes of any human rights violations through compliance mechanisms, instead of simply treating its symptoms [9].

2.2 Information

A key role for technology in supporting accountability can be found in collecting, collating and analyzing information about power wielder's compliance with standards. 'Worker voice' or 'worker empowerment' tools have received much attention recently, supporting the collection of data from supply chains, to serve due diligence as well as to provide workers with access to grievance channels. A recent landscape analysis by Berg, Farbenblum and Kintominas finds that the most common form of worker voice tool takes the form of a worker survey, using either automated calling or texting of workers, seeking feedback on a small set of questions around their working conditions [10]. There are few tools that aim to build capacity of private auditors or labour inspectors, to support their on-site labour inspections or audits (e.g. [11]). Berg *et al.* note three key concerns for the use of technology to gather information from workers. Firstly, they question the reliability of information gathered through the tools to inform decision making. Second, they question the value-add to workers in providing data to companies, noting that it may be used to benefit suppliers and not result in changes to structural causes of exploitation for workers. Finally, not only do Berg *et al.* suggest that workers may not receive any outcomes from participating in audits, but that participation may also create new risks of retaliation from employers.

The Worker Engagement Supported by Technology (WEST) Principles are a set of guidelines designed to support efforts to engage workers in global supply chains [12]. These principles guide across four phases of design, engagement, analysis, and use; mapping onto user-centered design approaches. For completeness the principles are included below (Table 1):

Table 1. WEST Principles (adapted from) [12]

Design	1. Start with Integrity and Purpose 2. Use Worker-Centric and Inclusive Design 3. Build Trust with Workers
Engage	4. Facilitate Uptake and Ownership 5. Manage Security and Risk
Analyse	6. Evaluate Outcomes and Processes
Utilise data	7. Inform Decisions and System Changes 8. Collaborate and Share Learnings

Despite initiatives such as the WEST Principles aimed at guiding the development of new tools to engage workers in global supply chains, Agre challenges the idea of technology as necessarily a positive (or negative) force to bring about change [13]. Instead, he notes that technology works as an amplifier of underlying positive or negative human intent and capacity. Toyama builds on this notion with amplification theory, viewing technology as a means to an end and not an end in itself, explaining that "People have intent and capacity, while technology is merely a tool that multiplies human capacity in the direction of human intent" [14, p. 77]. This idea was explored in a recent study regarding the development and adoption of a worker engagement tool used by front-line responders to screen workers in vulnerable situations [15]. Findings showed that, although the tool could support frontline responders in overcoming issues of language barriers, privacy and trust, the tool was not a solution to improve worker screening, but rather a tool to support this process, where the impact of positive and negative intentions of workers the frontline responders were critical on whether the tool was used for its purpose.

2.3 Social Compliance Audits

A social compliance audit is an instrument used to measure, monitor and evaluate the performance of an entity against a standard. Typical standards used include human rights standards such as SA8000[1], or ILO's Fundamental Principles and Rights at Work[2]. Social audits are often used as part of Corporate Social Responsibility (CSR) strategies, which aim at helping companies to be accountable to their stakeholders [16]. Critics of social compliance audits refer to them as ritualistic strategies, designed to maintain existing inequalities [17], promoting a false transparency while overlooking socio-economic drivers that set the ground for exploitative practices [18], ultimately contributing for a "human rights minimalism" paradigm" [19, p. 740]. Proponents note that when done well, they support democratic and legitimate governance processes [20].

Historically, audits have comprised document review, interviews with factory management, and site observations [20]. As due diligence actors seek to answer the corporate demand for identifying instances of labour exploitation, it has become widely accepted that workers need voice in depicting working conditions [21]. More recently, audits have included worker interviews, although these are not without their own logistical and practical challenges [22]. The success or failure of worker interviews often comes down to the quality of skills of the auditor. In a short space of time, auditors are required to gain the trust of workers, overcome language, culture and sometimes gender divides, and identify potentially hidden situations of exploitation. Yet, as Dellaportas explains, despite the precise and regimented nature of social auditing which derives from the accounting professional, "One unfortunate side-effect of accounting as a procedural technology is its capacity to deny the social aspects of business activities when accounting processes are separated from its social framework" because it "diminishes a manager's ethical ideal by disconnecting managers from the effects of organizational practice when accounting dwells predominantly on technical matters and organizational performance rather than organizational impacts" [23]. As a result, auditors' accounting training and focus on procedures can hinder the social aspects that are necessary to effectively conduct worker interviews, such as trust, that can lead to the reporting of situations of exploitation.

---

[1] https://sa-intl.org/programs/sa8000/

[2] https://www.ilo.org/declaration/lang--en/index.htm.

3   Research Methods

The research questions that this study aimed to answer are:

- What are the current worker feedback mechanisms used in in-person, social compliance audits?
- What are the key constraints to their worker feedback mechanisms?
- What role do stakeholders believe that technology could play to support in-person audits?

This section describes the research approach used in this study, detailing the selection criteria for participants and the research design.

3.1   Case Study

This study uses a critical realist case study approach that explores the problems perceived by key stakeholders in social compliance audits, as well as their perceptions on the use of technology to support their audits. Adherents of critical realism pose that aspects of the social world can only be understood within the context that they occur. Therefore, we used a mixed-methods approach, including expert interviews, document analysis and surveys to uncover not only what the participants did, but to interrogate the reasons that informed their actions. Critical theorists argue that qualitative studies cannot be focused simply at the level of everyday actions but must also interrogate the social and cultural structures that maintain and form them, in order to support informed action that could change them [24, p. 110].

Simons defines a case study as an in-depth study of a particular phenomenon in its 'real life' context [25]. It is research-based, inclusive of different methods and evidence-led, where 'The primary purpose is to generate in-depth understanding of a specific topic … to generate knowledge and/or to inform policy development, professional practice and civil or community action' [25, p. 21]. Case studies use multiple sources and methods of generating evidence to analyze different aspects of a phenomenon [26], and improve reliability, transferability (external validity), and trustworthiness (internal validity) of findings [27]. A case study is not only a technique for collecting data but a methodological approach that includes a number of qualitative and quantitative data-gathering methods [28, p. 103].

3.2   Research Design

This research study draws together the findings of expert interviews, document analysis, and survey aimed at answering the three research questions posed above.

- **Expert interviews.** Participants were recruited for the expert interviews using expert sampling, with one author reaching out to members of a Hong Kong-based business alliance to publicize and solicit participation in the research. Based on this, 15 supply chain experts from eight major corporations in the garment, toy and retail industries self-selected to participate in expert interviews. After consent was obtained, experts were questioned using a semi-structured interview process around the three research questions detailed above. These interviews lasted approximately one hour. After completing the interview, one author transcribed and analyzed the transcripts of the interview.

- **Document analysis.** Of the eight corporations that participated in the expert interviews, four provided copies of their worker interview questionnaires that are used in social compliance audits within their supply chains. We analyzed these questionnaires in order to understand the type of information collected during worker interviews. The questionnaires presented a mix of open-ended questions, and closed questions.
- **Survey.** One author advertised the auditor survey through a Hong Kong-based business alliance of 27 brands, resulting in 203 auditors from 16 countries across the Asia-Pacific Region self-selecting to participate. The 32-question survey was conducted in December 2018, aimed at collecting information on the several aspects of workers' interviews and access to technology [29]. These responses were analyzed using a combination of bottom up and top down coding techniques.

4 Results

This section presents the results of the study, according to themes that arose across the expert interview, document analysis and survey.

4.1 Current Feedback Mechanisms

During expert interviews, company representatives shared that they use a variety of social audit frameworks, such as internationally recognized third-party programs, their own, or a combination of both. While some corporations tend to outsource most or all of their auditing mandate to third-party service providers, some companies maintain in-house audit teams, and a few exclusively use internal auditors. Survey respondents noted that worker interviews are a mandatory component of any audit framework, a practice described by 99% (n = 201) of auditors. Almost all social compliance audits include interviews with workers, with 64% of auditors specifying that it takes them more than 10 min per interview. Challenges faced during worker interviews included not being able to interview a representative sample of workers given the size of some factories, time constraints and language barriers.

Our document analysis revealed that all questionnaires collected some personally identifiable information, such as the employee's name, identity documents (ID), badge number, assigned department, home country and date of birth. As well as collecting personally identifiable information, survey findings highlighted limited privacy for worker interviews, with only 12% of respondents indicating that they exclusively interview workers individually. Despite collecting personally identifiable information, experts raised concerns of factory owners being able to trace complaints back to individual workers. Eighty five percent (85%) of survey respondents said that they interview workers either individually or in groups. Survey respondents mentioned that interviews are conducted in places with little privacy, such as workstations (61%), during the workers' meal (17%), or in rooms with other people (4%).

When asked about their selection criteria for interviewing workers, the most common factor cited by auditors was their ability to speak the same language as the worker (76%). While this in itself should not be a surprise, it has serious implications for the inclusivity of worker interviews, limiting them to the language capabilities of the auditor. Other aspects mentioned were gender (70%), job post (35%), pregnancy (11%), ethnicity (proxy for migrant worker status) (7%) and physical condition (9%).

Across the different companies, experts described different approaches for conducting worker interviews. While some companies provide worker interview questionnaires (which were later forwarded to researchers for review), others shared that there is flexibility in the type of questions asked, leaving it up to the instincts of the auditor to steer the conversation. Survey respondents indicated that once collected, 41% used digital tools for storing data. Some respondents raised privacy concerns regarding how data was kept and handled.

Document analysis found that all interview questionnaires covered areas such as wages and benefits, working hours, health and safety and labour conditions. Although some questions were consistent with ILO's Indicators of Forced Labour[3], no questionnaire systematically included all indicators. This finding correlated to auditor responses on the survey. One key concern raised in expert interviews was the apparent coaching of workers by supervisors. They described different techniques they use to overcome these issues such as rephrasing questions and changing the order in which they ask questions to reduce the risk of 'workers reciting a script'. This concern was also raised in the auditor survey, where 40% of respondents described having encountered workers appearing to be coached during interviews.

During the interviews, most experts mentioned that auditors are trained on identifying exploitation and provided with standard operating procedures (SOPs) to follow. These SOPs include a thorough review of factory documentation, interviews with management staff, and further worker interviews. Although 91% of survey respondents indicated receiving training on how to select cases for further investigation, only 1% mentioned following guidelines for deciding on furthering investigation on a case, and 4% for when identifying a vulnerable worker that requires assistance. Survey respondents indicated a variety of drivers for investigation, including: unclear, inconsistent or suspicious information (34%); urgent, critical or unusual cases (17%); evidence (11%) and many workers reporting the same issue (8%).

When a worker is identified as vulnerable and requires assistance, 41% of the survey respondents indicated conducting further investigation, including increasing the sample of workers screened (4%). Twenty five percent (25%) indicated reporting and consulting with their team, clients or the facility management; ensuring protection of the worker or their information (15%); and finding potential solutions with the worker (12%) or comforting the worker (12%).

---

[3] ILO's Indicators of Forced Labour, presents a typography of exploitative conditions of work: abuse of vulnerability, deception, restriction of movement, isolation, physical and sexual violence, intimidation and threats, retention of identity documents, withholding of wages, debt bondage, abusive working and living conditions, and excessive overtime [30]. When we see forced labour simply as an end of a continuum of exploitation, we argue that these same categories can be used to understand exploitation in any work environment.

4.2   Constraints to Feedback Mechanisms

Based on the expert interviews and results of the auditor survey, we identify four key constraints to the worker feedback mechanisms currently used in social compliance audits:

- Time constraints. Worker interviews are one of many tasks that auditors are required to undertake as part of a factory inspection. This forces auditors to choose between interviewing few workers, or interviewing workers in groups.
- Privacy. There is often a lack of privacy in interviews, with workers being questioned in front of other actors (either in groups, or in public spaces). Very few factories have private spaces that can be used in order to hold individual interviews. Workers fear being overheard, and in many cases, participants note that factory employers teach them a script to recite to auditors.
- Communication. Auditors and workers face language barriers, which impact the inclusivity of worker interviews, and the accuracy of those that are undertaken despite the barriers.
- Training. While SOPs are provided by companies, auditors described using a gut feel. With well-trained auditors with expertise in a variety of different legal frameworks, this technique could provide excellent results. However, in cases where language barriers exist, or time constraints affect the amount of time auditors can dedicate to worker interviews, this lack of consistency could result in inaccurate findings.

4.3   Perceptions and Use of Technology

During the expert interviews, many of the participants knew about one or more existing worker grievance tools and mentioned that they would most likely only implement one tool (if at all) as using multiple platforms to collect worker feedback on top of their auditing report systems would be too confusing. They also mentioned that some factories already have their own worker engagement apps in place and that 'it is a challenge to get workers to download multiple apps.'[4]

Survey findings showed that all auditors had smartphones and internet access, although 19% reported weak signal and poor reception when trying to access internet during audits. Survey respondents indicated using their mobile phones at work for searching relevant information (33%) and keeping records (12%). A few respondents also mentioned using their phone for translation (5%) and for reporting bribery (4%). One respondent said: 'if a facility is offering bribe in that case the auditor may record the voice recorder in-order to collect evidence for the bribe offering.'

Our survey revealed that auditors have a strong positive perception of the benefits of technology for their work. One of the respondents said, 'The world is changing and it is the era of artificial intelligence and supercomputing, I am sure that the incorporation of technology will be helpful for the workers' condition assessment.' 98% of survey respondents agree that technology can be useful in their jobs and 92% think that technology could be useful to help to assess workers' conditions.' A respondent said that

---

[4] Stakeholder meeting, Corporate Representatives (Audit and Sustainability managers), Hong Kong, 21 June, 4 July and 10 August 2018.

'using technology in auditing can make evaluation more objective and effective.' Among reasons identified for supporting why technology can be useful in audits, respondents mentioned that technology allows to search and check for information (30%); makes evaluation more effective, transparent and objective (22%); is convenient and useful (15%); saves time (11%); improves communication (9%); facilitates data processing and storage (3%); and improves accuracy (3%). Another respondent said 'technology can help to save time for manually works and provide more accuracy or persuasiveness'. Other claimed 'technology may help processing the data fast and give a tentative picture'. 6% of survey respondents mentioned that technology empowers or supports workers as 'technology makes it easier for worker[s] to voice their needs'.

5   Discussion

This section provides a critical reflection on the role that digital technology, specifically worker voice tools, can play to unmask labour exploitation in supply chains. It builds on Agre's assertion that digital technology in itself can make no change, but at best, will amplify existing forces [13]. Building on this, Toyama notes that "while technology can be used to augment, improve, or streamline development capacity, it cannot make up for the lack of human intent and capability" [14, p. 76]. Toyama expands further, highlighting the mechanisms by which technology amplifies capacity: differential access, differential capacity, and differential motivation.

5.1   Differential Access

The notion of access refers to physical access as well as information accessibility. As an example, if a worker can only report cases of exploitation on their own internet enabled devices, then providing a tech-based solution further disadvantages the worker with a 2G phone (or access to an internet enabled device but with no data bundles). In these cases, the access burden of participation would rest heavily on workers. From our expert interviews and surveys, we found that unlike workers, almost all auditors have internet enabled mobile devices that they use regularly for work purposes. By targeting auditors with the burden of device ownership/maintenance/installation of worker voice tools, this means that there are no assumptions about access on the worker.

Turning to information accessibility, if worker voice tool targets workers from a specific demographic (either by assuming a level of literacy or by providing support in a limited set of languages), then tech-based solutions serve to further disadvantage illiterate (or illiterate in that language) workers. By supporting text free and voice interfaces, translated into multiple languages, differing information accessibility issues could be addressed. This would also serve to address key constraints identified by auditors of language barriers as well as privacy issues, when audio interfaces are played using a set of headphones.

5.2   Differential Capacity

Differential capacity refers to disparities amongst key stakeholders, including education, social skills, and influence [14, p. 77]. Applied to the context of social compliance audits, this refers to the differing ability of stakeholders to use technology for their own purposes, a factor that reinforces pre-existing power imbalances between employers and factory workers. To further support workers in their differential (and in most cases lesser) capacity, we use Rubenstein's framework of surrogate accountability to justify the need for surrogates to intermediate on behalf of accountability holders to hold power wielders to account. Rubenstein explains that, "the difficulties faced by accountability holders who are poor and vulnerable are exacerbated by the absence of accessible, fair, and efficient institutions that mitigate the effects of poverty and vulnerability" [5, p. 623].

Many current worker voice tools take the form of tip-off services (SMS based, hotlines, helplines), providing an electronic format for the traditional complaints/ suggestion boxes found at factories [12]. These tools should be applauded in their ability to support worker to privately disclose the exploitative conditions that they face. However, when considering the huge power disparity between workers and power wielders, our concern relates to the capacity or agency that workers believe they have to report exploitation without the support of an intermediary.

Instead, in this research we suggest a focus on building the capability of social compliance audits, especially involving independent auditors, as they are uniquely positioned to uphold the three elements accountability - standards, information and sanctions – on behalf of factory workers. Social compliance auditors measure workplace compliance against a particular set of standards. From our auditor survey, 99% of participants describe worker interviews as a key component of social auditing. They note that their current practice was complicated due to language barriers, time constraints, a lack of privacy, and issues identifying cases of exploitation.

From our survey, auditors suggested that their own capacity to identify cases of labour exploitation could be supported through the support of digital technology. Our findings suggest that a simple mobile application (to be installed on the auditors' mobile device) could provide a consistent manner to interview workers about the conditions of their work. When combined with a set of headphones, a set of simply worded, yes/no questions could be played in the workers own language, giving them a chance to respond privately (and anonymously) and report perceived exploitation at work. Multiple workers could be interviewed at the same time, simply by providing a further set of low-cost mobile devices (and headphones) to auditors. By combining responses across a group of workers, their privacy would be protected, and an auditor could use this information to inform the next stages of their in-person site inspection. For example, if even one worker who was interviewed reported an incidence of wages being withheld, the auditor could intermediate on behalf of workers, and request full documentation of payment stubs from factory officials.

5.3 Differential Motivation

In carrying out this research, we had the opportunity to work together with brands, corporate social responsibility experts and auditors who were intrinsically motivated to assess working conditions and remediate any cases of exploitation that were identified. However, it is not always the case that actors within supply chains aim to provide decent working conditions for workers.

Within the context of workplace inspections, the potential for technology to effectively uncover workplace exploitation depends on how auditors and workers use them. If both workers and auditors have positive intentions for its use, technology will amplify their intent and lead to an accurate identification of workplace conditions [15]. But if a well-intentioned auditor is faced with a report made by a worker with negative intentions – that is having a bad day or wishes to bring harm against their employer – then the auditor will use technology to and unwittingly lodge a false report. In the same way, if a positively intentioned worker wanting to report workplace exploitation is met by an unwilling auditor, the reporting technology tool may be used to bring about more harm to the worker, with the auditor sharing details of confidential reports with exploitative employers [15]. This shows that, despite the opportunities that technology offers in supporting accountability mechanisms in supply chains through social compliance auditing, whether it is in upholding standards, sanctions or collecting key information, it is also important to critically reflect on its real ability to bring about change.

While technology can play a key role in enabling effective reporting of exploitation and consistent ways to collect this information, it is not capable alone to make the structural changes necessary to achieve decent work environments. This is because "technologies are not embedded in a system of accountability ... they are just data gathering tools—it's tech in a vacuum if not a part of a sound ground game with safeguards, trust, feedback, and engagement" [21, p. 157]. When thinking about worker reporting tools used for social compliance auditing, Rende Taylor and Shih explain that "There is a flawed logic here that expects migrant workers to step up and claim the rights they don't have" [21, p. 157]. Business due diligence tools must purposely prioritise enhancing the workers' voices, and using that feedback effectively; otherwise, "their assumptions of pathways to impact may be flawed in their assumptions of the power of vulnerable populations to claim their rights in situations of labour exploitation" [21, p. 157].

Even if such technology was in place, Berg et al. present three concerns regarding its use to gather information from workers [10]. Firstly, the reliability of information used to make decisions, using Toyama's terminology, would be dependent on the workers' intent. This information could result in unfair sanctions on the one hand or serve to discredit real cases of exploitation on the other. Secondly, Berg et al. question the value for workers in participating and providing information for company due diligence purposes. If their input does not result in improvements in their working conditions (structural causes of exploitation), this may serve to break workers' trust in similar feedback mechanisms, potentially preventing them from reporting again.

The third concern refers to the safety of workers when using feedback mechanisms, particularly the risks of reprisals by employers for reporting wrongdoings. This highlights the importance of ethical handling of worker feedback to ensure the confidentiality of the reporting, as well guarantee the worker's privacy when technology is used.

Despite these concerns, our findings highlighted that if carefully designed and entrenched in a system that nurtures intent and capacity of key stakeholders, there is a role for a mobile app to support auditors to identify labour exploitation within social compliance audits in supply chains.

6   Conclusion

Worker voice tools are not a silver bullet. In and of themselves, they cannot 'solve' labour exploitation within supply chains. However, if carefully designed and used by well-trained and equipped auditors, they can help factory workers to overcome power asymmetries and report the conditions of their work. Of course, these tools in themselves are just one small component in a much broader social compliance auditing system, including the negotiation of standards, data gathering, and in some cases sanctions on exploitative working environments.

Drawing from a series of expert interviews, document analysis and a broad auditor survey, and with the three mechanisms of amplification in mind, the paper suggests a specific way that digital technology could be used to unmask labour exploitation in supply chains. Using Rubenstein's surrogate accountability, it identifies a role for intermediaries (or surrogates) to aid worker to overcome power asymmetries, holding power wielders to account for their conditions of work. This paper highlights key factors of human and institutional capacity and intent which are crucial to understand and support, to ensure that data that is gathered is used to promote justice and remediation.

References

1. Nicita, A., Ognivtsev, V., Shirotori, M.: Global supply chains: trade and economic policies for developing countries, p. 34
2. Grant, R.W., Keohane, R.O.: Accountability and abuses of power in world politics. Am. Polit. Sci. Rev. **99**(1), 29–43 (2005). https://doi.org/10.1017/S0003055405051476
3. Skřivánková, K.: Between decent work and forced labour: examining the continuum of exploitation, York, UK (2010). Accessed 01 Nov 2016
4. Global Migration Group: Exploitation and abuse of international migrants, particularly those in an irregular situation: a human rights approach, UNODC, Geneva (2013). https://www. unodc.org/documents/human-trafficking/2013/2013_GMG_Thematic_Paper.pdf. Accessed 04 Jan 2020
5. Rubenstein, J.: Accountability in an unequal world. J. Polit. **69**(3), 616–632 (2007). https://doi.org/10.1111/j.1468-2508.2007.00563.x
6. Reinecke, J., Donaghey, J.: The 'accord for fire and building safety in Bangladesh' in response to the Rana Plaza disaster. In: Global Governance of Labour Rights, pp. 257–277. Edward Elgar Publishing (2015)
7. United Nations: A/HRC/8/5 Protect, Respect and Remedy: A Framework for Business and Human Rights, 07 April 2008. https://www.business-humanrights.org/sites/default/files/rep orts-and-materials/Ruggie-report-7-Apr-2008.pdf
8. Bilchitz, D.: The ruggie framework: an adequate rubric for corporate human rights obligations? Int. J. Hum. Rights 12, June 2010. https://sur.conectas.org/en/the-ruggie-framework/. Accessed 21 May 2020
9. Sinkovics, N., Hoque, S.F., Sinkovics, R.R.: Rana Plaza collapse aftermath: are CSR compliance and auditing pressures effective? Account. Audit. Account. J. **29**(4), 617–649 (2016). https://doi.org/10.1108/AAAJ-07-2015-2141
10. Berg, L., Farbenblum, B., Kinitominas, A.: Addressing Exploitation in Supply Chains: Is technology a game changer for worker voice?. Anti-Traffick. Rev. **14**, 47–66 (2020). https://doi.org/10.14197/atr.201220144

11. Thinyane, H., Bhat, K.: Supporting the critical-agency of victims of human trafficking in Thailand. presented at the ACM CHI Conference on Human Factors in Computing Systems, Glasgow, Scotland, May 2019

12. West Principles: White Paper: Realizing the Benefits of Worker Reporting Digital Tools, March 2019. https://westprinciples.org/wp-content/uploads/2019/03/west_principles_white_paper-realizing_the_benefits_of_worker_reporting_digital_tools.pdf. Accessed 12 April 2019

13. Agre, P.E.: Real-time politics: the internet and the political process. Inf. Soc. **18**(5) (2002). https://www.tandfonline.com/doi/abs/10.1080/01972240290075174. Accessed 21 May 2019

14. Toyama, K.: Technology as amplifier in international development. In: Proceedings of the 2011 iConference, Seattle, Washington, 2011, pp. 75–82. https://doi.org/10.1145/1940761.1940772

15. Thinyane, H., Sassetti, F.: Towards a human rights-based approach to AI: case study of apprise (2020)

16. Blowfield, M.: Corporate social responsibility: reinventing the meaning of development? Int. Aff. **81**(3), 515–524 (2005)

17. Islam, M.A., Deegan, C., Gray, R.: Social compliance audits and multinational corporation supply chain: evidence from a study of the rituals of social audits. Account. Bus. Res. **48**(2), 190–224 (2018). https://doi.org/10.1080/00014788.2017.1362330

18. New, S.: Modern slavery and the supply chain: the limits of corporate social responsibility? Supply Chain Manag. Int. J. **20**, 697–707 (2015). https://doi.org/10.1108/SCM-06-2015-0201

19. Wettstein, F.: CSR and the debate on business and human rights: bridging the great divide. Bus. Ethics Q. **22**(4), 739–770 (2012). https://doi.org/10.5840/beq201222446

20. Courville, S.: Social accountability audits: challenging or defending democratic governance special issue on auditing in regulatory perspective. Law Policy **25**(3), 269–298 (2003)

21. Rende Taylor, L., Shih, E.: Worker feedback technologies and combatting modern slavery in global supply chains. J. Br. Acad. **7**, 131–165 (2019). https://doi.org/10.5871/jba/007s1.131

22. Rende Taylor, L., Latonero, M.: Updated guide to ethics and human rights in anti-human trafficking. Issara Institute, Bangkok, Thailand (2018). https://www.antislaverycommissioner.co.uk/media/1207/guide-to-ethics-and-human-rights-in-anti-human-trafficking.pdf

23. Dellaportas, S.: The role of accounting in mediating empathic care for the 'other'| Emerald Insight. Account. Audit. Account. J. **32**(6), 1617–1635 (2019)

24. Alvesson, M., Sköldberg, K.: Reflexive Methodology: New Vistas for Qualitative Research. SAGE, London (2000)

25. Simons, H.: Case Study Research in Practice. SAGE Publications (2009)

26. Denzin, N.K.: Sociological Methods: A Sourcebook. Transaction Publishers, New Brunswick (2006)

27. Rossman, G.B., Wilson, B.L.: Numbers and words combining quantitative and qualitative methods in a single large-scale evaluation study. Eval. Rev. **9**(5), 627–643 (1985). https://doi.org/10.1177/0193841X8500900505

28. Babbie, E., Mouton, J.: The Practice of Social Research. Oxford University Press, Cape Town (2001)

29. Thinyane, H., Mera, S., Sassetti, F.: Unmasking Labor Exploitation Across Supply Chains. United Nations University Institute on Computing and Society (2019)

30. ILO, ILO Indicators of Forced Labour: Special Action Programme to Combat Forced Labour, ILO, Geneva, Switzerland, WCMS-203832 (2012). http://www.ilo.org/wcmsp5/groups/public/@ed_norm/@declaration/documents/publication/wcms_203832.pdf. Accessed 18 Sep 2018

In Technology We Trust? Human Skills & Intermediaries in Digital Retail Banking

Soumyo Das[✉] and Bidisha Chaudhuri

Center for IT & Public Policy, IIIT Bangalore, Bengaluru, India
soumyo.das@iiitb.org

Abstract. Increasing use of ICTs in organisations has contributed to a resurgence of automation anxiety centred around issues of human skills and employability. Prior work, however, shows that human skill and knowledge are necessary for supervision, adjustment, maintenance, improvement and expansion of new technologies. Through our ethnographic case study of work practices of Front-End Executives in three retail bank branches in India, we find that customers continue to rely heavily on both technical and functional skills of these bank employees even with the increasing presence of ICT-based self-service technologies. We argue that human skills and intermediation help in the process of adoption of digital technologies in banking and thereby retain trust in digital banking despite substantial disruption caused by new technologies. The aim of the paper is to reiterate the importance of human skill in enabling meaningful engagement with new technologies for diverse actors across different strata of society.

Keywords: Automation · Digital banking · Human intermediation · Skill · Trust · Work practice

1 Introduction

Brynjoffsson and McAfee [12] argue that rapid and accelerating digitalisation will have a significant impact on the way work would be done going forward. Recent developments in automation technologies has led to a wide range of fears and concerns around job loss and restructuring of labour and skill, a resurgence of what Akst [3] terms *automation anxiety*. Such anxieties are centred on the implications of technology adoption on human skills and employability, deskilling and the process of redesigning occupations around automation processes. While in general, introduction of new information communication technologies (ICTs) for automation are premised on minimal human intervention [24], studies have shown that automated systems need human intervention for supervision, adjustment, maintenance, improvement & expansion [11]. Accordingly, both organisational studies and information system research have emphasised on the importance of exploring the role of human skills and agency along with new technologies in an organisational context [37, 40, 41, 54]. In these studies, ICTs are not treated as external artifacts leading to change in work, but as embedded in everyday work practices of

© IFIP International Federation for Information Processing 2020
Published by Springer Nature Switzerland AG 2020
R. K. Bandi et al. (Eds.): IFIPJWC 2020, IFIP AICT 601, pp. 281–294, 2020.
https://doi.org/10.1007/978-3-030-64697-4_21

employees within an organisational setup, shaping organisational relations, roles, and work practices [36, 38, 58].

When the implementation of new ICTs brings about changes in how people (customers, beneficiaries, etc.) interact with services provided by an organisation, the role of intermediaries have been shown to become critical [28]. The role of human intermediaries in implementing new technologies is even more pertinent in developing countries, where social endowment gaps (such as, illiteracy, low levels of education, gender, class, caste inequalities etc.), and inadequate infrastructures (e.g., connectivity, power systems etc.) continue to impede effective use and adoption of ICTs [13, 14, 18, 22, 31, 39]. The process of intermediation has been shown to be dependent on both technical and social knowledge that allows intermediaries to negotiate the dynamic organisational contexts of their everyday work to stabilise the diffusion of new technologies [14].

In this paper, we explore the concept of *'trust'* in human intermediation as a critical *'soft infrastructure'* [15] necessary to stabilise and sustain the use of ICTs in Banking, Financial Services, and Insurance (BFSI) industries. ICTs, including online banking systems, platform finance systems, and technologies like Artificial Intelligence are heralding a new approach to providing banking & financial services to customers [1, 20]. With a significant volume of customers increasingly moving towards digital banking channels [50], questions are being asked about the viability of brick and mortar retail branches, and importance of retail banking employees in the digital era. Against the backdrop of this debate, we focus on the role of retail bank employees in retaining customers' trust in banking despite facing the disruptive impact of new technologies. We specifically focus on the work practices of Front Desk Executives (FDEs)[1] and their interactions with customers. We argue that while ICTs allow for banking by bypassing retail branches, these very technologies bring a significant amount of customers to rely on FDEs within a physical bank branch.

The paper is organised into four major sections. In Sect. 2, we capture relevant literature that establishes the relationship between trust, human intermediation and skill. We follow this up with a brief note on our methodological approach. We then present our findings on interpersonal trust through everyday interactions between customers and FDEs in Sect. 4. In Sect. 5, we present a multi-dimensional analysis of the skills of FDEs as a basis for continued trust in banking infrastructure despite disruptive technologies. We conclude by delineating the relevance and scope of our research.

2 Relevant Work: Trust, Human Intermediation, and Skill

The concept of trust has been of interest to scholars across disciplines. When viewed as an attitude or expectation, trust has been shown to include an element of expectation regarding behaviour or outcomes: *"expectations of fiduciary obligation and responsibility, that is, the expectation that some others in our social relationships have moral obligations and responsibility to demonstrate a special concern for others' interests above their own"* [9, p. 15]. Another definition of trust is the *"willingness to rely on an*

---

[1] Front-Desk Executives are Retail Banking Employees who are responsible for providing financial services directly to customers.

exchange partner in whom one has confidence" [32, p. 315]. Meyer, Davis and Schoorman [30] show that the ability, benevolence, and integrity of a human actor are key factors to building trust and trustworthiness. The concept of trustworthiness is critical as it highlights that trust is not a zero-sum game, but rather that the level of trust between a trustor and trustee is a spectrum. This concept of trust is generally understood as a continuum where the perception of trust does not merely emerge from the properties of a system or institution, but is rather enacted through interactions with multiple actors within a larger social context [7].

A critical conceptualisation of trust, especially in contexts of development, is the goal-oriented nature of trust. It can be perceived as *"the ability of the trustee to perform an important action and the expectation of the trustor that the trustee will perform as expected or can be relied upon"* [27, p. 54]. This definition of trust works on the belief that an agent will help achieve an individual's goals in a situation characterized by uncertainty and vulnerability.

Studies on the interplay of trust and human intermediation have explored trust in internet kiosks and the intermediaries who mediate the services available [21, 44]; trust in ICT-enabled services or systems such as mobile banking or e-governance [33]; trust in information [15]; and trust in institutions, such as governments as providers of ICT services [26]. These studies have shown the relevance of institutional factors as a critical element of trust formation. For example, Rajalekshmis [44] argues trust to be dependent on perceptions of technology, information, or service provided, and the institutional mechanisms that secure transactions. She further shows how institutional membership of the intermediary is critical for successful e-governance service delivery. Similarly, Morawczynski and Miscione [33] discuss the emergence and sustenance of institutional trust in the context of mobile banking services (M-Pesa) in Kenya. When it comes to BFSI technologies, Ananda et al. [4] shows that institutional awareness plays a significant positive influence on adoption of digital banking technologies in India. Zhou [57] shows the relevance of institutional reputation as important for trust-building. Similarly, Deventer et al. [52] in their study of students' use of digital banking in the Philippines, shows that the perceived integrity of a banking institution plays a major role in rendering banking trustworthy. While convenience and enterprise image are considered to have positive effects on intention to use digital banking service [35], Sharma and Sharma [49] show how service quality plays a critical role in trust formation in online banking services in India. These studies indicate that skill of banking employees (especially those who are directly responsible for providing banking services to the customers) is intricately related to maintaining trust in banking institutions.

The term skill has often been clustered along with terminologies such as, ability and competency to signal a concept that enables an actor (human or technology) to have an influence within some specific domain [30]. Proctor defines skill as a *"goal-directed, well-organized behavior that is acquired through practice and performed with economy of effort"* [42, p. 18]. In a more general sense, skill as a concept is used to define a level of performance, with a sense of accuracy and speed in carrying out particular tasks. It also underlines the trustor's perception of the knowledge and skill of the trustee in a particular context [30]. We focus on how the different kinds of skills that a trustee, in this case FDEs, bring to their everyday work and how customers' perception of those skills builds and retains their trust in retail banking systems.

At a more general level, the implementation of ICTs are expected to lead to a direct substitution of jobs and tasks currently performed by workers, leading to unemployment and changes in organisational forms and functions [6, 23]. According to the World Bank [29], a significant volume of jobs are at risk in developing countries due to automation: 69% in India, 72% in Thailand, and 85% in Ethiopia. It is increasingly argued that digital technologies will eventually replace human service providers. For BFSI industries, increasing digitisation practices are raising the question of the relevance of retail banking employees in the 21st century - as intermediaries in the process of providing financial services to customers [2]. While our paper explores how employees' skill help retain customer trust, at a larger scale, our research highlights the importance of retail banking employees, and the importance of brick and mortar banking branches even in the era of digitalisation and automation of BFSI services, as necessary for customers, especially in developing regions.

3   Methodology

We study customer-Front-Desk Executive interactions in retail banking branches of Indian Standard Bank[2] and Indian Chartered Bank (See footnote 2) – two Public Sector Banks in India. Public Sector Banks in India are BFSI institutions owned & operated by the Government of India. Considered to be trustworthy institutions [47], these banks have a prime focus of providing financial products and services to all sections of the society in the country [45]. The organisational structure of a Public Sector retail bank, in general, consists of two layers – the client-facing Front-Desk Executives (comprising Tellers, Accounts Managers, Passbook Executives, Loans and Credit Officers and Customer Service Executives), and the back-end Administration Executives (comprising Operations Manager, Manager, Office Assistant etc.). Both these categories of employees use ICTs - Core Banking System and other generic-use ICTs for office work (e.g., scanners, printers etc.) to provide financial service to customers. Customers can also access financial services through three Self-Serviced ICTs - 1. Multi-Function Kiosks, 2. ATMs, and 3. Online Banking facilities.

This paper is based on an ethnographic case study [19] involving FDEs, support staff, customers, and retired employees of the banks. The fieldwork was undertaken between February and May 2019, and from October 2019 to January 2020, in three different retail banking branches of public sector banks located in Bangalore, Karnataka and in Kolkata, West Bengal. All three locations represent a diverse clientele, including people engaged in agriculture, construction, and other forms of informal work, as well as white collar workers and businessmen. The prominent languages spoken in field sites include Kannada, Bengali, Hindi and English. Our study adopted an exploratory single-case embedded design and included multiple data collection methods [10, 56] - including observations and interviews with key actors in the retail banking ecosystem and extensive interviews with customers (Table 1).

---

[2] Anonymised.

Table 1. List & count of respondents.

No.	Respondent type	Count
1	Front-Desk executives	18
2	Administration executives	6
3	Customers	23
4	Assistant to customers	17

The interviews were mostly semi-structured; there were also several informal conversations that occurred during the observations. The interviews lasted anywhere between 30–45 min, while informal interactions were much shorter and were conducted in between observations. Interviews with the FDEs took place over multiple rounds, with observations in each round shaping the discussions in the subsequent round. Given the sensitive nature of financial physical ecosystems (in terms of privacy and security), no recordings (audio or video) were taken. Furthermore, names of respondents and our field-sites have been anonymised for reasons of privacy. Case notes were written down at the time of observation and during interviews, which were later analysed using open coding methods. We divided our findings first on the basis of the customers profiles, based on their ability to understand and use banking services and ICTs. We then mapped these customer profiles onto their interactions with FDEs, based on their banking needs. While analysing the data on interactions between customers and FDEs, we identified major themes that recurrently emerged during interviews and observations. In this paper we focus on two such themes: *trust* and *skill*.

4 Digital Retail Banking and Human Intermediation: An Everyday Account of Interpersonal Trust

To explore how customers come to rely on FDEs for their day-to-day banking service requirements, we focused on the everyday interactions within bank branches. We found two categories of customers who visit retail banks on a regular basis: those who lack the skills to undertake financial services by themselves due to significant social endowment gaps attributable to age, literacy, digital skill etc.; and those who posses both banking knowledge and familiarity with digital technologies for banking, but still visit retail banking branches to feel *"more assured"* about their financial dealings. We elaborate on our observations across these two customer groups, through a few vignettes. These vignettes are chosen to provide the reader with an overarching understanding of retail banking processes and routine interactions that take place within a branch. They also provide a broader sense of the kind of problems people face in accessing services, their motivation to engage with bank employees and the ways they navigate ICTs in banking.

4.1 Customers with Limited Social Endowments

Interviews with our respondents highlight that a significant proportion of customers face issues with using digital technologies, which in turn impacts their ability to access financial services. Many elderly customers we interviewed argue that they do not have the necessary skills required to use digital technologies. Another set of customers reported to have limited literacy to undertake financial transactions by themselves.

Aman, a middle-school graduate and migrant construction labourer from Assam, who wanted to update the PIN number of his debit card, could not use the Multi-Function Kiosk as it displays instructions only in English - a language Aman was not quite comfortable with. After seeing him struggle, one of us (authors) tried to assist him with the process. Even after we translated the instructions for him, Aman was constantly unsure of how to proceed. It turned out that Aman had opened the bank account in Assam with his brother's SIM card and therefore, the OTP required to update the PIN would not reach him but his brother, thereby rendering futile, his effort to update the PIN without his brother's phone.. Aman said he had no idea that this was the process, or else he would have given his own phone number. At this point, the Accounts Executive intervened, and informed him that there is no way to bypass the OTP- PIN updating system, and following this, she took it upon herself to resolve the issue. As we observed the Account Executive assist Aman with updating his PIN, it became increasingly apparent that the process requires certain technical expertise and working knowledge of the system which would be difficult even for an educated person with significant levels of digital skill. Aman's case was not an aberration, rather a common occurrence where customers - illiterate/semi-literate, and/or with low/little digital literacy-struggle with digital technologies. Such instances highlight the need of FDEs to have a thorough knowledge of retail banking processes, technical skills, and to be aware of the diverse socio-economic backgrounds of their customers.

In another instance, Raghav, a customer, had come to the bank with his sister, Gayatri's passbook. He had attempted a withdrawal from her account at a nearby ATM the previous evening, but even though the money was debited from the account, the machine did not disburse the cash. The FDE informed Raghav of the process to be followed - which includes updating the passbook first in order to show that the money was indeed debited, and then filling up a form for further escalation. The Accounts Executive furthermore informed Raghav of the procedure that will follow, and reasoned to him that it will take up to seven working days to reimburse the money. A follow-up interview with Raghav reveals that he is not educated beyond middle school and Gayatri who works as a housekeeper is not literate. None of them are comfortable using digital technologies. Her employers prefer to pay her through bank deposit and not cash. Hence, Gayatri usually relies on Raghav for accessing an ATM to withdraw cash or to receive any financial services at the bank branch. During our discussion, Raghav says, *"Here it is easy - I can talk directly to Madam (referring to the FDE) and get my issues sorted." - "It is Indian Standard Bank, and hence the money will come back. Just that I wanted to know how much time it will take for the money to come back!"*

While Raghav's trust in the bank derives from its organisational reputation, on the ground it is mediated through his interactions with the FDEs. He feels reassured by the words of an expert human intermediary, which help reduce his worry of a misplaced transaction, and retain his trust in the organisation.

4.2   Customers with Requisite Capacities

A significant footfall in a retail bank consists of customers who are by and large, capable of using digital technologies but still prefer to visit the branch. All of them were aware of Self-Service Technologies and in some cases have also tried to use these technologies. When asked why they still come to the branch instead of doing financial transactions by themselves in the comfort of their homes, they argue that digital technologies are not stable yet, and hence problems persist with their usage. One customer informs us that, *"...they have this new app - ZOLO[3]...half the time it does not work!"*, while one employee, accepting the limitations of digital technologies, humorously responds that, *"....even the bank manager does not use internet banking!"*.

There are customers such as Rishabh, who could open an account for his wife online, but still chooses to visit a retail bank as he prefers a more personalised service experience. Rishabh works as a construction worker in the Middle East, and has come to the bank with his wife to resolve some queries pertaining to the joint-bank account he has applied for. He brought with him all of his documents (identification documents, education documents including his undergraduate degree etc.), and his wife's identity cards, in case they need to be submitted. The FDE informed him that no further documentation is required; however, she added that Rishabh and his wife could have gone for a different type of account - a specific savings account meant for women. That kind of an account, she informed, would provide a much higher rate of interest, a debit card with higher withdrawal limits, and according to prevailing national and bank- specific policies, would be easier to get a loan if required. An excited Rishabh agreed to reapply for this new account and requested the Accounts Executive to initiate the process for opening the same. When he asked the Accounts Executive why this information is not available online - she responded that the information is there, but is not advertised well enough.

We found updating passbooks as one of the most high volume work practices within a bank branch. While technically this is a fully automated straightforward task that should be performed by customers on a self-serviced machine, in all three branches we found a person dedicated solely to this task, called the Passbook Executive. In all three cases, we found out that their role goes much beyond. They also help in interpreting and explaining data to customers. Passbook Executives recounted examples of customers asking why a certain amount was debited or credited, or for why people could not see their recent transactions and so on. One Passbook Executive narrates an interesting incident - an elderly woman had come to the bank branch and raised a query as to why her daughter, a resident outside the city, had not received the money which she had sent through her son. After updating the passbook, the Passbook Executive realised that there was no history of any such transaction. He asked to contact her son. Only after she contacted her son, did she get to know that he had indeed not sent the money yet. The Passbook Executive uses this example to say that updating the passbook and getting a passbook with numbers on them mean nothing to the customers. Their requirements of coming to her are regarding the nature of the numbers - when a particular transaction was done/not done, whether the money was sent or not.

Above vignettes highlight the ways in which customers of various kinds and with diverse problems come to trust the retail banking employees. It is important to note that

---

[3] ZOLO is the digital banking app of Indian Standard Bank.

apart from the term '*trust*', customers also used phrases including '*believe in*' and '*know that they will*' as local connotations of the term '*trust*' to explain why they come to retail banks. Based on our study, we make a grounded argument that customers come to rely on the skills of these employees which shape the relationship of interpersonal trust between FDEs (as representatives of a trusted bank) and their customers. In the following section, we show how FDEs' skills become crucial in enabling customers to conduct day-to-day banking despite customers' limited understanding of ICTs in banking and hence, in retaining trust in banking institutions at large.

5 Digital Retail Banking and Human Intermediation: An Everyday Account of Interpersonal Trust

Skill allows us to achieve a specific goal with an economy of effort over a period of time [42]. With this understanding in mind, we categorise the skills of FDEs into two broad sets: technical skill and functional skill, and explain how each helps them gain trust of their customers. It is important to keep in mind, however, that these analytical categories of skill are not mutually exclusive and often overlap in practice.

5.1 Technical Skill

Williams et al. [53 p. 6] defines technical skill as the "*expertise or technical competence related to the field of work of an employee*". Such a skill is associated with the use of tools and technologies for efficient work and target achievement, which, in addition, requires specific knowledge of the work being done [16]. In an organisational ecosystem, technical skills should ideally refer to procedures that are easy to observe, quantify, and measure [55], and can be taught [48]. Overall, technical skills provide employees with the ability to perform work in a technically competent manner [43]. In our study, we found technical skills of FDEs to include both technology skills and domain skills in retail banking.

Technology Skills: Technology skills of FDEs require them to operate ICTs in order to get a desired output effectively. With increasing digitisation, FDEs need to understand and be able to work on different software and tools to access databases, interpret and process data, and to create and provide documentation. Despite the heavy presence of Self-Service Technologies that can be used by customers independently, a majority of customers lack the necessary skills and desired comfort to operate these technologies, which brings them to rely on the technology skills of FDEs.

Age also stands out as a critical factor leading to customers' lack of trust in digital technologies, due to the inability of elderly individuals (comprising a significant percentage of retail banking customers) in understanding how ICTs work. For example, one of our interviewees responded that "*...young people like you (referring to the researcher) have no problems with all these things - digital banking, internet banking, mobile phones - old people like me - I am not saying all of us - but most of us old people do not understand such things! And yet they expect us to use them?*". Some of them simply don't see any reason to use ICTs. "*It is not that I do not know how to use computers or mobile* *phones - but tell me this, I have been getting everything done for the past 40 years by coming to a bank. And now you tell me I have to learn something new just to get the same thing done? Not at my age, never!"* (Respondent).

It is this limited capacity coupled with anxieties of disruption on part of the customers that turns them to FDEs for help. In this sense, the very presence of ICTs in banking renders the human skill to navigate technology even more significant. For example, one respondent informs us that, *"...they have been doing this for a long time, they know what to do. Some of them are young, but they work better with computers than we do!".* Similarly, another respondent argues that, *"... (it) cannot be said (that) everyone is good, but they (referring to FDE) are by and by large capable people...everything is (done with) technology nowadays... they know what they are doing...not like earlier days...".*

Thus, technology skills of FDEs generate confidence and trust among customers. This interpersonal trust, one hand, draws on the institutional trust of an organisation and on the other hand, strengthens institutional trust through everyday work practices of the bank employees. This intersection between institutional and interpersonal trust becomes evident when one of the customers commented,

> *"Indian Standard Bank is the most respected bank in India! They won't sit (give the job to) anyone unless and until they are trained to deal with such people (referring to customers who need high assistance because of their socio-economic backgrounds)"*

Domain Skills: While the ability to use ICTs formed a significant part of their technical skill, FDEs also need to showcase their expertise in banking processes. They need to have specialised knowledge to understand what is a regular banking process, what rules and guidelines to follow, what constitutes an anomaly in financial transactions, and how to resolve specific problems as and when they arise. This knowledge, which Tricot & Sweller [51, p. 266] term as *'domain knowledge'*, is defined as *"memorised information that can lead to action permitting specific task completion over indefinite periods of time"*. The ability to use domain knowledge in contexts of work is what Anderson [5] terms *'domain skills'*. While the technology skills of an individual are general order skills, that is, they can be used across work domains, domain skills are related directly to the domain of work of an individual [5]. For example, for an Accounts Executive responsible for assisting customers with signing up for bank accounts, the domain skill would be the ability to assist a customer choose the right kind of a bank account based on their knowledge of the options available in relation to the customer's profile. While this knowledge comes out of being trained through set procedure, the ability to use domain knowledge as a skill comes as a result of lived experiences [5], an ability to convert their theoretical knowledge to a skill necessary for providing effective financial services..

As we observed in the case of Rishabh and his wife above, domain skill helps FDEs to provide a much more personalised service to their customers. This case is even more striking as Rishabh was well-versed with technology and could pick his choice online and yet chose to seek the advice of the FDE. It is his reliance on the specialised skills of FDEs that brought him to the bank. Another customer argues, *"..to be truthful, I can ask my colleagues to do these for me, but I trust them (referring to retail banking employees) in such matters (referring to online loan applications)...they know what to do".* Trust, in such circumstances, comes from customers' confidence in FDEs' domain expertise and the belief that they would use it effectively in the best interest of the customer.

5.2 Functional Skill

The official tagline of Indian Standard Bank is *'The Subcontinent Banks With Us'*, and it is probably only justified that FDEs of the bank would play host to one of the most diverse customer profiles with a very wide range of banking solutions. To this end, along with technical skills, FDEs need *'functional skills'*. Functional skills refer to general skills [8] or life skills [34] that fall outside the purview of formal technical training. These skills, while varying in quality depending on specific job roles and workplace environment, are widely required in all jobs in addition to technical skills [25, 46]. They include communication, creative thinking, problem solving, information management, leadership and organisational skills [34]. These skills are important for customer relation services and also for inter-organisational behavior among employees, including group effectiveness and teamwork capabilities [17].

Amongst the different forms of functional skills, communication and problem solving plays a key role, and becomes a critical reason behind people trusting one category of actors over another. In the case of Aman, who is unable to update a banking PIN on his own, the FDE not only showed technical skill but resolved the problem of their customer through creative thinking and effective communication. For example, since they could not speak in the same language, they managed to communicate through hand gestures and a smattering of commonplace English terms *('mobile', 'call', 'PIN'* etc.). It is also important to note that Aman could have asked anyone, including his colleagues who are more proficient with digital technologies. But he came all the way to the bank as he argues that since it is *"a matter of money, ...(he)...cannot even talk about it with anyone else"*, but a retail banking employee. We can argue that this is a case of Aman trusting the capability of employees to understand his situation, and trusting them for a safe solution.

Again, what we saw in case of passbook updating, the FDEs act as effective translators of the passbook, which ICTs alone cannot do. While FDEs' domain skill allows them to translate data from raw numbers to information, it is communication skill that helps them effectively explain their meaning to customers. This process brings a significant number of customers to resolve their queries with them. One customer argued that, *"...token is for all these counters (referring to Accounts, Loans, Credit etc.), but almost everyone goes to her (referring to Passbook Executive)!"* - highlighting the need for her intermediation in retail banking services. It is probably the reason why, in all the three banks we studied, the queue at the Passbook Counter happens to be the longest - as a majority of customers strike a conversation with Passbook Executives, trying to get a better understanding of their transactional histories.

Furthermore, our respondents argue that long standing relations with retail banking employees is one of the reasons they trust FDEs, and the reason why they still prefer to access services in person from retail banking branches. One customer explained, *"...they know me...I have been a customer here for a long time...the manager - we know him very well - he even came to our home this January during Saraswati Pujo*[4]*"*. Respondents argue that the long standing relations allow for greater interpersonal trust between the employees and the customers. This also meant that a strictly formal and transactional relationship was largely informal in practice, thereby allowing for greater personalised service provisioning. In many instances, customers discussed their personal experiences with FDEs and even sought financial advice from them. The functional skill of employees to negotiate and reduce organisational barriers in the formal relationship help them gain the trust of their customers.

We, therefore argue that FDEs provide much needed human intermediation to make digital banking more trustworthy for a diverse set of customers within public sector banks. The FDEs follow formal and informal methods of providing a financial service - by understanding a customer's problem, solving it through creative means, and by providing feedback through effective communication. Furthermore, we argue that this multidimensional understanding of FDEs' skills points out that a *'job'* does not necessarily correspond to a single-skill entity – rather, even seemingly the most menial of jobs, such as passbook updating, consist of multiple intersecting skills in practice. In retail banking, such skill sets range from domain knowledge to knowledge of ICTs, from communication skill to logical reasoning, from creativity to relationship management. These human skills become even more significant with increasing use of ICTs in banking, especially in retaining customers' trust in banking in the face of disruptive technological change.

6 Conclusion

Customers' perception of Front-Desk Employees' technical and functional skill forms the antecedent to building and retaining trust in them, and is a key reason why customers visited branches in person despite the ready availability of Self-Service Technologies for banking. Customers view these intermediaries not only as an extension of the retail banking ecosystem with adequate expertise and knowledge, but also as someone who can be trusted at a personal level to understand their needs and solve their problems. This trust becomes even more pronounced when FDEs help customers navigate through ICTs in banking, which often pose a barrier to their banking experiences.

Digital technologies such as, online banking, multi-function digital kiosks, are being introduced into a substrate of social relationships that lack both social and infrastructural resources to meaningfully engage with these technologies. FDEs fill in for this resource gap, and ensure successful utilisation of ICTs within given contexts. They become the *'soft information architectures'* [15], a catalyst in sustaining trust in banking ecosystems post the introduction of new technologies. Such a role becomes even more critical in developing regions, especially in public sectors banks, where the clientele is diverse, and their socio-economic conditions often pose barriers for effective use of ICTs. Our study captures the everyday experience of retail banking in such a setup. We find interpersonal trust to be a key factor towards the adoption of digital technologies in banking and argue that human skills of FDEs retains and sustains the trust in both ICTs and the organisations within which such ICTs are introduced.

---

[4] A local Hindu festival involving the worship of Goddess Saraswati.

While increasing use of ICTs in organisations has contributed to a resurgence of automation anxiety centred around issues of human skills and employability [3], our study reiterates the importance and resilience of human skill in affixing trust in new technologies, and in enabling meaningful engagement with technologies for diverse human actors coming from a wide strata of society. We argue that when it comes to technological innovation, one needs to place a greater focus on exploring what creates trust in ICTs in organisations, and pay greater attention to the role & importance of human skills in contributing to the same.

References

1. How is digital changing the finance industry. https://digitalmarketinginstitute.com/blog/how-is-digital-changing-the-financial-industry
2. What is finance automation, why it matters, and how to make it work, March 2018. https://www.teampay.co/insights/what-is-finance-automation/
3. Akst, D.: Automation anxiety. The Wilson Quarterly 37(3), 65 (2013)
4. Ananda, S., Devesh, S., Lawati, A.M.A.: What factors drive the adoption of digital banking? an empirical study from the perspective of omani retail banking. J. Financ. Serv. Mark. 25(1), 14–24 (2020)
5. Anderson, J.R.: Skill acquisition: compilation of weak-method problem situations. Psychol. Rev. 94(2), 192 (1987)
6. Autor, D.H., Katz, L.F., Kearney, M.S.: The polarization of the us labor market. Am. Econ. Rev. 96(2), 189–194 (2006)
7. Avgerou, C., Masiero, S., Poulymenakou, A.: Trusting e-voting amid experiences of electoral malpractice: the case of indian elections. J. Inf. Technol. 34(3), 263–289 (2019)
8. Awang, Z., Abidin, H.Z., Arshad, M., Habil, H., Yahya, A.S.: Non-technical skills for engineers in the 21st century: a basis for developing a guideline. Universiti Teknologi Malaysia, Skudai, Johor, Faculty of Management and Human Resource Development (2006)
9. Barber, K.S., Kim, J.: Belief revision process based on trust: agents evaluating reputation of information sources. In: Falcone, R., Singh, M., Tan, Y.-H. (eds.) Trust in Cyber-societies. LNCS (LNAI), vol. 2246, pp. 73–82. Springer, Heidelberg (2001). https://doi.org/10.1007/3-540-45547-7_5
10. Benbasat, I., Goldstein, D.K., Mead, M.: The case research strategy in studies of information systems. MIS quarterly pp. 369–386 (1987)
11. Bibby, K., Margulies, F., Rijnsdorp, J., Withers, R., Makarov, I.: Man's role in control systems. IFAC Proc. Volumes 8(1), 664–683 (1975). https://doi.org/10.1016/S1474-6670(17)67612-2
12. Brynjolfsson, E., McAfee, A.: The second machine age: work, progress, and prosperity in a time of brilliant technologies. WW Norton & Company (2014)
13. Cecchini, S.: Tapping ICT to reduce poverty in rural India. IEEE Technol. Soc. Mag. 22(2), 20–27 (2003)
14. Chaudhuri, B.: Paradoxes of intermediation in Aadhaar: human making of a digital infrastructure. South Asia J. South Asian Stud. 42(3), 572–587 (2019)
15. Chepaitis, E.V.: Soft barriers to ICT application in development: trust and information quality in Russia. J. Int. Dev. J. Dev. Stud. Assoc. 14(1), 51–60 (2002)
16. Damooei, J., Maxey, C., Watkins, W.: A survey of skill gaps and related workforce issues in selected manufacturing sectors: Report and recommendations. Workforce Investment Board of Ventura County, USA (2008)
17. DeLange, G.: The identification of the most important non-technical skills required by entry level engineering students when they assume employment. J. Coop. Educ. 35(2/3), 21 (2000)

18. Donner, J., Gitau, S., Marsden, G.: Exploring mobile-only internet use: results of a training study in urban south africa. Int. J. Commun. **5**, 24 (2011)
19. Fusch, P.I., Fusch, G.E., Ness, L.R.: How to conduct a mini-ethnographic case study: a guide for novice researchers. Qual. Rep. **22**(3), 923 (2017)
20. Gandham, S.: How digital technological banks can be more effective in the future of banking industry in india, March 2020. https://cio.economictimes.indiatimes.com/news/strategy-and-management/how-digital-technological-banks-can-be-more-effective-in-the-future-of-ban king-industry-in-india/74683508
21. Gomez, R., Gould, E.: The cool factor of public access to ict. Inf. Technol. People **23**(3), 247 (2010)
22. Heeks, R.: Information and communication technologies, poverty and development. Development informatics working paper (5) (1999)
23. Ilo, L.M.B.: Ilo global estimates on migrant workers: Results and methodology. Geneva: International Labour Organisation (ILO) (2015)
24. Kanade, T., Reed, M.L., Weiss, L.E.: New technologies and applications in robotics. Commun. ACM **37**(3), 58–68 (1994)
25. Kruger, S.: Developing non-technical skills through co-operative education. In: The Third VT Vittachi International Conference (2006)
26. Kuriyan, R., Ray, I.: Outsourcing the state? public–private partnerships and information technologies in india. World Dev. **37**(10), 1663–1673 (2009)
27. Lee, J.D., See, K.A.: Trust in automation: designing for appropriate reliance. Hum. Factors **46**(1), 50–80 (2004)
28. Lichtenthaler, U., Ernst, H.: Intermediary services in the markets for technology: Organizational antecedents and performance consequences. Organ. Stud. **29**(7), 1003–1035 (2008)
29. Maloney, W.F., Molina, C.: Are automation and trade polarizing developing country labor markets, too? The World Bank (2016)
30. Mayer, R.C., Davis, J.H., Schoorman, F.D.: An integrative model of organizational trust. Acad. Manag. Rev. **20**(3), 709–734 (1995)
31. Medhi, I., Menon, S.R., Cutrell, E., Toyama, K.: Beyondstrictilliteracy: abstracted learning among low-literate users. In: Proceedings of the 4th ACM/IEEE International Conference on Information and Communication Technologies and Development, pp. 1–9 (2010)
32. Moorman, C., Deshpande, R., Zaltman, G.: Factors affecting trust in market research relationships. J. Mark. **57**(1), 81–101 (1993)
33. Morawczynski, O., Miscione, G.: Examining trust in mobile banking transactions: The case of m-pesa in kenya. In: IFIP International Conference on Human Choice and Computers, pp. 287–298. Springer (2008)
34. Munce, J.W.: Toward a comprehensive model of clustering skills. National Society for Internships and Experiential Education (1980)
35. Nguyen, O.T.: Factors affecting the intention to use digital banking in Vietnam. J. Asian Finan. Econ. Bus. **7**(3), 303–310 (2020)
36. Orlikowski, W.J.: Using technology and constituting structures: a practice lens for studying technology in organizations. Organ. Sci. **11**(4), 404–428 (2000). https://doi.org/10.1287/orsc.11.4.404.14600
37. Orlikowski, W.J., Barley, S.R.: Technology and institutions: What can research on information technology and research on organizations learn from each other? MIS Q. **25**(2), 145–165 (2001). https://doi.org/10.2307/3250927
38. Orr, J.: Talking About Machines: An Ethnography of a Modern Job. Cornell University, New York (1996)
39. Parikh, J., Ghosh, K.: Understanding and designing for intermediated information tasks in india. IEEE Pervasive Comput. **5**(2), 32–39 (2006)

40. Pettigrew, A.M., Woodman, R.W., Cameron, K.S.: Studying organizational change and development: challenges for future research. Acad. Manag. J. **44**(4), 697–713 (2001). https://doi.org/10.5465/3069411
41. Poole, M.S., Van de Ven, A.H.: Handbook of Organizational Change and Innovation. Oxford University Press, New York (2004)
42. Proctor, R.W., Dutta, A.: Skill Acquisition and Human Performance. Sage Publications, Inc., Beverly Hills (1995)
43. Rahman, A., Fauzi, M.: Perception of Industry Towards Competencies of German-Malaysia Institute Graduates In Relation To Their Qualification For Highly Skilled Technician. Ph.D. thesis, Universiti Teknologi Malaysia (2000)
44. Rajalekshmi, K.G.: E-governance services through telecenters: the role of human intermediary and issues of trust. Inf. Technol. Int. Dev. **4**(1), 19 (2007)
45. Ray, D.: Development Economics. Princeton University Press, Princeton (1998)
46. Roger, M.: Non-technical essential skills handbook for apparel industry supervisors interpersonal communications (1996)
47. Roy, T., et al.: The economic history of India, 1857–1947. Oxford University Press, New Delhi (2011)
48. Shakir, R.: Soft skills at the malaysian institutes of higher learning. Asia Pacific Educ. Rev. **10**(3), 309–315 (2009)
49. Sharma, S.K., Sharma, M.: Examining the role of trust and quality dimensions in the actual usage of mobile banking services: an empirical investigation. Int. J. Inf. Manage. **44**, 65–75 (2019)
50. Suneja, R.: The grand digitization of the finance industry: How technology is paving the path towards the future, December 2019. https://economictimes.indiatimes.com/news/economy/finance/the-grand-digitization-of-the-finance-industry-how-technology-is-paving-the-path-towards-the-future/articleshow/72381230.cms?from =mdr
51. Tricot, A., Sweller, J.: Domain-specific knowledge and why teaching generic skills does not work. Educ. Psychol. Rev. **26**(2), 265–283 (2014)
52. Van Deventer, M., De Klerk, N., Bevan-Dye, A.: Influence of perceived integrity and perceived system quality on generation y students' perceived trust in mobile banking in south africa. Banks Bank Syst. **12**(1–1), 128–134 (2017)
53. Williams, D.M., Medina, J., Wright, D., Jones, K., Gallagher, J.E.: A review of effective methods of delivery of care: skill-mix and service transfer to primary care settings. Primary Dental Care **2**, 53–60 (2010)
54. Williams, R., Edge, D.: The social shaping of technology. Res. Policy **25**(6), 865–899 (1996). https://doi.org/10.1016/0048-7333(96)00885-2
55. Yahya, S., Ahmad, E., Abd Jalil, K.: The definition and characteristics of ubiquitous learning: a discussion. Int. J. Educ. Dev. ICT **6**(1) (2010)
56. Yin, R.: Designing case studies. Qualitative Research Methods, pp. 359–386 (2003)
57. Zhou, T.: Understanding users' initial trust in mobile banking: an elaboration likelihood perspective. Comput. Hum. Behav. **28**(4), 1518–1525 (2012)
58. Zuboff, S.: In the age of the smart machine (2010)

The Five-Dimensional Space of the Futures of Work: A View to 2030

Erran Carmel[1] and Steve Sawyer[2]([✉])

[1] American University, Washington, DC, USA
[2] Syracuse University, Syracuse, NY, USA
ssawyer@syr.edu

Abstract. We advance a structured view of the Futures of Work (FoW) using a futurist's lens to advance two goals: advancing core dimensions to the FoW while outlining the Futurist's approach to considering possible futures. Professional futurists point out that they do not predict the future, but rather, build a number of futures – in plural. These views of the futures are presented as scenarios to help decision makers consider alternatives and better understand interactions among the planning dimensions. The scenarios that drive planning are constructed by drawing on characteristics or dimensions that will shape our futures. It is these dimensions that we present here. We offer five foundational dimensions for the FoW, articulating them as opposing perspectives to frame the issue: (1) Virtuality versus Compressed working arrangements; (2) Atomistic work versus Holistic work; (3) Algorithmic versus Human decision-making; (4) Neoliberal capitalism versus Safety-net capitalism; (5) Übermensch versus Nihilists. We use these dimensions to provide scenarios to illustrate their use. We conclude by reflecting on the shock of the 2020 pandemic and the roles of firm size relative to the futures of work.

Keywords: Future of work · Scenarios · Foresight · Planning · Markets · Labor · Automation

1 Many Views of the Future of Work

The future earns its attention. Here, we focus specifically on the many possible Futures of Work (FoW) with an explicit attention to the structuring of that work, possible working arrangements, the working context and the expectations of workers. In this article we are theorizing on the framing of FoW, per Weick [1]. Our view is premised on the realization of multiple futures, acknowledging that there will be many future realities that build from our many current realities. And, while we cannot predict the future, we can use what we know to provide structured insight. To this, our theorizing on the FoW begins here by advancing five dimensions, detailed below, each of which builds from our present and serves to help shape or frame the unknown future. These dimensions help us to better understand that there exist many possible futures of work (which is why the article title is in plural). Using the dimensions, we can begin to construct multiple FoW scenarios

© IFIP International Federation for Information Processing 2020
Published by Springer Nature Switzerland AG 2020
R. K. Bandi et al. (Eds.): IFIPJWC 2020, IFIP AICT 601, pp. 295–309, 2020.
https://doi.org/10.1007/978-3-030-64697-4_22

to better understand the ways in which current arrangements implicate the future. These scenarios serve to evoke, rather than fully describe possible futures.

Our focus to the future is limited here to knowledge work: that which demands cognitive engagement, expertise and the mastery of a body of knowledge [2]. Knowledge work itself is a broad concept, spanning the work of Amazon Mechanical Turkers to design and other creative work that requires collaboration and interdependence as no one person can know enough about a problem or product to succeed [3]. We know that other known forms of work will be present in our future. For example, service work has been on the rise for decades and various forms of labor are now, and will continue to be, a substantial portion of the contemporary workforce – in developed and developing economies. Each of these forms of work will be part of all the futures we can envision. This noted, our focus to the FoW is the work and arrangement specifically designed to support the expertise- focused, digitally- enabled, collaboration- centered and often concept- reliant knowledge work.

Writing about the FoW has been increasing of late, given the rise of more open and global labor markets, increases in automation (now to include artificial intelligence), changes in demographics and urbanization. One stream of this work focuses on changes to the working arrangements and are often dystopian [4, 5]. A second stream focuses on the importance of structuring work and training [6] or particular innovations that are seen as redefining work [7]. A third stream, and the one we build from, develop structured views of the future that rely on scenario planning for analysis [8, 9].

As we consider possible futures of working, our future time horizon is 2030. Futurists typically look out 10–20 years from the present [10]. Ten years is far enough in the future that quantitative predictive methods are mostly impotent (with some important exceptions, such as population demographics and, separately, climate change). Yet, 2030 is not far enough into the future that it is indistinct. This time frame means that the future leaders in this time horizon are just entering the workforces of today. Today's 25-year-old worker will be a core part of middle management and charged with the operational goals of their firms and organizations. Likewise, the 3.7 million American students who finished their first year of middle school online in the pandemic will be entering the workforce[1].

To make our case for the FoW dimensions and planning approach presented here, this paper continues in four sections. In the next section, we advance our approach for how to consider the future, building out from methods developed by futurists and scholars involved in the broad intellectual space of Future Studies[2]. In the paper's third section, we build from our first contribution – structured thinking about the FoW – to articulate our second contribution: the five foundational dimensions that will be used to frame scenarios about the future. These dimensions serve to structure and frame the scenarios we advance in the paper's fourth section, noting that these scenarios are merely examples to demonstrate how the five dimensions are scaffold for policy and strategy.

---

[1] See https://nces.ed.gov/programs/digest/d13/tables/dt13_203.10.asp.

[2] This is also known as the discipline of Foresight. See https://wfsf.org/about-us/futures-studies.

2   Structured Thinking About the Future

Future Studies developed during the cold war decades as several factors converged. First, there was a need to understand the geopolitical terrain in a world in which global powers can target each other from afar. In the US, much of this futures study came out of the Rand Corporation, a government-focused think tank. Second was one of the first attempts – and a successful one – for a giant corporation, Shell Oil, to professionally prepare itself for the future. Finally, the maturation of computer information systems allowed thinkers to develop numerical forecasts, and simulations that were impossible a few years before. Such was the work of the Club of Rome, which gained considerable public attention in its 1972 seminal first report, "The Limits to Growth" [11].

Futurist methods are a mix of qualitative and quantitative approaches [12] or example, reliance on trends can be both quantitative, by building a predictive regression model, or qualitative, by interpreting multiple trendlines creatively into the future. Futurist studies are also characterized by attention to the synthesis or considerations of multiple forces, with the goal of articulating plausible or possible future arrangements across a range of factors or dimensions. This means that futurist approaches combine both the analyst's discipline of building from what is known and the innovator's willingness to build from circumstantial evidence [13].

The scenarios method is one of the most common foresight methods [14, 15]. Alexander [13] writes that a scenario is a work of creative fiction–a story. "Generally, we create scenarios by starting with some part of the present, such as a geographical area or organizational type, then imagine how it would change under the impact of one or several trends. ... They are narratives, clearly more art than science." One of the core reasons for using scenarios is, as Galer [16] notes, "…because humans are narrative creatures, stories can be powerful." That is, the act of consuming a scenario gives us a window into possibilities. At their best, scenarios allow adversaries to interact creatively in a safe space, such as with the 1991 Mont Fleur Scenarios, which helped South Africa move past apartheid [16].

Rhisiart et. al., [9] point out that scenario generation is intended as a policy support tool. They write that "Conceptions of the future structure the decision-making processes of the present. The way in which we use the future has a major influence on the possibilities and options that are revealed to us, both inside and outside government." They note that scenario building is a reaction to the weaknesses inherent in 'static' models in the strategy field, particularly where organizations have a 'pre-commitment' to a course of action. Johnston [17] articulates three goals of why scenarios are useful: informing – providing inputs – both conceptual and empirical to inform decision-making; enabling – developing the capacity to deal with uncertainty; and influencing – shaping policy and other outputs.

Building from this guidance, one goal of this paper is to advance an approach for theorizing on the future and to build theory and knowledge. Futurists typically write for a specific policy- making audience or in response to specific guidance from a funder or client. In contrast, our approach is guided more by our interests in the futures of work and a desire to advance scholarship in this area. To do this we draw Futures methods while focusing on the FoW. Following our discussion of the five dimensions that shape the FoW, we advance eight brief scenarios to validate the five dimensions' value.

3   Five Dimensions Framing the Futures of Work

Futures scenarios should build from a structure of knowns, drawing on characteristics to be used to shape possibilities: creating dimensions for consideration. Examples of possible dimensions are changing demographics, automation, climate change, or structural changes to policy (such as nationalizing health care). The goal of scenarios is to create plausible – but not necessarily probable – futures, that allow for planning and analysis. And, the dimensions used to structure these scenarios are the framing.

Futurist methods encourage developing these framing characteristics or dimensions as sets of contradictory possibilities [15]. For example, one might consider two possible futures: one where each person is responsible for their own personal safety (a 'wild west' view) and the other where the state provides complete protection and public safety prevails over individual liberty (a 'socialist's dreamworld'). These two views reflect how a characteristic (personal safety) can be developed into two contrasting dimensions: individual or collective action. And, we intimated in the evocative naming of these how these are plausible, not likely, serving to structure the scenario and establish a rhetorical position.

Wilkinson [18] calls these dimensions "uncertainties" and writes that when examining an issue (an issue in our case is the FoW), "… at first, all uncertainties seem unique. But by stepping back, we can reduce bundles of uncertainties that have some commonality to a single spectrum, *an axis of uncertainty*. If we can simplify our entire list of related uncertainties into two orthogonal axes" and to then use those two axes and build a 2 × 2 matrix with four very different, but plausible, quadrants of uncertainty. "Each of these far corners is, in essence, a logical future that we can explore."

To guide our selection of dimensions, we began by first using the extant literature to provide us an initial set of possibilities, discussing what we were finding. We used these discussions to guide additional literature work. This iterative process was driven by the competing tensions of future studies: to be guided by the evidence but open to emerging trends and issues. Our work with the literature led us to finding articles from a wide variety of disciplines. And, we drew on a number of industry and think-tank reports [19]. In doing this, we rejected dimensions that were focused on the environment and sustainability because with that kind of focus the future of work becomes a second order effect (even as it is critical for the human race). After much discussion, we did not create dimensions that create clear value choices (e.g., more inclusive work, work that provides for emotional safety), even as we stand by these as critical aspects of the future of work. The reality is that selection is a judgement call: we chose some of them because we felt that they were the right ones, that the dimensions we selected would challenge us and readers to consider these potential futures and to see these as viable axes of uncertainty [20][3].

One mechanism the Futurist approach employs is to frame the complexity relative to a smaller number of dimensions, then using these dimensions to emphasize differences. This is done by attending to the ends of a continuum or maximizing the differences in

---

[3] To this point, we appreciate the comments of all four reviewers, who and provided their own well-reasoned positions on our dimensions while suggesting relevant others. Their commentary has strengthened this paper!

a dyadic relation. This simplification serves both to articulate and magnify the ways in which possible futures might be characterized: the dimensions provide the framing for, the dyadic differences the scaling of, future scenarios.

The five dimensions that frame our scenarios about the FoW are summarized in Table 1 and detailed below. These dimensions reflect a synthesis of dimensions that are used to define other studies of emerging work arrangements, along with those papers containing analyses of FoW planning scenarios. The first dimension focuses on the nature of working arrangements, contrasting a more online-oriented and virtually-centered knowledge work with a second approach that relies on more informal engagement and interaction [8, 9]. The second dimension focuses attention to the structure of work and embodies the tensions between defined and task-centered work structures and more open-ended and interdependent approaches [7, 21]. The third dimension emphasizes the locus of decision-making and control, drawing on current discourses on AI and algorithmic management [5, 8]. The fourth dimension emphasizes the market structure that frames what firms and workers must consider [6, 22]. With the fifth dimension, we focus on the expectations for the kinds of workers for the knowledge-driven economy [4, 23]. Many readers will be familiar with the first three dimensions. In a broad FoW framing, the latter two of the five, in our judgement, deserve greater attention and more structured consideration, since they bring to the fore important debates on the structure of markets and the expectations the future has of the knowledge workers that will do the work.

Table 1. Five dimensions of the FoW

1. Virtuality versus Compressed Working Arrangements
2. Atomistic versus Holistic Work
3. Algorithmic versus Human Decision-making
4. Neoliberal capitalism versus Safety-net capitalism
5. Übermensch versus Nihilists

Dimension #1: Virtuality Versus Compressed Working Arrangements
This dimension emphasizes the spatial arrangements of work. This dimension focuses attention to the intertwined roles of space, place and both digital and personal connectivity [24]. The spatial arrangements of work reflects some of the mega-trends of population migration into dense super-cities and concerns with commuting and crowding [25]. Knowledge work can be disconnected from specific physical spaces, but it is often collaborative. So, co-location is more about exchange than access to scarce resources or heavy machinery. This is one of the reasons for the rise of dense open office designs, cubicle farms, coworking spaces and open seating [26–28].

We advance this dimension as changes to working arrangements have been core to discussions about the FoW. As work becomes more virtual and workers are more dispersed, do people need to be physically proximate? Even as work allows for more virtuality, the interdependence among knowledge workers encourages constant informal interaction. This, in turn, encourages workers to live closer together. But, moving is hard in crowded spaces, space is at a premium, and people have to learn to pursue their work wherever they find themselves. Thus, the rise in urbanization is both a bane for movement and commuting, and a source of informal interactions and connection.

Taken together, the FoW could be one where knowledge work is primarily pursued through virtual means, allowing people to work and live at a distance. Or, the knowledge work of the future could be pursued through the tight-knit social worlds of constant informal interaction that blurs work and non-work time, highlighting urbanization and spatial compression.

Dimension #2: Atomistic Versus Holistic Work
Atomization has two components, the structure of the task and the contractual relationship of the worker with the employer. Traditionally, the latter dimension – the contract – has received more attention. These fluid work arrangements are part-time, zero-hour and outcomes-oriented, flexible, temporary, freelance jobs, often enabled by a technology platform. From Tayloristic factories to today's gig economy this structure is not new, it just looks different today. The percentage of workers in atomized contracts has been relatively constant at 10% to 15% of the economy in both the USA and UK [29].

Increasingly, attention is being focused on atomizing tasks, not on the factory assembly line of Taylor factories, but in computer-enabled tasks. For example, software construction tasks can be decomposed and parsed to each individual designer, coder, tester, UI designer. At the extreme are the tasks of several minutes on Amazon's Mechanical Turk, gracefully detailed by [30].

Atomization has contentious benefits and costs. It benefits workers and employers by making work more adaptable. Some workers benefit from increased flexible lifestyles. Conversely, atomization may degrade humans by making them anonymous cogs in a machine, ghosts, that are expandable with any change in the employer's condition. Implicit in all this, is the inherent contradiction between specialization and collaboration future. Work is atomized because of the increased need for expertise, yet collaboration and teamwork are still required.

Dimension #3: Algorithmic Versus Human Decision-Making
This FoW dimension focuses attention to a core element of managing: decision-making. Managers and leaders who can combine experience and intuition to guide their decision-making are revered: books are written to help others understand their greatness. It seems a small step of 'ifs and thens' to see experience as data, intuition as some sort of advanced pattern-matching heuristic, and that a tuned algorithm, driven by machine learning, drawing on even more data, could be even more powerful, and certainly more rational and efficient.

There is evidence that contemporary society is growing comfortable with guidance based on machine-learning: we lean on systems for driving directions, music playlists and decisions about which food to eat. There is a growing literature focused on algorithmic or platformic management - the uses of data from participants on the platform to develop algorithms that determine or decide what is possible [21, 31]. Lyft and Uber's algorithms dictate how long drivers have to accept a ride, if they can get access to new customers in slow periods, etc. Algorithmic decision-making is embedded in fraud detection, loan-making and increasingly in hiring decisions. There are also clear concerns that include broad-scale and often valid worries of dehumanization (reducing people to fungible entities) issues with surveillance, and the lack of 'algorithmic transparency:' the ability to understand what data are being used and the ways in which these data shape a decision or output [32, 33].

In contrast to the logic of algorithms, we know that knowledge workers are creative entities. And, increasingly, are being asked (if not required) to make the decisions. The collections of digital devices, resources and data that knowledge workers pull together reflect patterns of need and idiosyncratic choices into what are termed "digital assemblages" or digital kits or, more obtusely, personal information systems [34–36].

Moving from the individual knowledge-worker as the locus of decision-making, entrepreneur thinking, start-up cultures, and the role of the innovator have amplified the need for risk-taking, decision-making groups, and the power of small and coherent leadership teams to disrupt and innovate [37, 38]. Human-centered decision-making may lead to mistakes, but also leaps of greatness. This dimension focuses attention to futures that rely on the high-speed and data-reliant approach of algorithmic decision-making or the reliance on the more experiential, intuitive, and varied approaches human of decision-makers.

Dimension #4 Neoliberal Capitalism Versus Safety-Net Capitalism

This dimension focuses on the economic context of work, building out from the role of markets. Markets provide a forum for exchange, connecting sellers and buyers. Markets have architectures: rules and norms that guide and structure the transaction [39]. We see the future as relying on market principles: What is in play is the set of rules and norms that structure these markets, advancing two different models. In the unfettered market of neo-liberal capitalism, the individual worker seeks work based on transactional arrangements: gigging for their life and livelihood [22]. In these markets, the firm seeks workers by posting for work, careful to make no promises beyond current needs. Both the firm and the worker act in their own best interests, based on transactions, unfettered by market constraints. This neoliberal arrangement locates all decisions to the transactors and companies value this flexibility from the marketplace [40]. Neoliberal markets are flexible, sterile, on-demand, unfettered from regulation, with no expectations to support, reward or sustain workers.

Another way to see the market space is one where the architecture - the policies and norms and systems - provide for distributions of risks and costs: there is a safety net built in for both firms and workers. Taxes and rules provide for social benefits and cover for underemployment, pay rates are capped at the upper end, and there is a minimum wage (if not a universal basic income) [23]. Employment is seen as a relationship between worker and firm: looking beyond a specific task or deliverable, with seniority providing for more security. Labor market protections in the form unions and employment laws extend beyond formal organizations. Firms are provided protection from market fluctuations through active state intervention (akin to the ways in which China have supported their large international firms [41]).

The essence of this dimension is the structure of the markets in which the FoW exists. Workers and firms will adjust to the incentives, adapt to the risks, and engage with other parties. Importantly, the markets of the FoW will be technologized: new platforms supporting interaction, expanded data collection and uses, and new forms of organizing will emerge. The choices made clear in this dimension focus attention on what kinds of markets we will see in the future.

Dimension #5: Übermensch versus Nihilists

This dimension focuses on the ethos or soul of the worker: what kinds of people are needed for the FoW? The FoW discourses advance fundamentally philosophical differences about who we are as human beings. We frame this as did Nietzsche: in dialectical terms. Are we fundamentally beings that aspire to higher goals and values? Or do we seek to make do and slide down to the easy, the nihilistic? The quest for meaningfulness in life and in work seems eternal: from Plato's views on the soul (as discussed in his *Phaedos*, per [42]) to death camp survivor Frankl [43] in his "Man's Search for Meaning." Scholars and philosophers aspire for all of us work that is meaningful. Going even further, the French philosopher Simone Weil aspired for us not just work, but hard work, as a moral calling. Work that is at the highest spiritual meaning - a metaphysical experience. Such workers would be 'Übermensch:' a superior person, one who rises above baseness and craven interests to pursue higher goals and purity. A FoW full of Übermensch would work together in seamless and ego-less ways, to all's best interests, acknowledging both shared and individual goals, attending the proper balance of work and life, caring for their employer's principal needs, and always with an eye towards higher goals of enlightenment, self-actualization and the social welfare.

In the face of these high-performing aspirations, many people report that they do not like their jobs and do not find their work meaningful. The management literature is full of approaches to motivate workers [44]. Kalleberg [45] calls this the mismatched worker, noting that what workers are asked to do often differs from what workers seek to provide. Still, many workers aspire to happiness, rather than meaning. And there, too, one can look at this through Nietsche, for he was also critical of mass culture and of the emerging utilitarian stream that our purpose in the world is to be happy. Gig workers report that flexibility to set their own working schedules, and to be away from office politics and commuting, are worth the precarity of temporary jobs and the loss of workplaces benefits such as retirement, vacation and health care [30].

We see this dimension as fundamental to the FoW because arguments about the FoW often assume that all workers who toil at work are Übermensch – or that they are repressed Übermenschers. And, that if the nasty boss, odd job roles, or cruel economic system, are removed, their true Übermensch will be able to surface. Yet, the evidence does not bear out these implicit beliefs. The dichotomy of the meaning of work is intertwined with the underlying assumption that work helps define who we are (in England one asks, 'where do you live?', as it indicates status. In the US, 'one asks what you do?').

4   Narrative Scenarios Exemplars

In Futures Methodologies, dimensions are structured to encourage thinking of non-obvious possibilities. In this section, we take four of the dimensions and create 2 × matrices, resulting in eight scenarios (see Table 2a and 2b). We then use the futures methodology approach of constructing a creative narrative of each of these futures. One of the key components of that is to create an evocative label, one that helps to convey the kind of future the scenario represents. In developing these futures scenarios, the focus is on plausibility: can we imagine a future like this? Plausible futures allow us to explore and consider the current trends, carried forward in time, to better assess what it might take to encourage or alter such paths. Plausibility also means these futures have roots in socio-technical processes and arrangements that are already evident today.

Table 2a. Future Scenarios; Examples using dimensions #1 and #2

	Virtuality	Compressed/f2f
Atomistic work	**M-Turk World**[#] Platform workers perform many tasks scattered in rich and poor nations [#] Named for Amazon's Mechanical Turk	**Back Office Gaanv**[#] Gaanv factories are better able to socialize and train workers in close-proximity [#]Gaanv is Hindi "for village"
Holistic work	**Immersive Virtual Office** Knowledge workers enter Mixed Reality work mode	**Artisan on Main Street**[#] Professionals come together in Manhattan and in main street to collaborate and feed off each other [#] Main Street represents the primary retail street of a village

Table 2b. Future Scenarios; Examples using dimensions #3 and #5

	Algorithmic decision-making	Human decision-making
Übermensch	**A world of Poets** Now that AI/robots do much of the labor and decision making, humans have time to create and read poetry	**AI serves humanity** AI is heavily regulated and is intermediated at important points by human decisions. Robots work alongside humans
Nihilism	**A world of Homer Simpsons**[#] Now that AI/robots do much of the labor and decision making, humans have time to sit on the couch and watch cartoons [#] Homer Simpson embodies base working-class stereotypes: crude, lazy, addicted to junk food and idly watching television	**Disneyworld Happiness** Humans work hard to collect currency to travel to the magic kingdom

These scenarios we designed to be generative: to invite readers to develop, to add details and consider implications. Futurists see scenarios as offerings, evocative sketches of possibilities: illuminating arrangements and raising discussion. Seen this way, details of the future are more for science fiction writers, hardly worthy of a journal article: framing the story is the real contribution [17]. Futurists also make the case that any detailed scenario-writing should be specifically situated in specific settings [11].

We expand on four of these scenarios by building on a practice that is common in foresight approaches [12, 18]. The writing of these narratives is disciplined creative work, educated fiction. The scenarios are stories of plausible futures that need to be both empirically and conceptually rooted in the milieu of the present. We expand these narratives here as a proof of concept and not for any other use. In and of themselves these narratives are cartoonish since they are extremes, but for policy makers they accelerate thinking.

Immersive Virtual Office: Knowledge workers do all their work through Mixed Reality (MR) work mode. Workers interact with documents, other humans, and objects via advanced headsets and new projection technologies. The worker is able to speak to and see their partner in much the same way regardless of distance. Offices and 3rd spaces have many noise and distraction cancelling features. Companies have reduced typical office space requirements from 20 m^2 to 10 m^2 as offices are used for occasional meetings, socializing, and showcases. Workers are commonly given a yearly grant to spruce up their home workplaces. They need to provide video evidence of their expenditures. MR works well in driverless cars much as we can work on our laptop in the passenger seat today.

Artisan on Main Street: Professionals come together in Manhattan and in main street to collaborate and feed off each other. The paranoia of corona subsided after cures and vaccines were found in 2022. Humans craved getting back into tight spaces and doing meaningful work together, feeding off the energy of proximity. At about the same time 3D printing technologies finally reached mass use, allowing more tasks to be done in small groups. Coworking made a resurgence, in spite of WeWork's multiple bankruptcies, driven by a number of competing and franchised multinational firms

AI Serves Humanity: AI is heavily regulated and is intermediated at important points by human decisions. Robots work alongside humans. The UN "Commission on the Future of the Human Species", chaired by historian Noah Harari, proposed a regulatory framework for AI that was, surprisingly, passed with some adjustments, by the EU and the USA. Blackbox decision-making was, from that point forward, approved on a case-by-case basis. This means that so-called 'algo work allocation' ('AGA'), such as Uber-like driver scheduling algorithms, are presented to FDA-like commissions for consideration ahead of use.

A World of Homer Simpsons: After two years of rolling coronavirus waves and stay-at-home orders, and now that AI/robots do much of the labor and decision making, humans have time to sit on the couch and watch cartoons. The economy is growing, yet unemployment remains at 25%. Universal basic income allows many to skip work partially, or fully – and be entertained. They need less human interaction because of an emerging genre of social AI – a new class of agents and robots called Friendz. Friendz are more advanced forms of software agent Alexa and robot Pepper.

This scenario essentially asks: why shouldn't we seek what the renowned futurist Arthur C. Clark desired? Namely, "full *un*employment[4]"? Or rephrased and simplified according to Keiper [45], there are two (extreme) narratives: (1) Techno-optimism. When technology (re: AI) allows us all to achieve self-actualization, and (2) Techno-Dummies: We all become couch potatoes like Homer Simpson. There is widespread assumption that the Homer Simpson future will be driven by AI which will play out in a range of increasingly more intelligent machines, ever-more pervasive computing, and the rise of cognitive computing.

5   What It Might Take to Reach These Futures of Work?

The five-dimensional space introduced above provides a framework to examine the FoW. These dimensions build from and extend contemporary studies of work and the literature engaged in conceptualizing possible futures of work [5, 6, 8, 9] These dimensions are our first contribution: a way to structure analyses about the many possible futures of work.

These five dimensions are advanced as dichotomies of the future: as if the future will be either one extreme or the polar opposite. And, some of contemporary public debate is about these extremes, such as the utopian and dystopian futures in the face of AI being hotly debated [46]. Likewise, Gershon's [22] treatise on neo-liberal market structures helps make clear these dimensions are both powerful structures about the future and that the framing we provide brings them into stark relief. We know the future is unlikely to present any of these in their extreme measure. Rather, our future will be at some midpoint of each of the five dimensions. That is, the FoW will reflect a reality bounded by this *five-dimensional space.*

The five-dimensional space framing the FoW must be seen in the context of larger social forces and other global events. We note two here: shocks and the power of size.

5.1   The Shock of the Coronavirus Pandemic: The Elephant in the Room

We write this article at the beginning of the 2020 pandemic era. It is risky to anticipate impacts from such broad-scale and fast-moving current shocks. Yet that is precisely what the tools of a futurist afford. The dimension most impacted is our first: "virtual or compressed". We present some implications based, in part, on [47]. It seems likely that office design will move away from crowded open space for some years to come. Knowledge workers will not want to work in open-work settings. Distances of two or three meter's spacing apart will be expected, even though this may be insufficient. Kitchen space for "collisions" will be impacted. More people will eat at their desk, fewer together. Traditional closed-door offices will be popular again, and partitions for cubicles will become much higher. Knowledge workers may decide to work from home more often, leveraging all that we are learning. Many firms, and knowledge workers may

---

[4] From interview of Arthur C. Clarke conducted by Gene Youngblood on 25 April, 1969, Los Angeles Free Press, Free Press Interview: A. C. Clarke author of '2001', Start Page 42, Quote Page 43, Column 4 and 5, Los Angeles, California. Retrieved from Digital Independent Voices Collection at revealdigital.com on 18 May, 2020.

opt to move out of crowded urban areas, leaving Manhattan, New York for Manhattan, Kansas.

5.2 The Impact of Company Size and the Tech Giants

A second social force to be considered is that of large multinational firms such as Walmart or Volkswagen – and particularly the five technology giants (Facebook, Amazon, Apple, Alphabet and Microsoft, or FAAAM). These firms represent service work, knowledge work, and manufacturing. Amazon is both one of the largest public companies in the world, one of the largest high-technology firms in the world, and one of the largest employers of service and low-wage workers. Increasingly these and other large firms have outsized impact, even as the share of employment of U.S. Fortune 500 firms, the largest public U.S. firms, is roughly the same today as in the 1950 s.

These firms seem like permanent fixtures, much like Bethlehem Steel seemed to be in the 1960 s, or General Motors in the 1970 s, or IBM in the 1980 s. In their moment, large firms can alter the ways in which policies and plans unfold, with an institutional presence much like the pull of gravity. Still, at the same time, the 21st century has been about entrepreneurialism: start-ups, unicorns, and innovation are seen as the moniker of the future. The five in FAAAM emerged beginning in the 1980 s (one since 2000).

We know there are powerful economies of production and scale for large organizations. They exist beyond any one person's views or effort: rules and systems get reified. Small firms come and go, forming and reforming: the essence of Schumpeter's creative destruction. Small firms are about connections and people (individuals) working together. The five dimensions do not dictate the future of organizing, they frame the ways in which future organizations will need to adapt, and we imagine that our FoW in 2030 will see both large and small firms thriving and failing, perhaps for different reasons than now.

6 Conclusion

Our first contribution comes in defining the key dimensions of our futures of work. Whether it be for future planning of a labor not-for-profit in Czechia, a consulting company in Japan, the Jobs and Small Business ministry in Canberra, or a FoW researcher in Chicago, we posit that the five dimensions framing the FoW, as detailed in Table 1, are a useful starting point and a useful foundation for disciplined thinking about 2030.

Our second contribution is to advance the Futurist's approach to disciplined thinking about the future. This approach draws on what is known to identify core dimensions that help to frame the future. Then the futurist's approach is to use these dimensions to create dichotomous perspectives that reflect plausible, not probable, futures. Done well, the dimensions force attention to intersections and interactions that shape future scenarios. These future scenarios, often constructed as 2 × 2 matrices to help illustrate tensions and choices, are then used for planning and analysis

To this point, the scenarios we developed in Table 2 are generative. We provide them as invitations to help envision possible futures that reflect the trends we can see emerging but cannot yet fully understand. Futurists traffic in doing this and we draw on their methods to consider the ways in which robotics, artificial intelligence, the shifts towards virtual and distributed work, population shifts towards mega-cities, reshaped work spaces that dichotomize the trend towards creating both larger and smaller organizations, and the increasingly pervasive roles that data and analytics will play in guiding technology and information-enabled work. As such, these scenarios serve only to illustrate our two contributions, they are simply examples.

Finally, we note the roots of the 2030 FoW are already evident today as we write this in 2020. And that is how it should be, as futurists always point out: the future is a blending of the present with the new. For example, we use powerful new mobile devices, but live in homes constructed in 1960, often with one power outlet per room. The seeds of our future are being sown, and our work serves to provide both a set of dimensions and a structured means to consider the FoW.

References

1. Weick, K.: What theory is not, theorizing is. Adm. Sci. Q. **40**, 385–390 (1995)
2. Drucker, P.: The new society of organizations. Harvard Bus. Rev. (1992)
3. Kleinman, D., Vallas, S.: Science, capitalism, and the rise of the "Knowledge Worker:" the changing structure of knowledge production in the United States. Theor Soc. **30**, 451–492 (2001)
4. Crowley, M., Tope, D., Chamberlain, L., Hodson, R.: Neo-Taylorism at work: occupational change in the post-Fordist era. Soc. Probl. **57**(3), 421–447 (2010)
5. Cottey, A.: The future of work: disciplined useful activity. J. Glob. Responsib. **10**(3), 271–286. (2019). https://doi.org/10.1108/JGR-11-2018-0075
6. McKinsey Global Institute: The Future of Work in America: People and Places, Today and Tomorrow. McKinsey & Company, McKinsey Global Institute, Brussels (2018)
7. Digital Future Society: The Future of Work in the Digital Era: The Rise of Labour Platforms. The Digital Futures Society (2019)
8. Boyd, J., Huettinger, M.: Smithian insights on automation and the future of work. Futures **111**, 104–115 (2019)
9. Rhisiart, M., Störmer, E., Daheim, C.: From foresight to impact? The 2030 Future of Work Scenarios. Technol. Forecast. Soc. Change **124**, 203–213 (2017)
10. Swanson, J.: When you think about the future, what's your time horizon (2019). https://knowledgeworks.org/resources/future-time-horizon/
11. Meadows, D.H., et al.: The Limits to Growth; a Report for the Club of Rome's Project on the Predicament of Mankind. Universe Books, New York (1972)
12. Schwartz, P.: The Art of the Long View: Planning for the Future in an Uncertain World. Currency Doubleday, New York (1991)
13. Alexander, B.: Academia Next: The Futures of Higher Education. Johns Hopkins University Press, Baltimore (2019)
14. Powers, D.: On Trend: The Business of Forecasting the Future. The University of Illinois Press, Urbana (2019)
15. Chermack, T., Lynham, S., Ruona, W.: A review of scenario planning literature. Futures Res. Q. **7**(2), 7–32 (2001)
16. Galer, G.: Scenarios of change in South Africa. Round Table **93**(375), 369–383 (2004). https://doi.org/10.1080/0035853042000249960
17. Johnston, R.: Developing the capacity to assess the impact of foresight. Foresight **14**(1), 56–68 (2012)

18. Wilkinson, L.: How to Build Scenarios, Wired, November (1995)
19. Bolles, G.A.: Why a Human Centric World of Work Matters, Presentation at Singularity University's The Changing Jobs, Workplace of the Future, Virtual Conference, May 2020
20. McGrath, J., Martin, J., Kulka, R.: Judgment Calls in Research. Sage, Beverly Hills (1982)
21. Vallas, S., Schor, J.: What do platforms do? Understanding the gig economy. Ann. Rev. Soc. **46**(16), 1–16.22 (2020). https://doi.org/10.1146/annurev-soc-121919-054857
22. Gershon, I.: Neoliberal agency. Curr. Anthropol. **52**(4), 537–555 (2011)
23. Piketty, T.: Capital in the 21st Century. Harvard University Press, Cambridge (2014)
24. Lee, H., Sawyer, S.: Conceptualizing Time, Space and Computing for Work and Organizing. Time Soc. **19**(3), 293–317 (2010)
25. World Bank: The Changing Nature of Work. World Development Report (2018)
26. DeMarco, T., Lister, T.: Peopleware: Productive Projects and Teams. Dorset House Publishing, New York (1977)
27. Pratt, M.: IT moves to open workspaces, but not everyone is happy, Computerworld, 6 October 2016
28. Morisson, A.: A typology of places in the knowledge economy: towards the fourth place. In: Calabrò, F., Della Spina, L., Bevilacqua, C. (eds.) ISHT 2018. SIST, vol. 100, pp. 444–451. Springer, Cham (2019). https://doi.org/10.1007/978-3-319-92099-3_50
29. Steward, S: Five myths about the gig economy, Washington Post, 24 April 2020
30. Gray, M., Suri, S.: Ghost Work. Houghton Mifflin, New York (2019)
31. Jarrahi, M.H., Sutherland, W., Nelson, S., Sawyer, S.: Platformic management, boundary resources for gig work, and worker autonomy. J. Comput. Support. Coop. Work **29**,153–189 (2020). https://doi.org/10.1007/s10606-019-09368-7
32. Murphy, H.: Algorithmic surveillance: the collection conundrum. Int. Rev. Law Comput. Technol. **31**, 225–242 (2017)
33. Rader, E., Cotter, K., Cho, J.: Explanations as mechanisms for supporting algorithmic transparency. In: CHI 2018: Proceedings of the 2018 CHI Conference on Human Factors in Computing Systems, April, Paper 103, pp. 1–13 (2018). https://doi.org/10.1145/3173574.3173677
34. Sawyer, S, Wigand, R., Crowston, K.: Digital assemblages: evidence and theorizing from a study of residential real estate. New Technol. Work Employ. **29**(1), 40–54 (2014)
35. Mainwaring, S., Anderson, K., Chang, M.: Living for the global city: mobile kits, urban interfaces, and UbiComp. In: Beigl, M., et al. (eds.) UbiComp, pp. 269–286 (2005)
36. Baskerville, R.: Individual information systems as a research arena. Eur. J. Inf. Syst. **20**, 251–254 (2011)
37. Bower, J., Christensen, C.: Disruptive technologies: catching the wave. Harvard Bus. Rev. (1995)
38. Christensen, C.: The Innovator's Dilemma: When New Technologies Cause Great Firms to Fail. Harvard Business Review Press, Cambridge (2015)
39. Bar, F.: The Construction of Marketplace Architecture, in Tracking a Transformation: E-commerce and the Terms of Competition in Industries, The BRIE-IGCC Economy Project Task Force on the Internet, Eds., pp. 27–49. Brookings Institution Press, Washington, DC (2001)
40. Commission, E.: Modernising Labour Law to Meet the Challenges of the 21st Century. Green Paper, Brussels (2006)
41. Hsueh, R.: State capitalism, chinese-style: strategic value of sectors, sectoral characteristics, and globalization. Governance **29**(1), 85–102 (2016). https://doi.org/10.1111/gove.12139
42. Claus, D.: Toward the Soul. Yale University Press, New Haven (1981)
43. Frankl, V.: Man's Search for Meaning. Beacon Press, New York (1946)
44. Hansen, M., Dacher, K.: Finding Meaning at Work, Even When Your Job Is Dull. Harvard Bus. Rev. (2012)

45. Kalleberg, A.: The Mismatched Worker: When People Don't Fit Their Jobs. Acad. Manag. Perspect. **22**(1) (2008)
46. Executive Office of the President: Artificial Intelligence, Automation and the Economy (2016). https://obamawhitehouse.archives.gov/sites/whitehouse.gov/files/documents/Artificial-Intelligence-Automation-Economy.PDF
47. Kretchmer, H.: 10 ways COVID-19 could change Office Design,' World Economic Forum, 22 April 2020. https://www.weforum.org/agenda/2020/04/covid19-coronavirus-change-office-work-homeworking-remote-design/

Humanoid Social Robots
and the Reconfiguration of Customer Service

Gabriella Volpe[1], Matthias Schulte-Althoff[1], David Dillmann[1], Emmanuelle Maurer[1],
Yannic Niedenzu[1], Philipp Schließer[1], and Daniel Fürstenau[1,2,3(✉)]

[1] Freie Universität Berlin, Garystr. 21, 14195 Berlin, Germany
arcgab.volpe@gmail.com
[2] Einstein Center Digital Future, Wilhelmstr. 67, 10117 Berlin, Germany
[3] Copenhagen Business School, Howitzvej 60, 2000 Frederiksberg, Denmark
dfu.digi@cbs.dk

Abstract. This paper reports on several studies in the context of implementing the humanoid social robot Pepper in a financial institution. The results show that the robot can affect the boundary relations between the roles of customer and service worker differently from common-sense expectations. While employees initially feared to be automated away by the robot, the results suggest that the relationship is more likely to change through an emotional bonding to the robot being projected to the company deploying it. Therefore, the robot might, at least partially, assume the role of the service worker as an ambassador of the company, which could recede more into the background in this regard. We discuss the implications of our findings in the context of current literature on the changing boundary relations through robot innovations.

Keywords: Humanoid robots · Actor-network theory · Emotions · Intelligence · Anthropomorphism · Attachment · Boundary relations

1 Introduction

Humanoid social robots are autonomous apparatuses that interact and communicate with humans or other autonomous physical agents by following social behaviors and rules attached to their role. These robots are now inhabiting everyday discourse on how artificial intelligence is changing the way in which we work, live, and interact [1, 2]. One the one hand, humanoid social robots are heralded for support in tasks such as lifting heavy objects and beings, like elderly humans [3], act as skilled workers [4], carers [5], or service workers [6, 7]. One the other hand, robot's introduction is often feared because of automation threats. There are fundamental human concerns to become obsolete, meaningless, dependent, and socially isolated [8, 9]. In a survey of 1,000 American adults, half of them were scared that robots will take away their jobs, and 81% refused to hand over even their menial tasks [10].

© IFIP International Federation for Information Processing 2020
Published by Springer Nature Switzerland AG 2020
R. K. Bandi et al. (Eds.): IFIPJWC 2020, IFIP AICT 601, pp. 310–325, 2020.
https://doi.org/10.1007/978-3-030-64697-4_23

Emerging scholarship has, however, started to provide more realistic accounts of the consequences of robot introduction. This work has found that robots, instead of automating job's away, they trigger changes in the boundary relations between already existing roles in work contexts [11–13]. Thereby, research has mostly considered how robots occasion changes in boundary relations among employees [e.g., 12, 14]. It thus remains to be investigated how humanoid social robots will affect the relationship between employees and customers in complex service situations. There is in fact little empirical evidence on how the boundary relationships between the employees and customers change with the introduction of a humanoid social robot.

The purpose of this paper is to investigate *how relationships between employees and customers change in result of the introduction of humanoid social robots in complex service contexts*. Through a theoretical lens of *techno-economic networks* [15], this paper considers an in-depth case study from a bank with whom we worked in an action research-like fashion to introduce the humanoid social robot *Pepper* [16] in a customer service context. Pepper is a 1.20 m high endearingly, or even cutely designed humanoid robot who can talk, move, and interact with humans. We conducted several studies with Pepper over a period of three years. Collected data from several qualitative and quantitative sources and perspectives, including the customer, employee, developer, and managerial point of view, present ample opportunity for tracing changes in the work relationships instigated through the implementation of this technology.

Against this background, our study finds that service robots do indeed change the way in which customer-employee relations are structured. While employees feared automation, the service robot in our case became an emotionally and anthropomorphically loaded actor, with which customers bonded, in turn changing the company perception as well. This dynamic brings robots in the customer relationship to the fore, while the robot may recede service personnel to the background. These results extend evidence that robots can affect people on an emotional level and hold theoretical implications for the reconfiguring of work relationships through robot innovations [11, 12, 14]. They invite speculation on how the dynamics of work relationships might change if future robots do not only emotionally bond with humans, but also influence employer perception, and how this potentially changes the role of the employee and their self-image.

2   Humanoid Social Robots Through an Actor Network Lens

Turning to Callon's [15] approach of techno-economic networks, this section prepares us how to think about boundary relations, what they are, and what different types of relations exist. As one of the founders of *actor-network theory* (ANT), Callon speculated on how *actors* of different kinds come into being and how they develop agency. He distinguished *actors* through the way in which they circulate and exchange *intermediaries*, such as texts and technical objects, but also skilled and knowledgeable human beings, or money. An intermediary is defined as *anything that is passed around*, such as a *product* creating a relationship between a *buyer* and a *seller*. In this way, both human and non-human objects can represent what Latour [17] calls *actants*. In other words, both humans and non-humans can turn into or act as either intermediary or mediator depending on their in-situ enactment [18].

The application of ANT has several advantages in the context of tracing the changes of work relationships in the customer-service context. First, it puts focus on the relational networks, allowing one to review the customer-service worker relationship and tracing its dynamics. It sensitizes us to the fact that new actors and relationships may emerge while others become abandoned. Second, it is open for non-human objects themselves to act as mediators, which is more attuned to the current reality of trading bots acting autonomously, social bots on the internet, and artificial intelligence excelling in human-mastery tasks, such as the board game Go, breast cancer detection, or self-driving cars, thus overcoming the issue of giving ontological priority to humans. Third, an ANT approach helps us to focus on "science in action" [19]. It allows us to consider not only a single viewpoint, such as the blackboxed artificial intelligence system presented to the customer, but also the multivocal voices and networks surrounding the creation of that blackbox, such as its developers, managerial sponsors, and service employees confronted with the system.

To begin, Fig. 1 shows the main boundaries and relations considered in this study, namely (1.) the relation between service worker and customer, (2.) the relation between service worker and robot, and (3.) the relation between customer and robot. The *relation between service worker and customer* is the traditional focus of customer relationship management. Within this relationship, a firm employs service workers using intermediaries – to use Callon's term – to create a relationship between the firm and the customer. As shown in Fig. 2, the traditional customer-to-service worker relationship is intermediated through conversations, texts, websites to which customers are directed, messages, eventually contracts, but also ways of informal conversations to bond, such as jokes. The role the humanoid robot assumes in this actor network is originally one as an intermediary in the relationship between service worker and customer and the empirical study will explore whether this relationship transitions into a more active one in which the robot becomes part of the actor network (as already indicated in Fig. 1).

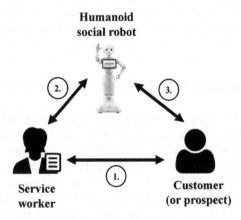

Fig. 1. Actor network considered in this study

To understand this, the *service worker-robot relationship* needs to be explored. In this context, robot's effects are different depending on the type of occupation [12].

While concerns about displacement have been raised for some job categories [20], recent work has highlighted that robots often reconfigure work relations in more complex ways [12, 14]. In the context, a robot augmenting human tasks often incurs changes to several occupational groups, for instance, pharmacists, technicians, and assistive workers [12]. We posit that it is important to consider (role, task, status) *boundaries* between occupational groups and also between customer and service worker, and how they change with the introduction of a new robotic technology. Similar to [11], we also situate our study in the context of complex services. In this context, it is possible for tasks to become enriched or impoverished in terms of demands and content, possibly having implications for the service worker's occupational status and role, depending on the actual role that the robot assumes in the relation between customer and robot.

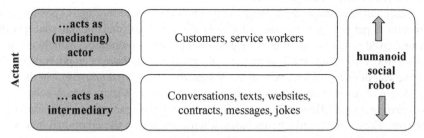

Fig. 2. Translation of concepts to our study context of customer services

The *relationship between customer and robot* needs to be explored more deeply. In our work, the notion of **attachment** comes to the fore. The premise is that human beings are naturally inclined to make and maintain lasting affectionate bonds. The quality and stability of such bonds impacts their emotional health and well-being throughout life [21]. Even given different intensities, attachment can be felt not only for family members and friends, but also for other targets, like pets or therapists [21–23]. This leads us to include that humanoids might also generate some form of "attachment." Investigating **customer attachment** like we do, Buttle et al. [24] state that feeling "satisfied" alone does not necessarily ensure a long-term relationship with whom induced that emotion. A managerial imperative is thus to identify approaches which might lead to a higher customer tenure and involvement [25]. In banking, several papers investigated customer-bank attachment [26, 27]. Recent work signals the importance of trust in attachment, for which two types of relations play a key role, namely **instrumental** and **relational** **(emotional)** attachment. Whereas *instrumental attachment* relies on convenience or access to a good deal, *relational attachment* connects customers to individual employees, branches, or the whole organization [28]. Here we make a key assumption regarding Pepper's role in the customer-service worker dynamic being explored – to investigate whether a humanoid robot can mediate (broker) the relation between service worker and customer. In our view, this will depend on whether the robot is able to effectively create instrumental and relational attachment.

Instrumental attachment concerns the physical strength, perceived intelligence, and language abilities determining the task spectrum of a robot regarding amount, variety, and depth of tasks that can be carried out. An instrumental robot is smart enough to adapt to our wishes, and to change its behavior if we don't like it. In the case of the robot Pepper, this kind of intelligence can be displayed by Pepper's dialog capacity (over the topic of sensing emotion from dialog, see among others [29]). Moreover, dialog can, even more strongly than the robot's appearance, influence how it is perceived. Dialogue can indeed lead to biased perceptions, making the users attribute qualities to the robot that might also be inaccurate [30]. When it comes to humanoids whose implementation is still ongoing, and whose principal use is for short-term interactions without deep content, it is useful to bring together only some of the above-mentioned aspects of intelligence. Following Picard [31], in this paper, humanoids' intelligence can be captured both according to their merely cognitive abilities (their capacity to give the right information), and according to the user's perception of its dialogical intelligence, such as the robot's capacity to listen and correctly interpret a users' intention.

Emotional attachment describes emerging bonds when a robot sparks positive emotions and is perceived as human. This boils down to two fundamental concepts that have received much attention in human-robot-interaction literatures, namely *emotions* and *anthropomorphism*. While different conceptualizations have been put forward [32, 33], we can define *emotions* here as *basic affective reactions to an event* in the sense of Eckman [34] based on six basic intercultural emotions – *happy, scared, calm, angry, surprised,* or *bored.* These reactions will likely influence perception and consequent behavior. Thus, they should be included when considering the emotional attachment that would be important for a robot to broker the relation between customer and firm.

In addition to emotions, the anthropomorphic, human-like aspect of a robot [35], should also be considered. According to Epley et al. [36], **anthropomorphism** can be defined as "the tendency to imbue the real or imagined behavior of nonhuman agents with human-like characteristics, motivations, intentions, or emotions". In robotics, "anthropomorphic design" usually refers to three parts: a robot's shape, behavior, and communication skills. Epley et al. [36] highlight sociality, effectance, and elicited agent knowledge to explain why human beings anthropomorphize. Sociality relies on human desire for social connection. Effectance refers to "the need to understand, control, and interact effectively with the environment" [37]. Elicited agent knowledge refers to the extent to which people apply relevant anthropocentric knowledge to objects or entities that might be targets for the attribution of human-like qualities [37]. A humanoid's morphological appearance might allow humans to recognize shared-traits with the robot, and thereby better interact with it [38]. It has also been demonstrated that the more anthropomorphic a robot is, the greater the human's receptivity is to advice provided to them by the robot [39], the extent to which humans will empathize with a robot [40], or engage in a joint human-robot task for successful task completion [41]. According to Broadbent et al. [13], robots with a higher similarity in appearance to humans, for example, are more likely to be attributed positive character traits (e.g., alive, sociable and amiable). However, as Duffy [38] makes clear, a robot's design should keep a certain amount of "robot-ness", so that the user does not develop the wrong expectations of the robot's capabilities. There is an "uncanny valley" as similarity to a living being becomes almost perfect. At this point, the subtle imperfections of the recreation become highly disturbing, or even repulsive. That is why caricatured representations, or humanoids like

Pepper, which still keep (both in their shape and in their color) a clear "robot-ness", may be more useful than more realistic designs.

3 Study Context and Methodological Approach

3.1 Study Context

Through an exploratory in-depth case study [42], we examined the changes of relationships regarding the introduction of Pepper in a bank. Prominent financial institution, Star Bank, had developed the social and economic desire to embark on a path of digitalization and innovation over the recent years. In collaboration with the research team, the innovation laboratory of the bank launched a project in October 2018 and purchased Pepper, a bright white-colored, cute, 1.2 m tall humanoid robot. Pepper was initially equipped with a simple software with basic features (Pepper 01), after which a second, smarter software with internet connection and more developed features (Pepper 02) was implemented by the research team. Pepper was programmed to ease the load of employees in accomplishing some of their easiest tasks, as well as offering customers specific experiences which they would not find at other banks, such as answering to common-sense questions, accessing the online banking website, or playing memory.

3.2 Design, Data Collection, and Analytical Strategy

We followed the Pepper project since its start. The first author of this paper was a part of the research team working on the first version of Pepper (Pepper 01) and followed the project since then. Four other authors were part of the research team that implemented the Pepper 02 robot. Two other co-authors supervised the Pepper 01 and Pepper 02 development and convoyed the robot throughout the study period to multiple events, including Pepper's performance at several employee and customer events. Several qualitative and quantitative studies were conducted, the most informative of which we present in this paper. Overall the study followed a mixed methods design, inspired by early studies on technology implementation in organizations [43]. We started with very open investigations consecutively narrowing them down were appropriate.

Data Collection. Beyond numerous participant observations, data was collected from five occasions. In a **first study** before the first steps of the software implementation started (October 2018), the first author and the Pepper 01 team collected voices of 22 customers in one of the firm's branches. The purpose of this initial investigation was for the research team to identify which features should according to the customers continue to be implemented regarding Pepper's intelligence and interaction-related capabilities, and which features were not well received. This helped gathering first insights into how customers perceived the robot. The conversations were supported by a picture of Pepper that was shown to the participants. In a **second study**, conducted in December 2018, the first author of this paper and the Pepper 01 research team interacted with seven employees in one branch of the bank. The conversations that took place during that day were structured by asking general questions followed by more specific, Pepper-related questions. The employees, who differed in age classes and gender, indicated to be open towards new technologies. Throughout the conversation, a picture of Pepper was shown to the respondents. In a **third study**, conducted in April 2019, a quantitative survey was distributed to 18 customers of the bank at an event were the robot was presented to customers. Participants responses before and after the interaction were recorded regarding emotional reactions as well as perceived intelligence of the robot. The age ranged from 25 to 65. Of the participants, 40% indicated that they knew Pepper before, for example from trade fairs, and most participants were interested in digital technologies. A **forth study** included experimental interactions with 19 probands. In January 2020, improvements to Pepper's software based on participant feedback were completed (Pepper 02). The experiment analyzed the emotions aroused by Pepper and correlations between the emotions and the perceived attachment to the company deploying it, and how a higher intelligence of the robot might influence these results. To prove the feasibility of this design, a small pretest had already been run with two respondents who had interacted with Pepper, from whom positive interactions and their feedback to the robot-interaction experience had been collected. Finally, a **fifth study** in February 2020 was based on further experimental interactions with probands. This simulated what would be a *spontaneous short-term interaction* with Pepper. in which groups of 15 to 17 people were invited to interact with the humanoid in as freely (casually) a way as possible. Each interaction took 10 to 15 min in order to give each participant a chance to interact either in an active or in a passive manner (such as a spectator may) with the humanoid. The experiment consisted of 54 participants across different age groups, genders, and nationalities. Participants varied in technological affinity and by their technological openness, indicating the degree to which they felt ready to introduce these technologies into their daily habits. Experiments expounded have been ethically certified from GfeW.

Analytical Strategy. Data was analyzed individually per study as well as combined. Reports were prepared per study in which the actual results were analyzed as well as general observations were shared with the study team. In addition, field memos were written by the researchers to reflect more on the overall learnings and observations. As we were involved in the implementation as participants, we could draw on our conversations and knowledge about the context and had access to additional documents and background information from different sources of the company. We used this knowledge in first preparing the individual study results as well as creating a case narrative capturing the most important phases of the implementation with regards to changes in boundary relations as we perceived it.

4   Results

Turning to results, we develop and present a comparative table, where we outline different periods and trace what the perceptions or actions of each group (employees and customers) of the robot in each period of implementation. In Table 1, we summarize from the employee and customer perspective the perceptions of and relations towards the humanoid robot which the rest of the section will explain.

Table 1. Main observations during the different phases of the implementation

	Employees	Customers	Robot
1. Initial enthusiasm	Most of the interviewed employees liked the humanoid's appearance and hoped for help with easy tasks. (Study 1)	Interviewed customers showed a highly positive attitude toward the introduction of the humanoid. (Study 2)	The robot acts as an intermediary between company and customers. No extra software implementation, only pre-integrated CMS. The robot was not deployed, only a picture of it was showed
2. Fear of automation	Many employees confessed to have initially felt scared of the robot possibly stealing their job. This fear was however antecedent the interview. (Study 1)	Customers hold general fear towards robots from popular narratives, but do not perceive Pepper a threat to job automation given its appearance (Study 2)	The robot acts as an intermediary between the company and the customers. No extra software implementation, only pre-integrated CMS. The robot had not been deployed yet.
3. Relief	After seeing the robot in action, employees felt relieved because they were now sure the humanoid could have never taken their job away. (Study 1)	Business customers felt amused, entertained and interested. The humanoid's perceived intelligence was relatively low and not scary (Study 3)	The robot acts as an intermediary between company and customers. Implementation of basic features: dancing, playing quiz, giving presentations, taking up poses
4. Enhanced perceived intelligence	Employees are curious to learn about new features but do not see new threats (when presented at event with research team)	Interviewed customers perceived robot as more intelligent, recognized its enhanced cognitive skills and showed overall sympathy toward it. (Study 4)	The robot becomes an actor itself Further features: internet connection, NLP/AI based system (Google Dialog-flow)
5. Reconfiguring emotional attachment	A humanoid robot might generate attachment to the company, like a human employee. (Study 5)	Respondents felt overall more attached to the deploying company after the interaction. Emotions and intelligence played a key role. (Study 5)	The robot becomes an actor itself. Further features: internet connection, NLP/AI based system (Google Dialog-flow)

Initial Enthusiasm. From both a customer and employee point of view, study 1 showed a positive attitude towards Pepper and showed that the fear of contact with the robot was very low (as one respondent remarked, "I would find it cool if Pepper would be here"). During the investigation, respondents' statements proved that especially younger people were very open to Pepper's introduction in the bank, whereas older respondents showed a little more resistance to the use of Pepper. These findings from study 1 confirmed that while neither the group of customers nor service workers were homogeneous, there was a general urge to interact, and that both roles anthropomorphized Pepper (as one respondent in the pre-test to study 4 noted, "I was very surprised how well Pepper was able to use his gestures. At times I felt as if I was talking to a human being"), although its speech and dialog capabilities were very limited.

Similarly, during study 2, employees expressed their first thoughts about the robot. It was noticeable that they had a very positive attitude towards the robot. Words such as "cute", "sweet" or even "friendly" and "appealing" were used to describe Pepper. Only few employees remarked that Pepper needs getting used to and looks very colorless.

Fear of Automation. While initial enthusiasm had been present in the early phases of the implementation, it was also noticeable that many employees stated that *they had felt at first worried that a robot might take their job away*: "It shouldn't do consultations, the customer relationship is my job", said one respondent. Customers in turn held general fear towards robots from popular narratives, but did not perceive Pepper a threat to job automation given its appearance (Study 2).

Relief. Throughout the progress of the project, it was interesting to hear how service workers had changed their mind about the introduction of the humanoid: many of the employees were relieved. Once they had seen the robot and tested its abilities, their fears had mostly dissipated: the humanoid would primarily be seen as a useful, entertaining tool addressing very basic tasks, but could not substitute them (neither in their consultancy work, nor in their interpersonal relationship with the customers). After seeing it, an interviewee stated: "Personally, I have no problem with the introduction of the humanoid, we're not redundant, he will definitely not take our job". In summary, employees showed an open, positive attitude towards Pepper's use.

From an ANT perspective, these results suggest that the employees feared that the humanoid social robot would *disintermediate* their relationship to the customer due to automation. However, the white, sweet and child-looking robot that the bank adopted was by no means capable of automating all tasks away. This led employees to be more comfortable with the robot and removed some of the initial barriers toward Pepper's adoption into the work environment.

A survey distributed to customers (study 3) asked about their emotional reactions to Pepper as well as how they perceived the intelligence of the robot after they had observed one proband interacting with the robot. Responses were collected on five-point Likert scales, where five indicated the highest approval. The results for emotional reactions were as follows: Emotional involvement was rated as 3.44. 'I feel well' was rated at 3.06. 'I feel amused' as well as 'I feel curious' were rated at 3.77. 'I feel uncomfortable' was rated at 2.0. Of the participants, 33% used the attributes 'cute' or 'nice' to describe the robot. Also, 20% used the attributes 'amusing' or 'entertaining' to describe it. These results indicated a high level of interest in the robot as well as generally more positive and comfortable feelings.

Regarding perceived intelligence, the average rating was 2.78 on the question 'do you find Pepper intelligent'. The respondents remarked that its capabilities should be improved through programming and that the interaction felt 'scripted'. Interestingly, some respondents anthropomorphized the robot, for instance by saying that 'she has expressed her will'. These first investigations suggested the relevance of our constructs such as emotional reactions, intelligence, and anthropomorphism, both on the customers' and on the employees' side, and informed further experimental investigations.

Enhanced Perceived Intelligence. After further features had been implemented, an experiment was conducted consisting of 19 participants' short-term interaction with Pepper accompanied by quantitative surveys (study 4). As can be seen from Table 2, probands rated the perceived competence of Pepper and perceived dialog capabilities significantly higher than the baseline. From this observation, it could be concluded that the integration of knowledge related to the bank was a most important factor to address perceived competence, which we see as a measure of intelligence. From the experiments, it could also be seen that Pepper aroused emotions, since participants felt sympathy regardless of its competency. Together, the results suggested that through the Pepper 02 implementation, especially instrumental attachment between customers and robot could be increased through enhanced intelligence of the robot, while emotional reaction played an important role across the entire implementation.

Table 2. Rating of the humanoid social robot's capabilities in different domains.

	Pepper 01 (Baseline)	Pepper 02 (Final system)	1 vs. 2: $p < 0.05$?
Competence	2.02	4.00	Yes
Dialog	2.40	4.05	Yes
Anthropomorphism	1.98	2.70	No
Sympathy	3.40	4.55	Yes

Reconfiguring Emotional Attachment. Study 5 mainly examined the influence of intelligence, emotions and anthropomorphism on company attachment. It was also considered whether the "smarter" software implementation developed by the research group (Pepper 02) had a higher positive influence as suggested by study 4. Worth pointing out is that the specific implementation (Pepper 01 or 02) did not count as highly – contrary to study 4. Yet the experiment had been affected by a slow connection to the internet, which made "smarter" Pepper slow down. Further, during the free interaction with the robot, participants were not always informed on the robot's complete feature set. Some extra features of Pepper 02 remained undiscovered. Based thereupon, Pepper 01 versus 02 differences were not further interpreted in this study.

As can be seen from Model 2 in Table 3, it was confirmed that *positive emotions* towards the robot (especially strong ones, like happiness) do generate a *higher attachment to the company* deploying the robot. The analysis of *Model 3* showed no support

Table 3. Regression models explaining company attachment (study 5)

DV: Attachment to company	M1: Controls only	M2: Emotions	M3: Emotions and appearance	M4: Emotions, intelligence, appearance
Intercept	2.222	−0.074	−1.019	−2.070
Controls				
Pepper 01 vs. 02	−0.103	−0.058	−0.153	−0.128
Gender	0.008	0.152	0.241	0.046
Citizenship	−0.669*	−0.140	−0.065	0.005
Age	−0.464*	−0.426*	−0.250	−0.330
Tech. openness	0.341*	0.086	0.038	0.074
Prev. experience	−0.801*	−0.395	−0.297	−0.364*
Comfortable place	0.236	0.120	0.127	0.306*
Explanatory var.				
Happy		0.608**	0.555***	0.431**
Calm		0.019	0.042	0.023
Curious		0.189	0.078	0.083
Scared		−0.349*	−0.319*	−0.263*
Angry		0.689**	0.558*	0.460
Bored		−0.121	−0.076	0.091
Robot's appearance			0.043	−0.334
Anthropomorphism			0.271	0.300*
Robot's intelligence				0.713**
N	54	54	54	54
df	7	13	16	17
R^2	0.33	0.60	0.65	0.78
Adj. R^2	0.23	0.47	0.50	0.67
Prob > F	0.0061	<0.001	0.0001	<0.001

* $p < 0.05$, ** $p < 0.01$, *** $p < 0.001$

for a relation between anthropomorphism and participants' attachment to the humanoid. However, in Model 4, including intelligence, anthropomorphism correlated positively with participants' attachment to the robot. Furthermore, as can be seen from Model 4, it was also apparent that intelligence was associated with company attachment. Intelligence was measured using the four variables non-verbal skills, verbal skills, naturalness, and degree to which the robot understands a users' intention. These were combined into a single factor after the factor analysis had confirmed the feasibility of this approach. In sum, the regression analysis had suggested a significant impact on participants' attachment a company that (a) the intelligence of the robot, (b) participants' happiness aroused during interaction, and (c) the anthropomorphic appearance of the robot the company deploying the humanoid.

Taken all together, the analysis suggested that the implementation went through five phases: (1) there were initial hopes in the implementation project, (2) fears of automation on the employee side, (3) relief when fears of automation proofed unjustified within first tests of reality, (4) further enhancements in the robots capabilities, such as perceived intelligence, and (5) finally the insight that bonding of customers with a robot also evokes bonding with the company, thus reconfiguring relations of customers and a company through a robot actor on an emotional attachment level.

5 Discussion

The purpose of this paper was to explore *how boundary relations change with the introduction of humanoid robots in the context of complex customer services.* This meant not only looking into technical automation potential, but to also research which emotional reactions the interaction with a humanoid could evoke in its interlocutors, and how their general attachment to the company deploying it was subsequently affected. Towards this aim, the paper presented results from five studies within the context of implementing Pepper, a humanoid robot, in a financial institution.

The results – especially of the fifth study – suggest that a humanoid can indeed increase people's attachment to the company the robot is employed by. Gender, citizenship, age, technology affinity, interaction environment, and previous experiences did not influence this attachment. The anthropomorphic aspect of the robot clearly played a significant role, but what had an even stronger impact on people's increased attachment to the bank institution were strong positive emotions evoked during the interaction with the robot (e.g. happiness), and the perceived intelligence of the robot itself.

Especially the perceived intelligence of the robot generated stronger attachment to the company. If we allow a comparison between a humanoid robot like Pepper, and a dog, the pet people tend to anthropomorphize the most [23], the findings align with what Kurdek [44] observed in his study about attachment towards pet dogs. Starting from the assumption that attachment is most likely to occur when positive interactions take place, he demonstrated that, together with energy, affection and emotional reactivity, a dogs' intelligence was key in generating owners' attachment to the animal. In a nutshell, our results suggest that a humanoid can become an embodied avatar of a company – more versatile than an animal ever can.

Together with unveiling the principal factors that might lead to a stronger attachment towards the company deploying a humanoid, i.e. pleasure generated during the interaction and perceived intelligence of the robot, the present work leads to a new, unprecedented observation. At the beginning of the Pepper project, voices of both customers and employees were collected. The results show that employee's initial skepticism towards introducing a humanoid had stemmed from their fear that the robot could away their current position. However, their initial skepticism had been quickly alleviated by employees' own assessment that a robot like Pepper was somewhat limited in its skills, and that it would have not be able to serve the bank beyond more simple tasks like reception, providing general information to and the entertainment of customers. Pepper might not be able to perform employees' main job, which is consultancy, nor substitute the interpersonal bond between customers and employees. The results of this paper show that a humanoid can generate, increase, or in general alter, a customers' bond to a company. Tasks that were originally done by humans can be automated, but from a different perspective than expected: not from a task level, but from an emotional level. The experiment ran in February 2020 shows that there is a category of machines (the humanoid robots) that can change or influence companies' identity among their customers, as well as the nature itself of customers' loyalty and bond to them.

In the sense of changing role descriptions, our work also confirms the main consideration of Barret et al. [12]. In fact, in their paper examining the influence of robotic innovation on the boundary dynamics among three different occupational groups working in a hospital pharmacy (i.e. pharmacists, technicians, and assistants), the authors showed that "the adoption and use of a robotic innovation by multiple occupational groups can reconfigure the boundary relations among them, with important implications for work practices, roles, and status" (p. 1464). In the same way, Oborn et al. [11] found similar results in their work looking into how the social and technical elements of robot applications can influence and restructure social dynamics. Our study adds to this stream of work the observation that a humanoid robot can not only alter boundaries across occupational groups but also boundaries between an occupation (service workers) and customers. A humanoid robot such as Pepper has the potential to automate very simple (instrumental) tasks but more importantly take over some emotional attachment functions of the service worker.

The present paper adds to research on human-robot interaction (and specifically research on humanoids in organizations) in two main regards. On the one hand it uses a novel research model to investigate the emotions people feel when interacting with a humanoid, as well as the factors influencing them, and the implications for the overall attachment they feel towards a company deploying the humanoid. On the other hand, it also provides a case study elucidating the path towards deploying humanoids in companies. The authors believe the opportunities to be twofold for a company like a bank deploying a humanoid like Pepper. The humanoid could both help improve the perceived innovativeness of the company, while also leading to stronger customer bonds. Organizationally and from a long-term perspective, this will also have consequences for the employees and their role, status, and tasks.

6   Conclusion

Human interaction with humanoid robots usually arouses emotions. If the humanoid looks sweet, funny, friendly and not too human-like (like Pepper does), these emotions are mostly positive. Studies point out that a customers' bond to a product can generate attachment to the company that this product is linked to. This led us to ask how a humanoid social robot could change the boundary relations between customers and employees in complex service situations. Our findings from study 5 suggest that perceived intelligence, positive emotions, and anthropomorphic characteristics of the robot are associated with greater emotional attachment to the company deploying the robot.

The results of our study also lead to a further consideration regarding our initial research question. As mentioned in the beginning, Callon [15] defines a techno-economic network as a "coordinated set of heterogeneous actors which interact more or less successfully to develop, produce, distribute and diffuse methods for generating goods and services" (p. 113). According to Callon, actors define one another through interactions, meaning in the intermediaries that they put into circulation (p. 135). So it happens, for example, that the interaction between a producer and the customer happens through the product. An actor takes the last generation of intermediaries and transforms (combines, mixes, concatenates, etc.) these to create the next generation (p. 141). In this case, importantly, that is the next generation of customers.

Applied to our case study, the original actors were the bank and its customers, and Pepper, while being a hybrid mixture of human and mechanical, was conceived to act only as an intermediary in the customer relationship with the bank. The results of our investigations show a shift in the role of a humanoid like Pepper within an actor network. One in which Pepper can be seen not only as an intermediary, but as an actor as well. By using texts, voice recognition, music, websites, etc. (all intermediaries), a humanoid can work as an actor itself. By arousing certain emotions and enhancing users' attachment to the bank, the humanoid is beginning to transform the network of the relationship between customer and service worker. It can change, or at least influence, a companies' identity, and the nature of customers' loyalty and bond to them.

References

1. McAfee, A., Brynjolfsson, E.: Machine, Platform, Crowd: Harnessing Our Digital Future. W.W. Norton & Company, New York (2017)
2. Agrawal, A., Gans, J., Goldfarb, A.: Prediction Machines: The Simple Economics of Artificial Intelligence. Harvard Business Review Press, Boston (2018)
3. The Guardian. https://www.theguardian.com/world/2018/feb/06/japan-robots-will-care-for-80-of-elderly-by-2020. Accessed 14 May 2020
4. Deming, D.: The Robots are Coming. Prepare for Trouble. The New York Times. https://www.nytimes.com/2020/01/30/business/artificial-intelligence-robots-retail.html. Accessed 14 May 2020
5. Mukai, T., et al.: Development of a nursing-care assistant robot RIBA that can lift a human in its arms. In: 2010 IEEE/RSJ International Conference on Intelligent Robots and Systems (2010)
6. Wirtz, J., et al.: Brave new world: service robots in the frontline. J. Serv. Manag. **29**(5), 907–931 (2018)
7. Mettler, T., Sprenger, M., Winter, R.: Service robots in hospitals: new perspectives on niche evolution and technology affordances. Eur. J. Inf. Syst. **26**(5), 451–468 (2017)
8. Dahlin, E.: Are robots stealing our jobs? Socius Soc. Res. Dyn. World **5**, 1–14 (2019)
9. Nam, T.: Citizen attitudes about job replacement by robotic automation. Futures **109**, 39–49 (2019)

10. Blumberg Capital: Artificial Intelligence In 2019: Getting Past the Adoption Tipping Point (2019). https://blumbergcapital.com/ai-in-2019/Blumberg. Capital's recent survey of 1,000 American Adults That Found about Half are Ready to Embrace New Tech, while the Other Half Fears it Will Take away their Jobs [Blumberg Capital, 2019]

11. Oborn, E., Barrett, M., Darzi, A.: Robots and service innovation in health care. J. Health Serv. Res. Policy 16(1), 46–50 (2011)

12. Barrett, M., Oborn, E., Orlikowski, J., Yates, J.: Reconfiguring boundary relations: robotic innovations in pharmacy work. Organ. Sci. 23(5), 1448–1466 (2012)

13. Broadbent, E., et al.: Robots with display screens: a robot with a more humanlike face display is perceived to have more mind and a better personality. PLoS ONE 8(8), 1–9 (2013)

14. Sergeeva, A.V., Faraj, S., Huysman, M.: Losing touch: an embodiment perspective on coordination in robotic surgery. Organ. Sci. 31(5), 1053–1312 (2020)

15. Callon, M.: Techno-economic networks and irreversibility. Sociol. Rev. 38(1_suppl), 132–161 (1991)

16. Softbank Homepage. https://www.softbankrobotics.com/emea/en/pepper. Accessed 14 May 2020

17. Latour, B.: Reassembling the Social: An Introduction to Actor-Network Theory. Oxford University Press, Oxford (2005)

18. D'Adderio, L.: The performativity of routines: theorising the influence of artefacts and distributed agencies on routines dynamics. Res. Policy 37(5), 769–789 (2008)

19. Latour, B.: Science in Action: How to Follow Scientists and Engineers through Society, 18th edn. Harvard University Press, Cambridge (1987)

20. Brynjolfsson, E., McAfee, A.: The Second Machine Age: Work, Progress, and Prosperity in a Time of Brilliant Technologies. W W Norton & Co, New York (2014)

21. Mikulincer, M., Shaver, P.R.: Attachment in Adulthood: Structure, Dynamics and Change. Guilford Press, New York (2007)

22. Siegel, D.J.: The Developing Mind: Toward a Neurobiology of Interpersonal Experience. Guilford Press, New York (1999)

23. Albert, A., Bulcroft, K.: Pets, families, and the life course. J. Marriage Fam. 50(2), 543–552 (1988)

24. Buttle, F.A., Ahmad, R., Aldlaigan, A.: The theory and practice of customer bonding. J. Bus. Bus. Market. 9(2), 3–27 (2002)

25. Laurent, G., Kapferer, J.-N.: Measuring consumer involvement profiles. J. Mark. Res. 22(1), 41–53 (1985)

26. Brown, K.A., Mitchell, T.R.: Organizational obstacles: links with financial performance, customer satisfaction, and job satisfaction in a service environment. Hum. Relat. 46(6), 725–743 (1993)

27. Bloemer, J., de Ruyter, K., Peeters, P.: Investigating drivers of bank loyalty: the complex relationship between image, service quality and satisfaction. Int. J. Bank Market. 16(7), 276–286 (1998)

28. Aldlaigan, A., Buttle, F.: Beyond satisfaction: customer attachment to retail banks. Int. J. Bank Market. 23(4), 349–359 (2005)

29. Klein, J., Moon, Y., Picard, R.W.: This computer responds to user frustration: theory, design, results, and implications. Interact. Comput. 14, 119–140 (2002)

30. Fong, T., Nourbakhsh, I., Dautenhahn, K.: A survey of socially interactive robots. Rob. Auton. Syst. 42(3–4), 143–166 (2003)

31. Picard, R.W.: Toward machines with emotional intelligence. In: Matthews, G., Zeidner, M., Roberts, R.D. (eds.) The Science of Emotional Intelligence: Knowns and Unknowns. Oxford University Press, Oxford (2008)

32. Barrett, L.F., Wager, T.D.: The structure of emotion: evidence from neuroimaging studies. Curr. Dir. Psychol. Sci. 15(2), 79–83 (2006)

33. Russell, J.A.: Core affect and the psychological construction of emotion. Psychol. Rev. **110**(1), 145–172 (2003)
34. Ekman, P.: Universals and cultural differences in facial expressions of emotion. In: Cole, J. (ed.) Nebraska Symposium on Motivation, vol. 19. University of Nebraska Press, Lincoln (1972)
35. Fink, J.: Anthropomorphism and human likeness in the design of robots and human-robot interaction. In: Ge, S.S., Khatib, O., Cabibihan, J.-J., Simmons, R., Williams, M.-A. (eds.) ICSR 2012. LNCS (LNAI), vol. 7621, pp. 199–208. Springer, Heidelberg (2012). https://doi.org/10.1007/978-3-642-34103-8_20
36. Epley, N., Waytz, A., Cacioppo, J.: On seeing human: a three-factor theory of anthropomorphism. Psychol. Rev. **114**(4), 864–886 (2007)
37. Crowell, C.R., Deska, J.C., Villano, M., Zenk, J., Roddy, J.T.: Anthropomorphism of robots: study of appearance and agency. JMIR Hum. Factors **6**(2), e12629 (2019)
38. Duffy, B.: Anthropomorphism and the social robot. Rob. Auton. Syst. **42**(3–4), 177–190 (2003)
39. Powers, A., Kiesler, S.: The advisor robot: tracing people's mental model from a robot's physical attributes. Presented at ACM SIGCHI/SIGART Conference on Human-Robot Interaction, Salt Lake City, Utah, pp. 218–225 (2006)
40. Riek, L., Rabinowitch, T., Chakrabarti, B., Robinson, P.: How anthropomorphism affects empathy toward robots. Presented at 4th ACM/IEEE International Conference on Human Robot Interaction, pp. 43–48 (2009)
41. Hinds, P., Roberts, T., Jones, H.: Whose job is it anyway? A study of human-robot interaction in a collaborative task. Int. J. Social Robot. **19**(1), 151–181 (2004)
42. Yin, R.K.: Case Study Research: Design and Methods. Sage, Los Angeles (2018)
43. Barley, S.R.: The alignment of technology and structure through roles and networks. Adm. Sci. Q. **35**(1), 61–103 (1990)
44. Kurdek, L.A.: Pet dogs as attachment figures for adult owners. J. Fam. Psychol. **23**(4), 439-46 (2009)

The Role of Social Capital in Mediating ICT-Enabled Peace Building Efforts: A Case Study from Kenya

Festus Mukoya[1,2]([✉]) and Arunima Sehgal Mukherjee[1,3]([✉])

[1] Department of Informatics, Universitetet i Oslo, Oslo, Norway
festusmukoya@gmail.com, arunimam@ifi.uio.no
[2] Free Pentecostal Fellowship in Kenya, Nairobi, Kenya
[3] HISP India, Noida, India

Abstract. Inter-ethnic violence has flared in recent years across Kenya's periphery due to struggles around processes of political devolution, corrupt systems of governance, elite sponsorship, cattle rustling, climate change, famine, land, politicization of ethnic relations and illicit arms. Violence has resulted in loss of life, loss of livelihood, increased hatred between communities and large-scale displacement. New ways of violence prevention are needed to achieve sustainable peace, and contribute to broader efforts of social development. This article analyses the implications of integrating ICT in mitigation of ethnic violence in Northwestern Kenya. The theoretical lens of social capital is used, with a focus on different forms of bonding, bridging and linking to analyse how ICTs can reduce those forms of capital that enhance violence and simultaneously promotes those that can promote peace. Our study finds that relatively simple ICT applications that can help inform anonymously on potential violent conditions and initiate speedy and effective response to them, can help promote binding social capital at the expense of bonding forms. This changing dynamics around the constitution of social capital has contributed to effectively promoting peace building efforts. The paper thus contributes to the important domain of 'ICTs for Peace' research and more broadly to ICT4D.

Keywords: ICT · Ethnic violence · Social capital · Kenya

1 Introduction

Inter-ethnic conflicts are a widespread problem on the African continent, with devastating effects on human security through loss of life and livelihood, and large-scale displacement [1]. Ethnic violence involves choosing victims based upon ethnic membership [2]. In Africa, the six worst-hit countries from such violence include Nigeria, Ethiopia, Somalia, Sudan, Kenya and Uganda [3], a trend increasing in recent years [3]. Kenya is reported to experience one of the highest levels of such violence [4], particularly following political devolution [5], often encouraged through elite sponsorship

R. K. Bandi et al. (Eds.): IFIPJWC 2020, IFIP AICT 601, pp. 326–340, 2020.
https://doi.org/10.1007/978-3-030-64697-4_24

[4, 5]. Other sources of conflict include cattle rustling, environmental degradation; drought, land related conflicts and the proliferation of small arms and light weapons (SALWs).

As ethnic violence continues to flare across the Low and Middle Income Countries (LMICs), peace activists are exploring ways of integrating ICTs in peacebuilding efforts [6], such as using mobile phones to help identify and map hate speech and rumours by citizens' perceptions of risk and conflict and providing early warning of potential risk situation [7, 8]. ICTs have been used to track violence in Latin America, for example, Infocrim in Sao Paolo has been credited with a fall in homicides from 12,800 to 7,200 in the period 1999–2005 [6]. Without communication networks, it is difficult and dangerous for civilians to inform on rebel groups, as they run the risk of being identified [9]. The Ushahidi platform has been used in Kenya to map election violence. There are also examples of other ICT applications being used for peace building in Kenya such as the Uwiano Platform for Peace, Umati for monitoring hate speech, Elections I witness and Sisi Ni Amani for monitoring election malpractices. However, the study of these applications have not focused on the role of citizens in implementing these efforts [4]. ICTs can also be used to facilitate organized violence, such as supporting the coordination amongst groups promoting violence [10], by enabling rapid sharing of information [11]. ICTs thus come with both opportunities and risks in peace building initiatives.

There is urgent need to develop more nuanced understanding of the role ICTs play in peace building efforts, and how these play out in particular social contexts. We explore these social dynamics around ICTs through the lens of social capital [12]. We explore this through the research question: *What is the interplay between ICTs and social capital in mitigation or not of ethnic violence?*

This paper is organised in seven sections. In the next section, we outline the theoretical approach based on a social capital perspective. In section three, we describe the methods, followed by the case study narrative. Section five presents the findings, and the analysis in Sect. 6. The conclusions are presented in section seven.

2 Theoretical Framework: A Social Capital Perspective

The use of ICTs in mitigating ethnic violence, are shaped by the social networks in which they are embedded including the shared norms and values, and how trust shapes processes of cooperative relationships within and among conflicting communities. The role of social capital has been highlighted by different academic disciplines, such as public policy and sociology, leading to its multiple conceptualizations and definitions (Hossam, 2009), focusing on the structure and/or on the content of the social [13–15]. We focus on the different mechanisms identified in shaping social capital, namely, bonding, bridging and linking and how these processes are mediated by ICTs. Social capital serves as the glue which can bind community based social networks and are important in shaping processes of technology development and use [16]. Social capital represents resources or assets rooted in an individual's or in a group's network of social relations.

We adopt the definition of social capital as networks, shared norms, and social trust that facilitate coordination and cooperation within or among groups for mutual benefit [15]. Putman emphasizes different means that shape social capital including processes of bonding, bridging and linking, which can both build and undermine social relationships. These means provide an interesting lens to understand the role of ICT in shaping social capital in peace building efforts, particularly in shaping social trust reflecting the level of confidence that people have that others will act in expected ways [17]. Trust indicates a willingness of a person to be vulnerable to another party either as a consequence of their belief of good intent [18]. Trust is embodied in structures of social relations and grows with increasing sense of personal or group security, and processes of accountability.

We study the means of building social capital within the context of a *social network* and seek to understand the level and type of engagement an individual has within the collective and the level of support he or she can obtain [19]. This is reflected in the *norms of reciprocity* between the individual and the collective [15]. In an interconnected group of people, social networks provide the foundation of personal and group interactions and how they unfold.

Bonding represents a means of building social capital in a collective characterised by high levels of similarity in demographics and social attitudes [20]. Bonding thus exists between 'people like us' such as in a family or close friends [21]. Bonding often escalates the polarization between communities increasing their vulnerability to violence, and simultaneously promotes violence against the perceived "other." *Bridging* social capital describes connections across a cleavage that typically divides society, such as ethnic or religious groups [17, 18]. Bridging helps to understand how can ICTs help peace actors to break constraining factors by enabling information flows between conflicting communities, and the building of consensus. *Linking* social capital describes norms of respect and networks of trusting relationships between people interacting across formal institutionalized power structures [22]. We use linking to understand the ICT-mediated relational dynamics among community members, non-state actors and state actors in the context of violence mitigation.

These three means of building social capital help to analyse the complex relationship between social capital and ICT-mediated violent mitigation efforts. We expect for conflict to increase tensions and decrease trust between engaged actors and also force them to rely and depend on each other. Social capital might be formed on the basis of solidarity in the face of an external threat, while relying on bonding processes. We analyse how ICTs reshapes elements of bonding, bridging and linking can enable or not peaceful coexistence of communities. [21] has argued that social capital can provide the basis for social belonging and constructive social interaction, enabling joint problem solving. However, Putman has not analysed the role of ICTs in shaping the different social capital processes, a gap which this paper seeks to address. However, imbalances in the bonding, bridging and linking forms of social capital can also lead to increased inequalities and subsequent conflicts [23]. Social capital can thus both lead to mitigating and promoting conflict [24], based on whether social capital is 'unresponsive' or 'exploitative' [25]. Social capital can both include or exclude groups [20]. Social capital therefore cannot be assumed to always act as a glue, since it can also function as a source of tension, and contributing to violence. How do ICTs like mobile phones redefine these dynamics, reflects our empirical quest.

3   Research Methods

This paper results from the work that is ongoing from 2018 in a Faith Based Organization (FBO) in Kenya, where one of the authors is involved as a leader for conflict mitigation efforts. The work involves formation and strengthening of community level peace structures, social contracting processes, strengthening community-authority relations and promoting early warning and early response using ICTs. The experiences and engagement is thus rich, intensive and ongoing and involving a diversity of learnings.

The study is based on the longitudinal research design (2018.2020), involving multi-stakeholder analysis based on qualitative data. The study employed a case study design to understand the role of ICT-based early warning and response system (EWERS) being implemented by the FBO in Kenya. The analytical focus of the case is on the role of ICTs in shaping peace building efforts of community groups in sites historically plagued by violence in Northwestern Kenya. We sought to understand how the social dynamics, viewed through the lens of social capital, shaped the use of ICTs in peace building efforts.

One of the authors, a member of the FBO, has been visiting the case study sites at least quarterly during the study period, while the other authors has made one visit each of the last two years. Data has been collected through various means of meetings, focus group discussions, and interviews. In 2020, given the travel restrictions, regular contact has been maintained between the authors and with the actors in the field over phone and Skype. Additionally, system reports were examined at periodic intervals, for example to see the changes reported in key indicators of conflict, such as related to cattle theft, domestic violence, prevalence of small arms, drug and substance abuse among others.

The study also applied a multi-stakeholder analysis approach in identifying stakeholders and classifying them, such as indicator monitors, community peace representatives and security agencies. We tried to investigate the relationships between stakeholders, and how these were being mediated by the EWERS application. The stakeholders were analysed at three levels: i) the first was the indicator monitors, also known as field agents that collect intelligence reports from the field; ii) the second was the system developers and analysts who received the data from the indicator monitors; and, iii) the third was the responders who mainly comprised of end-users, the government authorities and the other non-state actors who were expected to take peace building actions. For each group, we examined how members applied the ICT for peacebuilding efforts given their different roles. Peace building efforts were focused towards different ethnic communities engaged in conflict in two clusters: i) the Kipsigis, the Nandi and the Luo in Muhoroni conflict cluster; and, ii) the Bukusu, the Sabaot, the Iteso and the Kikuyu in Mt. Elgon conflict cluster. The analysis focused on interactions between community groups and exchange of ideas and goods. These clusters were organized through different groups, such as peace committees, community advocates and peace representatives, women peace associations and thematic committees.

Data analysis was broadly interpretive, helping to identify three key themes around the relationship between ICTs and social capital, shaped within the context of economic and power relations. We tried to reformulate stories narrated to us by different respondents, and related to concepts of bonding, linking and bridging social capital.

4 Study Context

The area under study covered Trans Nzoia, Bungoma, Kisumu, Nandi and Kericho Counties in Western Kenya, where there exists intractable ethnic violence. The FBO has been historically engaged in peace development efforts in these regions, including the use of ICTs. The communities under study were the Kipsigis in Kericho; the Nandi in Nandi and the Luo in Kisumu counties. While the Bukusu, the Sabaot and the Iteso in Trans Nzoia and Bungoma counties formed another conflict axis referred to as Mt. Elgon cluster (see Fig. 1)

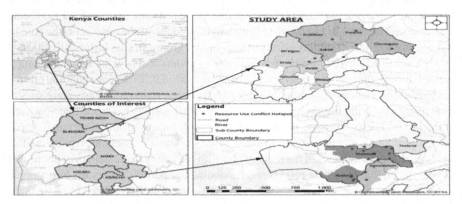

Fig. 1. Muhoroni and Mt. Elgon study areas

Communities in Mt. Elgon and Muhoroni clusters have been embroiled in violence since 1963. The causes include political dominance, land and boundary disputes, the proliferation of SALWs, and large-scale cattle theft. Existence of militia groups and IDPs is a threat to security, and there also exist high rates of corruption among some police and chiefs who also encourage drug and substance abuse. Ethnic discrimination in resource sharing was another cause of conflict.

The FBO registered in Kenya has been working on various development projects with a primary focus on peace and reconciliation projects. The FBO has designed and implemented an EWERS as a key tool in peace building efforts, based on the sending, receiving and processing of SMS. The EWERS receives information from field monitors and sends verified information to the mandated responders in time to take action.

The EWERS has three main components comprised of the monitoring, control and response units. The monitoring Unit comprises of a team of field agents knowledgeable about the violent hotspot areas. They are equipped with a simple feature phone and a reliable network provider for easy communication through both SMS and voice calls. Their primary role is to collect data in the hotspot areas according to pre-defined indicators of violence and relay the same to the control unit. The control unit is computer monitoring system with a web-based software. The personnel manning the system analyses, interprets and double checks the reports from the monitoring unit by calling the sender (field agents) and generating relevant reports for action by the response team. The response unit has a team of responders, including state security agencies, NGO's, local administrators, responsible for particular geographical areas and for types of incidents. They respond with appropriate action based on information of incidents received through their mobile phones. The system is schematically depicted in the Fig. 2.

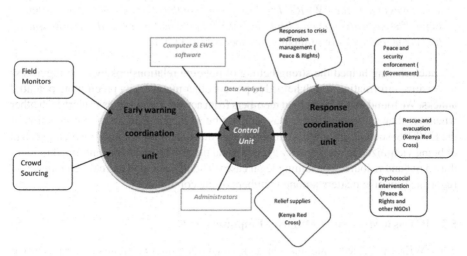

Fig. 2. The EWERS in use by the FBO

5   Case Description

This section describes the case study around key themes identified through the empirical work.

5.1   ICTs as a Platform of Sharing Sensitive Information for Peace and Security

The study established that the introduction and use of ICTs helped community members, particularly peace actors in Mt. Elgon, to overcome conditions constraining information flows between communities leading to better social relationships and improved mobilization of community resources. The EWERS, with its inbuilt features to anonymize the sender, motivated the field agents to share sensitive information to each other thereby contributing to saving lives and properties. For example,

> *"in Endebess a Turkana woman saw a group of some Pokot youths crossing the border from Uganda to attack the Bukusu and take away their animals and also smuggle in weapons. She sent the message to the system warning that the Bukusu farms will be attacked shortly. The police in collaboration with community leaders responded quickly before the culprits could carry out the attack."* (community member in KII).

In another case, "a Teso family had sold many bags of maize and had got lot of money. A group of Sabaot youths had noted this and were planning to attack this family at night. It was also an opportunity to evict them from their land which the Sabaot had believed that it was theirs. A Sabaot who got hint of the possible attack sent a message to the EWERS. The Teso family got the alert and moved away that night. The security agencies kept vigil at the home and arrested the youths who had come to attack" (community member part of FGD)

Such sharing helped the strengthening of bonding relationships by enabling access to sensitive information which helped to protect other members by preempting potential attacks. We found that ICTs helped members from across communities to alert each other whenever they sensed that there was going to be an attack. Prior to the introduction of the EWERS, such information went unreported due to fear the community members had of being victimized by the security agencies and the police, and to be embroiled in long-drawn out and resource consuming legal cases. The ICTs helped increase confidence of reporting sensitive matters among members of the community.

5.2   ICT as a Medium of Minority Empowerment

The EWERS provided a medium through which the minority groups could raise their voices and be included in peace building efforts. The EWERS facilitated flows of information, empowering the minorities to challenge the deeply entrenched power structures exercised by the majority groups. The prior lack of inclusion of minorities in these communities was a factor that had sustained the violence, and their inclusion contributed to increasing the levels of justice, as demonstrated in the example below:

"When appointing Assistant Chief in Kaplamai, the Nandi community noted that somebody from a different community was going to be appointed instead of their own. They started sending threats and complains which were captured in the EWERS. A Nandi woman received the alert message and opted to use her influence to support a woman candidate who was not a Nandi against the wishes of her community. The Kisii woman who was being supported by the Nandi woman got the position." (community member in KII).

The EWERS contributed to increasing leadership opportunities for women by enabling them to engage in different peace building efforts and help them to ascend to various leadership positions in their communities. Their engagement in response to the message alerts on issues of gender-based violence, corruption, SALW proliferation placed them at a vantage position to be appointed or elected into leadership. For example:

"The community in Chepchoina agreed to unanimously elect one of the most active member of the Peace network to a women leadership position. Everlyne Wasike has caused massive influence through response to the EWERS messages. She became so popular that the men in the community campaigned for her until the fellow women elected her to the chair of Maendeleo ya Wanawake. She was again later elected to the chair of the settlement farm (this position is normally a reserve

for men). Even recently three other women from Courageous women group were appointed as village elders." (community member in KII*).*

There were also increased opportunities for the empowerment of youth in the communities. The message alerts from the EWERS motivated regular interactions between the Chiefs and the youths from the affected communities, which also drew the attention of leaders to the economic plight of youths. Some chiefs started sensitizing the youth on the importance of peace and respect for the rule of law, and for them to focus on the development of entrepreneurial skills. This served as a means for youth empowerment.

"I have gone an extra mile to lobby the support of loaners such as Uwezo and women funds who lend the youth money to start business so that they can upgrade their livelihoods and as result of this, community members have gained trust in the administration and relates with me well." (Community Chief *in KII*)

5.3   ICTs as a Facilitative for Access to Economic Markets

The EWERS helped open up market spaces that had been before closed to community members, by linking then across ethnic divides and encouraging joint venture efforts. These connections led to new economic opportunities and business partnerships, for example, communities in Mt Elgon formed *chamas* and business groups in Saboti.

"We were brought together by EWERS to regularly respond to alert messages from the system. But with time we decided to also engage in joint business that has now become a SACCO whose membership is drawn from all communities living in Saboti." (community member in *FGD*).

Through the focus group discussions, we learnt that that business in the area had improved with the advent of the EWERS as it had facilitated a platform for interaction of diverse groups of people, enabling the opening up of new markets that had before been closed. The Sabaot harvest milk, honey and firewood and supply to the Bukusu who in return supply maize, cooking oil, sugar, soap. This had previously not happened due to high polarization between these two groups. According to a key informant, the Luo and Kalenjin had started to freely interact in the Sondu market leading to joint business ventures since both groups were included in the network engaged with responding to alert messages related to cattle theft.

"We exchange goods and services, for instance we the Kipsigis bring tomatoes that the Luo buy on credit and take it to Kisumu, and the payments done later." (community chief in *KII*).

5.4   ICTs as a Driver of Community Conversations for Peace

The early warning messages sent to the EWERS revealed polarized relationships between the Abagusii and Marakwet in the Trans Nzoia County. The persistence of messages drew the attention of national level government leaders who responded swiftly by forming community-based dialogue groups, helping the two communities to engage in reconciliation efforts. After peace was achieved, the communities made a social contract to be solving their issues amicably without being aggressive against the other through dialogue. A tree by the name *simatwet* became their symbol of peace where they would always meet whenever system alert messages pointed to possible dangers to security. Following such regular conversations, many people who had been earlier displaced, were recalled by host communities.

> *"The Abagusii IDPs have returned to their farms and were busy farming. The roads connecting between the areas occupied by the two communities had been closed but now they have been opened. Chepkaitit primary school located in the area between the Marakwet and the Abagusii had been vandalized and closed due to violence. None of the communities wanted their children to attend the school. The government repaired and reop-ened the school. Children from the two communities (Marakwet and Abagusii) started schooling together in Chepkaitit primary school. The school board now has members from both communities"* (community member in KII)

5.5   ICT System as a Tool for Recovery of Lost Assets in Conflict Situation

The ICTs facilitated the timely reporting of incidents encouraging timely response enhancing recovery of stolen goods and animals especially in the Muhoroni conflict cluster. Communities along the borderlines of Kisumu and Kericho collaborated with each other to ensure recovery of stolen animals and returning them to their rightful owners. One such example:

> *"Following the incident where animals were stolen and one person killed, as a community we all resolved that whenever stolen cattle is reported to have crossed to our area, we must search, find and return so that we breed good relationship with our neighbors and this has improved the relationship between us Kalenjins and our neighboring communities. As a chief, am ensuring that this is being enforced across the borders by members of the community and peace committees."* (community chief in KII).

5.6   ICTs Enabling Networking and Collaboration to Support Governance

ICTs facilitated the creation of a strong collaborative relations between the community members and the security agencies especially police. This trust emerged as a result of the sharing of information useful for each other. As there was increased flow of information between the community and the police, some of the barriers to trust were mitigated. According to one focus group discussion, earlier there used to be high level of mistrust between the police and the community members who feared intimidation. For example, a retired officer commanding a police division narrated,

> *"most junior officers are weak and can leak the information in regard to secret reports – thus they can easily pass over classified information that is so confidential to the criminals. They also tend to ask irrelevant questions such as how many criminals did you see? Which clothes were they wearing? For example, upon recovery of a cow, a civilian may not be interested to follow up the case in court due*

to such useless questions. Some policemen still threaten residents with penalties of being locked up. Such questions and threats are intimidating and scared members of the public from reporting. "(community member in FGD).

The above statement describes the constraining conditions that had previously affected the relationship between the police and community members, and the laxity of the police in responding to community distress calls. This constraining condition was reduced with the introduction of the EWERS with its inbuilt features of anonymization. Police officers from across the conflict divide now networked and jointly responded to the alerts. The EWERS helped in fast reporting which enhanced quick response from the police and other security teams leading to increased recovery of stolen livestock. Such response actions helped enhance trust between the police and community. The EWERS contributed to transformative changes in security management approaches, and the police started attending community forums such as church functions, organized seminars, and public security forums to interact directly with the public. They also started inviting some members of the public to give motivational talks to the members of the police force. In the same vein, through public and other community meetings, police officers educated the community on case reporting investigation processes and their respective roles and responsibilities. This resulted in greater bonding between the police and community leaders leading to improved reporting from the community which supported relevant and effective response. This attracted many community members to report accurately and boldly, as narrated by some key informants;

"The system helped to improve the image of the police as we sat together and shared challenges with the community leaders. The interaction of security teams at public meetings and community dialogues enhanced understanding among the parties. Through these meetings, more light was shed on best way of reporting, as a result, the senior officers agreed to share their numbers for reporting and further interaction with members of the community." (OCPD Mogere, KII). *"I was a policeman in Mount Elgon before retirement and it used to be rough due to absence of technology. Any information that was not IT- based was being leaked. Indeed, the area chief was killed due to absence of confidentiality. The EWERS enables pro-activeness from the security agencies which results in quick action and apprehension of criminals. The recent killings in Matungu Sub-County, Kakamega County almost extended to Bumula Sub-County in Bungoma County had it not been reports in the EWERS revealing actors behind threatening leaflets. While working as a policeman in Mount Elgon, I was threatened by criminals several times but the relay of information through the EWERS system always saved me."* (community member in FGD)

5.7   ICT as an Enabler of Accountability in Conflict Situations

The study established that the integration of EWERS in violence prevention process contributed to increased accountability of the government leaders especially the chiefs and the security personnel who were now expected to respond effectively raised security alerts. When the system relayed information to the police and local administration, the same was also sent to their concerned superiors who could hold them to account. Initially, most of the reported cases to local authorities were ignored or being silenced. Increased accountability helped to enhance trust building between community members and government administration. The trust between the government officials like Assistant Chiefs, Chiefs, Assistant County Commissioners and general members of the public improved due to the frequent interactions during response efforts to message alerts from the system. The trust was demonstrated in the ongoing levels of consultation and the inclusion of community members in key meetings. The Chiefs and their assistants regularly held consultative meetings with community leaders to deal with emerging issues, which has helped enhance transparency in how they were addressed cases of violence. For example:

> *"There is increased interaction between chiefs from Kalenjin side and chiefs from Luo side unlike before when we never used to work together. We collaborate especially on matters related to cattle theft and land and boundary disputes to ensure the two communities coexist peacefully. Whenever cattle theft has occurred on the Luo side and thieves are believed to be crossing to the Kalenjin side, the chiefs from the Luo side will inform the chiefs from the Kalenjin side and with their concerted efforts, the cattle are recovered. The same happens when there is boundary dispute, chiefs from both side would organize public barazas to address the issue."* (Chief Opiyo- KII). *"I received alert messages from the system complaining about the laxity of chiefs to respond to distress calls from the community members. To deal with these, I directed all chiefs in the region to establish security committees that will respond to distress calls within 5 mins. I have made sure this is enforced leading to improved relationship between the community and the administration."* (community member in KII).

6   Case Analysis

Our case highlights the different ways in which ICT contributed to increase trust and reciprocity within the social networks both in Muhoroni and Mt. Elgon clusters.

6.1   ICT –Enabled Social Networks – Peace Network as New Forms of Social Capital

We found various new peace networks emerged with the increase in social capital resources for violence prevention. The EWERS created a platform where community members could connect with the administration and the security agencies to engage in a cycle of responses to conditions of insecurity. This represents a form of linking social capital guided by notions of social trust [25]. Similarly, [26] describe linking social capital as networks of trusting relationships between people interacting across explicit, formal or institutionalized power or authority gradients in society. These emerging networks were characterized by trust and reciprocity, key features of social capital. The networks enabled the setting up of a bottom-up approach to peacebuilding and security governance by linking local initiatives with national plans. These networks enabled mechanisms that allowed local initiatives to inform and influence national peacebuilding efforts, and help ground them to the needs and conditions of the local context. These means that the ICTs created encouraged positive synergies towards transformations in peacebuilding efforts. For example, these networks contributed to the cultivation of a culture of peace and advancing of reconciliation efforts between the community members and authorities. These linking mechanisms enabled the creation of values such as of accountability, transparency, responsiveness, and tolerance, all of which are fundamental in mitigating ethnic violence. The linking peace network was sustained by the reciprocity between the community members and the administration. The police started to respond promptly to the alert messages leading to the recoveries of animals while the community members became increasingly motivated to willingly share sensitive data with the security personnel. Communication among the entities helped to improve coordination and even understanding of the nature of crimes experienced in the areas, helping to establish both a structural and intellectual dimension social capital as it created knowledge, skills and capabilities to operate in new ways [14]. These dimensions helped motivate the performance of the police to enhance peace building efforts.

The integration of ICTs helped better connect the different warring communities. Intractable violence had previously polarized the social relationships among different ethnic groups. Firstly, it helped to create an inter-connected peace network involving the village elders, chiefs, security teams, youths, women leaders, elders and business people across different ethnic divides. This ICT-enabled network of actors collectively engaged to report and respond to conflict escalating concerns like cattle theft, land grabbing, gender-based violence, smuggling and trading in illicit arms, drug and alcohol abuse, prejudicial tendencies and robbery with violence. The relationship was previously characterised by mistrust, non-cooperation, ethnic alignments to religion, political parties and biased economic activities. This polarization was characterized by higher levels of bonding social capital as compared with bridging and linking capital. The communities were more inward looking and self-centred in their activities, and the transcending of these inter-ethnic divided contributed to the expansion of bridging social capital by reducing levels of individual commitment and building greater inter-community orientation for their mutual benefits. This trend, as [20] has argued, that increasing bridging social capital reduces bonding relations. However, in ethical and moral terms, the action that leads to the benefit of the larger populace should be privileged over actions benefitting a minority. Therefore, reduction in ethnic bonding social capital worked for the general peace and welfare of the majority including those previously excluded..

6.2   ICTs Contributed to the Growth of Trust and Reciprocity Within and Among Ethnic Communities

Our study points to the growth or expansion of trust and reciprocity in many different forms including inclusion of the minority, strengthening of economic cooperation, enhanced tolerance of diversity and commitment towards reconciliation efforts. All these represent foundational principles of violence mitigation.

Inclusion of Minority: The dominant community had used the bonding relationship to unite against the minority from being appointed to leadership positions. However, the EWERS provided a platform where some members who were against this mission to report and support the minority, gained a larger voice. This required an imbalance to be created between bonding and bridging social capital, for justice to be promoted. While the dominant community lost to a minority group, it was unethical when people belonging to a different ethnic group were treated like "others", and as victims of stereotypes and prejudice. This led to discrimination and social exclusion. The stigma associated with discrimination and exclusion burdens people both as individuals and members of particular communities. Those discriminated and excluded suffer from feelings of guilt, helplessness, incompetence and reduced communal worth.

Bridging economic relationship was created when markets opened up to accommodate the members from across ethnic divides who had otherwise been denied such access. Within the bonding framework, individuals and communities had restricted freedoms in terms of interactions with other community members because of norms, values and cultural practices. [27] has argued that freedom or independence from being constrained by another's choice, the freedom of choice, is an innate human right. This freedom is to be respected and promoted, even when this choice is not exercised in rational or virtuous activities [27]. The use of the ICT application helped unlock the bonds to freedom of community members, and trusting relationships were developed with the growth of inter-ethnic economic partnerships, and the simultaneous weakening of bonding relationships.

Increase in Values of Tolerance of Diversity: A fundamental value for human beings to peacefully coexist is tolerance of diversity. The integration of EWERS in violence prevention contributed to increase in tolerance and acceptance of different people, values, and beliefs through contacts with diverse others leading to the growth in bridging relationships. This enhanced level of tolerance and acceptance amongst protagonist communities followed the increased flow of information between them and to external stakeholders.

Reciprocity as a Key Factor of Reconciliation: In this case, the act of returning the stolen animals to their rightful owners negated the value of cooperation for mutual benefit as those who survived on stolen animals may feel betrayed. However, analysing these consequences through Bentham's principle of utility, that the morally right action is the one that produces the best overall consequences with regard to the utility or welfare of all the affected parties (Crimmins, J. E., 2020). Within this framework, the results from the use of the EWERS can be justified.

7 Conclusions and Contributions

This paper concludes that ICT-integrated micro-based violence prevention systems that build on existing social capital mechanisms are effective in addressing ethnic based conflicts as they help offer local solutions to local problems. The study further concludes that the effectiveness or not of such ICT enabled efforts are well understood within a social capital framework and their means of bonding, linking and bridging. The study reinforces [24] argument that the networks that constitute social capital also serve as conduits for the flow of helpful information that can facilitate achieving goals for peaceful coexistence. The empirical evidence has demonstrated that ICTs facilitated the formation of peace networks in the conflicting communities that enabled the effective flow of information thereby contributing to reduce animosity.

The study concurs with [24] have argued that for social capital to contribute to the peacebuilding process or conflict management, there must be a balance of bonding, bridging and linking social capital. Many examples from the empirical study showed that in areas with stronger bonding social capital and weak bridging and linking social capital, injustices like discrimination of minorities in leadership, denial of access to markets and opportunities and exclusion thrive. The study shows that whenever bonding social capital reduces, there is a corresponding increase in bridging and linking social capital, leading to peace, new markets, new resources and opportunities. The study also demonstrates how ICTs can contribute in bringing better balance between these different forms of social capital.

The study concludes that for peacebuilding strategies to be effective in contributing to sustainable peace, the functional elements of social capital need to be factored in the design phase and monitored in the implementation process. The social networks form critical foundations through which violence can be pacified or assuaged. Social capital therefore cannot be assumed to always act as a glue, since it can also function as a source of tension

The paper contributes to ICT for Peace (ICT4P) research and more broadly to the domain of ICT4D. In addition, the paper contributes to ICT-enabled peacebuilding efforts that seek to strengthen linkages between state and non-state actors. The key vehicle for building these contributions comes from the adoption of the theoretical lens of social capital to study peace building efforts and the manner in which ICTs can mediate this relationship. The study demonstrates the inter-relation between the three forms of social capital, and how ICTs can mediate these relationships. For ICT4D researchers, there are implications for the design and development of bridging social capital be enabling the flow of information across ethnic divides. Building in robust features of anonymization of the field monitor's identity was an important device that promoted bridging. Enhanced bridging can lead to reduced bonding, with positive consequences on peace building efforts.

While this study has focused on particular conditions of violence in Northwestern Kenya, we believe our study also provides more generalizable finding for peace building efforts in other contexts. The social capital lens can be useful in diagnosing the underlying reasons for violence and in understanding how ICTs can be designed and implemented in a manner which reduces the reasons promoting violence and enhancing those that can potentially build more trust and mutual reciprocity across the warring groups.

References

1. Torbjörnsson, D.: Managing Communal Conflict in Africa (2016)
2. Horowitz, D.L.: Ethnic Groups in Conflict, Updated Edition with a New Preface. University of California Press, Berkeley (2000)
3. Brosché, J., Elfversson, E.: Communal conflict, civil war, and the state: complexities, connections, and the case of Sudan. Afr. J. Conflict Resolut. 12(1), 9–32 (2012)
4. Rohwerder, B.: Conflict analysis of Kenya. GSDRC University of Birmingham, Birmingham (2015)

5. Mbugua, J.K.: Inter-communal conflicts in Kenya: The real issues at stake in the Tana Delta (Issues Briefs N. 1). International Peace Support Training Centre, Nairobi (2013)
6. Kelly, L.: Uses of digital technologies in managing and preventing conflict (2019)
7. Perera, S.: To boldly know: knowledge, peacekeeping and remote data gathering in conflict-affected states. Int. Peacekeeping 24(5), 803–822 (2017)
8. Convergne, E., Snyder, M.R.: Making maps to make peace: geospatial technology as a tool for UN peacekeeping. Int. Peacekeeping 22(5), 565–586 (2015)
9. Berman, E., Felter, J.H., Shapiro, J.N.: Small Wars, Big Data: The Information Revolution in Modern Conflict. Princeton University Press, Princeton (2020)
10. Pierskalla, J., Fox, J., Vüllers, J., Strüver, G., Basedau, M.: Does discrimination breed grievances-and do grievances breed violence?: New evidence from an analysis of religious minorities in developing countries. Conflict Manag. Peace Sci. 34(3), 217–239 (2017)
11. Weidmann, N.B.: Communication networks and the transnational spread of ethnic conflict. J. Peace Res. 52(3), 285–296 (2015)
12. Haider, H.: Conflict: topic guide. Revised edition with B. Rohwerder. GSDRC, University of Birmingham, Birmingham (2014)
13. Lin, N.: Building a network theory of social capital. Connections 22(1), 28–51 (1999)
14. Coleman, J.S.: Social capital in the creation of human capital. Am. J. Sociol. 94, S95–S120 (1988)
15. Putnam, R.: The prosperous community: Social capital and public life. The American prospect, 13(Spring), vol. 4 (1993). http://www.prospect.org/print/vol/13. Accessed 7 April 2003
16. Yang, S., Lee, H., Kurnia, S.: Social capital in information and communications technology research: past, present, and future. Commun. Assoc. Inf. Syst. 25(1), 23 (2009)
17. Luhmann, N.: Law as a social system. Nw. UL Rev. 83, 136 (1988)
18. Nahapiet, J., Ghoshal, S., Goshal, S.: Social capital, intellectual capital, and the organizational advantage. Acad. Manag. Rev. 23(2), 242–266 (1998)
19. Grootaert, C.: On the relationship between empowerment, social capital and community driven development. World Bank Working Paper, (33074) (2003)
20. Narayan, D.: Bonds and bridges: Social capital and poverty (Vol. 2167). World Bank, Poverty Reduction and Economic Management Network, Poverty Division, Washington DC (1999)
21. Putnam, R.D.: Bowling Alone: The Collapse and Revival of American Community. Simon and Schuster, New York (2000)
22. Helliwell, J.F., Putnam, R.D.: The social context of well–being. Philos. Trans. R. Soc. Lond. Ser. B Biol. Sci. 359(1449), 1435–1446 (2004)
23. Goodhand, J.: Sri Lanka: NGOs and peace-building in complex political emergencies. Third World Q. 20(1), 69–87 (1999)
24. Coletta, N.J.: I Cullen (2000)
25. Putnam, R.D.: Bowling alone: America's declining social capital. J. Democracy 6, 65–78 (1995a)
26. Szreter, S., Woolcock, M.: Health by association? Social capital, social theory, and the political economy of public health. Int. J. Epidemiol. 33(4), 650–667 (2004)
27. Rauscher, F.: Kant's social and political philosophy (2007)

What Will the Future of Work Look like for IS Professionals? The Picture of Portugal

Anabela Mesquita[1,2(✉)], Ana Paula Camarinha[3], Filomena Castro Lopes[4], and Pedro Malta[5]

[1] Polytechnic of Porto, Porto, Portugal
sarmento@iscap.ipp.pt
[2] Algoritmi RC, Minho University, Guimarães, Portugal
[3] Centro de Estudos Organizacionais e Sociais do Politécnico do Porto, CEOS.PP, Polytechnic of Porto - ISCAP, Porto, Portugal
apteixeira@iscap.ipp.pt
[4] Research on Economics, Management and Information Technologies – REMIT, Univ Portucalense, Porto, Portugal
flopes@upt.pt
[5] NOVA Information Management School (NOVA IMS), Universidade Nova de Lisboa, Centro Algoritmi, Universidade do Minho, Braga, Portugal
pmalta@novaims.unl.pt

Abstract. Many professions, in the most diverse sectors of activity, have undergone great changes over time, largely due to the responsibility of technological evolution.

The rapid evolution of information technologies will, certainly imply, that employment in general and employment in Information Systems (IS), in particular, undergoes major changes both in terms of creating new professions and even for the extinction of others, as indeed it has already happened when professions such as telephone operators, typists, telegram distributors, typographers and even encyclopedias sellers disappeared.

The purpose of this article is to analyze the changes that can be expected in employment in IS for 2030 - how will work in IS be: what professions will be extinguished, which ones must adapt to the new reality and what the need for professions that do not yet exist.

After a review of the literature on the evolution of employment in IS over the years, realizing the trends of its evolution, a guide was elaborated for semi-structured interviews that were used in meetings with 6 (six) Portuguese organizations, in order to list their perceptions of the changes that are expected in the very near future.

From the analysis of results, it will be possible to have a clearer idea of the changes that are already occurring today, as well as what still needs to be changed. This answer will allow us to reflect on how to prepare tomorrow's professionals, in IS, for the job market in 2030.

Keywords: IS employment · Employment trends · Technical skills · Socio-behavioural skills

© IFIP International Federation for Information Processing 2020
Published by Springer Nature Switzerland AG 2020
R. K. Bandi et al. (Eds.): IFIPJWC 2020, IFIP AICT 601, pp. 341–358, 2020.
https://doi.org/10.1007/978-3-030-64697-4_25

1 Introduction

Due to technologies, we are witnessing great developments in society and organizations. Besides the changes being visible in the business models, in communication and collaboration, in the relationship between working and private life, in the structure and organizational hierarchies, technologies are also impacting the employment itself. This scenario requires citizens and employees to master the technologies as they constitute a fundamental pillar for any organization. In this changing context, employment in general, is a subject that deserves attention. As such, it is necessary to have a clear idea of the transformations that are taking place in order to be able to project trends, specifically with regard to the technical and socio-behavioral functions that support citizens' skills. Previous studies on the area of IS [4, 6, 7, 9] show that the skills required to carry out the different IS jobs have changed over time. According to Cheney et al. [6] job skills obsolescence has been a common topic of interest for many years. Some studies [2, 5, 6] have been carried out with the aim of anticipating which skills are more likely to be necessary for future employment. In this regard, there is no reason why the particular case of IS employment should be an exception. And by IS professionals, we understand those being experts in developing, applying, modifying, and strategizing technology to digitally change organizations. IS professionals work with other business professionals including computer scientists and engineers to create platforms that integrate digital technologies to design solutions that solve organizational problems [10, 18].

The youngsters who entered school in 2010 will be professionals in the decade of 2030. In the IS area, it is certainly expected this employment to be different from today as a result of various alterations being observed, such as technological evolution, globalization, and demographic change. The professions, and the skills to be displayed, should be in line with the needs of the 2030 labor market. Thus, it is necessary to understand the context where these changes are taking place, to have a clear picture of how we got here and the possible trends for the next 10 years. This should cover a complete and thorough understanding about the scientific knowledge, technical and soft skills that should be developed by each student during his education and training. While there is no consensus on how to categorize these different types of specific skills, in this work we will consider two different broad types of skills: technical skills and socio-behavioural sills. The former are often associated with disciplinary knowledge, while the latter are sometimes alternatively referred to as soft skills or individual foundation skills [9].

Knowing in advance what are the changes that might happen in a certain profession, will allow educational institutions to be ready and better prepared to educate and train students for a future that no one knows how it will be, by updating curricula and contents, more adequate for the uncertain moments we will face. And as changes do not take place all over the world at the same time and in the same way, we will focus our research in Portugal.

This article is structured as follows: the next section presents a historical evolution of IS employment followed by a perspective on the future of work in this area, together with a reference to the Structuration Theory that guided us in this research. The Methodology section presents the procedures used to collect data. Section 4 presents and discusses the results. Finally, we draw some conclusions, refer the limitations of the study and comments for future research.

2 State of the Art

2.1 History of the IS Employment

Although the IS area does not yet take us to go back many decades, employment in IS has changed over its short existence and is expected to continue to change [1].

In this section we look at the evolution of IS employment in the last 50 years. This historical overview shall help us understand the relationship between the main trends in IS employment over this period, as well as its transformation in terms of skills, from a merely technical to a more diversified set of skills.

In the 1970–80s, IS professionals were required to have strong technical skills and a very specialized nature for professions such as functional analyst, organic analyst, programmer, or systems administrator. These professionals, specialized and with funnelled disciplinary knowledge, worked in "islands" with some capacity for dialogue and professional understanding with the "side island". We lived in a phase in which the paradigm in which we believed, and which we followed, in the IS development, was the 'waterfall model'. Each professional performed a specific function at a certain stage in the cascade, thus narrowing the scope of their technical knowledge.

In the 1990s, IS professionals were also required to have business and organizational knowledge, in addition to their technological knowledge. This change coincided with the evolution of the IS role in organizations, from being seen as simply automating activities/functions to being seen as something that adds value to the business. Then, we started talking about other professions, such as systems analyst, IS project manager and database administrator.

Continuing the temporal crossing through IS employment, it can be said that in the last years, in addition to technological, management, and business knowledge the importance of socio-behavioural skills has become more widely acknowledged. Namely, teamwork, time management, communication, leadership, and conflict management, which begin to be evaluated and appreciated by employers. This is a period when the need for highly funnelled technological knowledge begins to decrease due to the growth of team projects, where different professionals dialogue with each other in the common attempt to solve a problem. In this context business analyst, CIO (Chief Information Officer) emerged as new IS professions.

There has been notable growth in the recognition of other behavioural competencies, such as creativity and critical thinking. This is not surprising since IS is beginning to be seen as a lever for innovation, and the concept of digital transformation has become commonplace. At the same time, there has been a rapid growth in new information technologies, which translates into the emergence of new professions, such as that of data analyst. Moreover, there is also a fragmentation of the programmer profession into a web, multimedia, and DevOps programmer.

However, the current need for rapid IS developments, coupled with the growth in the use of agile methodologies, has led to the integration of the function of systems analyst, requirements engineer, programmer, and tester. This means that IS professionals are now required to have a comprehensive range of technical skills which before were distributed among different specialized professionals.

Thus, it can be observed that, over time, the path of increasing specialization/funnelling of the skills of IS professionals has not taken place in terms of technological knowledge. On the contrary, there is an evolution towards increasingly broad requirements, in a multitude of technological, management, and business knowledge, also accompanied by an increase in the demands for socio-behavioural skills.

2.2   What Does the Literature Says About the Future of Employment in IS

It will be, at least partially, a futurology work, to identify the IS professions for 2030. Nevertheless, according to the market vision, it is recognized that information technology will be increasingly present at all organizational levels supporting and even replacing, some of the current professions [2].

We are all aware that some professions will disappear due to the growing presence of information technologies in organizations, but for the same reason, new ones will appear. Human beings, although they like to live in good conditions, which implies less work, more free time, and more profitability - factors where technology can act and contribute positively - will not, however let themselves be overcome by the machine [19]. Intelligence systems, among other emerging technologies, may seem frightening, particularly when associated with the forecasts for the evolution of employment until 2030. These technologies may lead us to fear that employment will disappear, become obsolete and replaced by robots, sensors, machine learning, chatbots, ... Certainly, improving living conditions will involve fewer hours of work, more free time, remote work, and an increase in productivity, aspects on which information technologies can and should contribute positively. Anyway, it is hardly believable that all human work can be replaced by machines [3], even if it has to be better prepared to witness significant changes, with ever shorter cycles [21].

According to the World Economic Forum [2] in general, an increase in employment in math and computer-related employment households, a moderate decline in manufacturing, and a large decline in jobs related to administrative work are expected in the next years. In addition, and more transversally, disruptive changes in industry and business models will also affect the quality and skills needed to perform any kind of task.

The analysis of several studies, such as Burns, et al. [4–10], reveals that talking about employment in 2030 is recognizing a set of skills necessary for people to contribute to and benefit from an inclusive and sustainable future. It is not unreasonable to recognize the growing importance of technical skills associated with the area of STEM (science, technology, engineering, and mathematics). However, competencies such as adaptability, creativity, collaboration, curiosity, autonomy, reconciliation of tensions, social responsibility, and ethics will also be needed. In parallel, accepting that the different areas will be increasingly supported by technologies means that it will also be necessary for IS professionals to be able to work in an interdisciplinary context. Thus, one is led to think that, in addition to the technical skills in the area of technologies, and in addition to the socio-behavioural competencies, these professionals should accumulate thematic skills, related to the specific areas in which they will exercise their activities (e.g. health, agriculture, law).

It is expected that IS professionals will be required to have, in the future, technical skills in areas such as digital experience, analytics, cloud, virtual reality, blockchain, cognitive technologies. One cannot forget that the information technologies that may have an important role and impact in business and society in general, is transitory, rapidly changing, being necessary to have skills allowing people to act, if possible, in a proactive and creative way, in this new digital world in constant change. However, literature also points to the future need for non-SI professionals to have more and more technological skills.

In a recent study provided by Blue [11], there are 5 things we need to know about the future of work: 1) technological skills will continue to dominate tomorrow's jobs; 2) human skills are still important; 3) with the evolution of jobs, women are locked out; 4) there is an untapped talent to fill the gaps in emerging jobs; and 5) networks still matter.

According to the Internet of Business [12], the IS jobs that will endure in the coming years are those related to data analysis, artificial intelligence and machine learning specialists, innovation and digital transformation experts, robotics professionals, user experience and interaction designers, process automation experts - all roles that machines will have difficulty replicating.

According to the Business Insider [13], the 13 (thirteen) best technology professions in the future are web developer, mobile applications developer, change manager, business intelligence analyst, change consultant (transformation consultant), data engineer, machine learning designer, software developer, business intelligence architect or developer, designer, developer or not engineer, cyber security engineer or analyst, network engineer or architect, security management specialist.

As can be seen from the above analysis, the trends are not conclusive, however, they all point to a different picture of IS skills and professions. In addition, taking into account the profiles and professions that seem to emerge, one can speak of a multidisciplinary range of competencies, pointing to the need to prepare "supermen", as mentioned by Nascimento [14].

Although in Portugal it continues to have one of the lowest percentages of professionals with specialized skills in Information and communications technology (ICT) in total employment and the number of the ICT graduates is low by EU standards [29], the trends within IS employment itself have followed the global trends.

To be sure, several studies have been recently published about digital skills, 21st century skills, e-competences, and the changing nature of work in the digital age, exploring what this may entail for the future of jobs and the labour market [2, 6, 8–10, 20–22, 28]. However, no significant research contributions of a similar nature can be found for the specific area of IS employment. This study offers a first contribution to start filling in this gap.

2.3 Structurational Model of Technology

Over the last decades there have been several the development of several lens through which one could look into an organization. The models of Technological Imperative and the Strategic Choice represented the two opposing ends of a continuum. The contribution of Giddens (1984) [30] allowed the emergence of another model, proposing an integrative meta-theory – the theory of structuration. This theory recognizes and accommodates both the subjective and objective dimensions of social reality and considers the duality and dependence of structure and action. Moreover, it also suggests that human actions simultaneously condition and are conditioned by institutional properties in social contexts. According to the Structuration Theory, organizational change is the joint effect of the actions of individuals interacting with institutional structures which enable and constrain the daily actions and thought processes of people, but do not completely determine them. People's choices are not independent of the structures where they take place as they can maintain, reinforce, change or destroy them. This interplay is seen as the duality of structure and is the basis that changes are not completely predictable.

Later, based on this theory, Orlikowski (1992) [31] proposed the Structurational Model of Technology, in which the dual nature of Information Technology (IT) is at the heart of the structuration process. As such, organizations are not only shaped by IT but they are also influenced by social and political processes and by the actions of members of the organizations. This theory comprises the following elements: a) human agents – technology designers, users and decision makers, b) technology – material artifacts, mediating task execution in the workplace and c) institutional properties of organizations, including organizational dimensions such as structural arrangements, business strategies, ideology, culture, control mechanisms, standard operating procedures, division of labor, expertise, communication patterns, as well as environmental pressures. This theory can be synthetized in the Fig. 1.

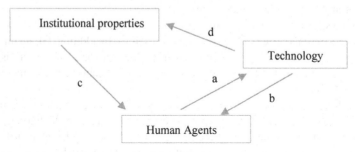

Fig. 1. Structurational model of technology Source: Orlikowski (1992) [31]

Technology is the product of human action (arrow a) and it comes into existence through human action and is sustained by human action through the ongoing maintenance and adaptation of technology. Moreover, human action constitutes technology through using it. This means that once created, technology is only given meaning when is manipulated by humans. It is only through appropriation of technology by humans that it plays a significant role.

Technology is the medium of human action (arrow b), because when it is used, it mediates the activities. One needs to be aware and recognize that technology cannot determine social practices. Human agency is always needed to use technology and this implies the possibility of choosing to act otherwise. Thus technology can only condition social practices by enabling and constraining them which are, by their turn, dependent on multiple factors.

One influence concerns the nature of human actions in organizations, which is situated action, and hence shaped by the organizational context (arrow c). When acting on technology, human agents are influenced by the institutional properties of their setting as they draw on existing knowledge, resources and norms to perform their work.

The final influence is related with the way in which human action, while using the technology, acts upon the institutional properties of an organization (arrow d), either by reinforcing them or by transforming them. The construction and use of technology is conditioned by an organization's structures of signification, domination and legitimation. The appropriation and use of technology implies the change or reinforcement of these structures and these effects are not, usually, reflected on by users. When users conform to the technology's embedded rules and resources, they are sustaining the institutional structures in which technology is deployed.

In the model proposed, structuration is seen as a dynamic process. While the main components and relationships are stable, their range, power and content will vary over time. Moreover, it is also considered to be a dialectical process as it assumes that their elements will interact recursively.

In the context of the present research it is possible to see that there is an appropriation of technology by organizations with a certain objective. Due to the characteristics of the technology, these have the power (in the sense of "possibility") to change the way people work and as such, their jobs as the processes and structures change accordingly. However, as also evident from the Model, these changes will be filtered (enabled or constrained) by the users, which are influenced, direct or indirectly by the characteristics of the organization, including its culture. According to this, it will be very difficult to point clear direction for the future of the IS job (as many factors are involved, including the interaction that will be established between the agents and the technology, mediated by the institutional properties). Yet, one can describe the present moment and draw some lines for the future, assuming that no other factors will influence this dynamic.

3   Research Methodology

After the identification of the main keywords taking into consideration the research question and the objectives, the work proceeded with the literature review which was based on a set of academic articles accessed via electronic databases (b-on) and, due to the nature of this investigation, also on articles prepared by management consultancies and international organizations, accessed online. The literature review allowed the preliminary identification of the major trends regarding employment in IS in Portugal for the future and the collection of information to be applied in complementary data collection techniques in order to further specify and characterize these trends and draw conclusions. Even so, there is no list of standard technical and socio-behavioural skills: the final list used in the interview guide is a compilation of the comparison of the lists found in research work carried out.

Based on the objectives to achieve in this research, the qualitative approach seemed to be the most appropriate methodology to adopt to further understand the phenomenon under study [15]: "… qualitative research aims a broader understanding of the phenomena". On one hand, the qualitative approach involves those who experience the phenomenon, in this case, those who deal with different human resources in the IS area; on the other, it allows the collection of information with the objective of obtaining all possible data, through the use of an adequate set of sources such as interviews (our main source of data collection), observations, of those involved (in this case, those dealing with employment in IS) [16].

Moreover, the case study method, often used in qualitative research, proved to be, also, the most appropriate methodology. It enables the researcher to answer "how" and "why" type questions [17] while studying how a phenomenon is influenced by the context within which it is situated. Case study research is compatible with the analysis of a broad range of data sources such as: documentation, archival records, interviews, physical artifacts, direct observations, and participant-observation. In this research, we relied on interviews to collect data. Content analysis was used to analyze data as it is referred, in the literature, as credible (Zhang and Wildemuth 2005) [32], with the consistency of the study process and the way of documenting, and also regarding the exposure of data that can be confirmed by third parties, readers and/or future reviewers.

Despite the literature review revealing the existence of some studies already carried out, we developed a set of questions and concerns based on the comparison of the lists found in research work conducted by other authors (as referred) which lead to the development of a script to be used in the semi-structured interviews: as we created the list of technical and socio-behavioural skills based on the studies found in research, we eliminated repeated assignments, to build the final sequence; for the professions the research focused in papers and in employability sites.

These questions allowed us to gather opinions about technical and socio-behavioural competencies, and to identify trends in Employment in IS in Portugal. In order to allow an interpretative analysis, we resort to staff from Portuguese business organizations linked to the areas of Recruitment and to Information Systems and Technologies, as these are respondents with more experience in this topic. The script guided the interviews made with the respondents to be mentioned: these are a useful means of data collection (in this case by the commented answers) as mentioned by Creswell (2003), [33] scientifically recognized (Castellan 2010) [34].

As said above, for the interviews, we identified respondents linked to the areas of Information Systems and Technologies and Recruitment from companies in different sectors. We contacted seven companies in Lisbon and four in Porto, but only four in Lisbon and two in Porto agreed to participate in the research (see Table 1):

The interviews took place in the interviewees' offices, and in the case of those that took place in Porto, the Human Resources Director was also present. After the interviews, the content was compiled on excel tables, and worked afterwards.

From the responses collected in the semi-structured interviews, it was possible to identify two evident broad categories: "Current IS Competencies" and "Future IS Competencies", to which were added the "Evolution of IS Competencies", the "Professions Issues" and the "Nature of Job Contracting" categories (see Table 2).

Table 1. Cases studies characterization

Sector	Role	Region
Food	Senior management with responsibility for human resource management	Lisbon
Information Systems and Technology	Senior management with responsibility for human resource management	Lisbon
Information Systems and Technology	Senior management with responsibility for managing team projects for its clients	Lisbon
Telecommunication Consultancy	Contractual functions in project management and its team	Lisbon
SPGS	Senior management with responsibility in the Information Systems area	Porto
Outsourcing in Information Systems Technologies	Managing Partners & Founder	Porto

Table 2. Competences category explained

Category	Purpose
Current IS Competencies	To identify current IS competencies using the lists prepared and exemplified in the script
Future IS Competencies	To identify future IS competencies using the lists prepared and exemplified in the script
Evolution of IS Competencies	To identify differences between current and future IS competencies listed in the script
Professions Issues	To identify job types, organization's areas, mastery degree of competences in actual and new collaborators and competences relevant in 2030
Professions Types	To identify which professions continuos to exist and the ones who disappear
Nature Job Contracting	To identify nature of job contracting

This work allowed us to identify the main contributions to the objectives of the research and for each category we can infer, in the light of the initial objectives, the information available after the interviews: the technique of propositional discourse analysis was applied to the interviews made [16].

In summary, after building the script and defining the number of respondents, the interviews reveal the views of those in the market about the current and future IS Competencies, as well as those that suggest adding as pertinent to the original list of the script and also relevant aspects about IS professions and forms of hiring. Analysis and results discussion is made in the next chapter.

4 Results and Discussion

This section presents the main results based on the 6 semi-structured interviews. The main objectives of the interview were i) to identify which are the most likely technical and socio-behavioural skills required to IS professionals in 2030 in comparison with those which are currently required, ii) to understand how the IS job is expected to change, and iii) to anticipate what new IS jobs may be created and, conversely, what IS jobs are likely to disappear. The section also discusses the main trends in IS employment till 2030 and, in this light, how to best prepare tomorrow's IS professionals.

4.1 Results

Regarding the current technical skills valued by the respondents, there was an unanimous reference to the importance of 8 of them, namely Data Analysis, Systems/business analysis, Analysis and evaluation of "user experience", Portfolio management, Project management, Risk management, Requirements identification and management, and Systems integration. However, in the case of the 2030 scenario, only one technical competence was referred by all the interviewees, namely Systems/business analysis.

Table 3 presents, for each technical skill initially considered, the number of respondents who chose it, taking into consideration its importance, now and in the future. The variation trend is also presented.

Table 3. Thecnical skills: Present and Future

Technical skills	Present	Future (2030)	Trend
DB administration and management	5	2	↓
Algorithmics	5	3	↓
Data Analysis	6	5	↓
System/business analysis	6	6	→
Analysis and evaluation of "user experience"	6	5	↓
Business and enterprise architecture	3	3	→
Network design and support	4	3	↓
Portfolio management	6	4	↓
Project management	6	5	↓
Risk management	6	5	↓
IS Governance	5	5	→
Requirements identification and management	6	4	↓
IT infrastructure	5	4	↓
Systems installation	3	3	→

(continued)

Table 3. (*continued*)

Technical skills	Present	Future (2030)	Trend
Systems integration	6	5	↓
Digital Marketing	2	3	↑
Mathematics	5	3	↓
Business and systems modelling	5	4	↓
Monitoring emerging technologies	4	3	↓
Software programming	4	3	↓
Information security	5	4	↓
Software systems	4	5	↑
Standards	1	1	→
Software tests	4	2	↓

Legend: ↓ decrease; ↑ Increase; → stable

When requested to order these skills by importance, both in the present and future outlooks, one company did not respond, and two others only did so for the 12 skills that they considered to be the most important. In any case, each of the companies where the interviews were made, identified a different skill as the most important one.

Seventeen new technical skills were added to the original list by the respondents; however, only one skill was identified by 2 different companies, this being Artificial Intelligence. Each of the other skills was added by a single company only. It was also noted that only three of these skills (Rapid Application Development, Continuous integration/delivery, Product management) were considered necessary today, but not for 2030. The justification for the need of these skills is associated with market trends, namely greater storage of data in the cloud, the growth of agile development and new technologies (such as artificial intelligent, predictive analysis, low code, services in demand, simplification of software development, application portability) already in use but expected to expand further in the future. However, the companies interviewed did not reveal unanimity in their responses. Responding companies also revealed that technical skills will be needed at all levels and functional areas of organizations and not only in the areas of software design/development.

When it comes to socio-behavioural skills (Table 4), it was found that 8 of these were listed by all companies as relevant today, but only 4 were expected to remain important in the future, namely Openness to opinions, Critical thinking, Problem solving and the Ability to listen.

Regarding the ranking of these socio-behavioural skills in terms of relative importance, both in the present and in the future, one of the companies did not respond. However, for each of those that responded, the rank for the importance of the socio-behavioural skills in the present was: Abstraction, Leadership, Collaboration, Assessment of the performance of oneself and others and Problem solving, with each of

Table 4. Socio-behavioural skills: Present and Future

Socio-behavioural skills	Present	Future (2030)	Trend
Openness to opinions	6	6	→
Abstraction	4	4	→
Adaptability	6	4	↓
Lifelong learning	4	3	↓
Assessment of the performance of oneself and others	6	4	↓
Collaboration	5	5	→
Written and oral communication	4	3	↓
Coordination	4	5	↑
Creativity	5	3	↓
Risk Management	5	5	→
Identification of new opportunities	5	5	→
Emotional intelligence	6	5	↓
Leadership	4	4	→
Critical Thinking	6	6	→
Systemic Thinking	5	5	→
Persuasion	5	4	↓
Problems Solving	6	6	→
Putting oneself into someone else's shoes	5	5	→
Ability to listen	6	6	→
Decision-making	5	5	→
Transmitting knowledge	6	5	↓

Legend: ↓ decrese; ↑ Increase; → stable

these skills having been singled out by a different company. Regarding future socio-behavioural skills, two companies gave greater importance to the Abstraction, and the remaining three chose each a different skill, namely Adaptability, Assessment of the performance of oneself and others, and Leadership. Only in one case was the ranking increased; the company that currently considers Problem solving as the most relevant socio-behavioural skills considers that, by 2030, it will be Adaptability.

Nine socio-behavioural skills were added to the original lists. It is observed that each company added different skills; however, only one company added skills which it considered would be needed for 2030 but were not yet needed today. These are: Interpersonal relationship and Strategic vision with interest/knowledge of the business in which one operates. The remaining skills added by the other respondents as needed today are also listed as important for 2030, namely: Entrepreneurship, Social responsibility/sustainability, Conflict management, Negotiation skills, Assertiveness, Learning from failures, Initiative and Proactivity. One company justifies the need to add other socio-behavioural skills due to market trends. Another company justifies that all technical skills (except skills in standards) combined with the socio-behavioural skills listed in the interview guide, plus two skills that they added to that list (Interpersonal relationship and Strategic vision and knowledge of the business in which it operates) will comprise the main characteristics of the IS professional of the future.

In general, the companies interviewed consider that technical skills are reasonably well-developed today in IS professionals; however, socio-behavioural ones could be better exploited. Companies emphasize that technical skills will remain important but will tend to lose ground to socio-behavioural skills, both becoming equally important in the future. A company considers that the employees' socio-behavioural skills will contribute to boost or constrain the development of technical skills; it is recognized that socio-behavioural skills are more difficult to change.

The Table 5 shows the number of responses for how companies anticipate the nature of IS employment in 2030 (1 unlikely to 5 very likely).

Table 5. The IS employment in 2030

Nature/Degree probability	No answer	1	2	3	4	5
Self-employed (individual)				2	1	3
Employment contract			1	4	1	
Part time	1		1	1	2	1
Full time	1		1	2	1	1
In the office			2	3	1	
Remote				1	3	2
Blended (in the office and remote)				1	3	2
Job for young people	1			1	3	1
Job for seniors (with several years of experience)					2	4

Regarding the 19 listed jobs, companies were asked to predict which ones are more likely to disappear by 2030 and why. Fifty percent of the respondent did not answer this question. The only jobs mentioned by more than one company were: Developer, Desktop or enterprise applications (3 companies), System administrator (2 companies) and Database administrator (2 companies). The jobs identified by a single company, were: Developer, full stack, Developer, back-end, Marketing or sales professional, Engineer, Site reliability, Data scientist or machine learning specialist and Chief information officer. The reasons given were the tendency of increasingly use the cloud, most of the systems being web, available as a service and the evolution from monolithic to simpler integrated systems.

As for the 5 jobs that they considered to be the most relevant, there is a trend towards the analytical component, which is now embedded in all employees (user experience), in the areas of security and integration. The importance, the security of information and systems, the holistic aspect of projects, and the digital transformation are the aspects pointed out as the reasons for the trend towards these professions in the future.

4.2 Discussion

This study suggests an almost generalized decrease of the importance, in the future, of those technical skills compiled through the review of the literature. However, this decrease is not significant. On the other hand, a new extended set of technical skills (17 in total) was advanced by the respondents, which attests the dynamic of the evolution of technological knowledge.

The growth of the cloud, accompanied by the progress of the automation and the artificial intelligence, will have repercussions in professions such as administrator and manager of data and network systems. Simultaneously, the market growth in the adoption of the so-called emerging technologies will justify the need for technical skills in the areas such as: Virtualization/Cloud, Automation/Artificial intelligence, Analytics/Business intelligence and Big Data.

Respondents recognize that the technical skills currently needed are, in general, reasonably well developed. However, there are still those who think they are lower than what is required. The dissatisfaction is greater when it comes to socio-behavioural skills, although there is the expectation that these skills will improve with younger generations. In any case, everyone agrees that by 2030, both technical and socio-behavioural skills will be required. In terms of socio-behavioural skills, there is a generalized growth in their importance and it is observed that four of them continue to be recognized as the most important ones: Openness to opinions, Critical thinking, Problem solving, and the Ability to listen. Among those listed, twelve socio-behavioural skills are expected to maintain their current importance, one is expected to become more important (Coordination), whereas eight are expected to become less important by 2030. Adaptability, Lifelong learning and Creativity, which are skills frequently associated with the so-called digital transformation era, showing a decrease in importance by 2030, even though one respondent considered Adaptability as the most important competence for 2030.

In addition, it is expected that the professional of IS will work remotely and that this professional will become a liberal one. There is no clear trend as to whether this will be a job for young people or for seniors, nor whether it will be carried out by full-time or part-time employees.

Finally, it should be noted that it is not possible to predict which are the five main IS professions. However, there is a trend towards security and systems integration. And, although It is also not possible to clearly identify which professions will have disappeared by 2030, the most likely candidates seem to be desktop developer, enterprise applications developer.

This study shows that information systems will increasingly become a commodity in organizations, where business and information systems and technologies will intertwine even more over time. Business professionals will start to develop their own systems and the development will be increasingly one of small systems that will be integrated with each other, according to the needs of its users. In this way, it is expected that the CIO, with the role and profile it currently has, will cease to exist, instead assuming a new, more diluted role within organizations, mainly concerned with organizational guidelines at the level of emerging technologies. These changes will be underpinned by the democratization of information technologies and low code tools. Consequently, even the profile of a system/business analyst, despite continuing to exist and playing an important role, will increasingly approach the end user owing to the need and importance of business knowledge.

Technical skills will remain important in the future, but they are not the only skills needed and may not even be the most needed skills. So, the IS curriculum must continue to offer three core types of skills as pointed by MSIS 2016 model graduate degree programs in Information Systems: Information Systems (i.e. technical) skills, individual foundational (i.e. socio-behavioural) skills, and skills in different domains of knowledge (predominantly business but also health, government, law, etc.).

Owing to constant technological evolution, the IS curriculum must be frequently reviewed so as to revise the technical skills it offers. This evolution also warns of the constant need for learning and developing new skills. So, the curriculum must be less rigid, offering flexible and elective modules, and more interdisciplinary, offering knowledge or practice in different knowledge domains.

In terms of socio-behavioural skills, the IS curriculum needs to continue to increase their relative importance. In addition, a more individual coaching and mentoring approach should be considered to help each future professional to develop the socio-behavioural skills that they need the most, and increase the use of problem-oriented learning methodologies, not only through internships in organisational context but also through the development of solutions for society and organizations

5   Conclusion and Future Research

The aim of this study was to have a perception of the trends regarding IS employment, towards 2030. In order to achieve the objectives of the research, a qualitative approach was used. A script was developed and experts from 6 different organizations were interviewed, allowing to obtain narrative summaries of the information collected through content analysis technique.

Results show that employment in IS will continue to last, opening up to new areas that do not yet exist, while, gradually, some professions with the profile and the name with which we currently know them, will subside and disappear. Automation will be a reality and will not only impact employment in other areas but will also promote changes in employment in IS. Automation will be used to reduce dependence on IT professionals, but the development of solutions will continue to grow. Moreover, information systems will increasingly become a commodity in organizations, where business and Information and systems technology (IST) will intertwine even more over time. Results also reveal that often, professionals with deep knowledge in a certain/specific area (technical, business, …) are also expected to have socio-behavioural skills.

Hybrid professional profiles are expected to grow in place of merely IS or IT profiles. This means that the "current" technologist will need more and more to raise requirements and the "current" business analyst will increasingly need to know about technologies.

IS employers recognize that the technical skills currently needed, in general, are reasonably well developed. However, there are still those who think they are lower than what is required. Regarding socio-behavioural skills, there is already a greater discontent, although believing that these will improve with the younger generations. Anyway, everyone agrees that in 2030, both technical and behavioural skills will be needed. In terms of the later, there is a generalized growth in their importance and it is observed that four of them continue to be recognized as the most important ones: Openness to opinions, Critical thinking, Problem solving and Ability to listen.

In addition, it is expected that within employment in IS there will be a trend towards distance work and for it to become a liberal profession. There is no clear trend as to whether this will be a job for young people or for seniors, nor whether it will be carried out by full-time or part-time employees.

Curricula within Universities must continually be adapted to the market needs. Organizations must blend traditional and new skills to effectively guide their organizations into the futures.

Finally, it should be noted that it is not possible to predict which are the five main IS professions. Anyway, there is a trend towards security and systems integration. It is also not possible to clearly identify which professions will disappear in 2030, however, the most likely candidates are developer, desktop, or enterprise applications.

As the limitations of this work, we would like to point out the fact that only experts, from 6 different organizations were interviewed. We strongly recommend the replication of this work, with more interviews and more organizations, from the IS sector and HR companies. Moreover, this study was carried out in Portugal, a small and peripherical country. As such, other studies should be done in other countries so we can have a clearer picture about the situation.

References

1. Pearlson, K.E., Saunders, C.S.: Managing Using Information Systems: A Strategic Approach. Wiley, Hoboken (2006)
2. World Economic Forum: The Future of Jobs Report (2018). http://www3.weforum.org/docs/WEF_Future_of_Jobs_2018.pdf. Accessed 26 May 2020
3. Vox: The big debate about the future of work (2017). https://newsvideo.su/video/7872482. Accessed 26 May 2020
4. Burns, T., Gao, Y., Sherman, C., Klein, S.: Do the Knowledge and Skills Required by employers of recent graduates of undergraduate information systems programs match the current ACM/AIS Information Systems Curriculum Guidelines? ISCAP (Information Systems and Computing Academic Professionals) (2018)
5. Teach Trends 2019 - Beyond the digital frontier, 10th anniversary edition. Deloitte Insights (2019)
6. Bakhshi, H., Downing, J.M., Osborne, M.A., Schneider, P.: The future of skills Employment in 2030, Pearson (2017). https://futureskills.pearson.com/research/assets/pdfs/technical-report.pdf. Accessed 26 May 2020
7. International Labor Organization: The future of work, Skills and Resilience for a World Change. European Political Strategy Centre Strategic Notes -Issue 13/2016, June 2016 (2016). https://www.skillsforemployment.org/KSP/en/Details/?dn=WCMSTEST4_176856. Accessed 26 May 2020

8. Dolphin, T.: Technology, Globalisation and the Future of Work in Europe Essays on Employment in a digitised economy. Institute for Public Research (2015). https://www.oxfordmar tin.ox.ac.uk/downloads/academic/technology-globalisation-future-of-work_Mar2015.pdf. Accessed 26 May 2020

9. OCDE: Future of education and Skills 2030 (2020). https://www.oecd.org/education/2030-project/teaching-and-learning/learning/. Accessed 26 May 2020

10. The World Bank: World Development Report 2019, The Changing Nature of Work, The World Bank (2019). https://www.worldbank.org/en/publication/wdr2019. Accessed 26 May 2020

11. Allen Blue: 5 Things we know about the jobs of the future. World Economic Forum, 24th January (2020). https://www.weforum.org/agenda/2020/01/future-jobs-and-skills-in-demand/. Accessed 26 May 2020

12. Middleton, C.: A.I will create 58 million jobs, decimate middle-class careers: World Economic Forum, Robotics, September 2018

13. Premack, R.: Information technology is one of the fastest-growing industries in America—here are the 13 best IT jobs of the future. Business Insider, June 2018

14. Nascimento, J.C.: Gestão e Sistemas de informação e os seus Profissionias. FCA, Lisboa (2006)

15. Fortin, M.-F., Côte, J., Filion, F.: Fondements et étapes du processus de recherché. Chenelière Éducation, Montreal, Canada (2006)

16. Bardin, L.: L'Analyse de contenu, Presses Universitaires de France, 5th edn., Edições 70 (1977). https://madmunifacs.files.wordpress.com/2016/08/anc3a1lise-de-contec3bado-laurence-bardin.pdf. Accessed 26 May 2020 (1977)

17. Yin, R.: Case Study Research. SAGE, London (2003)

18. Westfall, R.D.: An employment-oriented definition of the information systems field: an educator's view. J. Inf. Syst. Educ. **23** (2012). https://aisel.aisnet.org/cgi/viewcontent.cgi?article= 1187&context=jise. Accessed 30 July 2020

19. PwC: Workforce of the future, The competing forces shaping 2030 (2017). www.pwc.com/people

20. OECD: Measuring the Digital Transformation: A roadmap for the future. OECD Publishing, Paris (2019). https://www.oecd.org/publications/measuring-the-digital-transformation-9789264311992-en.htm. Accessed 30 July 2020

21. OECD: Preparing for the Changing Nature of Work in the Digital Era (2019). https://www.oecd.org/publications/measuring-the-digital-transformation-9789264311992-en.htm. Accessed 30 July 2020

22. Laar, E., Dijk, J., Deursen, A., Haan, J.: Determinants of 21st-century skills and 21st – century digital skills for workers: a systematic literature review. SAGE Open **10**(1), 1–14 (2020). https://doi.org/10.1177/2158244019900176

23. Cheney, P.H., Hale, D.P., Kasper, G.M.: Knowledge, skills and abilities of information systems professionals: past, present, and future. Inf. Manag. **19**(4), 237–247 (1990)

24. Osmani, M., Hindi, N., Al-Esmail, R., Weerakkody, V., Kapoor K., Eldabi, T.: Skills and attributes of IT graduates: evidence from employer's perspective. In: Twenty-Second Americas Conference of Information Systems, San Diego (2016)

25. ACM and AIS, IS 2010, curriculum Guidelines (2010). https://www.acm.org/binaries/con tent/assets/education/curricula-recommendations/is-2010-acm-final.pdf

26. ACM/AIS MSIS 2016 Task Force, MSIS 2016 Global Competency for graduate degree programs in Information Systems, 23 May 2017. https://doi.org/10.1145/3127597. Accessed 30 July 2020

27. Association for Information Systems and Temple University, Information Systems Job Index, Learn About Careers in Information Systems (2019)

28. CEN workshop agreement, European ICT professionals role profiles – Parte 1: 30 ICT profiles, August (2018)
29. European Commission: Indice de Digitalidade da Economia e da Sociedade (IDES) Relatório por pais de 2019, Portugal (2019)
30. Giddens, A.: The Constitution of Society: Outline of the Theory of Structure. University of California Press, Berkeley (1984)
31. Orlikowski, W.: The duality of technology: rethinking the concept of technology in organizations. Organ. Sci. **3**(3), 398–427 (1992)
32. Zhang, Y., Wildemuth, B.M.: Qualitative analysis of content, pp. 1–12 (2005). https://www.ischool.utexas.edu/~yanz/Content_analysis.pdf
33. Castellan, C.M.: Quantitative and qualitative research: a view for clarity. Int. J. Educ. **2**(2), E1 (2010). ISSN 1948-5476
34. Creswell, J.: Research Design - Qualitative, Quantitative and Mixed Methods Approaches, 2nd edn. SAGE Publications, Inc. (2003). ISBN 0-7619-2441-8

Author Index

Printed in the United States
by Baker & Taylor Publisher Services